The

Unbounded

Community

The Unbounded Community

Neighborhood Life and Social Structure

in New York City, 1830–1875

Kenneth A. Scherzer

Duke University Press   Durham & London 1992

© 1992 Duke University Press
All rights reserved
Printed in the United States of America
on acid-free paper ∞
Library of Congress Cataloging-in-Publication Data
appear on the last printed page of this book.

*To the Memory of David Herlihy
and William Barton McCash*

In this vast city . . . can be found promiscuously intermingled whatever can displease or delight the eye, sadden or render joyous the heart, please or prove corrupt the ear, cause the tear or excite the smile, and move to pity or upbraid to revenge. In one sense of the word every society is brought down to a common level—a mixture, wherein are brought to bear the high and low, rich and poor . . . the pious and profane. The rich nabob can be seen rolling in wealth, and so can the miserable outcast, rolling in disease, dissipation, and famine—forced to make the very gutter his resting place. . . . Riches may be displayed in a grand business-like manner; the varied charms of novelty may be seen; the avenues to business may be crowded, and money may be plenty— yet at the same time poverty moves on with the tide of affairs of men. All that the city of New York has for its inhabitants, *beings* of every order and degree of character, and whatever a man's pursuit may be . . . he will surely find kindred spirits with his own. . . . The changes of any city are as numerous as its inhabitants, and life itself shows its own effects. New York is a great metropolis, and the addition of every hour makes it greater. The good and bad hope to be rich—and all hope eventually to be saved.—John D. Vose, *Fresh Leaves from the Diary of a Broadway Dandy*

Contents

List of Tables and Figures

Tables

Figures

Preface

The neighborhood shapes how we view city life. The word neighborhood has become synonymous with community, and its mention can evoke nostalgic images of belonging, nurturing, and growing up. To those undaunted by the difficulties of life in older American cities, neighborhoods continue to represent the diversity of the city with their kaleidoscopic delights of smells, tastes, sounds, and sights. Yet specific neighborhood names suggest contested territory riven by divisions of class or race. Undoubtedly, the resurgence of ethnic neighborhoods by new waves of European, Latin American, and Asian immigrants will insure this continued clash of images for another generation. But are these popular images historically valid? Does a reading of past social geography reveal a clash of images and patterns as they do today? What are the roots of the urban neighborhood?

This book seeks to answer these questions. New York City during the nineteenth century was America's preeminent metropolis. While never typical of urban development in America, its staggering growth, stark social divisions, and seemingly insurmountable problems both fascinated and frightened the first generation to witness explosive urban growth, the emergence of an industrialized labor force, and large-scale immigration. Their effort to make sense out of these changes led to a reconceptualization of neighborhoods. By midcentury the language of space once reserved for discussions of health, morality, or the extremes of social class had evolved to describe residential areas in general. Beneath the surface, however, the reality of space often contained many surprises unappreciated by contemporaries. The patterns of who lived where were rarely as clear as the pronouncements of contemporaries lead us to believe. Discussions of immigrant neighborhoods invariably overlooked layered patterns of settlement, continued heterogeneity, and profound strands of nativism that underlay residence. Even the communal functions that many believed neighborhoods were supposed to perform often proved illusory given high rates of turnover and change. Like the tricks and traps of city life about which nineteenth-century visitors were often warned by guidebook writers, so neighborhoods presented their own deceptions that confounded those who wish to understand them. Through careful examination of representative areas during a period when New York's neighborhoods first developed, this book seeks to look behind the popular image to reassess nineteenth-century neighborhoods and how historians have viewed them.

During the research and writing of this study, the neighborhood proved a far more elusive subject than I had anticipated. Initially, I shared many of the same perceptions that I now criticize under the rubric of "neighborhoods of nostalgia." Like many who had enjoyed walking the streets of Manhattan in search of remnants of the nineteenth-century city in out-of-the-way places, I tended to think of neighborhoods in terms of iron, stone, brick, and mortar. I hoped to cover these physical places as encyclopedically as possible. However, in the course of my research, the neighborhood-as-place receded in my gaze to be replaced by a more abstract notion. The neighborhood now became something emblematic of the city dwellers' consciousness, their social interactions, and the complex world that city life was becoming. Even the subject of New York City itself faded in importance as I sought to understand the wider process of urban growth that many nineteenth-century cities underwent.

At the same time that my conceptualizations were becoming more abstract, my methodological focus came to be more concrete. In the late 1970s, when I began research for the dissertation that is the seed of this study, the hope still flickered for a successful melding between social theory and history. Where scholarship in history often seemed particularistic and narrow, sociology seemed to ask questions that I found interesting for the study of urban history. I hoped that my work would contribute to an expanding dialogue between the two disciplines. Yet the last decade has not been kind to such interdisciplinary cross-pollination. In subsequent revisions I have focused more upon addressing historical concerns and the debates among historians—most of which developed after I completed the dissertation. Nonetheless, many fundamental questions that I ask and the methodologies that I employ come out of urban sociology. Though no longer as intrusive in my text, theoretical discussion makes up the backbone of this book and figures heavily in the accompanying notes.

The length of notes and explication has, of necessity, forced them into endnotes for aesthetic reasons, although I still consider them integral to the discussion of this book.

Although my interest in New York City history goes back a long way, Kenneth T. Jackson was able to harness this interest while I was still a freshman at Columbia College and direct it into the study of urban history. Floyd Shumway, Norman Fainstein, and Chilton Williamson also encouraged my continuing exploration while I was still an undergraduate.

This book began as a dissertation supervised by Stephan Thernstrom at Harvard University. He always gave me the freedom to try new ideas, offered gentle encouragement, and through the long and sometimes arduous process of revisions, his continued interest and support proved invaluable. Network analysis of community and Granovetter's theory on weak ties was first suggested by Orlando Patterson. I shall never forget his call for the use of social theory to overcome historical "particularism" in the midst of my graduate oral examinations. And from the very beginning, another sociologist, James A. Davis, has served as statistical guru supplying technical expertise, software, and good-humored support. As second reader, he pushed constantly for clarity, a message that I was not always quick to receive. While still a graduate student, aspects of writing and methodology were also discussed with Sandor Schick, Jeffrey Adler, Ronald Formisano, Thomas Dublin, and J. Morgan Kousser. Initial funding for the research and computer time came from the Harvard History Department, the Charles Warren Center for the Study of American History, and the Harvard Sociology Department. Patricia Herlihy and the late David Herlihy provided an ideal environment at Mather House in which to write the dissertation. While not directly linked to the writing or revision of the manuscript, Frank Freidel provided friendship and psychological encouragement during difficult times in the job market. Without his support, I might not have remained an historian.

In addition to anonymous readers whose comments helped me improve the manuscript immeasurably, I am grateful to George Cotkin, Tom Sugrue, Olivier Zunz, Timothy Gilfoyle, Robert Hunt, and Kenneth T. Jackson for their feedback. At one critical juncture Sarah Elbert painstakingly dissected the entire manuscript and spent countless hours discussing changes. Her creative mind and sensitivity helped me refocus and sharpen every chapter. In the final stretch, the dedication of Lawrence J. Malley and the staff of Duke University Press have helped to sustain my enthusiasm for this project. Portions of the manuscript were presented at several forums: meetings of the American Historical Association and the Organization of American Historians, the Fraunces Tavern lunchtime lecture series, and a seminar sponsored by the Vanderbilt History Department. Illustrations and part of the production cost were funded by a generous grant from the Faculty Research Program of Middle Tennessee State University.

Many individuals and institutions have provided assistance and encouragement during my research. For access to their holdings and aid with uncovering varied and important materials, I would like to thank the staff of the New-York Historical Society Library, the New York Public Library Manuscript Division, the Columbia University Libraries, the Presbyterian Historical Society in Philadelphia, Ned Bunting of the Widener Library at Harvard University, and Kenneth Cobb of the New York City Municipal Archives. In several cases permission to microfilm material saved enormous amounts of time that I could then put into coding. Thanks go especially to Norman Goodman, then Clerk of Courts for the County of New York, for permission to film the 1855 State Census for New York City, to Judith Johnson of the Archives of the Episcopal Diocese of New York, to Phylis Barr of the Trinity Parish Archives, and to Russell Gasero of the Reformed Church Archives in New Brunswick, New Jersey.

In addition, the following ministers and priests opened their parish archives and took time from their busy schedules to aid me in examining parish records including: Rev. John Dyson Cannon of St. John the Evangelist Church; Bob Wolk of the Seaman's Institute; Rev. Vernoys of the Metropolitan-Duane Methodist Church; and Rev. Zorawick of Christ and St. Stephan's Church. I also would like to thank the pastors of St. Joseph's Catholic Church, the Central Baptist Church, and the New York Annual Conference of the Methodist Church in Rye, New York. Though of less importance in the book than the earlier dissertation, records of the Bowery and North River Savings Banks were also of use in evaluating individual wealth holding. My thanks to Steward Slocum, Mr. Anastadiades, Frank Pranzo, and Frank Bourne for allowing me to examine the contents of the vault at the original location of Bowery Savings Bank.

Finally, thanks go to my parents, who nurtured my childhood enjoyment of and interest in New York City even from the wilds of suburbia.

1   Toward an Historical
Understanding of Neighborhood

■■■■■■■■ As he looked back to his early years in New York's Lower East Side, where he had lived before his family moved to the "soulless waste-land" of Queens in 1949, writer Morris Dickstein remembered a small world, "remarkably self-contained" despite its lack of homogeneity. "Was there anything . . . that couldn't be bought within a five block radius?" "Everything seemed close by," and the "borders of the neighborhood were sharply defined," so that other nearby areas were "alien territory to my parents and off limits to me." This sense of growing up in a nurturing, supportive, and closed neighborhood community mirrored the sentiments of countless other New Yorkers whose childhood memories conjure a lost world. Yet for Dickstein, these memories meant something more, repre-senting "not only nostalgia for one's formative years" but also an appre-ciation of "the role neighborhoods play in the life of a city like New York." Urban dwellers in New York had long seemed to identify "less with the city than with their own neighborhood," and Dickstein noted how his life had "always been mediated by the neighborhoods I've lived in."[1]

Such is the "neighborhood of nostalgia"—candy stores, corner green grocers, stick ball, and fraternization on high stoops. To Jewish and other European immigrants, it is the tenement "world of our fathers" in which the "immigrant experience provided a set of common bonds: a shared cul-ture, common religion, family ties, and similar hopes for a better future." This reminiscence of pickles from a barrel, "thick-crusted pumpernickel and bottles of milk that had a generous head of cream"[2] is accompanied by and often masks a grief over lost innocence as the fear of crime and the influx of desperately poor newcomers, many of whom were Hispanic and black, prompted flight to distant boroughs and suburbs.[3] Heightened economic and racial polarization intermingles with a declining sense of community as Americans moved to suburbs in which social life became "privatized."[4] For black New Yorkers who predate the postwar waves of migration, the neighborhood of nostalgia is the Harlem of the 1920s and 1930s where a golden age of culture, supported by vibrant social and familial institutions, now seems a tattered memory amongst the rubble of abandonment. Areas like the Lower East Side have been left to newer groups or abandoned in the final stages of decay. Other less blighted areas have been "rescued from decay" through gentrification, and the result has been neighborhoods that while richer are "less humane, less concerned with the community, glitzier, and increasingly less interesting."[5] Less fortunate areas like the East Tremont section of the Bronx, so nostalgically evoked by Robert Caro, were simply bulldozed.[6]

With this erosion of former communities, the neighborhood of nostalgia has become a powerful cultural image. The sentiment grows that "everywhere we turn, the fabric of community life seems threatened." Filmmakers have rediscovered and now celebrate even the "mean streets" of New York "as if they could disappear any moment."[7] Nor is it surprising that political culture has attempted to tap the strong emotional currents underlying these sentiments. Politicians of varying ideological stripes have come to the rhetorical rescue of the neighborhood as if it were an endangered species. Ronald Reagan launched his bid for reelection by elevating "the strength of neighborhood" to the pantheon of "great American values" that he saw himself restoring,[8] and Jesse Jackson recalled growing up in a housing project where "we didn't have a neighborhood, we had a community."[9] These subjective and idealized conceptions of neighborhoods[10] sharply underscore the extent to which the concept of the neighborhood of nostalgia resonates throughout popular and political culture.

The Historians' Nostalgia

The idealization of neighborhood community has seeped into the writings of American historians as well, particularly recent studies of social and working-class history. Just as politicians have exploited the neighborhood of nostalgia for its appeal, so for many historians class-segregated neighborhoods embody a political question in the deepest sense.

Much social history over the last two decades has arguably been a reaction to the "end-of-ideology," consensus school of history that dominated scholarship over the preceding several decades (1930s–1950s). In proposing the existence of a unique American "liberal" ideology, consensus historians argued that historical circumstances—the abundance of land, the shortage of labor, and the gulf between America and Europe— spared American colonists and their descendants the class divisions and denied them the traditions of European working-class socialism. With such narrow social differences, it was argued, rich and poor Americans, native and immigrant alike, shared the same political spectrum and thus an ideological community.[11] Debate over the validity of consensus has served to heighten the importance of neighborhoods for the two principal movements in recent social history: the "new urban history" of the late 1960s and 1970s and the "new social history" of the 1980s. That both seek either to uncover or to deny the existence of community in the past has produced something of a consensus regarding the importance of neighborhood-based community. All these historians, whatever their ideological perspective, seem to agree that neighborhood community is a vital institution to urban democracy that determines how well urbanites adjust to their environment. The disagreements lie in whether neighborhoods were constructed out of class or ethnic ties or whether transiency actually prevented the formation of neighborhood communities.

In recent years historians influenced by work on class formation in eighteenth- and nineteenth-century Great Britain, particularly that of E. P. Thompson, have challenged the assertion of the consensus school that American workers lacked a distinctive class-consciousness or tradition of radicalism. Much of the resulting new social history has illuminated previously overlooked facets of the making of an American working class, and this has helped revitalize American social history by focusing attention on changing social modes of production, the emergence of industrial capitalism, and, in particular, the cultural lives of the urban working class. As one scholar has noted, class relations have begun to be appreciated "as part of a human achievement in which men and women struggle to comprehend the social relations into which they were born (or entered involuntarily) and in which, by collective exercise of power, they sustain or challenge those relations, in every phase of social life."[12]

For several analysts of early industrial capitalism, neighborhoods have held a special importance in defining working-class community. It is widely argued that neighborhoods are as much a material manifestation of class formation as the division of labor and the debasement of crafts are in the workplace. Marxist historians have even claimed that "tightly knit units like the family and community neighborhood remained immune to the culture of capitalism and thus served as counterhegemonic enclaves."[13] In the case of New York City the retreat of the "haute bourgeoisie" to exclusive enclaves and the emergence of impoverished areas

like the Five Points, which housed practitioners of debased crafts, produced neighborhood divisions that paralleled those of class. "Navigating a
course through the uncertain waters of Manhattan's real estate" that separated the wealthy "inner Republic of the Fifteenth Ward" and Broadway
from the "artisan republic" on the Bowery required, in the words of Peter
Buckley, "a relocation of consciousness as well as bodies and belongings"
to deal with "new distinctions between work and leisure, between areas
of masculine and feminine power, and between public and private action."
Location therefore provides the historian of the nineteenth-century city
"convenient access into the lived experience and consciousness" of both
the elite and the workers.[14]

Elizabeth Blackmar's detailed study of early patterns of residential development, for example, challenges Sam Bass Warner's essentially consensus view[15] that "spatial concentration and integration" in the preindustrial
city "encouraged and supported social cohesion, cooperation, and defer-
ence." By the end of the eighteenth century, Blackmar counters, traditional
household modes of labor organization that integrated work and living
space were in decline as master craftsmen ceased to provide accommodations for their workers. This gave rise to a bifurcated housing market in
which large property owners were increasingly separated from their tenants. Displaced journeymen and unskilled workers experienced increasing
"detachment" and "transience." "The interchangeability of rental housing
as a commodity, like the interchangeability of labor power to capitalist
production, forced working-class tenants to move around in order to find
accommodations within the price limit set by wages." The result was the
emergence of "class neighborhoods" in the "form of 'class streets' or even
parts of streets divided into 'respectable' and 'non-respectable' blocks."
Tenant areas came to be collections of slums while genteel districts of
middle-class houses arose that promised "convenience to a separate workplace, healthfulness, and family comfort."[16] While "Manhattan did not
develop a highly differentiated class geography reinforced by transportation systems," the "relations that could not be defined through physical
distance" came to be expressed through new ways of asserting social distance. This gradual "melding of social and spatial neighborhoods" in turn
"laid the ground for new modes of class interaction."[17]

The existence of class-segregated neighborhoods has became for historians of nineteenth-century New York the sine qua non to any understanding of social geography. A few notable enclaves of wealth and of poverty
show New York's underlying class polarization in the 1840s: For the
rich, there were the "residential enclaves along Broadway at the southern
portion of the city," places where "they dined in each other's homes and

married into each other's families." For the laboring poor, there were areas such as Bancker Street in the Fifth Ward where "poor blacks crammed into tumbledown houses, where overcrowding and poor sanitation led to periodic outbreaks of disease and fever"; Corlears Hook, to the east, where "the sailors' resort became a lower-class haven"; and most infamous of all, the Five Points district, where the abandonment of clapboard homes by their "original artisan owners" produced a "vaporous neighborhood" constructed upon the soggy fill of the former Collect Pond.[18]

To be sure, such studies eschew the rosiness of the modern neighborhood of nostalgia. It is difficult to be nostalgic for cellar apartments, high mortality, and ramshackle tenements—although Dickstein's reminiscences were actually triggered by a reminder that the beloved neighborhood of his youth was (as it had long been) a slum. Still, life in nineteenth-century working-class neighborhoods has been romanticized by scholars who emphasize the strength of working-class community. This is true of a recent study by Christine Stansell that seeks to integrate the evolution of class relations in New York under industrial capitalism with the gender relations of the working poor. Like many labor historians, she dates the increased segregation of New York's neighborhoods to the Federalist era when the city began to separate into two areas: the "small, self-enclosed enclave of the wealthy and urbane" and the "riotous world of the laboring poor" located in the "dark, dirty, overcrowded little plebeian neighborhoods along the East River." By the 1830s "the enclaves of laboring people were coming to constitute separate territories, so extensive and distinct that they seemed to genteel observers something like a foreign domain."[19] The strength of working-class communities combined with class-based patterns of gender relations to produce a peculiar "moral economy of the tenements." The disappearance of urban domestic production in nineteenth-century slums pulled men further out of the household and allowed poor women to create a new and unique form of women's community. Thus "even within the male-dominated structures of tenement life, married women found in the urban neighborhoods a female milieu that offered help in their dealings with men." They were, in other words, "shifting communities of cooperation and contention" counterpoising a "sexual delineation of urban geography" with one based purely upon class.[20]

This special concern of labor historians with neighborhood communities has much in common with that of the earlier historiographic movement, the new urban history.[21] Like other "new" histories of the 1960s, this movement reflected optimism about the possible merger between history and the social sciences.[22] However, its hope of treating the city as "an arbitrary container of some socioeconomic activity" ended in failure, and "what looked like the wave of the future in the late 1960s began to resemble," in the words of Charles Tilly, "spent foam on a littered beach only a decade later."[23] Yet it is easy to forget that both labor history and the new urban history both tackled the same fundamental question of whether America had developed a class conscious radicalized working class. Unlike those who essentially sought to Americanize the findings of E. P. Thompson or retroactively search for communal institutions, historians like Stephan Thernstrom and Peter Knights accepted the basic premise of consensus historians and utilized new methodologies and quantitative tools borrowed from sociology to explain why America had failed to develop the radicalized working class that it should have under industrial capitalism.[24] Where labor historians assigned a crucial role to neighborhoods in cementing class-consciousness, many urban historians denied this role; they concluded from high rates of geographic mobility and unexpectedly low rates of residential segregation that neither stable, cohesive neighborhood communities nor meaningful working-class radicalism had any chance to form for most Americans. Socialism was in effect stillborn through a combination of transiency, the satisfactions of home ownership, and incremental upward mobility.[25] Thus the new urban history also embraced elements of the neighborhood of nostalgia by assuming, like many sociologists from whom they drew their methodological inspiration, that stable neighborhoods were prerequisites for community and that high levels of transiency invariably produced alienation and anomie.

Its failure to handle the question of social inequality has unfortunately obscured what should have been its most durable contribution: the use of successive manuscript censuses to trace individuals, allowing historians to uncover high levels of geographic mobility in nineteenth-century America.[26] In a path-breaking study, Thernstrom estimated that 157,862 families moved into Boston during the 1880s as 138,572 simultaneously left, which suggested that upward of 800,000 people might have passed through the city in a single decade.[27] While these estimates were flawed by inadequate attention to mortality among out-migrants and by some inaccurate data, the volatility of populations in eastern cities was nonetheless remarkable. Yet, while the quantitative extent of mobility and the role of kinship in directing it are now better understood, its qualitative meaning remains largely a matter of conjecture—fed by suppositions linking mobility to social disruption. One scholar noted that the "restless and footloose" character of American city dwellers produced a "felt lack of community" and a sense of rootlessness, while another argued that transiency "worked against the development of a local sense of community cohesion and integration."[28] If the constant flow of newcomers sometimes fostered cosmopolitanism, its chief effect may have been to promote anomie which in turn "contributed to the inward concentration—the intensification of domesticity—that became the hallmark of the modern family."[29] The picture presented by urban historians portrayed migrant Americans as uprooted souls—the products and prisoners of a disrupted social environment more likely to create alienation, isolation, and apathy than solidarity, community, and resistance.[30]

Other findings about immigrant ghettos compounded this already gloomy picture. Since the early twentieth century, writers had characterized these neighborhoods as a "closed unchanging space, symbol of immigrant isolation for a few months, a few years, or life." Having lost their village-based communities when they left Europe, these uprooted inhabitants huddled together in festering slums until upward socioeconomic mobility or assimilation into American culture allowed them to escape.[31] In more recent years, this depiction had been revised to stress the function of residential communities in the sheltering and socializing of immigrants with the aid of kinsmen, countrymen, ethnic institutions such as churches and local voluntary associations, and, in politics, through the ward leader.[32] But with the discovery of geographic mobility, it seemed that newcomers moved too often to develop either the negative effects of "ghetto culture" or, for that matter, the positive effects of neighborhood-based institutions in fostering group cohesion. Furthermore, ecological studies of residential patterns in nineteenth-century cities indicated that many if not most immigrants actually congregated within small residential clusters rather than large homogeneous neighborhoods.[33] These findings suggested that urban neighborhoods played little more than a *symbolic* role in the transmission and preservation of ethnic culture, by housing institutions that seemed to foster solidarity and by helping to define the alien culture to both group members and the wider society.[34] The question of how social cohesion could have been maintained was never adequately answered.

Laboring under the weight of these preconceptions, the analysis of both urban and "new social" historians suggested that little remained to be said on the subject of neighborhoods. Ethnic historians assumed that the clustering of ethnic schools, churches, clubs, and fraternal societies constituted cohesive neighborhood communities.[35] Neo-Marxist historians accepted the existence of neighborhood-communities as an article of faith in their search for class-consciousness. Other labor historians who stressed residential stability over mobility spoke of neighborhoods that were so "culturally isolated" that they formed "insular communities" that prevented urban working-class populations from "unifying across racial, ethnic, or territorial boundaries."[36] And social scientific historians tended to deny a role to neighborhoods altogether by equating mobility and residential heterogeneity with social dislocation. Each of these conclusions rested to a large extent upon assumptions associated with the neighborhood of nostalgia.

Without denying the importance of neighborhoods as material manifestations of class or ethnic cohesion, this book seeks to examine New York neighborhoods afresh and in greater detail than before while at the same time seeking to redefine the meaning of urban neighborhoods that historians have used. Instead of following preconceived definitions, I want to treat neighborhoods as a tabula rasa, a newly emerging, always dynamic phenomenon in the early-to-middle nineteenth century. Neighborhoods in the 1850s were not the same institutions that they were later in the nineteenth century or, for that matter, in the 1920s and 1930s when urban sociologists began to decry their decline and disappearance. The automatic equation of neighborhood with community is thus intrinsically ahistorical because it fails to explain either the fragility of neighborhoods when they did form or the strength of social bonds that survived transience.[37] Gary Nash's call for a new direction in community studies also applies to the study of urban neighborhoods. "Rather than nostalgically tracing the eclipse of community we need to trace the continuously evolving process of community," by which Nash meant "the kinds of structural changes occurring in the cities" which "encouraged—even necessitated—the fabrication of communities within communities by energized and mobilized groups that had previously often been politically and socially quiescent." Homogeneity and smallness are not "indispensable" elements of "community and visible social relations."[38]

Flawed Models

What went wrong with so much historical scholarship on neighborhoods? The principal problem was that many assertions about neighborhoods rested upon sparse evidence uncritically examined.[39] British urban historians have warned of "the semantic, methodological and ideological problems associated with attempts to establish the existence of urban 'communities' in nineteenth- and twentieth-century towns and cities." As Jeremy Bolton noted, "an ideological bias often colours much research in the urban field," so that "perceptions about the actual local basis of social activity" have become linked with "the desire to promote such a basis."[40]

Such "retrospective application of methods" yields sharply different pictures of urban life. Historians using literary accounts constructed working-class communities dominated by the sizable number of "way-farers" who "worked casually or seasonally and who slept rough," while historians who relied upon statistical accounts ignored the *lumpenprole-tariat* in favor of the "respectable" working class who "rarely figured in the graphic descriptions of social investigators."[41] Furthermore, the assumption of neighborhood solidarities to posit a citywide working-class community has failed to prove that ties of class were stronger than those of the local neighborhood community.[42] Third, neighborhood communities are particularly difficult to define, for they exist as products of social relations and states of mind (consciousness which may or may not be related to class, ethnicity, transiency, or gender) *and* as *things* that have names, particular kinds of people inhabiting them, and physical boundaries.[43]

Lastly, the spatial segregation of nineteenth-century European cities, where many neo-Marxist historians turned for their model, was different from the social geography they ascribed to American cities. Engels viewed Manchester's divergent social geography as, to use the words of David Ward, "an unavoidable outcome of the adversarial class relationships of industrial capitalism," with geographical patterns directly representing the conflict between the working and the middle classes.[44] Yet when such descriptions of Victorian towns as "dichotomous socio-geographic arrangements of rich and poor or middle class and working class" were tested empirically, they were found to be "somewhat misleading." Furthermore, this pattern was not a product of industrial capitalism at all but instead dated back to the eighteenth century and the era of mercantile capitalism. The vast majority of skilled, semiskilled, and unskilled inhabitants were actually "less differentiated from one another in 1871 than they were in 1841 and 1851." Social bifurcation—at least in residence—seemed chiefly to be the result of the "theoretical and ideological" perspectives of contemporary observers.[45]

The relationship between social segregation and the existence of working-class community is also highly ambiguous in American cities. Labor historians who otherwise agreed on the evolution of urban class-consciousness have reached conflicting conclusions on the relationship between neighborhood and community. Paul Johnson's examination of Rochester, New York, in the 1830s traced the decline in sense of community that fueled the great religious revivals to the creation of class-based neighborhoods. "In 1820," he argues, "most Rochesterians worked, played, and slept in the same place. There were no neighborhoods as we understand them: no distinct commercial and residential zones, no residential areas based upon social class." By the 1830s "the social geography of Rochester was class-specific: master and wage earner no longer lived in the same households or on the same blocks."[46] But Paul Faler, in his study of Lynn shoemakers, argued that the rise of industrial capitalism did not create neighborhoods but rather eroded them. Together with family life, "the customs and traditional activities" of different neighborhoods had "tended to inhibit the formation of relationships based on one's occupation." When opportunities of shoemaking crafts dried up under industrialization—thus locking workers into different strata of production—"the neighborhood as the basis of social affiliation" was actually weakened.[47]

The new urban history was likewise shackled by certain presuppositions it had made about neighborhoods. Urban sociology long sought to trace the disruption and decline of "homogeneous, unified, and stable communities by the forces of industrialization, urbanization, and immigration."[48] As historians themselves first drew upon the work of sociologists such as Tönnies and Wirth and, later, Park and Burgess, it is hardly surprising that much of the historical scholarship on community decline dealt with the same effects of the segmentation of roles—the replacement of personal by impersonal modes of production.[49] Some urban historians blamed urbanization for the disruptions of traditional familial and communal controls over the individual and saw the replacement of cohesive neighborhoods by a "series of tenuous segmental relations superimposed upon a territorial base with a definite center but without a definite periphery."[50]

The Neighborhood Redefined

Many urban historical studies persist in applying this Wirthian model of social fragmentation that portrays city life as a disrupted or, at best, a bifurcated community divided between mobile and nonmobile urbanites. But over the last several decades, sociologists have substantially modified this view and empirical community studies have consistently uncovered remnants of surviving communal solidarities in ethnic "urban villagers."[51] Despite the dominance of an industrial bureaucratic system which was presumed to have disrupted social ties, kinship continues to function as a major provider of emotional support for residents.[52] Most importantly, sociologists have applied social network theory, drawn from the work of anthropologists, thus shifting the focus of empirical sociological study away from its traditional emphasis upon urban ecology and the assumption that psychosocial satisfaction was linked to physical space and residential stability. This has resulted in a greater appreciation of nonlocal social ties anchored in friendship and kinship. Even if "urban life in large measure takes place within smaller universes—family, neighborhood, firm, sect, gang, or whatever," urban anthropologist Ulf Hannerz reminds us that "we must forever be aware of their openness to other areas of urban life, at least until we have convinced ourselves that they have in some way become closed."[53]

Urban sociologists and anthropologists now accept the conclusion that transiency and the lack of residential homogeneity do not automatically produce dislocation or social fragmentation. They have repeatedly found "more persistent proliferation of personal relations than should be there" given the previous equation of proximity with social community.[54] This discovery has, in turn, changed the way in which the city itself has been viewed, challenging the importance of neighborhoods in defining the character of their inhabitants. With the involvement of urbanites in a variety of overlapping, ever-widening communities—a "network of networks"— migration and urbanization need not be destructive of social cohesion.[55] In an era of high geographical mobility, urbanites were able to find all the necessary support of a social community outside of neighborhoods, in a ramified network of kin and friends.[56]

Labor and social historians have also tended to overlook the multidimensional nature of the urban neighborhood.[57] These dimensions encompass a series of overlapping social relations that include three crucial elements: the internal spatial organization of the city; the operation of the local area as a crucible for social relations for the urbanites who live there, and the symbolic (cognitive) significance that these neighborhoods hold for their residents. By ignoring these, historians have neglected critical questions on the relationship between neighborhood and community. Is the "aspatial community" described by urban sociologists merely a twentieth-century phenomenon, the result of the decline of neighborhoods in the age of the telephone and the automobile? And given what urban historians have told us about the fluid nature of urban populations, was the maintenance of cultural continuity in nineteenth-century cities— the cohesive institutions and culture of urban newcomers—facilitated by a form of community that may not have been determined by spatial homogeneity? In other words, were historical neighborhoods also unbounded communities?

Buffet's Enigma

The multidimensional character of community membership in urban neighborhoods is illustrated by the case of August Buffet. A former resident of New York's Fourth Ward, Buffet was murdered during a visit to his old neighborhood from New Haven in September 1853. As the circumstances of his murder unfolded, glimpses emerged of the durable ties of friendship that were maintained at a distance and of Buffet's virtual anonymity in his former neighborhood. These details also offer a glance at how the social community of the urban neighborhood might function to separate residents from outsiders.

Buffet visited Louis Bannard, an old friend he had made while residing in New York between 1848 and 1849, at 27 Greenwich Street. Initially he planned to return to Connecticut after three days, but he chose to stay an additional day at the house of Joseph D. Tavier, where he was boarding. Late in the evening of the third day, having downed several glasses of claret, Buffet ventured out onto Gold Street in the impoverished Fourth Ward. Suddenly he was confronted by a group of drunken men and, in the brawl which ensued, he was stabbed to death. To the bystanders who witnessed the murder, the victim was a stranger. Neither Margaret Brost, who together with her husband ran a saloon and boardinghouse at 53 Frankfort Street, nor Mary White, who was home caring for her sick child across the street, knew Buffet. But Brost and White knew one another, as did two other neighbors, Joseph Besancom and Antoine Lortel. In their testimony at the inquest, each of these witnesses referred to the others by name. The evidence suggests that August Buffet was an outsider in a place where neighbors at least were acquainted with one another. Yet he was no stranger or casual tourist, having had a place to stay, a friend to visit, and knowledge of the area from the time of his previous residence in the city.[58]

Buffet's fate points to the heart of the social operation of urban neighborhoods. In nostalgia and in fact, neighborhoods were integral parts of how the urban environment was divided and defined. Even though Buffet had moved to Connecticut, he retained a familiarity with certain areas of New York as well as a set of old friends that made him part of an extended neighborhood. But in death he was a stranger to all the witnesses who seemed to know who belonged to their neighborhood and who did not. Buffet's murder showed the bridge between migrant and neighborhood, and that with transiency, neighborhoods operated on several different levels.

The nineteenth-century process of spatial differentiation by which residential patterns fitfully moved from heterogeneity to homogeneity was neither linear nor a simple matter of class or ethnicity. The period 1830–1875 covered by the present study catches New York at a critical stage when such revolutionary developments as the emergence of distinct business and residential areas, rapid growth, and immigrant influxes converged to create a new type of spatially differentiated city. A second dimension illuminated by Buffet's murder is the distinction that existed in all neighborhoods between being an outsider and being a member—a relationship that went well beyond ownership of the means of production.[59] Lastly, neighborhoods existed cognitively. Buffet's awareness of social geography and the paradox that he, as a stranger, hardly doubted that he belonged suggest that transiency as a fact of daily life—in the nineteenth century as today—might have stretched the meaning of neighborhood to extend, like Buffet's travels, well beyond one small geographical area.

This multilayered picture of urban neighborhoods builds upon but also modifies prevailing historical definitions of neighborhood life. If, as has been suggested, residents of cities constructed neighborhood communities by living in common localities, by demonstrating a common set of activities and sentiments, and by forming "networks of interpersonal ties" for support, this book argues that support and sentiment generally operated with little reference to locality.[60] First, segregated residential areas were still exceptional in antebellum New York despite the profound change that the city's basic spatial configuration was undergoing. Those neighborhoods which existed were the preserves primarily of self-segregated New Yorkers of native stock, of the relatively small members of the upper classes, and of the very poor. The working-class areas that came to comprise vast districts of the city actually remained complex mixes of trades, classes, and nationalities. This diversity made class and cultural unity harder to accomplish within neighborhoods. If the overall pattern of spatial evolution moved slowly toward greater homogeneity, mental perceptions of neighborhood—the feeling that space socially defined the character of inhabitants—remained primitive until midcentury. And given extraordinary levels of geographical mobility, interpersonal ties of social networks operated with little regard to space. This book thus seeks to reexamine these functions in light of mobility and unceasing residential change.

An Alternative Path

How can neighborhoods be examined without falling into the trap of past assumptions—sociological and historical? The urban sociologist Albert Hunter has pointed to three dimensions that might help shape the historical study of neighborhood: (1) an ecological dimension determined by who lives where, (2) a symbolic dimension in which urban space reflects a cognitive awareness by residents of social divisions within the city, and (3) a social dimension involving spatial limitations upon voluntary institutions and social networks—in other words, how neighborhoods shape who knows whom. For Hunter (as for August Buffet) urban neighborhoods possess both a concrete and a symbolic identity; they exist both as a collection of individuals segregated according to certain attributes and as a set of overlapping social relations. In this manner, the community can be viewed not only as a "functional spatial unit meeting sustenance needs," but also as a unit of "patterned social interaction" and "cultural-symbolic collective identity"—a state of mind—with social status, stage of the life cycle, and ethnicity each helping to shape the individual's choice of neighborhood.[61] Finally, the neighborhood derived its institutional coherence from membership groups such as local voluntary associations.[62]

Sociologists thus remind us that the ability to evaluate surroundings—what they refer to as the symbolic-cultural function of neighborhoods as an "object of orientation"—is an indispensable element to understanding community membership and attachment to place in the modern metropolis. It is equally important to understanding the antebellum city. The reaction of nineteenth-century urbanites to the new phenomenon of segregated neighborhoods yields evidence of a new form of spatial consciousness that went beyond that of class.[63] In addition, the historical dissection of neighborhoods in antebellum New York uncovers a structure of overlapping communities that clearly shows that neighborhoods as social entities extended well beyond the boundaries of any specific locale. Such evidence of aspatial community has too often been overlooked through a reliance upon records of voluntary associations that were primarily local in scope.[64] Social clubs, fraternal organizations, and charitable societies may well serve to anchor communities, but they comprised only one aspect of the "patterned social interaction," an aspect that served only a narrow segment of urban populations during the nineteenth century. The analysis offered here examines not only these formal ties, but informal relations of kinship and friendship which proved of far greater value in rooting the day-to-day social lives of highly mobile neighborhood residents in urban social networks.

The following chapters on nineteenth-century New York City are grouped into three sections, each of which corresponds to a different facet of the interaction between physical and social space.[65] The first section discusses the ecological roots of community as revealed by: the ethnic and transient basis of settlement, the importance of wealth and occupational status in shaping residential differentiation, and the role of the urban household (kinship and boarding) in neighborhood choice. A second section utilizes qualitative sources to probe nineteenth-century perceptions of the "symbolic community," with special emphasis upon four sample wards. And a third section explores the relationship between formal and informal social interaction on the one hand and urban space on the other to discover how well antebellum neighborhoods actually functioned as social communities.

PART I

The Ecological

Neighborhood

2 Moving Day

▮▮▮▮▮▮▮▮ A frustrated enumerator of the 1855 state census confided: "I should think one third of the Population of the District are In the Habit of Moving from once to four times a year rendering it Impossible for the Marshall to Render an Ackret account of Deaths" since "friends of the Desiest" had "moved to some other Part of the citty [sic]."[1] "Of all the civilized people on the face of the earth," wrote Lawrence Goulding in the preface to his 1875 city directory, "the inhabitants of New York appear to be the most inclined to move about." The massive task of compiling this directory made Goulding aware also that New York was "the American rendezvous of cosmopolitans who come and go by the thousands," ranging from the farmer's son fresh from the country to new arrivals from Europe who had just set foot at Castle Clinton.[2]

This constant ebb and flow of transients was nothing new. Even in the 1830s, well before famine and political upheaval in Europe had unleashed waves of Irish and German immigrants, one observer was already warning of "the influx of immigrants from New England and Europe" that might soon "overspread and characterize the whole."[3] Although relatively few of the 3,641,481 immigrants passing through New York between 1820 and 1860 actually stayed, New York continued to be a city of newcomers throughout the nineteenth century.[4] These newcomers—and many others—changed residence with great frequency. How did the urban neighborhood emerge as an institution from the clutter and disorder of the earlier mercantile city? "May-Day" is the key to understanding this question.

It must have seemed as though everyone moved on May Day. This practice, unique to New York, replaced the joyous celebration of morris

"New York City—An Incident of Spring-Time—A Canvasser For A City Directory Collecting Names In the Fourth Ward." This illustration suggests that
directories' canvassers did not ignore poor areas, although middle-class canvassers were met with abuse. From *Frank Leslie's Illustrated Newspaper*,
17 May, 1879.

dances around maypoles with frenetic activity. Even established Knickerbockers, descendants of the city's early Dutch settlers, shared with the
newly arrived and the working classes an irresistible drive to abandon old
neighborhoods for new. This restless spirit was epitomized by the ritual
of Moving Day, which fell for most on the first of May because of a city
ordinance requiring all tenants who failed to renew their leases to vacate
the old dwellings by nine o'clock and be moved into their new homes by
three.[5] Starting in January, landlords would set rents for the coming year,
leaving tenants the option of either remaining or seeking new residences
elsewhere. The result, one contemporary observed, was that it was not
uncommon to meet people "who resided in a dozen different houses in
as many years; and yet who speak of their wishes to try the advantage of
another quarter of the city when the proper season arrives."[6] "From the
peep of day till twilight," exclaimed a startled English visitor, "may be
seen carts, which go at a rate of speed astonishingly rapid, laden with furniture of every kind, racing up and down the city, as if its inhabitants were
flying from a pestilence."[7] Some flew indeed from increased rents; others
flew out of a love of variety.

More than wanderlust, Moving Day has come to symbolize for some historians the hardening of neighborhood boundaries that increasingly segregated the working class from the districts dominated by the emerging class of wealthy merchant capitalists. At the same time, the first of May has served as a barometer of dislocation because of the emergence of a rental housing market. "Despite the disruption," noted Elizabeth Blackmar, "the 'anarchy' of moving day carnival ultimately confirmed market rules of property relations."[8] These two interpretations of Moving Day share the assumption that the existence of a "large floating population" was invariably a sign of a "society in which opportunities are restricted and in which geographical rather than social mobility" showed success or failure.[9]

Nineteenth-century cities like New York came to be sharply divided between a vast working class or "strolling poor" that drifted in and out of cities largely invisible to keepers of public records (such as assessors' rolls) and a stable, wealthy elite of successful artisans and merchants. One scholar noted how the first of May, together with the first days of February, August, and November—"quarter days," when quarterly leases expired—were "awaited with dread" by journeymen for whom "any kind of setback could make it impossible to pay for lodging." Workers moved either to find cheaper lodging or to escape the payment of back rent—notwithstanding the frequent imposition of "distrainment of property" or liens by landlords.[10] For Edward Spann, May Day embodied the "diversity and anonymity of life in a large metropolis and the necessary disruption of life and home associated with a fast-growing, transforming commercial city." New York had become, he argued, a city of "a-social and occasionally anti-social individualism," its people little more than "floating atoms in turbulent space" and its "rootless character" a discouragement to the "development of a strong sense of community."[11]

Yet such negative assessments of Moving Day overlook a psychological dimension that marked it as a time of hope for a fresh beginning.[12] Certainly affluent residents, undoubtedly seasoned movers, greeted the opportunity to move with excitement and treated May First as a festive (if hectic) occasion. Indeed, the push of rising real estate values in lower Manhattan and the pull of new construction uptown proved hard to resist. After selling his house on Broadway in 1836, Philip Hone wrote that "I shall leave this delightful house with feelings of deep regret . . . but $60,000 is a great deal of money." The following day he and a friend walked out to inspect new lots on Second Avenue, St. Mark's Place, Tompkins Square, and Lafayette Place (a walk of over two miles in either direction). He wrote:

"May 1st in the City," a humorous view of moving day in New York. From *Harper's Weekly*, 30 April, 1859. Photograph courtesy of Duke University Library.

> I am turned out of doors. . . . Almost everybody downtown is in the same predicament, for all the dwelling houses are to be converted into stores. We are tempted with prices so exorbitantly high that none can resist, and old downtown burgonmasters [sic], who have fixed to one spot all their lives, will be seen during the next summer in flocks, marching reluctantly north to pitch their tents in places which in their time, were orchards, cornfields, or morasses a pretty smart distance from town, and a journey to which was formerly an affair of some moment, and required preparation beforehand, but which constitutes at this time the most fashionable quarter in New York.[13]

When his father's home was demolished eight years later, Hone may have "mourned over the departure of an old acquaintance," but he mainly expressed surprise that the "old house stood so long."[14]

The abandonment of Lower Broadway and Wall Street to commerce by former residents might also suggest that May Day destroyed a way of life based upon informal sociability where one might bring "business associates back, often unannounced for dinner and an early game of whist" and replaced it with a new one of alienation and "social promiscuity." It has been suggested that beneath the seeming whimsy of Hone's account lurks a sorrowful lament for the passing of an older form of urban sociability and the need to recreate a new "social circle of friendship" through "new techniques."[15] But if this were the case, one finds little support for it in the testimony of another wealthy refugee from the financial district, George Templeton Strong.[16] In 1848 Strong described a vague "feeling of self-reproach" at his lack of regret about moving. "How *can* I abandon all these old usages and leave the dirty, rat-infested loaferine Greenwich Street and everything that I've grown up among and got used to, and yet feel no sorrow about it; give up all my old friends here . . . this inconvenient house where alone I can remember living, and change so cheerfully?" he asked. Despite the ties to be broken and the experiences to be left behind, what attachment he felt for his old home was easily supplanted by an overriding belief in the inevitability of progress. Given the rapid expansion of the once-suburban sections of Manhattan—offering grander quarters in less crowded surroundings—it is not surprising that old attachments could so easily be broken. Strong merely reflected the feelings of many other mobile New Yorkers when he confided in his diary: "It seems to me as if I were parting from my oldest and best friends for ever and ought to be unhappy about it: but somehow I a'nt a bit."[17]

One can also overstate the trauma of Moving Day for the city's working classes. Walt Whitman observed how many poor New Yorkers greeted May Day with "anticipation and foreboding months before the day,"[18] but even for those who were driven to find new lodging more by the high rents, the chronic shortage of housing, and the uncertainty of employment than by the vanity of fashion, Moving Day became an occasion for ritual celebration marked by dancing in the streets and bonfires. The satirist Seba Smith, speaking through the rustic dialect of his mouthpiece Major Jack Downing of Downingsville, described how residents in some of New York's poorer neighborhoods turned the practice of disposing of old belongings prior to their move into a joyous saturnalia.[19] When Downing first encountered the fires in the streets, he thought it might be an expression of some longstanding animosity between tenant and landlord, even an indication of class warfare. He wondered whether "the tenants had come off so bad in the battle with the landlords this time" that "they might be layin' a plan to burn the whole city at once." The light came not from the flames of burning tenement houses but, instead, from bonfires consuming old bedding. "Just burning up the old straw beds—everybody burns up the old straw to-night," one resident told the surprised Downing.

Rowdy displays in the streets of working-class neighborhoods were not unusual. For poor New Yorkers, like their counterparts in other cities, the streets were frequent locations for public rituals, ceremonies, and parades. The streets were "shared more equally than other space" as places for broadcasting messages, for asserting claims to respectable status, and for performing "rites of local solidarity."[20] The "burning the old straw" stood in sharp contrast to the images of clattering wagons dashing through streets and of hapless residents anxiously waiting atop all their worldly belongings for the cartman to arrive routinely pictured in contemporary accounts of May Day.[21] It marked a bold assertion of working-class dominion of the streets where bonfires blazed, not to mention the sharp gulf between the downy feather bedding of the wealthy and the coarse straw-filled bedding of the poor that made this seemingly ritualized cleansing a practical necessary. As boys danced around the flames holding sticks and poking in fresh clumps of straw they chanted: "Whorah . . . Whorah; now for roast bed-bugs and fleas. Hark, only hear the fleas roar, and the bed bugs crack and snap like burning hemlocks." Festivities finally wound up with brazen sexual dalliance and playful taunting that would have been alien to the middle class. "Hold your tongue, you sassy brutes," responded the girls in mock indignation, and the boys responded by taking "after 'em full chisel with handfuls of burning straw, and the gals run as if a catamount was after 'em till they got into the house." If May Day was greeted with foreboding, the "burning of the old straw" suggested that fear was tempered with hope. The boisterous street rituals of the poor may have differed from the calm resignation of rich merchants like Hone or Strong, but for both mobility was an accepted part of urban life in the nineteenth century.

Above all, "moving day should also warn us," Stuart Blumin has noted, "that there is a dynamic element in the urban spatial structure that a static description of neighborhoods is likely to miss." Not only does the movement of urban population reveal the emergence of "real differences between the class and ethnic composition of various neighborhoods," it also sheds light on the "question of specialization of urban land usage."[22] Moving Day was integrally linked to—indeed it derived from—the rapid development and expansion of the central business district. New York's spatial character was profoundly altered as the marriage between residential and commercial land use, long the hallmark of the mercantile city, was finally dissolved. In the city's lower wards, the "march of improvement" replaced elegant private homes with "splendid business structures," while elsewhere, "where, until of late years, there were but a few private residences," large tenement houses appeared.[23]

Out of the disorder of these frantic annual "removals" and the ever-changing nature of New York's population—which suggested chaos to natives and visitors alike—would eventually come the order of a new spatial character. In 1830 the settled part of the "nation's metropolis" consisted only of the southernmost mile or so of Manhattan, bounded at the north by Fourteenth Street, beyond which was pastureland and suburban country estates. Among the earliest American cities to develop a discrete central business district, New York's social configuration outwardly continued to resemble that of the classic antebellum walking city where transportation was expensive and pedestrians reigned.[24]

The Great Fire of 1835, which consumed most of New York's financial district, helped clear the path for the replacement of the chaotic spatial plan of the old mercantile city by the segmented order of the modern metropolis. The narrow windings of the downtown streets and alleys survived—as they mostly survive today—but the arrangements of countinghouses, stores, and residences were now quite different than before, with businesses starting to cluster according to economic function and the type of industry. While most merchants continued to conduct businesses grossing $100,000 to $250,000 per annum in countinghouses on the ground floors of their homes, grocers were already beginning to cluster along Front Street, and the lower stretches of Pearl Street were rapidly becoming the headquarters for New York's many dry goods jobbers.[25] But the fire merely served to accelerate the spatial sorting of commercial activity that dated back to the period before the American Revolution, when mercantile warehouses clustered along the East River and crafts and small industry tended to be found further inland.[26] This geographical divorce of retailing from wholesaling may have occurred as early as 1780, and a clearly defined center for the retailing of luxury goods existed early in the nineteenth century. The financial district finally came into being sometime between 1805 and 1810, when the city's population stood at 80,000.[27] By 1840, as Allan Pred has noted, "All evidence indicates that the morphology of the mercantile city was already characterized by 'discrete districts segregated by function.'"[28]

Much the same pattern of *specialization* held true for New Yorker's residential neighborhoods. The origin of the neighborhood as a meaningful social unit can be traced to the late seventeenth century when the Dongan Charter divided lower Manhattan into five wards (North, South, Dock, East, and West) plus an Out Ward. Though New York remained a small, unified town based upon face-to-face relations between members of an essentially classless society, the distribution of institutions such as markets, churches, and taverns had begun to transform wards into neighborhood communities. Early in the eighteenth century, the clustering of Dutch residents in the North Ward and English in the East led to the formation of rudimentary ethnic communities anchored by neighborhood churches. Throughout the eighteenth century, residents lived in small spatial clusters inhabiting homes that combined residence and workplace. Nonetheless, wards remained mixed in ethnic and economic composition, and by the end of the century the level of ethnic segregation had actually diminished save for new migrants and minority residence (blacks and Jews).[29]

By 1730, when New York was a trading town of only 7,045 whites plus 1,577 slaves, there were "distinctive patterns" of clustering by "religious identification" and "economic composition" in various parts of the city.[30] New York at the eve of the American Revolution could be divided into "residential neighborhoods of different status characteristics," with "its upper classes" living "within the commercial district and adjacent to it," the artisans residing and working in "a broad band across the center of the city," and the "poor or transient population settling at the fringes."[31]

The formation of residential neighborhoods may have started in the late eighteenth and early nineteenth century with the replacement of older integrated shops and houses by single-family dwellings and the subsequent subdivision of housing often resulting in commercial conversions. During the eighteenth century, weak ethnic communities were replaced by neighborhoods divided by trade and by class. In trade neighborhoods, craft shop owners moved to cheaper land north of Chambers Street, establishing centers for maritime crafts and shipbuilding in Corlears Hook, printing near Franklin Square, and nuisance industries like brewing and tallow-making in the Sixth Ward. In the early nineteenth century, systematic locations of industry helped to create industrial districts along the northern fringe that expanded as the city grew. At the same time, developers who combined Georgian private parks from London with restrictive residential covenants created residential areas like Gramercy Park surrounded by blocks of uniform, single-family housing that catered to the wealthy.[32]

But the fact remains that well into the 1840s—if not beyond—the primitive nature of New York's industry also inhibited the formation of separate residential districts, for most of the city's artisans continued to labor in places "identical to or in close proximity of, their places of residence." Improvements in public transportation, which pushed daily ridership up to 25,000 by the late 1830s, had little impact upon the physical layout of the city. Despite the proliferation of omnibus and railway lines—Manhattan boasted thirty separate horsecar lines and six street railway companies by 1855—fares remained beyond the reach of most residents, and in 1840, according to one estimate, only "23 per cent of New York's industrial workers were employed outside of their homes."[33] The handicraft nature of urban industry and the expense of transportation dampened the formation of residential neighborhoods only for awhile, however. By 1875 such neighborhoods had largely formed.

As New Yorkers moved uptown, the settled areas of the city expanded up the length of Manhattan, engulfing rustic farm hamlets. In 1818 landowners from Greenwich Village petitioned the New York Common Council over street regulations, citing the fact that their settlement would soon "become united to" and make "a component part of the thickly populated part of the city."[34] Just seven years later—and three years after the ravages of a Yellow Fever epidemic had driven much of the city to relocate its banks and stores in makeshift structures erected along Bank Street—the *Commercial Advertiser* observed that "Greenwich is no longer a country village." "Such has been the growth of our city that the building of one block more will connect the two places; and in three years time, at the rate building has been everywhere erected during the last season, Greenwich will be known only as a part of the city, and the suburbs will be beyond them."[35]

Within two decades the notion that Greenwich had ever been a village distinct from New York City already seemed ridiculous to many residents. Major Jack Downing even questioned the appellation "Village," exclaiming, "If I was to die, I couldn't tell it from the city."[36] By mid-century virtually all residential construction occurred north of Fourteenth Street. By 1870 the city's geographic center lay at Union Square, with 85 percent of all New Yorkers living within a two-mile radius.[37] New York City now showed many of the patterns of ethnic, class, and familial segregation which categorize the modern city.

In the forty-five years following 1830, New York grew from a thriving but modest commercial city of 197,112 to a preeminent world metropolis with a population of over one million. At the same time, the force of intra- and intercity residential mobility had redefined the spatial relations of housing and business. This was the crucial period in the evolution of the city's neighborhoods, when heterogeneity gave way to differentiation and New Yorkers became acutely aware of a new social geography. The line of development continuously pushed northward, so that Fourteenth Street, once a dividing line, now seemed as much a part of the teeming city as Wall and Chambers Streets—two former city limits of the eighteenth century. By 1875 much of the haphazard residential and commercial intermixing had given way to discrete areas marked by their different uses of land and distinct patterns of settlement. Some of these areas pushed beyond the bounds of Manhattan.

Even in the "heyday" of the mercantile city, New York's population was

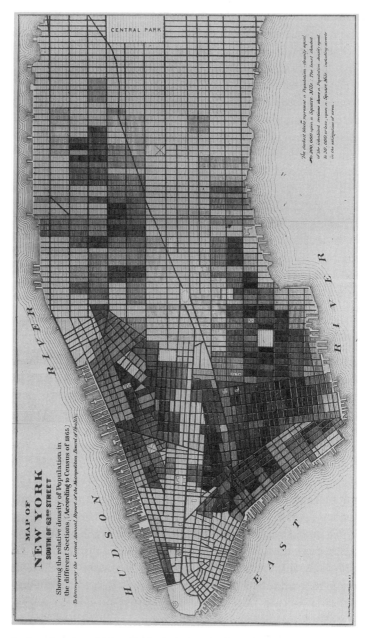

Population density of New York City south of 63rd Street, 1865. From Metropolitan Board of Health of the State of New York, *Second Annual Report*
(New York: Union Printing House, 1868), facing p. 295. Photograph courtesy
of the General Research Division, New York Public Library, Astor, Lenox, and
Tilden foundations.

expanding into the upper reaches of Manhattan and beyond its boundaries into New Jersey and Brooklyn, incorporating them into a nascent metropolitan area many decades before the consolidation of the five boroughs.[38] While antebellum residential areas remained heterogeneous with regard to ethnicity and wealth, most already showed the signs of social differentiation that ultimately would produce neighborhoods defined by social status, family type, and ethnic composition. To be sure, intermingling of a wide spectrum of groups still characterized the city's older wards despite the arrival of large numbers of Irish and German immigrants in the late 1840s and 1850s. But in the new residential areas that sprouted up north of Fourteenth Street during the antebellum period, the axis of differentiation emerged with increasing clarity, as real-estate development and improvements in transportation led to residential clustering. Finally, the flow of people in and out of the city gave rise to early suburbs in the emerging New York *metropolitan* area and promoted regional specialization that mimicked the developing pattern of neighborhoods within urban boundaries.

Neighborhoods in Motion

Residential mobility provided the mechanism for specialization within New York's neighborhoods—and, as will be shown later, over its metropolitan region—but how should its progression be measured?[39] Some of the methods employed by historians to study residential change reveal the difficulties of such an effort. For instance, attempts to trace urban growth and development in New York architecturally through the uptown march of countinghouses and row homes reveals little about the changing composition of the people who lived in the houses.[40] Such an approach to neighborhood evolution misses how quickly residential patterns shifted— a rate too rapid and a pattern too fine for housing changes to reflect. When it comes to understanding where nineteenth-century New Yorkers actually lived, we often know more about the buildings than the people who inhabited them. Even where it is possible to reconstruct "where people lived and who, occupationally and ethnically, they lived near," such geographical calculus risks imposing "a static pattern on a fluid reality." Also it may be that levels of segregation contemporary historians find significant had a different meaning to nineteenth-century observers. Modern writers tend to "assume that 'community' is based on class and therefore more likely to develop as segregation increases"—a very different view from that of contemporaries who often "assumed that 'community' required social mixing and therefore declined as segregation intensified."[41]

Nevertheless, most urban historians agree that the relationship between socio-ethnic factors and residential location is critical to an understanding of the overall spatial organization of cities.[42] In the 1920s sociologists such as Robert E. Park and H. W. Zorbaugh of the "Chicago school" borrowed terminology from biology in their effort to view residential differentiation as an evolutionary process that sorted the various sections of the city into "functional niches" according to land use. Unfortunately, most of their analysis merely succeeded in replacing the biological struggle for survival with an economic one based upon land usage. But in the 1950s, through the work of Esref Shevsky and Wendell Bell, this deterministic approach was supplanted by "social area analysis," a technique that treated the development of urban-industrial society and the emergence of the large-scale urban metropolis as if they were two identical phenomena.

Since Shevsky and Bell held that the evolution of segmented social groups found direct expression in the emerging spatial configuration of the city, neighborhoods were the key to understanding the process of urbanization. Spatial differentiation could thus be understood through the use of factor analysis to examine the interaction among three factors that corresponded to the three principal divisions believed to characterize society: (1) social-economic status, (2) family status and life cycle, and (3) geographic mobility and ethnicity (transiency and origin).[43] Some proponents of factorial ecology hoped that this technique might provide a key to understanding the process of "modernization" by measuring the transition from the undifferentiated preindustrial city to that of the modern metropolis with its neighborhood segregation according to class, ethnicity-transiency, and familial orientation.[44]

Factorial ecology can indeed help to pinpoint the emergence of socially distinct neighborhoods from the diversity that characterized the antebellum walking city.[45] The methodology of social area analysis sub-divides the city into geographic sub-areas, which are scored to produce variables measuring the three main factors of differentiation: first, occupation, income, education, and the value of residential dwellings (each of which has been shown to be highly correlated in their spatial distribution by urban demographers); second, age, gender, marital status, and fertility; and third, ethnicity, race, and transiency.[46]

Foundations of Residence

With the development of working-class, ethnic, or wealthy enclaves, neighborhoods became special places, each possessing a characteristic social identity. Factor analysis reveals these patterns when used to contrast a variety of sample areas by sifting through demographic and social indicators in search of underlying factors. While most statistical techniques involving two or more variables presume each variable to be "unique" (e.g., one variable being dependent upon one or more independent variables) and "to measure a single aspect of any problem," there are some latent characteristics for which "a single variable is unlikely to be an accurate measurement." Factor analysis assumes that indicator variables are correlated and that each indicator consists of two components: a common element associated with some underlying latent variable and a random element not related to the latent factor. When multiple factors exist for a set of indicator variables, some of which are correlated with one factor but not another, factor analysis can be used as an *exploratory* technique to study the number of latent factors and the strength of the relationship of indicator variables with these factors.[47] This is especially useful for the study of urban residential patterns where such indicators as the proportion of servants or elderly in a given district might not directly predict who lived where, but might instead help to reveal such underlying residential factors as class or family status. The examination that follows utilizes samples drawn from the 1855 manuscript state census and the published returns from the lost 1865 census to compare fourteen enumeration districts drawn from four wards, with each ward representing a distinctive example of neighborhood growth and change in terms of household composition, occupational structure, length of residence, ethnicity, and life-cycle stage.[48]

The Fourth Ward was a waterfront district that had long been one of the city's poorest wards. It served as home for sailors and large numbers of craftsmen associated with the shipbuilding industry along the East River. While many of its early inhabitants had been Irish immigrants, the bulk of its population in 1830 was native-born. By the 1870s the area had become one of the most densely packed Irish neighborhoods in New York, with a reputation for poor sanitation exceeded only by its moral depravity, a distinction that it shared with the notorious Five Points in the adjacent Sixth Ward. Here could be found the notorious Gotham Court slum described by numerous reformers. In essence the Fourth was the home of a transient population; its household and community structure reflected its role as the point of arrival for impoverished immigrants.

By contrast, the Fifth Ward was one of New York's most prestigious addresses in 1830, and one of its sample districts contained the most elegant private greenspace in the city, St. John's Park. However, despite the affluent Knickerbockers who occupied the high-stooped brick row houses around the park, the social composition of this area was complex and unstable. Even from its earliest period, the Fifth Ward housed a large proportion of the city's blacks, and, with the influx of immigrants in the 1850s, it also became a center for impoverished Germans. By the 1860s many of the fine old homes had been converted into boardinghouses, brothels, and tenements. The purchase of St. John's Park in 1867 by Cornelius Vanderbilt, and its subsequent transformation into a railroad freight depot, marked just another step in a long process of decay which saw this area gradually absorbed into the expanding central business district. Thus the Fifth Ward was a neighborhood in flight. Its older native population had neither the attachment to space nor the social cohesion to successfully resist the encroachment of warehouses and small industry, and, with seemingly little regret, they abandoned their old homes for ones in the newer, more fashionable neighborhoods uptown.

The other two clusters of sample areas offer further contrasts. The Ninth Ward, which comprised much of New York's first suburb, the western part of Greenwich Village, had the reputation of being New York's "American" neighborhood because of its high concentration of English, native-born, and Knickerbocker residents. Greenwich may have lacked the elegance of a St. John's Park or of a Washington Square, but it was also one of the city's most solidly middle-class areas—respectable without being ostentatious. Despite small pockets of poor Irish who had resided in the Ninth Ward as far back as the 1820s, the abundance of Protestant churches and roomy brick houses erected during the building boom of the 1820s, 1830s, and 1840s attested to the dominance of its native population. The Tenth Ward, located in the center of the Lower East Side, also started as a predominantly native neighborhood, but by the 1870s most of its early residents had moved elsewhere, to be replaced by German immigrants who made this area the nucleus of their "Kleindeutschland." While the Ninth Ward remained remarkably stable, the Tenth underwent a dramatic ethnic transformation.

If heterogeneity had been the hallmark of New York residential life for most of its history, by 1855 one could find clear signs of the formation of distinct neighborhoods based on segregation by class. This pattern of growing homogeneity amidst continuing diversity is shown in a factor analysis of census data. Had New York neighborhoods resembled the classic pattern of spatial differentiation described by factorial ecologists, the associations between variables (indicants) designed to measure socioeconomic, familial, and ethnic characteristics would have produced patterns of underlying relationships (unobserved factors) in which class variables

were significantly correlated under one factor, those for family under a
second factor, and those for ethnicity under a third.

The results of the factor loadings for 1855 (which used samples at the
electoral-district level for the four sample wards) reveal considerable overlap among indicants rather than the clearly defined axes of differentiation
that we would expect in modern cities (table 2.1).[49] The tables show the indicators used in the factor analysis, which indicant correlated significantly
with which factor, and the relative importance of each factor as shown
by variance. If factor analysis is supposed to summarize the interaction of
observed variables in terms of unobserved factors, the meaning of many of
those factors was often unclear—particularly those associated with indicants for ethnicity and familial status. Wealth often mixed with various
nonstatus variables such as concentrations of British and Scottish residents or the absence of young children. Indeed, factor III—which might be
labeled as "proportion-of-working-women"—was highly ambiguous despite tapping several other important indicants of socioeconomic status.
While this factor suggests that residence was shaped by the proportion of
women in the work force, the fact that so many women were employed as
servants leaves unclear whether the clustering of families with servants
operated independently of social status.[50] The ambiguous meaning of this
and several other factors suggests (if nothing else) that the eighteenth-
century pattern of chaotic intermingling of wealth, ethnicity, transiency,
and family status continued well into the nineteenth century.

Yet one factor closely approximated the patterns of independence found
in modern cities: socioeconomic status (I). In the factorial solution, class
operated on three different levels: (1) through occupation, (2) through the
quality of neighborhood housing as measured by the value of each dwelling divided by the number of its residents and the proportion of families
residing in single-family homes, and (3) through the employment of servants.[51] In factor I the high correlations among indicants for single-family
homes, managerial and white collar employment, mean per capita wealth,
property ownership, and the proportion of domestics suggest that housing
quality and occupational status were both prime determinants of who
lived where. Factor I was also stronger than other factors. Not only did
it contribute 27.7 percent to the overall variance compared with the next
largest factor (II), which captured significantly less (21.7 percent), but nine
of its eleven indicants (variables with significant correlation coefficients
levels of ± 0.30 or more) clearly represented either social status or housing
characteristics.[52]

Thus while the factor analysis of New York neighborhoods demon-

Table 2.1   A Factor Analysis of Residence,
Four Sample Wards, New York City, 1855

(A) Indicants used in analysis sampled at the enumeration-district level

No.	Variable
	Socioeconomic characteristics
1	Percentage of male work force, professional and managerial
2	Percentage of nonprofessional male work force, clerical
3	Percentage of work force, skilled
4	Percentage of male work force, unskilled
5	Percentage of work force, female
6	Percentage of female work force, skilled and professional
7	Percentage of families with servants
8	Mean per capita wealth by household
	Family characteristics
9	Percentage of population 20–64, male
10	Percentage of adult population aged 65 and over
11	Percentage of population 0–64 under 20 years
12	Percentage of female population 15 years and over not married
13	Percentage of male population 15 years and over not married
14	Fertility ratio (children under 5 years to married females 20–49 years weighted by age distribution)
15	Percentage of females 15–64 in work force
16	Percentage of males widowers
17	Percentage of females widowed
18	Percentage of families with boarders
	Ethnic characteristics
19	Percentage of population New York City-born
20	Percentage of population U.S. but not New York state-born
21	Percentage of population Irish-born
22	Percentage of population German-born
23	Percentage of population British and Scottish-born
24	Percentage of population black
25	Percentage of population resident 1–3 years
26	Mean years resident for non-New York City-born
27	Percentage of eligible aliens unnaturalized
	Housing characteristics
28	Percentage of population in single-family homes
29	Percentage of families that own property
30	Percentage of families in single-family homes

Source: New York State Census for 1855 (manuscript), wards 4, 5, 9, 10.

Table 2.1   (*continued*)

(B) Rotated Seven-Factor Solution (Varimax criterion)

Indicant*	No.	I	II	III	IV	V	VI	VII	h²
Pop. in single-family house	28	94	—	—	—	—	—	—	97
Families in single-family houses	30	92	—	—	—	—	—	—	97
British and Scottish	23	82	—	—	—	—	—	—	82
Skilled female	6	−74	—	—	—	36	—	—	86
Male nonprofessional clerical	2	70	—	—	—	−30	34	—	75
Mean per capita wealth	8	66	—	—	—	—	—	—	56
Families with servants	7	65	—	69	—	—	—	—	94
Professional/ managerial	1	63	—	—	—	34	61	—	99
Property ownership	29	47	—	43	—	−61	—	—	82
Females not married	12	36	—	76	—	—	—	—	91
Under 20 population	11	−30	—	—	—	−62	—	−44	86
Aged 65 and over	10	—	91	—	—	—	—	—	87
New York City-born	19	—	80	—	—	—	—	−33	84
Mean years resident	26	—	75	44	—	—	—	—	91
Population 20–64 male	9	—	−64	—	—	56	39	—	91
Non-New York U.S.-born	20	—	60	—	—	−39	—	57	92
Males not married	13	—	−57	46	—	—	−33	−30	82
Irish-born	21	—	−56	—	62	39	30	—	99
Percentage females in workforce	15	—	—	81	46	—	—	—	95
Percentage work force female	5	—	—	77	—	—	—	—	89
Fertility	14	—	—	51	50	—	—	−36	80
Resident 1–3 years	25	—	—	−41	—	79	—	—	91
Skilled work force	3	—	—	—	−87	—	—	—	89
Unskilled work force	4	—	—	—	83	—	—	—	87
German-born	22	—	—	—	−77	—	30	—	91
Families with boarders	18	—	—	—	—	82	—	—	80

Table 2.1   (*continued*)

Indicant*	No.	Factor Loading							h²
		I	II	III	IV	V	VI	VII	
Widowers	16	—	—	—	—	67	36	48	85
Unnaturalized aliens	27	—	—	—	—	—	79	—	67
Widows	17	—	—	—	—	—	—	84	86
Blacks	24	—	—	—	—	—	—	83	78
Percentage of factor variance		27.7	21.7	19.8	11.2	8.1	7.0	4.6	(100.0)
Percentage of total variance		24.4	19.2	17.5	10.3	7.6	6.6	4.6	(90.2)

*Only coefficients of +/− 0.30 or more are indicated.

strates the ambiguity characteristic of cities in an intermediate state of development, social rank was emerging as the most important—and only distinct—determinant of residential choice during this early period of neighborhood development. Increasingly sharp class boundaries brought by industrialization, the influx of Irish and German immigrants, and the aggressive invasion of an expanding central business district into adjacent residential areas forcibly altered traditional forms of urban organization to create a degree of social segregation hitherto unknown in the neighborhoods of Manhattan.

Socioeconomic rank continued to shape residential choice in 1865 in much the same manner as it had a decade before. A factor analysis of ward-level data from the 1865 state census[53] shows once again that factor I, which contained high loadings for indicants of social status, accounted for nearly twice as much variance as any other (table 2.2). Likewise, the underlying dimension of differentiation for ethnicity and family status remained indistinct and the separation between factors blurred. While wards varied according to the number of skilled workers, servants, laborers, and upper-level professionals they contained, even factor I showed confusing correlations between social status and indicants of "familialism" and ethnicity such as marital status, levels of fertility, New York City-born, and the presence of Germans.

Yet if the 1865 results offer further evidence of the survival of pre-industrial vestiges associated with the walking city amidst the progress of "industrialization," they also offer a glimpse of two aspects of citywide neighborhood development not apparent in the 1855 data: (1) the eclipse of older native enclaves near New York's business center in the face of commercial encroachment and invasions of newly arrived immigrants and (2) the development of new suburban neighborhoods. Declining neighborhoods adjoining centers of commerce—typified by factor II—housed large numbers of young single men holding clerical jobs in numerous hotels and boardinghouses—together with the domestics who served them. The negative loading in the factor for population under age twenty and for New York City-born suggests that transitional neighborhoods were also places inhabited by aging parents whose grown children had departed for more fashionable areas leaving "empty nests." By contrast, newly emerging neighborhoods (factor III) were strongly native, prosperously white-collar, and family-oriented (as measured by fertility). Many of these new areas, which lay on the outskirts of the developed city, also served as home to large numbers of Irish immigrants who settled in such ethnic enclaves as Hell's Kitchen or in the shanty towns that fringed the built-up sections of the Upper East and West Sides.

The factor analyses for 1855 and 1865 thus reveal two simultaneous processes which underlay the development of the modern neighborhood: one worked at the level of the local areas to create well-defined districts under three principal axes of social differentiation, and the other operated citywide to transform New York's overall spatial structure. Like other American cities of the time, the concentration and chaos characteristic of the walking city rapidly gave way to an ordered array of nonresidential business districts and residential neighborhoods. But New York's emerging spatial order differed markedly from that of other cities in one fundamental respect: the extent to which class shaped residence when compared to other factors including ethnicity.[54] Certainly, by the early 1850s attributes such as wealth, ethnicity, and even, to a lesser extent, age and marital status exerted considerable influence upon who lived where, but the prerogatives of class—the employment of servants and residence in uncrowded housing—were the earliest determinants of neighborhood to emerge. The impersonal, invisible hand of the marketplace intervened to limit the freedom of immigrant and native New Yorkers to live among their countrymen.

This same economics of land development could be found at work in the new commercial and industrial centers that sprang up in Manhattan's sparsely populated lower wards and along both river fronts, driving out residents from the emerging central business district. Ethnicity, to the extent it shaped residential choice, functioned under the constraints of the real-estate market and the broader pattern of commercial development. Indeed, during much of the nineteenth century, most immigrants settled in small clusters with their fellow countrymen rather than in seg-

Table 2.2   A Factor Analysis of New York City Residence, 1865

(A) Indicants used in analysis, sampled at the ward level

No.	Variable
	Socioeconomic characteristics
1	Percentage of work force, professional and managerial
2	Percentage of nonprofessional work force, clerical
3	Percentage of work force, skilled
4	Percentage of work force, unskilled
5	Ratio of servants to total number of families
	Family characteristics
6	Percentage of males widowers
7	Percentage of females widows
8	Percentage of total population over 65 years
9	Percentage of population 0–64 under 20 years
10	Percentage of population 21–64, male
11	Fertility ratio (children under 5 years to 1000 females 15–44 years)
12	Percentage of population married
	Ethnic characteristics
13	Percentage of population black
14	Percentage of population Irish-born
15	Percentage of population German-born (includes Prussia)
16	Percentage of population New York City-born
17	Percentage of population New York state but not New York City-born
18	Percentage of population U.S. but not New York state-born
19	Percentage of foreign-born population naturalized
	Housing characteristics
20	Mean value of dwellings (in dollars)
21	Mean number of families per dwelling
22	Gross population density (people per square mile)
23	Percentage of population increase 1855–65

Sources: Computed from Secretary of State, *Census of the State of New York for 1865* (Albany, 1866); Franklin B. Hough, *Statistics of Population of the City and County of New York as Shown by the State Census of 1865* (New York, 1866). Variable 22 from State of New York, Metropolitan Board of Health, *Second Annual Report* (New York, 1868), p. 97.

regated institutionally complete ethnic "ghettos." Though the influx of large numbers of Germans and Irish in the decade preceding the Civil War did produce areas classifiable by nationality, these neighborhoods were more often centers for immigrant cultural institutions serving a scattered community than they were residential enclaves for a single segregated

Table 2.2   (continued)

(B) Rotated Five-Factor Solution (Varimax criterion)

Indicant*	No.	Factor Loading					h²
		I	II	III	IV	V	
Ratio of servants	5	−89	30	30	—	—	98
Married	12	84	—	—	—	—	79
Skilled work force	3	83	—	—	—	—	86
Unskilled work force	4	−81	—	—	36	—	88
Mean dwelling value	20	−81	—	33	—	—	81
Population density	22	72	—	31	—	33	79
Fertility	11	66	46	—	−47	—	93
Irish-born	14	−58	49	—	53	—	86
Under 20	9	55	−37	−61	−30	—	95
German-born	15	47	—	—	56	45	90
Professional/managerial	1	−46	80	—	—	—	88
New York City-born	16	38	37	−55	−35	—	77
Non-New York state U.S.-born	18	−34	88	—	—	—	100
Aged 65 and over	8	—	74	—	—	—	59
Mean families per dwelling	21	—	70	—	—	42	81
Naturalized foreign born	19	—	−69	—	—	—	57
New York State-born outside N.Y.C.	17	—	66	—	—	−41	64
Population increase	23	—	33	−62	—	—	64
Clerical work force	2	—	—	76	—	—	63
Male 21–64 years	10	—	—	65	—	—	44
Blacks	13	—	—	41	—	−31	37
Widows	7	—	—	—	83	—	74
Widowers	6	—	—	—	—	60	37
Percentage of factor variance		47.5	24.5	14.4	8.3	5.3	(100.0)
Percentage of total variance		36.2	19.4	12.0	7.6	5.6	(80.9)

*Only coefficients of +/− 0.30 or more are indicated.

group. Fewer than half of New York's Germans could be found in Kleindeutschland or its adjacent wards in the Lower East Side, despite the fact that nearly half the city's population lived in this area. With the exception of clusters of poor, recently arrived immigrants in the Fourth and Sixth Wards, the proportion of Irish inhabitants varied little from area to area. The greatest ethnic segregation occurred not in immigrant but in native wards, where Knickerbockers congregated hoping to escape the influx of newcomers.

Consequently suggestions that an "immigrant city" preceded the more modern class-based "industrial city" (as in places like Detroit) certainly did not hold up for eastern seaport walking cities where ethnic neighborhoods were often a transitional stage in spatial evolution that followed the imposition of the more basic geographical structure of class and specialized land use.[55] The clustering of jobbers and the growth of the central business district preceded ethnic differentiation and operated independently of the forces of immigration.[56] Ethnic clustering was determined by broader real-estate pressures that determined rent levels that immigrants could afford, as well as where available housing might be located.

Neighborhoods, Mobility, and Region

The turmoil of Moving Day did not stop at the city limits. As the internal movement of inhabitants on May Day contributed to the internal ordering of the urban environment, so the movement of in- and out-migrants led to the emergence of the urban "system," in which suburban towns and satellite industrial cities became integrated into a larger metropolitan region. A knowledge of destinations for New Yorkers who left the city thus makes geographical mobility a measure of the process of metropolitanization.

Our understanding of "the historical rhythm of geographic mobility" and the movement of people beyond municipal boundaries remains somewhat unclear.[57] Despite scholarship on levels of persistence and the role of "chaining" or kinship ties in shaping migrant destination, the historical debate continues over how to measure out-migration, the direction of mobility, its causes, and its implications.[58] As residents "shifted about once, twice, several times a year," adrift in New York's regionally based labor markets, the extraordinarily high levels of mobility (estimated at between 44 and 70 percent per decade) make questions about the "peregrinations of those who moved about" particularly difficult to answer. They perhaps await "some massive computer study."[59]

The motivations for such "peregrinations" are indeed complex, encompassing employment and other factors that draw or repel migrants, not to mention the rich array of kinship or friendship ties that bind residents to a neighborhood or provide the social network to facilitate an escape.[60] The *direction* of moves can be systematically studied to ascertain where New York out-migrants settled.[61] Church records offer a source of data that, while limited in its focus on a small number of relatively prosperous parishioners, nevertheless avoids the problem of data linkage (e.g., locating information on names drawn from one source in other records). Using Catholic church records, Jay Dolan showed that three out of five

German and Irish immigrants died or left the city within a twenty-year period, with only one in four Irish remaining. But Catholic records disclosed nothing about destinations.[62] However, membership records from Protestant churches, particularly letters of transference provide a wealth of information on the origins, directions, and timing of much geographical mobility beyond New York City's borders.[63]

Destination was influenced by a number of things including the timing of the move, the changing nature of the neighborhood in which the church was located, and, to some extent, the ebbing and flowing of religious sentiment among Protestant churchgoers. But one thing is clear: effective neighborhood boundaries for church members extended well beyond the city's limits into the broader metropolitan area.

A breakdown of 325 church transferal records by the years during which ministers dismissed parishioners to other congregations shows that more members departed in the decades of the 1840s and the 1860s than at any other period (table 2.3). In the 1840s membership rapidly rose and fell in the wake of religious revivals which swept New York, the emotional intensity of evangelism dividing congregations and many members leaving to found or join other churches. Most of the departures of the 1860s, on the other hand, were clearly the result of the changing character of the native Protestant wards in which church members lived. As waves of immigrants rapidly invaded the lower wards, many established churches moved uptown after having experienced losses in their congregations. Parishioners unable to move—particularly those from the strongly native Lower West Side—were left with the hard decision of whether to continue their memberships from afar or to transfer to other closer churches.

Most of the intracity migrants who departed during the 1850s moved to the newer, rapidly developing middle section of the city between Fourteenth and Fortieth Streets including the districts of Chelsea and Gramercy Park. In the 1860s the more northerly wards above Fortieth Street came to equal old Midtown in popularity.

Nearly half of those dismissed by downtown churches left New York City entirely (which was then Manhattan), although few of these were moves of a long distance. Thirty percent settling in the areas adjacent to Manhattan which comprised a nascent New York metropolitan region.[64] New Jersey was the usual destination, accounting for over 16 percent of all dismissals. Few of these moves seem to have been directly related to industrial employment. From the early 1830s onward more than one out of ten individuals who left the Lower West Side crossed the Hudson River to settle in Hoboken, Jersey City, or the other small communities within easy access of Manhattan, rather than in developing manufacturing cen-

Table 2.3   Destination by Date of Departure, Protestant
Church Members, Sample Areas, New York City, 1830–75.

Variables: Destination: location of church that member was dismissed to.
            Date of departure: year that letter of dismissal was sent (grouped by
                decade).

Terms of Model (controlled for)	χ^2	d.f.	significance
(All associations)	95.4	60	.0027

Table for destination by date dismissed (raw data)

Destination	Date dismissed (% across)						N (row)	% Down
	1830	1840	1850	1860	1870	1880+		
Lower West	18.2	44.4	5.1	22.2	5.1	5.1	99.0	30.5
Lower East	34.8	39.1	13.0	8.7	0.0	4.3	23.0	7.1
Mid. Manhattan	0.0	11.1	44.4	25.9	14.8	3.7	27.0	8.3
Up. Manhattan	0.0	5.6	27.8	38.9	16.7	11.1	18.0	5.5
Brooklyn	10.3	27.6	17.2	20.7	24.1	0.0	29.0	8.9
New Jersey	9.3	20.4	14.8	18.5	25.9	11.1	54.0	10.6
N.Y. State	16.0	28.0	24.0	24.0	8.0	0.0	25.0	7.6
North suburbs*	0.0	28.6	7.1	35.7	21.4	7.1	14.0	4.3
South U.S.	20.0	20.0	20.0	20.0	20.0	0.0	5.0	1.5
West U.S.	0.0	0.0	50.0	25.0	25.0	0.0	4.0	0.0
New England	12.5	25.0	12.5	12.5	25.0	12.5	16.0	4.9
Midwest	20.0	30.0	10.0	20.0	20.0	0.0	10.0	3.0
Mid-Atlantic	0.0	0.0	100.0	0.0	0.0	0.0	1.0	0.0

N (table) = 325.0

*Westchester and Rockland counties.
Source: Membership records for sample churches (see appendix A) for wards 4, 5, 9, and
10; New York City, 1830–75.

ters like Newark or Paterson. By the postbellum period the Garden State
accounted for nearly a third of all moves. Brooklyn was an early suburban
refuge from the bustle of Lower Manhattan, but seemed to have lost some
of its popularity with well-to-do Protestant out-migrants in the 1880s,
after the opening of the Brooklyn Bridge made that city more accessible
to the working class. After 1860 Rockland and Westchester counties also
attracted many of the out-migrants who settled in such small pastoral
hamlets as Morrissania and Fordham (later to become the Bronx). Twenty
percent of the church members departed the New York metropolitan area
entirely. The favored destinations of these migrants were the Hudson Val-

ley, Albany and, to a lesser extent, the Mohawk River Valley. A few even made it to California in the wake of the Gold Rush.

The reasons for these varied moves are difficult to ascertain given the limited information provided by the church records. Occupational and residential distinctions apparently made little difference as to who moved where, for a model comparing destination and vertical occupational rank produced no significant associations, and, similarly, current address had no measurable correlation with the direction of moves.[65] Length of church membership, however, did correlate with destination (see table 2.4). Brooklyn (including Long Island), New Jersey, and the upper reaches of Manhattan attracted migrants with a greater length of tenure than any other residential district of New York City. Churches in such areas as the Lower

Table 2.4   Destination by Tenure of Church Membership, Protestant Church Members, Sample Areas, New York City, 1830–75

Variables: Destination: location of church that member was dismissed to.
           Tenure: length of church membership by category.

Terms of Model (controlled for)	χ^2	d.f.	significance
(All associations)	29.0	18	.0479

Table of destination by tenure (raw data)

Destination	Tenure (% across)			N (row)
	Short 0–4 yrs.	Medium 5–14 yrs.	Long 15+ yrs.	
Lower West Side	47.5	45.5	7.1	99.0
Lower East Side	82.6	8.7	8.7	23.0
Middle (14th–20th St.)	44.4	40.7	14.8	27.0
Upper Manhattan (above 40th St.)	38.9	50.0	11.1	18.0
Brooklyn	39.3	50.0	10.7	28.0
New Jersey	34.5	45.5	20.0	55.0
N.Y. State	60.0	36.0	4.0	25.0
North suburbs*	57.1	35.7	7.1	14.0
Other	35.9	56.4	7.7	19.5
New England	51.6	45.2	3.2	15.5
N (table) = 324.0				

*Westchester and Rockland counties.
Source: Membership records for sample churches (see appendix A) for wards, 4, 5, 9, and 10; New York City, 1830–75.

East Side, which had experienced decline in status among natives with the rapid influx of immigrants, experienced corresponding drops in transfers of churchgoers who had been members for more than five years. Destinations in the Midwest and South, on the other hand, attracted members who had presumably remained in the city long enough to accumulate the resources necessary for long-distance migration, suggesting that migration was a function of life cycle and age (though the church dismissal records say nothing explicitly about either of these two factors). Suburban moves frequently reflected the desire of older migrants to retire to the country or to join kin. Marital and occupational opportunities likely influenced moves to the hinterland.[66]

Thus despite their often elite bias, Protestant church membership records nonetheless confirm the extent to which urban decentralization had become an established part of New York's growth and development by the antebellum period. The movement to suburban New Jersey and in Brooklyn Heights had begun early in the nineteenth century. One historian found that Brooklyn had already begun to outdistance New York in terms of growth by 1810, and, "on the opposite shore, Newark, Jersey City, Hoboken, Hudson, and Elizabeth were, in percentage terms, outgrowing New York by the 1840s." For well-to-do professionals, the distance between residence and work increased rapidly as early as the decade of 1835–1845.[67] An 1818 visitor observed that "Brooklyn on Long Island and Paulus Hook in New Jersey on the other side of the Hudson" (lying only one quarter of an hour away from New York by steamboat) could be "regarded as suburbs because of the constant and easy transportation."[68]

The rivers separating New York from New Jersey and Brooklyn probably facilitated the rapid development of these "ferry suburbs." Compared with the high cost of omnibus transportation, steam ferries were quick, efficient, and inexpensive.[69] One aristocratic English visitor marveled at the Hudson ferries, which ran all hours of the day and were "as comfortable as bridges, for persons in carriages need not alight, but may drive into the boat, and remain there undisturbed to the end of the passage, and drive on shore again." Passengers without carriages were accommodated in "pleasant cabins with warm and comfortable fires."[70] Another traveler credited the "well regulated communication" which departed for Brooklyn every three minutes and for New Jersey every ten.[71]

The declining status and rapid depopulation of formerly prestigious Lower Manhattan areas such as the Fifth Ward, which prompted many merchants and professionals to stop residing above their countinghouses, were the by-products of this early suburbanization.[72] A downtown minister lamented the force of the "two strong currents" that were carrying away the "protestant and christian populations" leaving Jews and Catholics behind as "driftwood." One of these was the "up town current bearing the rich to more eligible parts of the city," and the other was "the popular current appealing to the purse and bearing the middle classes to the rural districts."[73] Long-term residents stranded in the wake of this outmigration by a refusal or inability to move seemed more and more to be quaint relics in their changing neighborhoods. Under the grim shadows of the New York Central train yard that replaced the stately beauty of St. John's Park in 1867, John Ericson, inventor of the warship Monitor, stubbornly refused to abandon his Beach Street home. On the East River side of Manhattan, in the decaying Rose Street area of the Fourth Ward, old-style merchant John Allan seemed little more than an "antiquary," living a "hermit-like existence" in an "old-fashioned house . . . encircled by factories, sailors boarding-houses and mansions of questionable repute."[74]

By the 1850s suburbs had begun to attract a broader cross-section of New Yorkers, including larger numbers of the working class who moved not to seek status but rather to escape Manhattan's rising rents. A London workingman who seemed to like little of what he saw during his American stay found the crowded tenements so unbearable that after "a fortnight in one of these horrible dens . . . we were glad to cross to Brooklyn, where houses are smaller, and things have not got such a pitch of dirt, discomfort, and indecency."[75] To some reformers, suburbs appeared to be antidotes to the expense and poor housing conditions of the settled city. Samuel Halliday urged working-class families with children to "push to the upper parts of the island" or, better yet, to Brooklyn or to New Jersey, "where respectable cottages are to be had for the same rent that will hire a single floor in the city."[76] Many immigrants had already settled there. Even before the massive influx of the "forty-eighters" (German immigrants who arrived in the wake of the 1848 revolutions), Williamsburg was over two-thirds German and, across the Hudson, other small settlements thrived in Jersey City and Hoboken. Large numbers of Irish similarly departed Manhattan for the relative comfort of Brooklyn, and by the 1870s these outlying cities accounted for four-fifths of the metropolitan area's growth (table 2.5).[77]

So strong was the outward flow that newspaper editorialists in the 1860s and 1870s voiced increasing concern over the flight of native "bank clerks, bookkeepers, and salesmen" to "New Jersey, Staten Island, or Westchester to secure attractive and comfortable homes." "New York is practically losing the best part of its population," warned The Evening Post.[78] Edward Crapsey, an early criminologist, went so far as to argue that the flight to the suburbs "denuded" the city of "that invaluable balance-wheel to political action, the middle class," which brought prosperity and virtuousness

Table 2.5   Comparative Population Increases for New York
City, Brooklyn, and Hudson County, New Jersey, 1830–75

Area	Population					
	1830	1840	1850	1860	1870	1875
N.Y.C.	197,112	312,710	515,547	805,358	942,292	1,041,886
Brooklyn	20,535	47,618	138,882	279,122	396,099	509,154
Hudson County	4,651*	8,327	12,282	53,826	118,143	405,903
Newark	10,953	17,290	38,844	51,711	105,059	123,310
N.Y. metro area (excl. Newark)	222,298	368,650	666,711	1,138,306	1,456,534	1,956,943

*Includes Bergen County.

	Net and Percentage Increases Decennially				
	1830–40	1840–50	1850–60	1860–70	1870–75
N.Y.C.					
Net	115,598	202,837	289,811	136,934	99,594
%	58.6	64.9	56.2	17.0	10.6
Brooklyn					
Net	27,078	91,268	140,240	116,977	113,055
%	131.9	191.7	101.0	41.9	28.5
Hudson County					
Net	3,676	3,955	41,544	64,317	287,760
%	79.0	47.5	338.3	119.5	243.6
Metro area					
Net	146,352	298,061	471,592	318,228	500,409
%	65.8	80.9	70.7	27.9	34.4
Newark					
Net	6,337	21,554	12,867	53,348	18,251
%	172.8	124.7	33.1	103.2	17.4
Suburbs as % of metro growth	21.0	31.9	38.5	57.0	80.1

Source: New Jersey, Department of State, Compendium of Censuses, 1726–1905 (Trenton, N.J., 1906). Secretary of State, Census of the State of New York for 1875 (Albany, 1875)

to New Jersey, Long Island, and "contiguous counties" at "the expense of the metropolis of the western world":

> Every man of moderate income saw that when he could house his family more decently and at less cost in any one of the suburban towns of New Jersey, he could reach them sooner and with less hardship, even if twenty miles away, than he could if they were only a tenth of that distance up-town. Therefore an exodus began to these towns, which has continued for several years, to the detriment of the city to a degree that is hardly realized. Thousands of men who during business hours engaged in our marts, became rooted in foreign soil, had all their home-associations elsewhere, were utterly indifferent as to the conduct of municipal affairs, and spent or invested without the city the money they acquired within it.[79]

Crapsey's prediction that the laboring populations would be brutalized by criminals as a result of the exodus of a noble citizenry never came to pass, but out-migration did become a leading force behind urban decentralization.

Conclusion

From the enormous flux and apparent chaos of Moving Day, the city's neighborhoods were undergoing a transformation that left them ultimately more distinctive and homogeneous. By 1865 the essential axes of residential differentiation had already emerged. First wealth, and later, ethnicity and family composition determined who moved where. But if clearly defined neighborhoods housed only a minority of New Yorkers during the antebellum period, a sign of how incomplete the process of neighborhood differentiation remained even into the mid-1860s, the overall direction of this change was clear.

The centrifugal force of geographic mobility also extended to suburbs and satellite manufacturing cities, forming "metropolitan" environments that expanded the range of neighborhoods available to residents. Within Manhattan's boundaries, the exodus of established residents from transitional areas in the path of the expanding central business district to newer more fashionable areas farther uptown (as shown by the 1865 factor analysis) reversed the traditional social geography of the city. Affluent residents now settled in suburban neighborhoods and commuted into the central business district. Rich and poor, natives and newcomers increasingly led lives in separate neighborhoods. The only constant was change itself. No sooner had these neighborhoods developed than they began to change. The lesson of May Day is thus not merely the creation of order out of flux, but ultimately the dynamism and fragility of neighborhoods—a point that a bifurcated view of New York's spatial geography all too easily overlooks.

3　Patterns of Neighborhood Change

■■■■■■■■ At the close of the antebellum period, shocked reformers and clergymen discovered two profound changes that had radically altered the urban environment in New York, threatening to leave them strangers in their own city. First, the propensity of immigrants to settle in distinct enclaves fragmented the Metropolis and placed the newcomers beyond the beneficent influence of native social control. The New York Association for Improving the Condition of the Poor observed in its 1867 report: "The fact is obvious and indisputable, that the social relations of the foreign to the native population have, in late years, materially changed. They no longer, as formerly, melt away, or so blend with the native stocks as to become incorporated." Now the Irish and Germans, who composed the bulk of the foreign population, showed a "clear tendency to segregate" into their own "distinct communities almost impervious to American sentiments and influences, as are the inhabitants of Dublin or Hamburg."[1]

The second change was the astronomical rise of real-estate values, which drove the wealthy from socially diverse areas in the center city to newer, more homogeneous neighborhoods uptown and put pressure on working people. The exodus of New York's Knickerbocker elite from its ancestral homes along Whitehall, State Street, and lower Broadway attracted the attention of *Putnam's Monthly*:

> Aristocracy, startled and disgusted with the plebeian trade which already threatened to lay its insolent hands upon her mantle, and to come trampling into her silken parlors with its heavy boots and rough attire, fled by dignified degrees up Broadway, lingered for a time in Greenwich-street, Park Place, and Barclay-street, until at length find-

ing the enemy still persistent, she took a great leap into the wilderness above Bleecker-street. Alas for the poor lady, every day drives her higher and higher; Twenty-eighth-st is now familiar with her presence, and she is already casting her longing eyes still further on.[2]

For residents of lesser means also, the rapid burst in land speculation and commercial development in the 1850s meant escalating rents and of course housing scarcities. As early as the 1830s, well before the great influx of Irish and German immigrants, one New Yorker complained that inflation had pushed the cost of housing up 33 percent in just two years until it was "next to impossible for a man in a moderate income to support a wife and children." With their earnings being diverted to rent and "nothing left wherewith to purchase food, clothing, and fuel," city dwellers would have to "turn their backs upon the city and seek residence elsewhere" if they hoped to avoid impoverishment.[3]

Throughout the two decades to follow, this same complaint would be heard in good times and bad as the influx of immigrants accelerated. In 1860 a retired cartman lamented that "with all her glitter of prosperity, and all her rapid increase in wealth and population, New York is not now the place for a poor man that it first was" in the 1830s. Then, craftsmen's wages were higher, "the necessities of life were low in price and better in quality than they are at present," and a good, comfortable apartment could be found for $75 a year; "*now* the same accommodations will cost twice that amount."[4] Walt Whitman, then employed as a journalist, declared: "In no other city in the whole world, does rent occupy so large a proportion of expenditures as in New York." The price of accommodation was, according to his estimation, two to four times as high as in London, with a brownstone-fronted row house costing $2,000 and lesser dwellings averaging $700. Because the "competition on the narrow island for dwelling-places is so keen," only New York's "better classes" could afford the luxury of ownership, while most of the poor were forced to live in tenements that were "cheap and nasty."[5]

Class and Ethnicity

It has become common wisdom that the tightening supply of housing and the clustering of immigrants helped to establish ethnic background and employment (rank and classification) as important predictors of residential location, thus making neighborhood an important badge of social rank that revealed "a new structure of class relations within the city's social landscape."[6] With "social distance" (stratification) serving as an increasingly important symbol of "class standing and as a means of maintaining the existing distinction between ranks," wealth and address together came to provide valuable information on an occupant's "likely social characteristics."[7] While the class composition of neighborhoods suggested a city in which "not all wards had fashionable neighborhoods and not all wards had slums but few had neither and probably half had both," the wealthy increasingly found their homes through social circles that promoted residential clustering based upon "feelings of class exclusiveness."[8] As we have already seen, labor historians have also treated neighborhoods as cradles of class-based community.[9]

Yet these views overstate residential homogeneity and exaggerate the importance of neighborhoods in fomenting class divisions. Save for the elite's ability to afford housing in the newly evolved residential neighborhoods, the actual extent of class-based segregation in New York is uncertain. The differentiation that did exist was often "both imprecise and unstable" due to the rapid expansion of commerce and the growth in the number of poor.[10] Economic differences may well have "manifested themselves within buildings and blocks rather than *between* neighborhoods, with the very poorest residents living in sunless rear buildings, cellars and attics and the more prosperous housed in apartments on the lower floors"—a "Parisianization" of Manhattan housing.[11] Not until late in the nineteenth century, one geographer noted, "did socially mobile people move in substantial numbers to exclusively residential additions to the city that catered to the needs of both the lower middle class, and, eventually, to the more securely employed levels of the working class."[12] Even many wealthy New Yorkers lived in "wards inhabited by families of modest means, with plebeian alleys, streets and blocks typically bordering the neighborhoods of the wealthy."[13]

Likewise the alarm that social reformers expressed at the perceived segregation of New York's foreign population was doubtless exaggerated, for the same complex pattern of residential diversity also held for immigrant neighborhoods.[14] One study using data drawn from the 1860 census to examine the distribution of Germans and Irish in ninety-three enumeration districts concluded that "although a limited number of districts housed proportionately larger numbers of the two major foreign groups," the proportion of Irish and Germans in most areas varied little.[15] Indeed, while Germans tended to cluster more than the Irish, the overall rate of dispersal for both groups was remarkably uniform. Not until the second great wave of immigration later in the nineteenth century would two ingredients essential to the formation of immigrant ghettos exist in sufficient quantities to foster ethnic segregation: a generous supply of centrally located

housing and jobs for unskilled labor in the central business district.[16] High
population turnover and an ethnic labor mix actually delayed the formation of tight concentrations until later in the century. Like London's Irish
population who "lived in enclaves inside English working-class territory,
worked in English areas and traversed English areas to visit other Irish
enclaves," few foreign-born New Yorkers ever lived in any area even resembling the classic immigrant "ghetto." In both cities "community was
essentially ethnic rather than geographical," extending beyond one's residential location.[17]

Lastly such a contrasting picture of continued ethnic and class heterogeneity contradicts the basic description of urban neighborhoods that historians have offered for other cities.[18] Antebellum New York City not only
differed in its high level of ethnic diffusion and low degree of occupational
differentiation, it also lacked the other crucial ingredient in neighborhood formation: widespread home ownership.[19] Manhattan in the 1850s
(as today) was composed overwhelmingly of renters, not homeowners. In
half of the fourteen enumeration districts sampled, fewer than 3 percent of
all households owned property. Only the Ninth Ward, whose largely native
population belonged to the "middle class of people, composed mainly of
trades-people, clerks, mechanics of the better class, etc.," did levels of
ownership reach between 9 and 17 percent.[20] By 1840 the wave of speculative building had swept beyond Greenwich Village, and most new housing
erected in Manhattan now went up either in the Lower East Side or along
the city's edges. Those new units constructed south of Fourteenth Street
were almost entirely composed of tenements. Single-family housing—
residences most likely to be owner-occupied—were built chiefly for the
white-collar classes in suburban wards, where few New Yorkers lived.[21]
Even this new housing was intended primarily for rental.[22]

Given these low levels of ownership and continuing high degree of heterogeneity, how did the process of residential differentiation take shape?
As we have seen, the rise of residential neighborhoods thus involves a
number of factors including the shift from central to peripheral residence
among the wealthy, the separation of commercial from residential function, and the emergence of axes of differentiation in residence corresponding to class, ethnicity, and family status. How ethnicity shaped neighborhood is the subject of the following section.

Cohorts and Countrymen

The residential attraction of any given area in a city largely depends on
the availability of employment, the cost of housing, and the existence of

established residents with whom the newcomer can feel secure. For immigrants, decisions about where to settle are restricted by their newness to the city and the degree to which their group has been assimilated into the dominant culture. Their age also is an important factor, because the networks of friends, coworkers, and relations who supply much of the information required for finding a job or making a move are age-specific. These network ties, combined with the cultural background of the newcomer, constitute what the early New York sociologist Thomas Jones has called "consciousness of kind"—for example, group identity.[23] But the concept of social cohesion applies equally well to natives as to immigrants. Given this fact, ethnicity should be divided for analysis into two separate components, one encompassing cultural background, and the other, transiency.

Such indicants of transiency as the general age at arrival in New York and the timing of migration are no less important than cultural heritage in explaining how particular neighborhoods were settled. For example, an area fashionable with German newcomers in the 1830s might differ from one attracting Germans in the 1850s. In addition, variations in when particular immigrants arrived might also point to the existence of "zones of emergence" that drew more established immigrants.[24] Coupled with the traditional concept of "ethnic dominance" (e.g., predominance of ethnic groups in particular areas) first articulated by early spatial ecologists, the use of arrival cohorts allows us to study the processes of neighborhood stability and transition.[25] Similarly, variations in arrival ages for pre- and postfamine Irish can serve as a rough measure of employability and ease of adaptation. Intragroup variations among arrival cohorts and in ages at arrival for residents of mid-nineteenth-century New York neighborhoods show a more complex picture of ethnicity as a factor in residence than has heretofore been recognized.

Before famine and revolution brought waves of foreigners to America, only one of the four sample wards had a large foreign population (table 3.1). The 1845 state census—the first canvas to record the exact nativity of New Yorkers—showed the Fourth Ward to be only 48.6 percent native-born (38.4 of its population coming from Ireland).[26] Immigration in the decade 1845–1855 strongly altered the ethnic composition of these wards. The percentage of native-born residents fell from 48.6 percent to 30 percent in the predominantly Irish Fourth Ward and from 68.9 percent to 52.4 percent in the Fifth. The strongly native Tenth Ward experienced the most striking transformation, dropping from 72.1 percent native to 49.1 percent native in just ten years. Only the character of the Ninth Ward remained nearly intact, dropping only 11.9 percent.

Table 3.1   Principal Nativity, Four Sample Wards, New York City, 1835–75

	1835*		1845**		1855		1865		1875	
	%	N	%	N	%	N	%	N	%	N
Ward 4										
Aliens	28.1	2,433	23.6	4,955	47.1	10,785	26.3	4,558	6.2	1,285
Native-born	—	—	48.6	10,211	30.0	6,860	43.4	7,533	48.1	10,018
German	—	—	6.0	1,253	11.7	2,688	11.8	2,049	10.2	2,115
Irish	—	—	38.4	8,061	45.6	10,446	38.1	6,605	32.1	6,681
Ward 5										
Aliens	39.6	2,570	14.9	3,041	34.5	7,462	26.9	4,906	4.8	759
Native-born	—	—	68.9	14,035	52.4	11,322	51.4	9,353	52.7	8,410
German	—	—	3.7	746	12.2	2,633	13.5	2,464	13.2	2,099
Irish	—	—	28.4	5,779	22.5	4,866	24.3	4,380	27.5	4,380
Ward 9										
Aliens	13.5	1,339	12.1	4,239	23.4	9,346	14.3	5,494	3.4	1,688
Native-born	—	—	77.7	24,029	65.8	26,317	69.1	26,602	68.3	33,723
German	—	—	1.3	920	5.5	2,192	6.6	2,524	7.2	3,577
Irish	—	—	20.4	6,320	19.8	7,909	16.5	6,348	16.7	8,259
Ward 10										
Aliens	12.4	1,246	12.0	2,531	38.7	10,783	26.9	8,478	7.9	3,283
Native-born	—	—	72.1	15,131	49.1	12,945	49.6	15,644	46.2	19,284
German	—	—	10.9	2,281	28.6	7,536	33.8	10,649	34.7	14,484
Irish	—	—	15.2	3,198	13.0	3,442	10.0	3,139	5.8	2,435
Total City										
Aliens	21.0	27,669	16.4	60,946	37.0	232,790	20.9	151,838	4.6	48,305
Native-born	—	—	63.7	236,567	47.7	297,278	56.1	407,312	57.2	595,843
German	—	—	6.6	24,416	15.7	97,573	14.8	107,269	15.8	165,021
Irish	—	—	26.0	96,581	19.0	175,735	22.2	161,334	19.1	199,084

Source: Secretary of State, *Census for the State of New York*, for 1845, 1855, 1865, and 1875.
*Ethnic breakdown unavailable for 1835.
**Since no separate figures are available for the Irish population in 1845, the figures for this year actually refer to Great Britain (incl. Ireland, England, Wales, and Scotland).

Immigrants did not settle in a single large concentration but rather formed many small residential clusters scattered with remarkable uniformity throughout the city. Actually, the standard description of segregated ghetto neighborhoods applied best to areas inhabited by *native-born* New Yorkers. Indeed, the evidence presented here suggests that only the high level of segregation of blacks exceeded that of native-born whites.[27] The 1855 census, taken just after the highest levels of immigration had begun to subside, shows the dispersal of immigrants throughout different broad sections of the city (table 3.2). Irish immigrants resided in every neighborhood, with their population levels averaging 30.9 percent (only the Tip of Manhattan shows a concentration exceeding the mean by more than one standard deviation). Although clusters of German settlers were also scattered, this immigrant group was considerably more concentrated, with high proportions to be found in the Lower East Side and the Upper West Side between Fortieth and Eighty-sixth Streets (percentages of 22.3 and 21.0 versus a mean of 13.3, with a standard deviation of 5.5). Levels of segregation for other immigrant groups varied in inverse ratio to their numbers, with Scandinavians, Eastern Europeans, and Southern Europeans showing the strongest tendency to cluster.

The warnings of reformers, if exaggerated, were heeded by one group: their fellow natives. Residential segregation among natives who congregated in so-called "American" wards was far more striking than that for any immigrant group.[28] Indices of dissimilarity computed from the 1855 census for fourteen sample enumeration districts suggest that the desire of native-born New Yorkers to avoid coresidence with the foreign-born was even stronger than the tendency of immigrants to draw inward into their own communities (table 3.3).[29] Such a withdrawal of native-born New Yorkers to segregated neighborhoods suggests a residential "nativism" that may have run even deeper than nativistic political and labor sentiment.[30] Both native New Yorkers and such small foreign-born groups as Scandinavians, Western, Southern, and Eastern Europeans proved to be significantly more segregated than either the Irish or Germans. The dissimilarity figures also show that with the rare exception of an occasional Southerner or Midwesterner, native New Yorkers preferred to live side-by-side with another native-born American or, to a lesser extent, with an Englishman, a Welshman, or a Scotsman with whom they shared a common language. Other native-born migrant groups, such as those from other Middle Atlantic States than New York (mainly New Jersey), similarly preferred neighborhoods dominated by natives of the city. "Consciousness of kind" was clearly a more powerful force behind ethnic cohesion and residential selection for the natives experienced in the culture, employment, and housing markets of Manhattan than it was for most immigrants who, out of necessity, took what they could find.

The relationship between ethnicity and residence was highly fluid over time, fluctuating with changes in residential taste and shifts in the availability of housing. These changes reflected variations between successive waves of migrants and immigrants over several decades. Bonds of membership in a group of arrival cohorts, for instance, often clashed with (in

Table 3.2   Nativity Distribution by Area, New York City, 1855

Neighborhood	New York City	New York State	New England	Mid-Atlantic	South U.S.	West & Mid-West	Canada
			Birthplace (% across)				
Tip of Manhattan (wd. 1,2,3)	27.8	3.8	4.0	2.7	.5	.3	.4
Lower West Side (wd. 5,8,9,15)	40.3	7.9	4.7	5.8	.8	.3	.6
Lower East Side (wd. 4,6,7 10,11,13,14,17)	35.3	3.1	2.2	1.7	.4	.1	.4
Middle West Side (wd. 16,20)	40.8	6.5	3.3	4.0	.4	.2	.5
Middle East Side (wd. 18,21)	39.5	5.3	3.5	4.2	.6	.4	.4
Upper West Side (wd. 22)	36.4	4.3	2.2	2.8	.2	.1	.3
Upper East Side (wd. 19)	37.9	3.4	2.0	2.7	.4	.1	.5
Suburbs (wd. 12)	36.0	5.4	2.9	2.2	.4	.3	.7

Source: Secretary of State, *New York State Census,* 1855, pp. 110–15. Excludes individuals with unknown birthplaces and those born at sea.

some cases, proved more cohesive than) bonds of nativity alone when it came to choosing a neighborhood.

The absence of census data prior to 1850 makes it necessary to work backward from the 1855 manuscript census using a cross-sectional sample of residents not born in New York grouped according to date-of-arrival in order to approximately determine which areas successive waves of settlers favored. A multivariate analysis of variables—such as ethnicity, age at arrival, the estimated year of arrival in New York County, and whether one resided in one of the four sample wards—most clearly shows the strong relationship between ethnic origins and the timing of one's arrival.[31] Yet these two variables also strongly influenced where one resided in 1855 (table 3.4).[32] Neighborhoods underwent changes in desirability even among subsequent waves of the same ethnic group. The propensity of each group to migrate at a different stage of the life cycle acted indirectly through the

				Birthplace (% across)					
England & Wales	Scotland	Ireland	Germany	Scan-danavia	West Europe	East Europe	South Europe	Other	N
3.3	.7	39.5	12.4	.8	1.9	.1	.2	.2	25,166
4.5	1.9	21.9	8.2	.1	2.3	.1	.3	.4	119,663
3.3	.8	27.3	22.3	.2	1.2	.4	.3	.2	271,466
5.0	3.2	30.6	12.3	0.0	.9	.2	0.0	.2	89,008
3.4	1.0	34.0	7.5	.1	.7	0.0	.2	.3	76,834
4.0	1.9	25.4	21.0	.1	1.0	0.0	0.0	0.0	22,589
3.6	1.0	35.8	10.2	0.0	.5	0.0	0.0	.3	17,432
3.7	.9	33.0	12.2	.1	.9	0.0	.2	.4	17,574

factor of ethnicity to influence the demographic composition of neighborhoods.[33]

Percentage tables computed from the modeled data (Base Model Two) show how each ward attracted a different mix of native migrants and immigrants from Great Britain, Ireland, and Germany over the forty years leading up to 1855. Native migrant and immigrant residents formed hierarchies of old-timers and new settlers within respective nativity groups, each composed of members of different arrival cohorts. From this information, we can reconstruct different scenarios of settlement for each of the four wards in the sample.

The Fourth Ward, long a magnet for Irish settlement during the first half of the nineteenth century, initially attracted a wide range of immigrant groups. Even controlling for the changing composition of general immigration, only a third of the early settlers were Irish-born, with native-born

Table 3.3   Indexes of Dissimilarity in Residential Distribution among Ethnic and Migration Groups for Fourteen Sample Electoral Districts, Wards 4,5,9, and 10, New York City, 1855

Area	I NYC	II NYS	III NE	IV MidA	V South
I New York City	—	38	32	20	53
II New York State (excl. N.Y.C.)		—	24	33	51
III New England			—	32	41
IV Mid-Atlantic States				—	43
V South U.S.					—
VI Mid-West U.S.					
VII Canada (incl. Nova Scotia and Newfoundland)					
VIII Great Britain (incl. Wales)					
IX Scotland					
X Ireland					
XI Germany (incl. Prussia)					
XII Scandinavia					
XIII Western Europe (Holland, France, Belgium and Switzerland)					
XIV Eastern Europe (incl. Austria, Poland, Russia)					
XV Southern Europe (incl. Spain, Portugal, Italy, Greece)					
XVI Other					

Source: New York State Census for 1855 (manuscript).

and British migrants accounting for 23.5 and 21.0, respectively, of the pre-1830 cohort group. In the 1830s the number of British and native-born arrival cohorts fell sharply. Those for the Irish nearly doubled. With the passage of time, however, the composition of newcomers into this area became less and less diverse until Irish came to overwhelmingly dominate. The increase in Irish immigration starting in the 1830s and reaching its extraordinary peak in the late 1840s and early 1850s progressively discouraged potential in-migrants from other groups. The percentage of native migrants declined to 7.4 for the 1830s, rebounded briefly in the early 1840s, and dwindled to negligible levels during the decade of Potato Famine migration.

The Tenth Ward also showed a sharp division between long-term residents, most of whom were British or American, and the overwhelmingly German newcomers. Yet a tiny but important cluster of German settlers

VI MidW	VII Can	VIII GB	IX Scot	X Ire	XI Germ	XII Scan	XIII WEur.	XIV EEur.	XV SEur.	XVI Oth	Segregation Index
48	37	38	35	48	68	91	70	72	74	62	42
27	23	26	36	31	24	80	52	68	63	56	21
33	35	39	36	31	48	82	53	59	61	49	24
42	40	36	37	45	55	92	53	73	77	58	36
38	54	48	52	56	60	90	38	76	71	29	49
—	27	21	37	37	39	88	48	67	61	38	23
	—	29	36	44	45	88	61	74	74	51	24
		—	29	31	35	81	44	58	55	46	20
			—	36	54	91	52	63	65	52	34
				—	49	59	64	64	47	51	31
					—	77	49	58	61	64	36
						—	88	77	49	81	77
							—	59	38	44	47
								—	60	70	62
									—	62	57
										—	52

in the pre-1830 arrival group had provided the seed for the area that came to be known as "Kleindeutschland." That number increased in the 1830s and 1840s, so that even before the arrival of the "Forty-Eighters," a third of each arrival cohort group was German-born. Yet the Tenth Ward continued to attract many American and British settlers through the late 1830s (22.5 and 24.6 percent, respectively). Starting in the early 1840s the Tenth Ward experienced a surge in settlement from all immigrant groups, but the rapid acceleration in German in-migration after 1850 thinned the ranks of the Irish moving into the area. By 1855, post-1845 newcomers—most of whom were German-born—had come to outnumber both American-born and British. Native residents remaining in the Tenth Ward found themselves stranded in an area whose character had altered dramatically. In the period between the end of the Civil War and the 1880s outside Protestant churchmen bemoaned the fate of the few survivors of the Anglo-American

Table 3.4   Nativity, Arrival Characteristics, and Neighborhood among Residents Not Born in New York City, Four Sample Wards, New York City, 1855

Variables: Ward: 4, 5, 9, and 10.

Nativity: non-New York City-born (U.S.), Great Britain (incl. Scotland), Ireland, Germany, other.

Year of arrival: Computed x = (1855 − length of residence). Categories: pre-1830, 1830–39, 1840–44, 1845–49, 1850–55.

Age at arrival: Computed x = (age − length of residence). Categories: 1–14, 15–19, 20–24, 30+ years.

Terms of Model (controlled for)	χ^2	χ^2 d.f.	χ^2 signif.	Difference χ^2	Diff. d.f.	Difference signif.	Coef. of determination
Base I							
All 3-way associations (Ward, nativity, arrival	179.9	192	0.7253	—	—	—	—
year) (Nativity, arrival year,	278.6	240	0.0440	98.75	48	0.0001	0.3543
age) (Ward, nativity, age)	251.4	256	n.s.*	—	—	—.	—
(Ward, arrival year,	247.2	240	n.s.*	—	—	—	—
age) All associations	229.4	240	n.s.*	—	—	—	—
excluding 3-way (Ward, nativity, age)	620.3	396	n.s.*	—	—	—	—
Base II							
(Ward, nativity, arrival year)+							
(Ward, age)+(nativity, age)+							
(Arrival year, age)	370.8	352	0.2353	—	—	—	—
(Nativity, age at							
arrival)	491.5	368	0.0001	120.7	16	0.0001	0.2456
(Arrival year, age)	423.9	368	0.0233	53.1	16	0.0001	0.1252
(Ward, age)	398.6	364	n.s.*				

*Probability over 10% (.1); n.s. = not significant.

Table from modeled data (controlling for effects between ward and arrival age): ward by year of arrival, grouped by nativity

Nativity	Ward	Year of Arrival (% across)					N
		1820–29	1830–39	1840–44	1845–49	1850–55	
U.S.	4	15.2	13.6	20.0	15.2	36.0	62.5
U.S.	5	9.9	16.6	16.6	19.4	37.5	177.5

Table 3.4 *(continued)*

Nativity	Ward	Year of Arrival (% across)					N
		1820–29	1830–39	1840–44	1845–49	1850–55	
U.S.	9	14.4	18.2	12.3	25.8	29.4	502.5
U.S.	10	16.7	16.0	6.3	13.0	48.0	134.5
Great Britain	4	10.8	19.7	9.6	15.9	43.9	78.5
Great Britain	5	5.4	19.8	23.4	9.0	42.5	83.5
Great Britain	9	10.4	17.2	13.8	28.0	30.6	148.5
Great Britain	10	19.3	27.5	14.6	18.1	20.5	85.5
Ireland	4	2.3	11.8	9.2	32.2	44.5	582.5
Ireland	5	4.4	6.3	10.1	31.0	48.2	262.5
Ireland	9	4.5	12.6	8.2	25.7	49.0	321.5
Ireland	10	5.8	9.9	13.2	30.2	41.0	147.5
Germany	4	1.9	8.0	5.7	17.1	67.3	131.5
Germany	5	1.3	5.5	5.5	26.9	60.8	191.5
Germany	9	4.6	8.7	6.7	24.1	55.9	97.5
Germany	10	1.3	6.5	4.7	23.8	63.7	498.5
Other	4	8.8	17.0	14.3	15.6	44.2	73.5
Other	5	2.7	12.4	4.9	26.5	53.5	92.5
Other	9	15.3	25.4	8.5	11.8	39.0	29.5
Other	10	8.0	6.2	8.0	16.8	61.1	56.5

N = 3758.0

Source: New York State Census for 1855 (manuscript).

community, who clung tenaciously to their aging row houses that were now sandwiched in between new, dark tenements, and who begged constantly for financial support from prosperous uptown Protestant congregations to maintain their now empty Methodist, Baptist, and Episcopal churches.[34]

In the decade preceding 1855, the rapid influx of immigrants put tremendous pressure on the entire stock of housing in Lower Manhattan and produced competition among ethnic groups for living quarters. The competition was fierce enough to temporarily reverse the historical trend toward greater residential homogeneity. The proportion of native in-migrants, in sharp decline for several decades, stabilized and for a time actually increased in areas that were mainly composed of immigrants. In some cases the proportion of Irish-born among the 1850 arrival cohorts actually declined. Adding to this competition for rental housing was German immigration which peaked several years behind that of the Irish. In the Fourth Ward, the drop in the percentage of Irish from a high of 77 in the late 1840s to 59.3 in the 1850s was largely offset by the arrival of German settlers, who now composed 20.2 percent of the population.

Notwithstanding the marked increase in Irish and German immigration, strongly native wards maintained their earlier ethnic homogeneity. The Ninth Ward, long considered a pocket of calm in a sea of residential change, continued to attract the highest proportion of native- and English-born settlers in Lower Manhattan.[35] To be sure, among the 1850–1855 cohort group who moved into this area, more than half were either German or Irish, and only 46.2 percent were Anglo-American. But Greenwich Village differed markedly from other areas of New York in the stability and longevity of its old-time inhabitants. Despite the fact that the majority of the Ninth Ward's in-migrants were now foreign-born, recent arrivals accounted for only 37.9 percent of the area's residents, compared with between 47.1 and 53.6 percent for other sample wards. Nearly half of the area's in-migrants had resided in New York City for more than ten years, and a quarter for longer than fifteen.[36]

Like the Ninth, the Fifth Ward had also shown a predominance of American and British settlers among its early arrival cohorts. However, after the exodus of many of its wealthy residents commenced in the late 1830s, the proportion who remained in the Ward declined to only 26.5 percent—a level comparable to that of many immigrant wards. While nearly half of the pre-1830 settlers were of Yankee stock, by the late 1840s the composition of this area had become exceptionally diverse. Of this arrival cohort 32.1 percent were Irish, 29.5 percent were German, 16.9 percent were of native stock, and 9 percent from Great Britain. Although the Fifth Ward ceased to be a solidly Anglo-American enclave after 1845, high levels of transiency and a diverse ethnic mix prevented any single ethnic group from establishing dominance as had been the case with the Irish in the Fourth Ward and the Germans in the Tenth.

As changing preferences shaped neighborhood composition over several decades for successive waves of arrival cohorts, so did variations in arrival ages (used as a rough estimator of migration age), though indirectly. Age-at-arrival produced significant demographic differences among neighborhoods because of its strong correlation with ethnicity. An analysis comparing ethnicity, age-at-arrival, and sex showed nativity to be the strongest predictor of residential location (table 3.5), but arrival age varied directly with nativity—a fact that underscores how ethno-cultural differences shaped neighborhood demography as well as timing of arrival for immigrants and migrants coming to New York City.[37]

Ease of travel and availability of supportive ties over a broader span of the life cycle facilitated the migration of native-born children at an

Table 3.5   Nativity, Arrival Characteristics, Gender, and Neighborhood among Residents Not Born in New York City, Four Sample Wards, New York City, 1855

Variables: Ward: 4, 5, 9, and 10.

Nativity: Non-New York City-born (U.S.), Great Britain (incl. Scotland), Ireland, Germany, other.

Age at arrival: Computed x = (age − length of residence). Categories: 1−14, 15−19, 20−24, 30+ years.

Terms of Model (controlled for)	χ^2	χ^2 d.f.	χ^2 signif.	Difference χ^2	Diff. d.f.	Difference signif.	Coef. of determination
All 2-way associations	143.71	136	.3085	—	—	—	—
(Ward, nativity)	1359.24	148	.0001	1215.53	12	.0001	.8943
(Age, nativity)	293.26	152	.0001	149.55	16	.0001	.5100
(Sex, nativity)	191.05	140	.0024	47.34	4	.0001	.2478
(Ward, age)	171.53	148	.0903	27.82	12	.0061	.1622
(Ward, sex)	170.24	139	.0364	26.53	3	.0001	.1558
(Sex, age)	164.26	140	.0789	20.55	4	.0006	.1251

Table from modeled data (all 2-way associations):
sex by age at arrival grouped by nativity

Nativity	Sex	Age at Arrival (% across) 1–14	15–19	20–24	25–29	30+	N
U.S.	Male	38.0	13.6	18.3	11.2	18.8	417
U.S.	Female	38.5	17.8	15.7	9.1	19.0	430
Great Britain	Male	30.7	12.5	22.9	14.0	19.9	199
Great Britain	Female	31.5	16.8	19.9	11.4	20.4	168
Ireland	Male	23.1	22.1	23.4	13.9	17.5	555
Ireland	Female	22.9	29.1	19.6	11.0	17.4	729
Germany	Male	16.6	14.8	26.5	18.9	23.2	485
Germany	Female	17.1	19.9	23.4	15.5	24.1	403
Other	Male	22.7	12.6	24.1	17.5	23.1	135
Other	Female	23.3	17.2	21.2	14.3	23.9	87

N = 3608

Source: New York State Census for 1855 (manuscript).

early age relative to foreign-born immigrants. More than half of American immigrants arrived before their twentieth birthday, and 38 percent came before the age of fifteen. And since a move from New Jersey, upstate New York, or New England involved far less hardship than a move from Ireland or Germany, it is hardly surprising that American migrants often moved as family groups including young children. English-born immigrants likewise migrated in family units (as shown by the comparatively high proportion of children aged one to fourteen—31 percent), but arrived at somewhat older ages than Americans. By contrast, Irish immigrants arrived young; the well-known tendency of Irish families to send older children in advance is borne out by the smaller numbers of children under fifteen relative to those in their late teens or early twenties. At the other extreme, German immigrants were older when they arrived in New York City; only 17 percent of Germans arrived as children compared with between 22 to 30 percent for other foreign-born groups, and the most common age of arrival was the early twenties, with many continuing to arrive into their late twenties and thirties.

Gender also shaped the timing of migration within ethnic groups, although to a much lesser extent. For every group, women arrived at younger ages than men. Even though no significant difference could be found in the numbers of girls and boys who arrived in New York under the age of fifteen, the principal age of migration for women was in the late teens, compared with the early twenties for men. There were differences among ethnic groups. Over 17 percent of native-born female migrants arrived in New York between the ages of fifteen and nineteen and 15.7 percent between the ages of twenty and twenty-four, compared with 13.6 percent of native-born males in their teens and 18.3 percent in their twenties. Among Irish settlers, however, 29.1 percent of women and 22.1 percent of young men immigrated in their late teens.[38] This discrepancy is not hard to explain if it is remembered that the peak ages of employment for servants were the late teens and that 28.8 percent of the Irish in this age group worked as domestics, compared with only 4.6 percent among the sampled Americans.[39]

Differences among arrival cohorts thus shed considerable light upon the process of neighborhood development and change during successive waves of migration. Likewise variations in ages of arrival among ethnic groups elucidates three separate patterns in the timing and demographic composition of migration related to the process of "chaining," where immigrants came to join friends or relations. First, ease of migration and the existence of a wider range of opportunities favored the young. Planned individual migration aimed at improving economic opportunity or enhancing marriageability—in other words moves apart from "catastrophic" mass migration—tended to occur in childhood, particularly among the native and English newcomers to New York. Second, during migration periods sparked by mass demographic or economic catastrophe, families sent adolescent members in the prime of their employable years to scout conditions in the new land (and/or to ease the economic burdens on those who remained behind) before sending other members to follow (particularly common among the Irish). Finally, where emigration occurred for reasons other than pure economics, older family members in their twenties and thirties constituted a large share of the migrants, as was commonly the case with German immigrants. In each of these scenarios, different patterns of migration obliquely influenced the social and demographic character of neighborhoods through variations in age and gender composition. American family migrants with children, unattached teenage Irish men and women, and mature skilled German immigrants thus helped to form richly layered residential neighborhoods that, despite outward appearances to reformers of ethnic homogeneity, were demographically diverse. Only "American" residents of New York demonstrated levels of segregation that matched the dire predictions.[40]

Employment Location, Ethnicity, and Residence

We have seen how the growing segregation of immigrants in shantytowns on the city's periphery or in downtown areas of declining respectability was the result of many factors: the withdrawal of native-born New Yorkers to exclusive enclaves, internal demographic cleavages among ethnic groups, abrupt changes in residential fashion, the development of a central business district, and the workings of a tight rental market strained to its limit by the influx of newcomers. Disentangling ethnically determined choice from impersonal economic forces related to industrial location and the emergence of an urban working class has proven a thorny problem for historians. Starting with the work of Oscar Handlin and Moses Rischin, ethnic historians emphasized the creation of "ghetto" neighborhoods as the natural product of ethnic affinities.[41] Most urban studies have echoed this basic focus, although this view has been increasingly tempered by an awareness of ethnic divisions within particular trades.[42]

On the other hand, some revisionist students of ethnic residence together with many new labor historians have treated ethnic neighborhoods as the result of industrial location or class. One study of late nineteenth-century Philadelphia argued that ethnic neighborhoods were not the product simply of "abstract, natural law put forth by the classical ecologist" or of "the desire of people with a common cultural heritage to live close to one another" but rather of "decisions made in the local, regional, and national economies" that determined the location of industries.[43] Labor historians have argued that spatial differentiation was principally a sub-process to the paramount formation of a distinctive working class. While acknowledging a division within trades by ethnicity, their studies have stressed the emergence of "class-specific" social geography based upon the growing gap between rich and poor—between master and journeymen.[44]

Recent findings on working-class community in nineteenth-century New York City have shown the artificiality of approaches that failed to integrate class and ethnicity with the economic spatial evolution of the antebellum city. Spatial differentiation was, as Richard Stott has argued convincingly, tied both to industrial location and the "retirement of the city's middle and upper classes," which "left areas of the city almost totally to workers," thereby insuring "the development of distinct working class residential areas." This process of differentiation operated within the metropolitan region: Manhattan became the "commercial and labor-intensive center" of the region, while heavy manufacturing concentrated in the suburbs.[45] To be sure, some industries like shipbuilding, sugar boiling, iron founding, and publishing which congregated along waterfront areas or in neighborhoods adjoining the central business district promoted corresponding residential segregation. But unlike employment in a mill town, residence in New York was not entirely subordinated to industrial employment, with many employers locating themselves in the midst of residential areas. If New York was a place, as some contemporaries observed, where "almost every branch of business seems to have its own locality," the resulting patterns of industrial location produced a highly complicated system of warehouse areas, residential districts, and waterfront quays.[46]

Data from the industrial and population censuses suggest the industrial foundations upon which residential patterns in Lower Manhattan were built. The clustering of particular industries in different areas strongly in-fluenced the residential composition of the surrounding neighborhoods, as workers tried to live within close proximity to their places of work.[47] For example, the Fourth Ward, with its high concentration of grog shops, boardinghouses, and workers employed in transportation (not to mention unenumerated brothels), was the sailor's home at shore.[48] The low popu-lation density and ample room for industrial development in the Ninth Ward compared with other wards made this section of Greenwich Village a haven for workers in the building trades, many of whom were employed by the local lumberyards and factories that produced ready-made staircases, banisters, and other materials for construction.[49] The Tenth Ward reflected the occupational diversity of the Lower East Side, where residences were interspersed with small manufacturing establishments producing ready-made clothing, shoes, cigars, jewelry, furniture, and lager beer. In each of these wards, the spectrum of employment varied widely, ranging from merchant to tradesman to laborer, all living in close proximity to work.[50] The working population of the Fifth Ward was especially diverse, and most of this neighborhood's residents worked as butchers and produce sellers in the stalls of Washington Market, prepared fancy sweets for the affluent clientele of such popular Broadway establishments as Taylor's Ice Cream Parlor and Thompson's Saloon, or sweated over boiling cauldrons of sugar in the area's many refineries.[51]

Other evidence points to increasing social differentiation that transcended ethnicity. Unskilled laborers, a major constituent of the working population in neighborhoods adjoining the central business district, were scarcely to be found in the Ninth and Tenth Wards, where unusually large proportions of skilled workers and merchants lived. Conversely, white-collar workers and their retinues of domestic servants tended to reside on the West Side of Manhattan across town from the worker-dominated East Side.[52]

Much the same pattern held not only for the sample wards, but also for the city as a whole. An examination of residential locations for 312 occupations drawn from the published state census of 1865 (table 3.6) shows how the location of industrial employment crudely divided New York into four general districts: (1) areas where commercial use was replacing mixed residence and industry, in the Tip of Manhattan and Dry Dock (high standardized residuals for private/domestic service, public service, and hotels which were support industries of commerce); (2) areas where occupational division mirrored the growing polarization between middle- and upper-class natives on the one hand and working-class immigrants on the other, such as the Lower East and West Sides (high residuals for commerce and private/domestic service on the lower West Side and high residuals for clothing and metal work on the East); (3) areas of ongoing development north of Fourteenth Street, the East being the location of fashionable residences while the West housed assorted industries (high residuals for manufacture and textiles on the West Side and for commerce, professionals, and private/domestic servants on the East Side); and (4) the periphery, inhabited by a strange mix of impoverished shantytown squatters and suburban gentry (disproportionate concentrations of laborers, government workers, educators and other professionals). Within this overall structure of industrial division were individual patterns of clustering like

Table 3.6 Industrial Classification and Residence, New York City, 1865

Terms of Model (controlled for)	χ^2	d.f.	χ^2 signif.
(All associations)	35551.56	279	.000

Table A: percentages from raw data

Industry	Area (% down)				
	Tip Manhat.	Dry Dock	Mid Lower	Lower West	Lower East
Agriculture	.2	.1	.1	.1	.2
Food	3.6	4.4	4.8	4.5	6.8
Food Prep.	1.2	.5	1.9	1.1	.6
Tobacco	.5	1.0	.7	.9	3.9
Liquor	6.6	2.8	3.9	2.4	2.6
Hotels	2.5	1.4	.8	1.1	.3
Leather	.1	.9	.8	.6	.9
Clothing	7.9	13.3	18.6	9.7	18.4
Textiles	.2	.2	.3	.3	.4
Drygoods	.0	.1	.5	.2	.4
Metal Work	1.6	4.8	5.3	4.3	7.3
Jewelry	.4	.8	1.3	1.2	1.1
Wood Work	1.5	3.2	3.6	2.2	2.4
Furniture	.3	.8	1.9	1.3	2.8
Building	1.5	4.7	5.4	5.4	7.6
Shipbuilding	.3	3.8	.4	.4	2.0
Fuel	.1	.2	.4	.3	.2
Chemicals	.1	.3	.2	.5	.6
Misc. Prods.	.1	.3	.4	.3	.5
Printing	1.1	3.5	3.0	1.9	2.3
Manufacture	.4	1.0	1.1	.8	1.2
Commerce	12.4	11.5	11.5	18.8	12.0
Transport	7.6	11.0	3.3	6.8	3.9
Arts	.2	.2	1.1	.9	1.2
Professions	.9	.6	.6	2.3	1.3
Clergy	.2	.2	.2	.3	.2
Education	.2	1.0	.7	1.0	.8
Government	1.6	1.2	1.1	1.6	.9
Military	1.4	.4	1.0	.6	.5
Priv. Serv.	21.1	9.3	7.9	17.9	6.3
Publ. Serv.	6.3	4.1	6.1	3.8	3.4
Laborers	18.2	12.8	13.0	6.5	7.0
	100.0	100.0	100.0	100.0	100.0
Number	5934	19165	14338	38954	59575

		Area (% down)				
West Side	East Side	Upper West	Upper East	Suburb	(down)	N
.1	.1	.2	.3	.5	.2	343
5.3	3.6	6.8	5.2	3.5	5.2	12241
.7	.5	.4	.5	.9	.7	1651
.7	.6	.8	1.0	.3	1.5	3623
1.6	1.1	2.2	2.3	1.7	2.3	5354
.3	.6	.4	.3	.5	.7	1542
.8	.5	1.0	.8	.4	.8	1785
12.0	8.5	8.5	6.3	6.4	12.5	29458
1.1	.3	2.2	.3	.1	.5	1177
.2	.1	.3	.2	.0	.2	548
5.8	4.8	4.6	4.0	3.7	5.4	12594
.6	.5	.6	.8	.5	.9	2049
2.4	1.6	2.5	3.2	1.4	2.4	5619
1.6	1.4	1.4	9.4	1.1	2.1	4986
10.5	7.1	10.3	9.5	8.1	7.3	17203
.2	.2	.4	.3	.3	1.0	2414
.5	.4	.5	.4	.4	.4	823
.5	.4	.5	.5	1.1	.5	1154
.6	.3	.8	.3	.8	.4	1014
1.0	1.2	1.0	1.4	.7	1.9	4359
2.0	.9	2.0	.7	.7	1.2	2743
13.4	15.1	12.4	13.9	13.7	13.9	32630
5.4	4.1	6.2	5.8	4.0	5.5	12938
.5	.5	.5	.5	.4	.8	1792
1.5	2.7	1.3	1.8	3.0	1.7	3919
.3	.3	.3	.2	.3	.2	524
1.1	.9	.9	1.2	2.5	1.0	2244
1.2	1.2	1.5	1.9	3.3	1.3	3113
.5	.3	1.2	.5	1.3	.6	1412
14.4	30.2	13.7	12.9	22.9	14.5	34182
3.7	2.2	1.6	2.2	1.6	3.4	8055
9.4	8.1	13.0	11.4	14.1	9.3	21957
100.0	100.0	100.0	100.0	100.0	100.0	
33639	30520	13162	12036	8123		235446

Table 3.6   (*continued*)

Table B: standardized residuals from log-linear model*

	Area									
Industry	Tip Manhat.	Dry Dock	Mid Lower	Lower West	Lower East	West Side	East Side	Upper West	Upper East	Suburb
Agriculture		−2.8	−2.5				−2.9	3.0	5.1	7.9
Food	−5.3	−4.7	−2.1	−6.0	17.4		−12.3	7.9		−6.8
Food Prep.	4.1	−3.3	3.9	8.4	−2.2		−5.3	−4.1	−2.5	1.9
Tobacco	−6.6	−5.9	−7.5	−10.7	45.5	−12.0	−13.6	−7.3	−4.9	−8.7
Liquor	22.0	4.5	5.6		4.6	−7.9	−14.2			−3.7
Hotels	17.7	11.9		11.6	−10.6	−8.6		−3.7	−4.5	
Leather	−5.9	2.5		−2.9	5.3		−5.4	3.4		−3.5
Clothing	−10.2	3.0	20.4	−15.5	40.9	−2.7	−20.0	−12.9	−19.3	−15.7
Textiles	−3.4	−6.0	−3.1	−6.8	−4.5	14.6	−6.3	28.1	−3.9	−5.2
Drygoods	−3.3	−2.9	7.6		7.0	−2.6	−5.3			−4.3
Metal Work	−12.6	−3.6		−9.0	20.8	3.6	−4.0	−3.6	−6.6	−6.5
Jewelry	−3.9		5.3	7.5	6.2	−4.6	−8.0	−3.1		−3.7
Wood Work	−4.2	6.8	9.6	−2.8			−8.6		5.7	−5.7
Furniture	−9.5	−12.4		−10.8	11.5	−7.1	−8.9	−5.4	55.2	−6.4
Building	−16.7	−13.6	−8.3	−14.3	2.2		21.6	12.8	9.0	2.8
Shipbuilding	−5.7	37.5	−7.4	−11.6	24.5	−14.9	−14.2	−7.3	−7.9	−6.9
Fuel	−3.4	−3.5			−4.5	5.7	2.7	3.6		
Chemicals	−3.8	−3.0	−5.3		3.5					7.7
Misc. Prods.	−3.6			−5.4		4.9	−4.1	6.7		4.8
Printing	−4.5	16.5	10.1		8.6	−10.9	−8.0	−7.0	−3.3	−7.6
Manufacture	−5.5	−2.2		−6.2		14.6	−4.6	8.8	−4.6	−3.5
Commerce	−3.0	−8.8	−7.7	26.3	−11.9	−2.1	5.8	−4.4		
Transport	7.0	32.5	−11.3	11.3		−16.2	−10.7	3.3		−5.8
Arts	−4.7	−8.8	5.3	4.0	13.0	−5.7	−4.4	−3.9	−3.5	−4.1
Professions	−4.2	−11.2	−9.6	10.1	−6.6	−2.1	13.7		−3.2	9.5
Clergy					−3.8		2.9			
Education	−6.1			−3.0	−4.6				2.8	14.6
Government				5.2	−8.6	−2.3	−2.4	2.1	5.3	15.6
Military	7.6	−4.1	5.9		−3.6	−2.2	−5.9	8.3	−2.1	8.1
Priv. Services	13.2	−19.1	−21.0	17.8	−52.6		71.9	−2.6	−4.6	19.7
Pub. Services	12.0	4.9	17.6	3.8		2.5	−11.2	11.0	−7.2	−8.9
Laborers	22.2	15.7	14.5	−18.3	−18.4		−7.1	13.8	7.5	13.9

Variables: Area: Tip of Manhattan (wards 1, 2, and 3), Dry Dock (wards 4 and 7), Middle Lower (wards 6 and 14), Lower West Side (wards 5, 8, 9, and 15), Lower East Side (wards 10, 11, 13, and 17), West Side (wards 16 and 20), East Side (wards 18 and 21), Upper West Side (ward 22), Upper East Side (ward 19), Suburb (ward 12).

Industrial classification: Agriculture, Food, Food Preparation, Tobacco, Liquor, Hotels, Leather,

Table 3.6 *(continued)*

Clothing, Textiles, Drygoods, Metal Work, Jewelry, Wood Work, Furniture, Building, Shipbuilding, Fuel, Chemicals, Misc. Products, Printing and Publishing, Manufacturing, General Commerce, Transportation, The Arts, Professions, Clergy, Education, Government, Military, Private/ Domestic Service, Public (Other) Service, Laborers.

*Standardized residuals: (Observed-Fitted)/SQRT(Fitted). Since standardized residuals are normally distributed, numbers greater than +/− 1.96 are significant to the .05 level. Only significant values are shown.

Source: Franklin B. Hough, *Statistics of Population of the City and County of New York As Shown by the State Census of 1865* (New York: New York Printing, 1866).

shipbuilding in the Dry Dock area, tobacco in the Lower East Side, textile production in the West and Upper West Sides, and furniture making in the Upper East Side.

The central business core near the Tip of Manhattan had declined in population since the 1830s as tradesmen moved to the Lower East Side. At roughly this same time merchants, lawyers, physicians, and others among the city's more affluent professionals left for newer centers of fashion in Washington Square, Bond Street, and Lafayette Place.[53] Those skilled and semiskilled workers who remained in the central business district were usually employed in the service sector that catered to the needs of business commuters (who by day ran the countinghouses and wholesaling establishments and by night escaped to residences located in Brooklyn, New Jersey, or Uptown). Many of these worked in restaurants, tended saloons, or ran hotels and boardinghouses for businessmen. Others served the district's seamen and accommodated newly arrived Germans and Irish.[54] But the largest proportion of residents in this area consisted of unskilled laborers who found inexpensive housing in decaying structures that surrounded the business area. The nearby waterfront quarters, known as Dry Dock, comprised a second industrial district that stretched along the East River from the edge of the commercial area to Corlears Hook. Here could be found unskilled laborers and workers involved in shipbuilding, leather industries, and clothing as well as the seamen who boarded in the numerous sailor's boardinghouses.[55]

North of the Tip, Broadway divided Manhattan both geographically and socially between the East and West Sides. To contemporaries the social division was apparent in the caliber of retail stores. If Broadway and the West Side south of Fourteenth Street catered to the rich, the Bowery attracted the "modest purse, the *demi-mode.*"[56] Compared to the marble dry-goods palaces of Broadway, the Bowery, Chatham Square, and the narrow length of Catherine Street offered working-class shoppers less fashionable stores selling a wide variety of inexpensive goods.[57]

The location of retail stores reflected the residential character of the surrounding neighborhood. The Lower West Side housed a large proportion of the city's clerks and small merchants within walking distance of the dry-goods palaces and early department stores. The Lower East Side contained large numbers of peddlers, grocers, bakers, and other petty-proprietors selling "goods of extreme convenience" ranging from food to clothing to hardware to their local clientele. Such a division, historian Stuart Blumin has suggested, insured that "business commuters and well-to-do shoppers" never crossed from West Side to East and that "non-manual proprietors impinged but little on the consciousness of those who lived, worked, and shopped in more prosperous parts of the city."[58] But Broadway divided more than retailing; the West Side was also a key residential enclave for merchants, professionals, and their domestic servants. The area east of Broadway (including the middle-lower wards and the Lower East Side) was undeniably the residential center for skilled workers. Relatively few domestic servants or service workers inhabited this dense band of settlement surrounding New York's commercial center. Rather, craftsmen worked in small workshops scattered throughout their tenement neighborhoods rolling cigars, stitching clothing, cobbling leather goods, metalworking, turning out furniture, or commuting to publishing and shipmaking jobs in other neighborhoods.

The social order was reversed in newly emerged residential neighborhoods north of Fourteenth Street. The East Side was the domicile of wealthy merchants, doctors, and lawyers, professionals who commuted to work in the financial district. The large proportion of domestic servants—highest of any in the city—attested to its wealth. By contrast, residents across town, many of whom lived in the areas that later would be known as Hell's Kitchen and the Tenderloin, were much poorer. Where many East Side residents were engaged in commerce, blue-collar trades such as construction and manufacture employed the bulk of workers on the West Side.[59] Last of all, undeveloped wards on the outskirts of Manhattan, including those suburbs north of Fortieth Street, housed four different groups: businessmen and professionals who lived on suburban estates; building tradesmen involved in new housing construction at the city's edge; workers employed by "nuisance" industries such as fat-rendering, chemical production, fuel, and leather tanning; and laborers who lived as squatters. With its poor residing in the center or on the periphery, and with other classes located in sectors that radiated northward from the central business district, New York City only vaguely displayed the classic pattern of urban development described by Chicago sociologists during the 1920s where areas of increasing wealth radiate outward from the central business district in concentric zones.[60]

These findings underscore the relationship between industrial location and residential composition.[61] At the same time, much of the impact of industrial location upon residence was also the result of ethnic division within employment.[62] In New York City, workers of common backgrounds and skills levels tended to reside closest to jobs in familiar industries (table 3.7).[63] American-born workers were disproportionately clustered in skilled crafts such as jewelry-making, wood- and metalworking; in the building trades; and, as a legacy of the former protective municipal licensure of carting, in land-based transportation (many sailors were also Yankee, sharing the seas with a diverse array of other nationalities, most notably Norwegians and Portuguese).[64] And Yankees dominated commerce, in all levels from clerking to merchant. Among foreign-born workers, the English most closely approached the American success in commerce, and their high level of work skills led to employment in such crafts as metalworking and printing. German immigrants gravitated toward the apparel industry, the woodworking trades, particularly furniture and cabinet making (including musical instrument production), food sales and preparation (grocery proprietors, butchers, and confectioners), tobacco, and liquor (as producers of both lager beer and distilled spirits). Irish occupied the bottom rungs of the occupational ladder. Though many could be found in tailoring ready-made clothing, lasting shoes, or as petty-proprietors (operating saloons, grog shops, and grocery stores in the Fourth Ward), Irish employment in domestic service (28.8 percent) was more than twice as high as for any other group, and for unskilled labor the percentage (14.4) was nearly four times as high as that of the Germans.[65]

If ethnic differences in employment and the intricate pattern of industrial location cloud how class shaped residential patterns, to what extent can class be said to have *independently* shaped neighborhood choice? And how did the residential impact of class compare with ethnicity and demographic factors? These questions can largely be answered by reexamining the occupational basis of residence employing classifications based upon occupational rank (drawn from the Philadelphia Social History Project) rather than industry.[66] Despite the difficulty of inferring class from measures of stratification,[67] the use of occupational rank makes it possible to statistically separate the impact on residence of occupational rank (e.g., class) from those of other closely related factors such as nativity, age, and gender (table 3.8). The statistical procedure known as linear-flow modeling allows us to examine the multivariate interaction of several variables

Table 3.7   Industrial Occupation, Residence, and
Ethnicity, Four Sample Wards, New York City, 1855

Variables: Ward: 4, 5, 9, and 10.
　　　　　Industrial classification: Food, Food Preparation, Tobacco, Liquor, Hotels,
　　　　　Leather, Clothing, Textiles, Metal Work, Jewelry, Wood Work, Furniture,
　　　　　Building, Shipbuilding, Misc. Products, Printing and Publishing, Manu-
　　　　　facturing, General Commerce, Transportation, Professions, Education,
　　　　　Government, Domestic Service, Public (Other) Service, Laborers.
　　　　　Ethnicity: U.S., England-Scotland, Ireland, Germany, Other.

Terms of Model (controlled for)	χ^2	χ^2 d.f.	χ^2 signif.	Difference χ^2	Diff. d.f.	Difference signif.	Coef. of determination
All 2-way assoc.	289.53	288	.4637	—	—	—	—
(Nativity, industry)	953.37	384	.0001	663.84	96	.0001	.6963
(Ward, nativity)	758.43	300	.0001	468.90	12	.0001	.6182
(Ward, industry)	550.58	360	.0001	261.04	72	.0001	.4741

*Probability over 10% (.1).

Table from modeled data: industrial classification by ethnicity

	Nativity (% down)									
	U.S.		Great Britain		Ireland		Germany		Other	
Industry	%	Resid.*	%	Resid.*	%	Resid.*	%	Resid.*	%	Resid.*
Food	5.3		3.6		4.7		9.7	4.0	1.9	
Food Prep.	0.8		0.9		0.9		1.4		3.1	
Tobacco	0.8		0.9		0.4	−2.1	2.9	3.6	3.1	
Liquor	0.6		1.8		0.9		3.3	3.5	1.9	
Hotels	0.6		2.3		1.1		1.0		5.0	4.6
Leather	0.6		1.8		2.4	2.1	1.0		1.3	
Clothing	10.0	−3.3	12.3		13.5		24.7	6.2	13.8	
Textiles	1.5		2.7		1.3		1.0		1.3	
Metal Work	5.5	2.0	6.4	2.1	2.7	−2.0	3.3		2.5	
Jewelry	4.7	2.7	1.9		1.8	−2.0	2.9		3.1	
Wood Work	4.7		1.9		1.8	−2.0	2.9		3.1	
Furniture	1.1	4.7	2.3		0.6	−2.8	4.9	5.2	1.9	
Building	11.2		8.2		3.6	−3.5	4.3		6.3	
Shipbuilding	1.4		1.8		0.8		0.6		1.9	
Misc. Prods.	1.2		1.4		1.1		0.8		1.9	
Printing	2.9		4.5	2.0	2.2		1.2		1.9	
Manufacture	0.6	−3.3	1.8		0.6	5.9	0.8	−2.3	1.3	
Commerce	18.3	6.3	14.5	2.2	4.7	−5.5	7.2	−2.2	11.9	
Transport	13.0	3.8	9.1		7.5		2.5	−4.8	16.3	3.4
Professions	3.9	2.0	4.1		1.1	−3.0	2.3		5.0	

Table 3.7 (continued)

Industry	U.S. %	Resid.*	Great Britain %	Resid.*	Ireland %	Resid.*	Germany %	Resid.*	Other %	Resid.*
					Nativity (% down)					
Education	1.7	2.1	1.8		0.3	−2.0	0.8		1.2	
Government	2.9	3.7	1.8		0.5	−2.3	0.4		1.3	
Priv. Serv.	4.6	−6.9	7.7	−2.3	28.8	10.0	12.6		2.6	−3.9
Publ. Serv.	1.8	−1.9	2.3		3.2		3.3		6.9	3.1
Laborers	2.8	−4.0	1.4	−2.9	14.4	7.6	3.9	−2.3	1.9	−2.3
N (Columns)	722.0		222.0		785.0		514.0		160.0	
N (Table)	= 2401.0									

*Standardized residuals: (Observed-Fitted)/SQRT(Fitted). Since standardized residuals are normally distributed, numbers greater than +/− 1.96 are significant to the .05 level. Only significant values are shown.
Source: New York State Census for 1855 (manuscript).

and to separate direct effects of one variable upon another from those that might be either indirect or spurious (effects decomposition).[68] This technique (also known as D-system) produces results resembling those of path-analysis but for nominal data. Since both dependent and causal variables are categorical, D-system requires a very tight ordering of variables in forming a model to be tested and considerable care in interpretation. Constructing such a model requires a series of logical assumptions on how the variables being tested shaped residential choice: first, that the ethnic background of New Yorkers influenced their tendency to be of a certain gender (since employment patterns of women varied from one ethnic group to another); second, that ethnicity and gender in turn both influenced the age of residents (as we have seen with variations in age-at-arrival); third, that all three of these variables determined occupational rank; and lastly, that the four of these taken together shaped residence. With such a model, we can control for various interaction to produce "path-like" coefficients that allow us to measure the extent to which nativity, to take just one example, directly influenced one's choice of ward and how it influenced where one resided indirectly through ethnic differences in sex, age, or occupation.[69]

Analysis of coefficients for the model partially confirm the importance of class in residential decision and supports a view that New York was becoming a city in which workers lived in their own distinctive neighborhoods. But ethnicity appears to have shaped residence even more than class (coefficients of .2542 versus .1954 for occupation). Since ethnic background strongly influenced occupation, much of the sharp neighborhood

Table 3.8   The Impact of Occupational Rank Upon
Residence, Four Sample Wards, New York City, 1855

(A) An effects decomposition of a dichotomized linear
flow model measuring the impact of ethnicity, age,
gender, and occupational rank upon residence (D-system)[a]

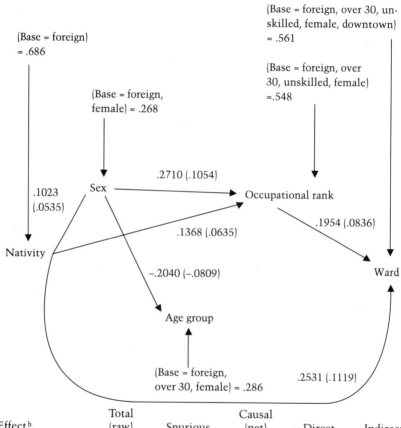

(Base = foreign)
= .686

(Base = foreign, over 30, unskilled, female, downtown)
= .561

(Base = foreign,
female) = .268

(Base = foreign, over
30, unskilled, female)
=.548

.2710 (.1054)

.1023
(.0535)

Sex

Occupational rank

.1954 (.0836)

.1368 (.0635)

Nativity

Ward

−.2040 (−.0809)

Age group

(Base = foreign,
over 30, female) = .286

.2531 (.1119)

Effect[b]	Total (raw)	Spurious	Causal (net)	Direct	Indirect
Nativity-sex	+.1023	—	+.1023	—	—
Nativity-age	−.0443*	—	−.0443*	−.0285*	−.0158*
Sex-age	−.2162	−.0122	−.2040	—	—
Nativity-occup.	+.1674	—	+.1674	+.1368	+.0310
Sex-occup.	+.3318	+.0414	+.2904	+.2710	+.0194
Age-occup.	−.0572	−.0486	−.0086*	—	—
Nativity-ward	+.2542	—	+.2542	+.2531	+.0011
Sex-ward	+.0038*	−.0277	+.0315*	+.0173*	+.0142
Age-ward	−.0151*	−.0071*	−.0080*	−.0374*	+.0294*
Occup.-ward	+.1721	−.0233	+.1954	—	—

Table 3.8 (*continued*)

[a] Numbers are *d* coefficients and intercept values. Values within parentheses are two-sigma confidence limits, with variances doubled to correct for multistage sampling. See James A. Davis, "Analyzing Contingency Tables with Linear Flow Graphs: D-Systems," in D. Heise, ed., *Sociological Methodology*, (San Francisco: Jossey-Bass, 1976), pp. 111–45.

[b] Categories: nativity—native, foreign; Sex—male, female; Age—under 30 30 and older; Occupational Rank—upper (professional, proprietary and skilled), lower (semiskilled, unskilled, and others); Ward—downtown (Wards 4 and 5), uptown (Wards 9 and 10).

[*] Pearson χ^2 not significant to the .10 level (10%).

(B) An effects decomposition of a full (nondichotomized) linear flow model measuring the impact of ethnicity, age, and occupational rank upon familial residence $(\chi)^2$

Effect:	Total (raw)	Spurious	% [b]	Causal (net)	Direct	% [c]	Indirect	% [c]
Ethnic-sex	150.25	—		150.25	—		—	
Ethnic-age	27.25	—		27.25	14.69*	53.9	12.56	46.1
Sex-age	53.65	2.71	5.1	50.91	—		—	
Ethnic-occup.	331.32	—		331.32	278.66	84.1	52.66	15.9
Sex-occup.	247.21	72.53	29.3	174.68	145.67	83.4	29.01	16.6
Age-occup.	33.65	15.83	47.0	17.82	—		—	
Ethnic-ward	627.39	—		627.39	531.57	84.7	95.82	15.3
Sex-ward	24.33	1.69	6.9	22.64	7.59*	33.5	15.05	66.5
Age-ward	2.25*	.00*	0.0	2.25*	2.23*	99.1	.02*	.9
Occup.-ward	147.29	40.75	27.7	106.54	—		—	

[a] Categories: ethnicity—native, English-Scottish, Irish, German, Other; age—under 30, 30 and older; occupational rank—professional, proprietary, skilled, semiskilled, unskilled, and others; Sex—male, female; ward—4, 5, 9 and 10.

[b] Figures are percentages of total (raw) χ^2 that are spurious.

[c] Figures are percentages of causal (net) χ^2 that are direct and indirect effects.

[*] Pearson χ^2 not significant to the .10 level (10 percent).

[**] Pearson χ^2 not significant to the .05 level (5 percent).

Source: New York State Census for 1855 (manuscript).

division between New York neighborhoods was actually an indirect result of the massive influx of immigrants, many of whom happened to be poor.[70] When a separate model was analyzed for nondichotomized variables, the impact of ethnicity on residential choice relative to occupation was even more pronounced (table 3.8). While oblique causal effects, such as the sharp drop-off of female labor force participation relative to men older than thirty (sex-age) and the rigid segregation of working women in a narrow range of jobs (sex-occupation), also proved significant—and sometimes more powerful than that of occupation upon ward—the importance of all other factors paled when compared with ethnicity.

To the extent that occupational rank influenced residential choice, modeled data controlling for ethnicity (table 3.9) show the Fourth Ward to have been the most proletarian of the four neighborhoods, with unusually high numbers of semiskilled and unskilled workers but relatively few professionals or skilled tradesmen. The Tenth Ward, whose working-class residents tended to be skilled (58.9 percent) rather than semiskilled or unskilled, was proletarian without being poor. The Fifth and Ninth Wards were considerably more wealthy: the former contained proportionately more professionals (8.9 percent) but fewer skilled workers (36.7 percent), while the latter housed significantly fewer skilled or unskilled workers (39.3 and 6.1 percent) but more who could be classified as semiskilled (29.7 percent).[71]

But the way in which class influenced residential choice was mediated by other variables, most notably ethnic background. If the role of occupational rank upon neighborhood is examined statistically, controlling to remove interactions with age, gender, and ethnicity, the picture of class and neighborhood that we have just observed, while quite similar, is subtly altered. Had the Fourth Ward not contained such a large concentration of Irish immigrants, to cite one example, it would not have contained the concentration of poor unskilled laborers for which the ward was notorious (although other categories of occupational rank would have remained largely unchanged).[72] In other neighborhoods, ethnicity actually masked deeper class differences. Modeling data for the Fifth Ward to remove ethnic differences in residence and employment boosted the proportion of professionals and unskilled residing in the Fifth Ward to 9.2 and 14.1 percent, respectively. And in still other areas like the Ninth Ward in Greenwich Village, eliminating effects for ethnicity also wiped out any distinguishing characteristics in terms of occupational rank.

Together these findings strongly suggest that elements of both views of neighborhood—those of ethnic and labor historians—are simultaneously true. On the one hand, the development of particular patterns of industrial location, the separation of work and residence especially among the wealthy, and the nascent forces of spatial differentiation, intensified residence based upon class. On the other hand, though far from complete, the ethnic division of labor indirectly created status neighborhoods. But ethnicity was a more important determinant of residence than class. Indeed, New York's neighborhoods subsumed class to ethnicity even though none were entirely self-contained economic units.[73] The most distinguishing characteristic of the "American Ward" was its degree of ethnic segregation

Table 3.9 Occupational Rank, Ethnicity, and
Residence, Four Sample Wards, New York City, 1855

(A) Occupational rank and residence, controlling for ethnicity, gender, and age

	Ward (% down)								
Rank	4	S.R.*	5	S.R.*	9	S.R.*	10	S.R.*	All
Professional	3.5	−2.6	8.9	3.5	5.7		4.7		5.5
Proprietary	15.8		16.9		16.6		18.3		16.8
Skilled	35.8	−4.1	37.5	−2.5	44.1		54.1	5.9	42.75
Semiskilled	34.4	6.4	20.6	−2.4	25.4		16.4	−5.0	24.9
Unskilled	10.6		16.2		8.2		6.5	−3.1	10.1

(B) Age and occupational rank, controlling for ethnicity and gender

	Occupational Rank (% across)										
Age	Profess.	S.R.*	Propr.	S.R.*	Skilled	S.R.*	Semi-skill	S.R.*	Unskill	S.R.*	N
15–29	4.4	−2.3	16.8		43.9		26.8	2.1	8.1	−3.1	1154.7
30+	6.6	2.3	16.8		41.6		22.9	−2.1	12.1	3.1	1068.3
Total	5.5		16.8		42.8		24.9		10.1		2223.0

(C) Occupational rank and gender, controlling for ethnicity and age

	Occupational Rank (% across)										
Sex	Profess.	S.R.*	Propr.	S.R.*	Skilled	S.R.*	Semi-skill	S.R.*	Unskill	S.R.*	N
Male	5.5		18.9	4.4	45.7	4.7	8.4	−11.8	11.5	3.8	1636
Female	5.4		11.1	−4.4	34.6	−4.7	43.0	11.8	6.1	−3.8	587

(D) Occupational rank and ethnicity, controlling for age and gender

	Occupational Rank (% across)										
Ethnicity	Profess.	S.R.*	Propr.	S.R.*	Skilled	S.R.*	Semi-skill	S.R.*	Unskill	S.R.*	N
Native-white	8.1	3.3	23.1	4.9	47.9	3.0	18.3	−4.4	2.6	−7.2	612
Black	11.8	2.7	15.5		23.0	−3.9	36.4	2.6	13.3		91
British	8.9	2.2	21.9	2.0	42.7		21.4		5.1	−2.5	203
Irish	2.2	−4.6	9.7	−6.1	35.2	−4.9	32.3	5.5	20.6	11.2	699
German	2.8	−3.0	16.9		53.0	5.1	21.0	−2.2	6.4	−3.0	481
Other	10.9	2.9	18.0		36.2		27.5		7.4		137
Total	5.5		16.8		42.8		24.9		10.1		2223

*Standardized residuals: (Observed-Fitted)/SQRT(Fitted). Since standardized residuals are normally distributed, numbers greater than +/− 1.96 are significant to the .05 level. Only significant values are shown.
Source: Table 3.8.

rather than its wealth, a fact which indicates that ethnic residence itself was something of a luxury in a real-estate market strained by an influx of immigrants. For recently arrived immigrants who clung precariously to their new jobs, residence closely followed employment. Native-born New Yorkers possessed greater cultural and economic resources (and perhaps greater security) which in turn gave them a wider range of residential choice—although most, to be sure, clustered in affluent neighborhoods.

Crowding, Servants, and Status

To nineteenth-century New Yorkers, social status was a matter not only of job level but also of what people owned, where they rented, and whether they could afford domestic servants.[74] We know that consumption (conspicuous or otherwise) operated even under the tightest constraints of working-class budgets.[75] Indeed, some observers were shocked by what they saw as the lavishing of extravagant sums by immigrants on consumer items, particularly on fancy clothing.[76] With real-estate ownership beyond the reach of most New Yorkers, disposable income not spent on necessities was invariably channeled into the consumption of goods which served the function of display and "security" (because of their portability), much as home ownership functioned in other cities.[77] Burglary reports and inventories of stolen goods compiled by police in the Tenth Ward between 1855 and 1856 not only list goods such as junk, "old rope, scrap iron and lead" pilfered for "quick redemption for cash" in "a peculiar black market," they also describe at length belongings taken from the homes of area residents that illuminate the material component of working-class status.[78]

Many of the goods commonly reported stolen were pieces of clothing. Considering that the wages for regularly employed male adults ranged only from $7.50 to $15.00 per week, garments were surprisingly expensive.[79] John Mayshopher, who lived in the front basement of a tenement at 37 Essex Street, lost a clock, a Turkish cap, a carpet bag with a shirt, and a pair of silk pants which he valued at $32.50. William Boyle's front room and first floor domicile was entered into and robbed of a black coat valued at $25, a pair of black pants worth $6.50, several vests which ranged in value from $3.00 to $3.50 each, and a silver flute worth $20. An apartment in a two-story tenement, where clerk Matthew Farrell lived, was robbed of a silk dress worth $25, a pair of pants valued at $5, a $1.50 vest, and $20 in bills. Frederick Whittemeyer had $60 in clothing taken from his tenement, including four coats and two pairs of pants.[80]

Gold jewelry, pocket watches, and currency that had been stashed away in drawers, trunks, or even under mattresses comprised the bulk of stolen property. John Kolp, a mason residing in a third-floor tenement, reported a gold breast pin valued at $34, along with assorted clothing, as missing. H. C. Richardson lost $200 in jewelry and clothing. Henry Weil, a cabinet-maker from 97 Rivington Street, was the least fortunate of the crime victims: he was robbed of over $500 in diamond and gold jewelry. Pocket watches, a leading symbol of social status, were also a popular target of theft, with retail prices that ranged from $15 for silver plate models to $125 for fancy gold.[81]

The range and value of such stolen objects suggest that a sizable propor-tion of the disposable income of New Yorkers was stashed away in drawers in the form of bank notes or was expended upon status consumption in the form of jewelry, the ubiquitous pocket watch, and fancy clothing.[82] Disposable income that was not hidden away or lavished on clothing and jewelry was channeled into investments and savings. Building and loan societies multiplied in the 1850s by promising small investors a quick and high return from land speculation, but these were risky investments at best and "speculative frauds" at worst.[83] Savings banks were a more reliable form for investment, and their popularity soared in the late ante-bellum period. As a result of the increased flow of immigration and the discovery by neighborhood-based businessmen of the lucrative potential of thrift institutions, the number of these savings banks increased to eigh-teen in 1861, to twenty-three in 1866, and to thirty-two in 1868, when an estimated 356,081 accounts held $106,638,090 in deposits.[84]

Given what is known about the volume of savings and the subterranean market in stolen goods that existed among the nineteenth-century work-ing class, it is odd that so little is understood about the impact of wealth-holding upon residence and neighborhood development except in relation to the upper classes, for whom residential addresses defined both wealth and status.[85] For most of the city's population, income gaps among neigh-borhoods were relatively small. So it would seem that wealth constituted yet another *indirect* factor in the evolution of neighborhoods, secondary to more important *direct* factors such as nativity and occupational rank. Thus considerable social diversity existed within neighborhoods, where there was nothing anomalous in finding, for example, Henry Vanderwater, a weigher by trade, residing with his wife, five daughters, and a servant in a single-family home surrounded almost entirely by tenements in the highly crowded Tenth Ward.[86]

When two additional variables for social status—(1) housing density (the proportion of household heads living in single- or dual-family houses)[87] and (2) the employment of servants—are introduced into a model measur-ing the impact of ethnicity and occupational rank upon residence, only

Table 3.10   A Model of Social Rank, Ethnicity, and Residence among Household Heads, Four Sample Wards, New York City, 1855 (Three Measures)

(A) An effects decomposition of a dichotomized linear flow model measuring the impact of ethnicity, occupational rank, single-family residence, and employment of servants upon residence (D-system)[a]

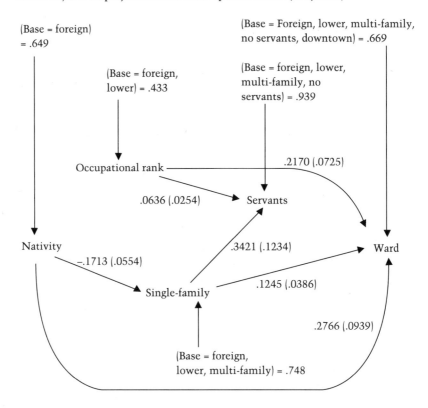

Effect[b]	Total (raw)	Spurious	Causal (net)	Direct	Indirect
Nativity-occupation	+.0401*	—	+.0401*	—	—
Nativity-single-fam	−.1660	—	−.1680	−.1713**	+.0033
Occupation-single-fam	−.0297*	+.0057*	−.0354*	—	—
Nativity-servants	+.1029	—	+.1029	+.0373*	+.0656*
Occupation-servants	+.0602**	−.0034	+.0636**	+.0451*	+.0185*
Single-fam-servants	+.3883	−.0018	+.3901	—	—
Nativity-ward	+.2899	—	+.2899	+.2766	+.0133
Occupation-ward	+.1760	−.0110	+.1870	+.2170	−.0300
Single-fam-ward	+.1610	−.0510	+.1100	+.1245	−.0145
Servants-ward	+.0983**	+.0800**	+.0183*	—	—

Table 3.10 *(continued)*

[a] Numbers are d coefficients and intercept values. Values within parentheses are two-sigma confidence limits, with variances doubled to correct for multistage sampling. See James A. Davis, "Analyzing Contingency Tables with Linear Flow Graphs: D-Systems," in D. Heise, ed., *Sociological Methodology* (San Francisco: Jossey-Bass, 1976), pp. 111–145.

[b] Categories: nativity—native, foreign; occupational rank—upper (professional, proprietary, and skilled), lower (semiskilled, unskilled, and others); single-family—one- or two-family homes, three+ family homes; servants—yes, no; ward—downtown (wards 4 and 5), uptown (wards 9 and 10).

[*] Pearson χ^2 not significant to the .10 level (10%).

[**] Pearson χ^2 not significant to the .05 level (5%).

(B) An effects decomposition of a full (nondichotomized) linear flow model measuring the impact of ethnicity, age, and occupational rank upon familial residence χ^2 [a]

Effect:	Total (raw)	Spurious	% [b]	Causal (net)	Direct	% [c]	Indirect	% [c]
Native-occup.	120.79	—	—	120.79	—	—	—	—
Native-single	55.09	—	—	55.09	45.29	82.2	9.8	21.6
Occup.-single	54.96	10.75	19.6	44.21	—	—	—	—
Native-servant	38.32	—	—	38.32	12.92**	33.7	25.40	66.3
Occup.-servant	65.22	9.91	15.2	55.31	36.62	66.2	18.69	33.8
Single-servant	171.28	56.32	32.9	114.96	—	—	—	—
Native-ward	265.24	—	—	265.24	172.27	64.9	92.97	35.1
Occup.-ward	76.88	21.87	28.4	55.01	59.62	108.4	−4.61	−8.4
Single-ward	21.51	6.37	29.6	15.14	15.27	100.9	−0.13	−0.9
Servant-ward	4.87*	3.50*	71.9	1.37*	—	—	—	—

[a] Categories: nativity—native, foreign; occupational rank—upper (professional, proprietary and skilled), lower (semiskilled, unskilled, and others); single-family—one- or two-family homes, three+ family homes; servants—yes, no; ward—downtown (wards 4 and 5), uptown (wards 9 and 10).

[b] Figures are percentages of total (raw) χ^2 that are spurious.

[c] Figures are percentages of causal (net) χ^2 that are direct and indirect effects.

[*] Pearson χ^2 not significant to the .10 level (10%).

[**] Pearson χ^2 not significant to the .05 level (5%).

Source: New York State Census for 1855 (manuscript).

the first showed any significant relationship with that of ward. In both dichotomized and polytomous models (table 3.10), weak effects for housing density were dwarfed by much stronger relations among ethnicity, occupation, and residence. The employment of servants had no significant residential impact at all.

Results from this analysis largely confirm what we have already observed: the important influence of ethnicity and occupation upon residential selection. Not only did people select neighborhoods chiefly because of consciousness of kind, but such ethnic clustering had social ramifications. For example, the social composition of the Fourth and Tenth Wards reflected both ethnic patterns of residential concentration (Irish in the former and Germans in the latter and, less directly, immigrant patterns of occupational clustering—Irish at the bottom of the occupational ladder and Germans filling skilled trades). Likewise, much of the middling status of the Ninth Ward was the result of its strong concentration of Yankees. Yet the results also demonstrate that occupational rank was capable of shaping residence independent of ethnicity (albeit to a lesser extent). Even though much of the wide occupational lacuna between rich and poor neighborhoods vanishes when controlling for ethnic differences, significant gaps still separated the largely semiskilled Fourth Ward from the skilled Tenth, or the Ninth Ward with its many nonworking heads of households ("other" in table 3.11).

The results also suggest yet another socioeconomic factor shaped the social composition of neighborhoods operating independently and in conjunction with ethnic status and occupational rank: the distribution of uncrowded housing. Given the emerging residential housing market, the luxury of space varied with the composition of housing stock from ward to ward, as well as with the ability of residents to afford less crowded homes within each ward. The Fourth and Fifth Wards possessed a disproportionate number of tenements (71 percent), while the Ninth Ward contained a greater share of single- and dual-family homes (41.4 percent) than would have been expected had the housing market operated uniformly (table 3.11).[88] But even here, ethnic cohesion was a greater cause of residential crowding than geography. Regardless of where they lived, Germans and Irish were particularly vulnerable to crowding in multi-family tenements. This pattern contrasted sharply with that of native-born and British families who tended to reside in dwellings housing fewer than three families (79.5 percent of Irish and 73.1 percent of Germans lived in tenements, compared with only 58.2 percent of native-born and 53.7 of British). By comparison, occupational rank had only a small effect upon housing status, with professionals and proprietors living in the least crowded homes.[89]

In sum, status variables such as the employment of servants and housing density, although tightly interrelated with one another, operated independently of ward. The propensity to employ servants varied little among ethnic groups or between neighborhoods. While 45 percent of all house-

Table 3.11   Social Rank, Ethnicity, and Residence, Four Sample
Wards, New York City, 1855 (Three Measures)

(A) Ethnicity and single-family residence, controlling for occupational rank. *

| Ethnicity | Family Residence | | | | |
	1–2 Family	S.R. *	Multi-family	S.R. *	N
Native-white	41.9	3.7	58.1	−3.7	397
British	46.4	3.0	53.6	−3.0	126
Irish	21.9	−5.5	78.1	5.5	317
German	30.1		69.9		268
Other	41.3		58.7		123
Total	34.7		65.3		1241

(B) Ethnicity and employment of servants, controlling for occupational rank and single-family residence. *

| Ethnicity | Servants | | | | |
	None	S.R. *	1+	S.R. *	N
Native-white	74.0		26.0		397
British	69.3		30.7		136
Irish	79.0	2.6	21.0	−2.1	317
German	72.9		27.1		268
Other	63.2	−2.7	36.8	2.7	123
Total	73.5		26.5		1241

(C) Occupational rank and single-family residence, controlling for ethnicity. *

| Rank | Family Residence | | | | |
	1–2 Family	S.R. *	Multi-family	S.R. *	N
Professional	57.5		42.5		73
Proprietary	42.1		57.9		185
Skilled	26.9		73.5		416
Semiskilled	26.5		73.5		188
Unskilled	32.9		67.1		110
Other	41.9		58.1		269
Total	34.7		63.3		1241

(D) Occupational rank and employment of servants, controlling for ethnicity and single-family residence. *

| Rank | Servants | | | | |
	None	S.R. *	1+	S.R. *	N
Professional	48.3	−5.0	51.7	5.0	73
Proprietary	67.6		32.4		185
Skilled	79.6	3.5	20.4	−3.5	416
Semiskilled	76.9		231.1		188
Unskilled	70.4		29.6		110
Other	73.7		26.3		269
Total	73.5		26.5		1241

(E) Single-family residence and employment of servants, controlling for ethnicity and occupational rank. *

| Family Residence | Servants | | | | |
	None	S.R.	1+	S.R.	N
1–2 families	55.0	−10.7	45.0	10.7	430.3
Multifamily	83.3	10.7	16.7	−10.7	810.7
Total	73.5		26.5		1241

Table 3.11   *(continued)*

(F) Occupational rank and residence, controlling for ethnicity, single-family residence, and employment of servants.*

Rank	4	S.R.*	5	S.R.*	9	S.R.*	10	S.R.*	All
					Ward				
Professional	5.5		5.3		6.9		5.5		5.5
Proprietary	13.9		14.2		15.6		15.5		14.9
Skilled	25.7	−3.0	26.9	−2.7	37.0		41.9	3.6	33.55
Semiskilled	24.0	4.5	12.8		15.5		9.2	−3.3	15.1
Unskilled	9.3		12.6	2.5	8.8		5.1	−2.6	8.9
Other	21.7		28.2	3.0	16.3	−3.2	21.7		21.7
Total	260.1		282.2		396.6		302.1		1241.0

(G) Single-family residence and residence, controlling for ethnicity, occupational rank, and employment of servants.*

Family Residence	4	S.R.*	5	S.R.*	9	S.R.*	10	S.R.*	N
					Ward				
1–2 Families	29.3	−2.0	29.0	−2.3	41.4	3.4	35.8		34.7
Multifamily	70.7	2.0	71.0	2.3	58.6	−3.4	64.2		65.3
Total	260.1		282.2		396.6		302.1		1241.0

ᵃ Standardized residuals: (Observed-Fitted)/SQRT(Fitted). Since standardized residuals are normally distributed, numbers greater than +/− 1.96 are significant to the .05 level. Only significant values are shown.
Source: See table 3.10.

holds in single- and dual-family residences had servants, only 16.7 percent of those in multifamily tenements did (table 3.11). Only the distribution of uncrowded housing, the propensity of certain industries to congregate in certain areas, and the ethnic division of labor imposed class order on any but the very richest or very poorest neighborhoods.

Homeless

Ethnicity and occupational rank not only influenced the ability of residents to hire a maid, to live in a private dwelling, or to select a neighborhood of their choice, but more fundamentally whether one lived in a residence or on the streets. Among the lowest classes of New York's poor, the homeless *lumpenproletariat* temporarily were housed on floors and benches of police station houses. Here social rank meant the difference between poverty in a tenement house and utter destitution. Not belonging to any set neighborhood, the homeless lodger and vagrant floated from one address to another, slept out of doors, or sought shelter in district police stations. An Aldermanic committee charged with reorganizing New York's police department in the early 1840s estimated that in addition to 350,000 permanent residents, New York also harbored a floating population of 50,000 "who, at no time, possess home or house."[90] Under the existing police system, large numbers of homeless men and women had been sheltered in the city's four watch houses and, in times of good weather, in Battery Park. With the reorganization of the department in 1845, the newly established metropolitan police began sheltering these individuals temporarily in seventeen stations scattered through the wards.[91] In 1853, when the city had twenty precincts, the police accommodated 24,892 destitute people during one six-month period alone.[92] With the implementation of the Metropolitan Police Act in 1857, the number of police stations grew to thirty, and on especially cold nights between 1,000 and 1,200 homeless were sheltered, and another 600 to 800 were turned away from each station house.[93] By the 1860s an average of 86,214 lodgers per year, "the most wretched of our population," were supplied with "naked wooden platforms without beds or bed clothing, in rooms kept sufficiently warm to secure them from suffering or danger and cold."[94] Though it is difficult to assess the causes or composition of nineteenth-century homelessness, contemporaries noted that they were of "both sexes, all ages, nationalities, and it might be said, of all conditions." Much of this destitute population was chronically homeless— "regulars," "rounders," or repeaters—who moved from station house to station house as "habitually homeless, penniless, friendless," or simply down on their luck.[95]

The two surviving police blotters from antebellum New York offer information about how homeless men and women lodging in precinct houses in the 1850s—and presumably overlooked by city marshals during censuses—compared with their more fortunate neighbors.[96] A comparison between lodgers sampled from Tenth Ward police blotters for the years 1855–1856 and the population in the surrounding ward as enumerated in the manuscript state census indicates that the homeless were mostly immigrants who were disadvantaged in their age and timing of arrival.[97] Police lodgers were less likely to be "fresh off the boat" than other ethnic residents, having arrived earlier and at an older age than their countrymen (table 3.12). Indeed, it was more common for British and Irish lodgers to have arrived during the periods 1830–1834 and 1840–1844 than non-lodgers.[98] The ages at which lodgers immigrated were significantly older than for other Tenth Ward residents (table 3.13). While 57 percent of Ger-

Cross-section view and elevation of the Gotham Court tenements at 34 and
38 Cherry Street in the Fourth Ward. Each of its 144 apartments was divided
into two rooms, a living room of 14 by 10 feet and a bedroom 14 by 7 feet.

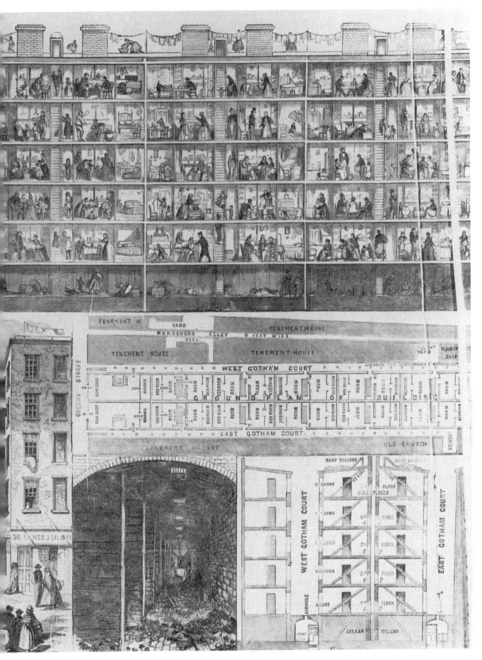

Built in 1850, it was one of the most notorious slums in the city until it was demolished in 1895. From *Frank Leslie's Zeitung*, June 1867. Photograph courtesy of the New-York Historical Society, New York City.

"Homeless in the New York Station House," a view of homeless women lodged in a shelter operated by the police. From *Harper's Weekly*, 13 December, 1873. Photograph courtesy of Duke University Library.

man, 72 percent of Irish, and 73 percent of British immigrants normally arrived before the age of twenty-five, among lodgers comparable figures were 41 percent, 59 percent, and 58 percent, respectively. This admittedly sketchy evidence nonetheless suggests that foreign vagrants were not (or should not have been) strangers to American ways, having been in America longer than most of their neighbors. Still, their older ages-at-arrival seemed to have placed them at a disadvantage both in adjusting to the new culture and finding employment compared with other immigrants. Women may have arrived too old to be hired as domestics and men too old to learn skilled trades. Both also seem to have lacked the supportive ties of friendship or family that were commonly available to younger migrants.

Police lodgers (the vast majority in the sample were women) differed markedly from other residents of the Tenth Ward in terms of occupation rank. While only one out of ten male residents of the Tenth Ward could be classified as semiskilled or unskilled, more than a third of homeless men belong to these categories. As for women, 55.6 percent of residents who worked clung to the bottom rungs of the occupational ladder, compared with 78.9 percent among the homeless (table 3.14).

Similar differences existed between residents and the homeless within

Table 3.12 Ethnicity and Homelessness Among
Arrival Cohorts, Tenth Ward, New York City, 1855–56

Variables: Nativity: foreign-born nationality—British (incl. Scotland), Irish,
German, other (Canadian, French, Dutch).

Year of arrival: before 1820, 1820–29, 1830–34, 1835–39, 1840–44,
1845–49, 1850–55 (or 1856 for some vagrants).

Homelessness: no (inhabitants with residences according to 1855
manuscript state census); yes (derived from the Tenth Ward Police
Blotters for 1855 and 1856). For the sake of analysis, the two models
were initially assumed to constitute separate populations.

Terms of Model (controlled for)	χ^2	χ^2 d.f.	χ^2 signif.	Difference χ^2	Diff. d.f.	Difference signif.	Coef. of determination
All 2-way assoc.	19.3	18	.3723	—	—	—	—
(Nativity, arrival)	159.7	36	.0001	140.4	18	.0001	.8791
(Homeless, nativity)	210.5	21	.0001	191.2	3	.0001	.9082
(Vagrancy, arrival)	38.1	24	.0335	18.8	6	.0048	.4932

Table from modeled data (all 2-way associations):
homelessness by period of arrival, grouped by nativity

Homeless	Nativity	Period of Arrival (% across)							N
		Pre-1820	1820 –29	1830 –34	1835 –39	1840 –44	1845 –49	1850 –55/6	
No	Gt. Britain	6	11	9	16	18	20	21	78.5
No	Ireland	2	3	4	6	10	29	45	143.5
No	Germany	1	1	3	3	4	21	68	544.5
No	Other	2	6	4	2	5	14	67	48.5
Yes	Gt. Britain	3	15	15	15	23	14	11	22.5
Yes	Ireland	1	6	12	7	17	26	31	118.5
Yes	Germany	0	2	9	4	7	23	55	14.5
Yes	Other	1	13	12	2	9	14	48	7.5

Sources: New York State Census for 1855 (manuscript), Ward 10; and New York City
Police Department, "Tenth District Police Blotter" (manuscript).

the same ethnic groups. Vagrants were two or three times as likely to
have low status jobs than their fellow countrymen. Even among Irish immigrants, one in five of the homeless held skilled or white-collar jobs,
compared with 53.8 percent for those with homes.

When combined with data on age and arrival cohorts, these figures reinforce our picture of predominantly female vagrants beyond the prime
ages of domestic employment. While most female domestics had ceased

Table 3.13   Ethnicity, Homelessness, and Age
at Arrival, Tenth Ward, New York City, 1855–56

Variables: Nativity: foreign-born nationality—British (incl. Scotland), Irish,
German.
Age at arrival: in years—1–14, 15–19, 25–29, 30–34, 35–39, 40+.
Homelessness: no (inhabitants with residences according to 1855
manuscript state census); yes (derived from the Tenth Ward Police
Blotters for 1855 and 1856). For the sake of analysis, the two models
were initially assumed to constitute separate populations.

Terms of Model (controlled for)	χ^2	χ^2 d.f.	χ^2 signif.	Difference χ^2	Diff. d.f.	Difference signif.	Coef. of determination
All 2-way assoc.	18.4	12	.1036	—	—	—	—
(Homeless, nativity)	245.2	14	.0001	226.8	2	.0001	.9250
(Nativity, age)	48.4	24	.0025	30.0	12	.0031	.6200
(Homeless, age)	35.3	18	.0088	16.9	6	.0098	.4787

Table from modeled data (all 2-way associations):
homelessness by age at arrival, grouped by nativity

Homeless	Nativity	Age at Arrival (% across)							N
		1–14	15–19	20–24	25–29	30–34	35–39	40+	
No	Gt. Britain	32	17	24	6	10	4	6	76.5
No	Ireland	23	28	21	12	6	5	6	138.5
No	Germany	18	18	21	16	13	6	8	489.5
Yes	Gt. Britain	25	8	25	7	19	4	11	21.5
Yes	Ireland	19	14	26	15	12	6	10	118.5
Yes	Germany	13	8	20	18	22	6	13	15.5
N= 860.0									

Sources: New York State Census for 1855 (manuscript), Ward 10; and New York City
Police Department, "Tenth District Police Blotter" (manuscript).

work for married life by the age of twenty-five, older homeless women
continued to list themselves as domestics—this at a time when the
city's intelligence offices (as employment offices were called) were already
crowded with immigrant women in search of employment.[99] Here the data
raises more questions than it answers, especially questions concerning
the composition and conditions of prefamine immigrants from Ireland
and the cracks in family support that left certain individuals adrift. Yet
the older age of many vagrants upon arrival compared with other residents

Table 3.14   The Occupational Basis of Homelessness: Sex,
Nativity, and Occupational Rank among Resident and
Homeless Populations, Tenth Ward, New York City, 1855–56

Variables: Nativity: U.S., Great Britain (Incl. Scotland), Ireland, Germany, Other.
Sex: male, female.

Vertical Occupational Rank: professional (I), pettyproprietary (II),
skilled (III), unskilled specified (IV), unskilled unspecified (V), site
only (VI).

Homelessness: no (inhabitants with residences according to 1855
manuscript state census); yes (derived from the Tenth Ward Police
Blotters for 1855 and 1856). For the sake of analysis, the two models
were initially assumed to constitute separate populations.

Terms of Model (controlled for)	χ^2	χ^2 d.f.	χ^2 signif.	Difference χ^2	Diff. d.f.	Difference signif.	Coef. of determination
All 2-way assoc.	75.21	69	.2839	—	—	—	—
(Sex, occupation)	237.07	74	.0001	161.85	5	.0001	.9250
(Homeless, nativity)	146.54	73	.0001	71.32	4	.0031	.6200
(Nativity, occupation)	130.08	89	.0032	54.86	20	.0098	.4787
(Homeless, sex)	109.60	70	.0020	34.39	1	.0001	.4218
(Homeless, occupation)	97.96	74	.0324	22.74	5	.0006	.2322
(Sex, nativity)	97.96	73	n.s.*	—	—	—	—

*Probability over 10% (.1);

Table from modeled data (all 2-way associations): vertical
occupational rank by homelessness, grouped by sex

Sex	Homeless	Vertical Occupational Rank (% across)						
		I	II	III	IV	V	VI	N
Male	No	2.9	17.4	66.2	6.7	3.2	3.6	433.0
Males	Yes	3.3	9.4	48.5	13.9	21.8	3.2	73.0
Female	No	2.7	10.9	26.0	54.6	1.0	4.8	90.0
Females	Yes	2.0	3.9	12.5	74.3	4.6	2.8	133.0

N = 728.9

Table from modeled data: vertical occupational
rank by homelessness, grouped by nativity

Nativity	Homeless	Vertical Occupational Rank (% across)						
		I	II	III	IV	V	VI	N
U.S.	No	5.8	20.3	53.2	13.0	2.5	5.3	136.0
U.S.	Yes	6.4	10.1	34.3	36.3	7.8	5.1	34.0

Table 3.14   (*continued*)

| Nativity | Homeless | Vertical Occupational Rank (% across) | | | | | | |
		I	II	III	IV	V	VI	N
G.Britain	No	2.8	17.3	57.2	14.3	2.5	5.8	46.0
G.Britain	Yes	3.0	8.5	36.1	39.2	7.7	5.5	24.0
Ireland	No	1.3	10.6	41.9	37.2	6.3	2.7	75.0
Ireland	Yes	0.9	3.3	16.9	64.8	12.5	1.6	122.0
Germany	No	1.2	14.6	70.1	9.4	2.0	2.7	238.0
Germany	Yes	1.4	8.2	50.8	29.4	7.2	2.9	16.0
Other	No	7.8	24.3	46.6	12.6	3.4	5.3	28.0
Other	Yes	8.4	11.9	29.5	34.6	10.5	5.0	10.0
N= 728.9								

Sources: New York State Census for 1855 (manuscript), Ward 10; and New York City Police Department, "Tenth District Police Blotter" (manuscript).

suggests that for some immigrants, inopportune timing and the lack of adaptability may have hampered their life chances and doomed them to destitution on the streets.

Conclusion

Differences within ethnic groups as to the timing and age at which immigrants arrived, coupled with shifts in neighborhood fashion, make it difficult to generalize about the impact of ethnicity upon residence in antebellum New York and force us to reexamine some prior assumptions about the spatial dispersal of natives and newcomers. The diverse social composition of older areas often masked fundamental transitions so that closer examination of seeming heterogeneity reveals that neighborhoods were composed of several different groups in transit: old-time residents whose hold on the neighborhood was waning, immigrant or migrant newcomers who were establishing ethnic dominance, and other newcomers who had little choice over where to settle given the tight housing market in Manhattan during the early 1850s. Superimposed on this overall pattern were the anonymous transients who slept on street corners or sought lodging in police stations during harsh weather.

Nor did this process of ethnic settlement proceed toward homogeneity in a linear fashion. Indeed, data on settlement patterns among arrival cohorts make it clear that many neighborhoods actually experienced *de-*

clines in homogeneity because of the tight competition for housing between natives and newcomers in the 1850s. This housing shortage would
not begin to be addressed until the post–Civil War boom that once again
continued the earlier march toward homogeneity.[100] Most importantly,
while native reformers commonly talked of the "tendency" of immigrants
to "segregate" within "distinct communities," the clearest tendency in
this direction occurred among a group that native reformers easily overlooked: Anglo-American natives like themselves. Native areas were ethnically more homogeneous and their segregation largely stemmed from a
conservative—and at times nativisitic—desire to bond together and maintain the city as they had known it against the fearful onslaught of foreigners. By comparison, "consciousness of kind" among immigrants and
the desire to maintain old-world culture was weak.

For the majority of New Yorkers of all ethnic groups, work location
shaped where one lived. With the development of a central business district, the separation of work from residence and the clustering of certain
trades, such as sugar-refining, printing, construction, and shipbuilding,
made industrial location a critical force in neighborhood development.
Likewise, occupational rank and, to a lesser extent, the quality of housing
stock became badges of status on their own. Yet even here, despite the
existence of rich and poor areas, class was not an unambiguous predictor
of neighborhood type. Working-class neighborhoods remained heterogeneous in character. This fact should temper efforts to locate class consciousness in the residential patterns of neighborhood. While such consciousness undoubtedly existed and made its presence known in ever more
frequent clashes in city streets, it was not until the Civil War (with its
bloody Draft Riots) and beyond that the flight of the wealthy and the influx of Southern and Eastern European immigrants completed the pattern
of homogeneity in spatial organization that had begun to develop in the
antebellum period.

The findings have suggested that the reality of New York spatial organization combined elements of both rival views of community development.
While it is true that residence increasingly did serve to define class for
those who could afford the luxury of single- or dual-family dwellings, the
changing attraction of certain neighborhoods among arrival cohorts revealed how the forces of cultural continuity and ethnic identity had, since
early in the century, channeled people to different local communities.
Ethnic divisions in employment further reinforced the spatial segregation
based upon consciousness of kind. But New York's ethnic neighborhoods,
despite their collection of churches, business, clubs, and associations,

were neither insular nor, strictly speaking, institutionally complete. And the rudiments of an ethnic division of labor failed to translate into economic self-sufficiency since the conscious building of community was a luxury that few immigrants could afford.

4 Children and Boarders—The Familial Basis of Neighborhood

■■■■■■■■ The 1880 edition of *Appleton's Dictionary of New York City* reminds us of an important residential institution in nineteenth-century New York: "Within the past five years, the efforts made to induce people of moderate means to live in apartments, and abandon boarding-houses and hotels, in which a large proportion of the population had there[to]fore resided, has met with a marked degree of success." Before being replaced by apartments, boardinghouses and hotels had been a significant factor in the city's residential patterns.[1] In particular, there was a mutual avoidance between boarders and young families. Boarders typically eschewed areas housing large numbers of families with young children for boardinghouses located in areas adjoining the central business district. By the same token, families embarking on child-rearing choose more distant neighborhoods.[2] How people elected residence on the basis of life cycles is one of the least understood aspects of neighborhood formation in nineteenth-century New York residence.[3] This chapter attempts to shed light on this question by exploring (1) the culture of boarding; (2) the processes of transition from adolescence through semiautonomy to marriage; and (3) the forces which, along with family structure, played a determining role in where people lived during such life-cycle transitions.

Boarders

Much historical work on the urban family sees the household as a haven in an increasingly heartless world during the antebellum period,[4] but the desire for domestic privacy was no more important a city-building force than its neglected negative image: the desire of young men and women to spend their few years of freedom between childhood and marriage away from families and children.[5] Such semiautonomy was peculiarly characteristic of the mid-nineteenth century, when older forms of domestic production were yielding to the industrial era, and universal education had not yet emerged as an alternative to family life for young adults. This was still a time when, as Joseph Kett has discovered, "adolescence . . . as the period after puberty during which a young person is institutionally segregated from casual contacts with a broad range of adults" scarcely existed.[6] With apprenticeship on the wane and households losing their function as productive units, young men and women were forced out of their households into this semiautonomous stage prior to marriage.[7] Just as the nineteenth-century city witnessed the separation of residential neighborhoods from business districts through the divorcement of work from residence, so families witnessed the separation of their traditional preindustrial functions: production, child-rearing, and residence.[8]

If any institution embodied semiautonomy, it was the boardinghouse.[9] Life as a boarder in an augmented family or a professional boardinghouse offered newly arrived and long-established inhabitants alike accommodation, meals, and the pleasures of camaraderie outside the encumbering boundaries of one's own family. The practice was "universal among unmarried of all classes, male and female."[10] As a social institution, boarding provided both cohesion and shape to the lives of unrelated individuals. As a familial practice, the augmented household was especially attractive to newcomers because of their confusion, their economic needs, "and the need for socialization into the ways of the city."[11] Boarding marked the only stage of an individual's life free from the obligations to parent or to child. Particularly as it was experienced in the professional boardinghouses, this usually temporary residence joined freedom from family constraints with the extreme fluidity of a transient population to produce a peculiar urban subculture.[12]

As a neighborhood phenomenon, the concentration of boardinghouses in the city's lower wards adjoining the central business district served as a symbol of community change.[13] And as several historians have shown, boarding was also linked to fundamental changes in New York's housing and labor markets. First, as employers abandoned the practice of lodging employees in their own houses, the "internal adaptations of houses to create specialized living space for boarders not connected to household production prefigured the external separation of work and living space and the production of living space as a commodity for a general market." Second, the provision of meals and lodging in formal establishments "offered the first systematic multi-tenant housing solution from within the mechanic classes" to the problem of escalating rents and housing shortages. Finally, "the management of boarding houses transformed domestic labor into a service commodity" by allowing women to generate additional household under the cloak of domesticity (women operated three-fifths of boardinghouses).[14]

Initially, the spread of boardinghouses for sailors, day laborers, and journeymen served as "wedges of movement of masses of the poor into the east side streets."[15] By antebellum days, contemporaries automatically associated their proliferation to the ebbing fashionability of the neighborhoods in which they appeared. "The boarding house," noted one observer, was usually the "cast off mansion of gentility." Another writer noted how they had become as "thick as leaves in Vallambrosa."[16] Describing the areas of St. John's Park, Houston Street, and Bleecker Street, Walt Whitman observed that "whole neighborhoods of Boarding-houses" stood in "localities formerly as aristocratic as 'Fifth Avenuedom.'"[17] The extent of boardinghouse concentration is apparent when one examines the addresses of the nearly one thousand such establishments listed in *Trow's New York City Directory* for 1854–1855. A comparison between boardinghouse location and the aggregate population (by household) in wards south of Fortieth Street shows that proportionately few of these houses were listed in wards located either on the northern fringes of New York's residential expansion or in the tenement-infested Lower East Side (table 4.1).[18] Rather, most clustered in the First, Fourth, and Fifth Wards. In Manhattan, as in other cities, boarding thrived in formerly affluent residential districts that were undergoing a pattern of invasion and succession.[19]

Family and institutional boarding represented two essentially different forms of transient residence. Professional boarding establishments, for example, could house a larger number of boarders than the family that might take in one or two outsiders.[20] Half of the professional establishments, comprising only 6 percent of those households with boarders, accommodated five or more transients. By contrast, about nine out of ten "augmented families" housed fewer than four boarders, with half having only one.[21] But the chief difference was that professional establishments provided lodgers a greater degree of openness, since there were no prerequisite occupational, kinship, or ethnic ties.[22] Furthermore, since boardinghouses served as both hotels and restaurants, eating times were not as closely linked to the schedules and work patterns of individual host families. Finally, the size and structure of these establishments provided for a greater diversity among residents in terms of age, occupation, ethnic background, and life-cycle stages; it was not uncommon to find boarding families and unmarried singles sharing the same dinner table.[23]

Table 4.1   Distribution of Professional
Boardinghouses by Ward, New York City, 1854–55

Variables: Wards: 1 through 22
Boardinghouse: Boardinghouse, presumed non-boardinghouse.*

Terms of Model (controlled for)	χ^2	d.f.	χ^2 signif.
(all associations)	878.42	21	.0001

Ward	Boardinghouses %	S. R.**	Non-Boardinghouses %	S. R.**	Total N	Total %
1	11.44	19.81	2.02	−1.73	2646	2.08
2	2.54	11.71	.33	−1.02	934	.74
3	3.28	8.63	.78	−.75	1012	.80
4	12.29	13.52	3.67	−1.18	4732	3.72
5	11.76	14.08	3.28	−1.23	4233	3.33
6	5.61	2.22	4.13	−.19	5241	4.12
7	5.08	−.40	5.38	.04	6811	5.36
8	9.64	5.23	5.55	−.46	7066	5.56
9	3.92	−2.74	6.14	.24	7745	6.10
10	4.13	−.67	4.61	.06	5825	4.58
11	3.18	−6.25	9.44	.55	1893	9.36
12	.00	−4.08	1.86	.36	2335	1.84
13	3.28	−2.09	4.78	.18	6040	4.75
14	3.50	−.85	4.07	.07	5143	4.05
15	4.34	2.59	2.90	−.23	3690	2.90
16	4.13	−2.79	6.44	.24	8125	6.39
17	4.34	−5.55	10.08	.48	12708	0.00
18	2.86	−3.91	5.99	.34	7551	5.94
19	.00	−4.48	2.23	.39	2796	2.20
20	2.97	−5.51	8.08	.48	0178	8.01
21	1.17	−4.62	4.33	.40	5451	4.29
22	.53	−5.18	3.90	.45	4903	3.86
Total	100.00		100.00			100.00
N	944		125614		126058	

*The ratio of professional boarding and lodging houses to the total number of house-holds in the ward was computed by subtracting the number of these establishments from the total number of families listed for each ward in the published state census. The location of professional boardinghouses was determined by sorting those houses listed in the business section of *Trow's New York City Directory* for 1854–55 according to location by ward.

**Standardized residuals: (Observed-Fitted)/SQRT(Fitted). Since standardized residuals are normally distributed, numbers greater than +/− 1.67 are significant to the .10 level and greater than +/− 1.96 are significant to the .05 level.

Source: Trow's New York City Directory, 1855 (New York: H. Trow, 1854) and Secretary of State, *Census of the State of New York for 1855* (Albany, 1857), p. 8.

Nineteenth-century evidence suggests that the freedom that formalized boarding offered from the encumbrances of life with a private family
was important to potential boarders.[24] Thomas Gunn's satirical volume,
The Physiology of the New York Boarding-Houses, offers perhaps the
best descriptions of the qualitative differences between institutional and
family boarding.[25] Gunn viewed life with a private family as a halfway
step that would appeal only to an individual reluctant to experience full
autonomy—one who harbored a "wholesome distrust of boarding houses"
and who desired "a nearer approach to domestic felicity." Thus family
boarding provided a "compromise" solution. As a hypothetical lodger with
the Brown family discovered, however, such a compromise could lead to
an unpleasant loss of privacy: "Being treated 'exactly as one of the family,'
it is tacitly expected that you will let pass, without comment or objection,
whatever may conflict with your own tastes and inclinations. . . . [Conse-
quently] The Boarder in a Private Family usually quits on general grounds
of discontent and incompatibility of temper. He has, in fact, been so much
'one of the family' that he has lost claim to his own individuality."[26]

Loss of privacy was actually common in both types of boarding and
was offset by one paramount factor: the chance at affordable housing in
a tight housing market. Boarding particularly benefited the middle class
by offering them adequate service at a time when "good" servants were
hard to find. Because real-estate ownership rates were low, middle-class
New Yorkers were driven into boarding to escape rents that could range
up to $3,500 a year for a large house.[27] Walt Whitman observed that "thou-
sands of young or 'moderately well off' people, absolutely unable to find
the right residence for them, hire a house quite too large, and eke out
the rent by subletting one, two, or three, or more rooms, or entire floors,
to such lodgers as they can find." This custom prevailed everywhere:
"Fifth Avenue, Fourteenth Street, from river to river, Twenty-Second and
Twenty-third Streets and nearly every other respectable portion of the
city."[28] But boarding also benefited the working classes. One visitor called
the professional boardinghouse "a real blessing to the industrious poor"
that furnished them with "comforts, conveniences, and social appliances
which people of moderate means cannot hope to command in their private
establishments."[29] Another resident, writing in the 1890s, remembered
paying 10 shillings a week for board when his daily salary as a mechanic
was 8–12 shillings in the 1830s. In 1840 a British immigrant's guidebook
noted that good boarding could be found for $2.50 (10s 6d) a week, and
first-class accommodations for $3.00–$3.50, including three meals a day.[30]
The standard cost at a boardinghouse ranged between $4 and $7 a week for
working-class accommodations, and $12 and $15 for simple middle-class

rooms. For luxurious residential hotels the rate could be $150 dollars a week—this at a time when a laborer might earn $1 a day.[31]

For many visitors to the city during the first half of the nineteenth century, the "peculiarity of living in boarding-houses, instead of keeping house, or occupying private lodging," was considered to be one of the "most distinguishing features of society in New York."[32] While some have suggested that "most immigrants" found the "pseudo-family of the boardinghouse" to be "no substitute for the real thing,"[33] the freedom that boarding offered to "unmarried men" by replacing long-standing kinship obligations with temporary quasi-familial ties was an "unquestionable" attraction that impressed both residents and travelers. After a stay in New York, Swedish Baron Klinkowstrom praised boardinghouses for the easy social contacts that they offered. "At such lodging places people can always find company at home and do not need to seek it elsewhere," he observed. "Hence they avoid great expenses."[34] One affluent British visitor observed how "it was no uncommon occurrence for us to converse, on the same day, with individuals from many different parts of the globe."[35] Some of these social contacts extended beyond boarding life. A young woman— herself a veteran of boarding life—wrote that "often lasting and valuable friendships are founded by those thus thrown together."[36] Nor was this lively company limited to wealthy foreign visitors or to cosmopolitan middle-class natives. An itinerant Irish book peddler described life in Mrs. Fleming's boarding establishment at 177 Grand Street during the mid-1850s:

> All Mrs. Fleming's boarders emigrated from the Emerald Isle, with the exception of one American of the name Taylor, with whom I was exceedingly well pleased during our acquaintance. The ladies who boarded there supported themselves respectably by their superior skills in needlework, and made themselves distinguished and admired by various accomplishments, all young and unmarried. A gentleman of the name Mr. David O'Kavanaugh, one of the boarders and a

Scenes satirizing New York boardinghouse life: (a) arriving for an interview at a boardinghouse; (b) prospective lodger poring over responses to newspaper advertisement; (c) scrutiny at a "high" boardinghouse (d) montage showing landladies of various appearances, ages, and characteristics; (e) inspecting less-than-perfect quarters; (f) lunchtime flirtation (and over-eager service) at a fashionable boardinghouse; (g) "boisterous animal indulgence" at a medical students' boardinghouse, underscoring the fraternal nature of boarding life; (h) jigging in a sailors' boardinghouse. From Thomas Butler Gunn, *The Physiology of New York Boarding-Houses* (New York: Mason Brothers, 1857).

countryman of mine, played beautifully on musical instruments, and one of the boarding ladies also played to perfection on the piano, so when they played in concert, time passed insensibly away. As a community we lived indescribably happy, clear of sorrow, of sickness, and hunger, and it is to be hoped sinless.[37]

Despite the occupational and ethnic mixing found in some establishments, most were extensions of specific ethnic and craft communities and served a crucial function in helping to acclimatize newcomers. In some cities such as Milwaukee, two-thirds of the lodgers resided in the home of a countryman, and two-fifths had occupations which matched those of the families' heads.[38] A study of Boston boarders for the 1880s likewise uncovered a "significant tendency towards occupational clustering" together with a "strong connection between the boarders' places of origin and those of their household heads."[39] Much the same was true for boarders in New York City several decades before. Journeymen early in the nineteenth century had recourse to craft boardinghouses where, for a rent of three dollars a week, newcomers could find a bed, information on possible opportunities for employment, and easy access into the formal and informal social life of the artisan community.[40] And antebellum descriptions of boarding, including Gunn's *Physiology*, cataloged houses that catered exclusively to Germans, Irish, English, and Chinese. Several Jewish houses served exclusively kosher fare. And there were regional houses for Bostonians, Southerners, and "Down Easterners," interest-based houses for the pious and "serious," vegetarian houses, "Tip-Top" houses for dandies, "theatrical boardinghouses," "artists'" houses, medical students' houses, and sailors' houses. Gunn even listed a house for believers in spiritualism.[41]

The descriptions by contemporaries of highly cohesive boarding establishments are borne out by the residential patterns of 784 boarders and lodgers in the four sample wards. Germans were the most tightly segregated group, with nearly 80 percent boarding in a "gasthaus," while for other groups the figure ranged from 42.9 percent for boarders born in England and Scotland in English houses to 61.5 percent of Irish-born boarders in Irish-run houses.[42] When it came to class and craft ties, higher status workers generally chose to board in the houses of individuals having a similar social status. A third of professionals boarded with other professionals while avoiding families headed by skilled workmen. Petty-proprietors were even more exclusive, boarding only with their own group or in professional houses, while steadfastly avoiding skilled and semi-skilled households. Likewise, skilled, semiskilled, and unskilled workers tended to avoid houses of a higher rank. Skilled workers emerged as the most self-segregated occupational group with more than half boarding with fellow tradesmen.[43]

This ethnic and occupational homogeneity, together with the community spirit that it fostered, was to a great extent the result of the boardinghouse keeper's selectivity and temperament. That is to say, the eternal vigilance of the landlady who wished to maintain the reputation of her establishment made "membership" in these houses selective for boarders sharing similar backgrounds. Jeremiah O'Donovan had to present Mrs. Fleming with a letter of introduction from Judge McKenna of Philadelphia, who knew the "comfort and protection her house offered to every one who valued her dignity and reputation," before he could gain entrance.[44] Potential lodgers usually found accommodations by placing advertisements in one of several daily newspapers and waiting for the responses to come in from Manhattan, Brooklyn, and Hoboken.[45] One could follow vacancy signs posted in front of boardinghouses, which were at some times of the year (in the words of one character from a nineteenth-century novel) "almost as thick as lawyers' shingles in Philadelphia."[46] Though New Yorkers frequently complained about the annoyance of having to submit references to boardinghouse keepers, one observer defended them, calling references "absolutely necessary" to keep the houses free of such "improper characters" as thieves and prostitutes.[47] If Bleecker Street houses required "most unexceptionable references," proprietors in other areas were not always so careful: "the requirements of propriety" were often "satisfied by a limited regard to appearances, and a general free and easy kind of semi-morality prevails, as a result of freedom from restraint, and the presence of contaminated influences." Occasionally, prostitutes did slip through this security, and some establishments were undoubtedly run as houses of assignation.[48]

It was also not uncommon for clashes among inmates to disrupt the happy community of boardinghouses, due to the loss of privacy in close quarters. One guide to finding a proper boardinghouse written in the late 1870s advised "strangers and others engaging board" to "carefully avoid engaging their rooms for longer than from week to week, as the presence of disagreeable people or the contingencies frequently make it desirable to change, and an arrangement for a longer term is sure to result in trouble."[49] In one case a startled visitor watched as an argument between a German and an American boarder turned into a "fracas" which led to the American's departure to another house "with all possible precipitation."[50]

Nonetheless, the absence of children and the predominance of adults made the boardinghouse a peculiar environment in which freedom replaced responsibility. Frequently, the boarding subculture fostered a system of mutual support between lodger and host. In a familial situation, a boarder might take "charge of the house" in the head's absence.[51] Or a boardinghouse keeper might act as a surrogate parent, as was the case of Frederick and Margaret Eckle, who in 1850 witnessed the marriage of George Bohner, a sailor who resided in their home at 330 Water Street.[52] But boarding mainly functioned as a means of escaping family obligation. In this regard, institutional boarding was markedly antifamily. An English hatter living in Newark asked his employer why he and his family boarded: "I asked him if he did not feel many restraints of a domestic nature in the house of another person, which he would necessarily be free from in a home of his own. He answered me by saying that 'his wife had a hundred relations, and that he had about the same number himself, who, were he in a house of his own, would eat him up in a month,' so he found it more economical to board."[53]

The aversion to family life was compounded by the fact that most boarders were young singles, many of whom took a dim view of families boarding with children. As one lodger noted in the late 1860s: "Children are rated a nuisance by the majority of boarding-house keepers." Many establishments flatly refused to admit children under the age of four or five, while in those that did, suspicious landladies were known to make "sudden and unexpected raids on rooms which they occupy, for the purpose of ascertaining to what extent they are injuring the furniture." Under such tight control—and under the constant watch of the host and other boarders—the "poor disconsolates" had little else to do but to "amuse themselves with indoor toys, or slide down the banisters in mortal fear of the threats of the irate mistress of the house, and finally go to bed to kill time."[54] Nor was it uncommon to find youngsters barred from sitting rooms.[55] The lesson was simple: "To persons with families, boarding house life ought to be intolerable," declared one writer. "The troubles which these 'encumbrances' cause are so great that the wife and mother comes to the conclusion that more children will simply add to her difficulties of this kind, and so she commences to 'regulate' her family, and the little ones cease coming."[56]

For all the allure of lodging free from the aggravation of crying children, amidst the convivial company of peer members around the dinner table and in the sitting room, boarding life was not without its problems. Boarders continually griped about the rudeness and tightfistedness of landladies, the paucity and bad quality of the food, and the frequent poor repair of furniture and rooms. Some resented being slaves to the dinner bell that summoned boarders, like prison inmates, to meals of "beef

of tougher consistency and more *veiny* construction than was desirable"
and of potatoes which "exhibited as many eyes as Argus" (usually downed
in extreme haste). But this complaint was not universal, for it was not
uncommon to find houses praised for their "well spread" tables. Even one
normally caustic critic of boarding conceded that "probably the *cuisine*
of the boarding-house is the great attraction to married people who could
never afford such daily bills of fare in their own homes."[57]

Other problems, however, are not so easily dismissed. From the end
of the eighteenth century onward, many had viewed boardinghouses and
their footloose inmates as threats to the public morals and health. In the
wake of yellow fever epidemics in 1799, city fathers singled out "sailors
boarding houses and tipling houses" for municipal regulation, noting that
they were often "the resort of sailors and the lower class emigrants, and
other disorderly persons; where drunkenness and debauchers [sic] of every
kind are committed, which often produces disease of the most serious
nature, especially during the summer months."[58] In 1804 and again in
1810 the Common Council passed ordinances requiring the keepers of
boardinghouses and lodging houses to report the number of apartments
to be let so that the municipality could issue licenses stipulating a maximum number of boarders per dwelling. And during the summer months,
when the risk of disease was greatest, the law required each boardinghouse keeper to submit to the City Inspector's Office a list of any new
lodgers, together with the names of any boarder taken ill, under penalty
of a stiff fine.[59] A petition filed in 1805 before the Common Council by
Molly Wakefield, requesting relief from a fine for noncompliance, testifies
to the stringent enforcement of these regulations.[60] Throughout the period
of recurrent epidemics in the early 1820s, medical inspectors continued to
view boardinghouses as breeding grounds for disease, noting that yellow
fever "proved remarkably fatal where air must have been from necessity
impure and surcharged with human effluvia, as in *boarding houses*."[61]

After real-estate development finally drained and filled Lower Manhattan's swampy sections, which had long been breeding grounds for yellow
fever, criticism of boarding shifted from public health to morality. Aside
from the obvious threat posed to female boarders by the free intermingling
of coeducational boarding, a threat which some contemporaries blamed
for many a virtuous girl's fall into prostitution, critics of what Hareven
and Modell characterized as the "lodger evil" attacked boarding as the
very embodiment of social breakdown among the urban family.[62] In antebellum New York, the very convenience of boardinghouse life that made
semiautonomy so appealing was attacked for eroding the desire of young
men and women to get married and set up housekeeping on their own.

One British visitor dryly noted that the *"table d'hote"* and the "public drawing-room" were "not the conditions which to an Englishman's mind are conducive to the true happiness and charm of wedded life."[63] Another of his countrymen echoed these sentiments, observing that

> like the clubs of London, boarding-houses in America indispose men to form attachments, or to contemplate a more permanent settlement. To the young married couple it is also a convenience . . . but its disadvantage is much greater to them in the end; for when they become parents, and separate establishments are more necessary—the wife has acquired no experience in housekeeping, and both her husband and herself are adverse to the trouble, care, and anxiety of a separate house and separate servants; besides finding it less exciting and agreeable to sit down to breakfast and dine alone, and pass the evening without companions, to which they were accustomed while living at the boarding-house.[64]

The independence that undoubtedly accounted for much of the appeal of boarding to young middle-class men was to blame, in the view of one critic, for their lost adolescence. With youths spending so many of their formative years living unsupervised in boardinghouses, it was hardly surprising that "the children in this country are prematurely men and women." Freed from the "restraints of parental authority" by parents who unwittingly relinquished control out of pride "in seeing their children precocious and smart, like the boys and girls of 'other people,'" children seemed to be seeking work and lodging on their own at tender ages. This particular observer testified to having "met with several young boys and girls who were boarding in houses only a short distance from their homes."[65]

To their most extreme critics, boardinghouses were "hot-beds of vice and every species of immorality" and a "serious blot on the national character."[66] Behind such obvious exaggeration lay an element of truth. As has already been noted, boarders spurned children as they reveled in their temporary freedom from familial obligations. For single women and girls, living on their own was often available only through prostitution and casual sex, which made boardinghouses synonymous with bawdy houses and houses of assignation.[67] Respectable female boarders undoubtedly found boarding life to be plagued with unpleasantness, most attributable to a lack of privacy. "At first I was delighted with my boarding-house—it was quite genteel, and the young men were very polite to me," one female bookbinder reflected. But "after a while it became unpleasant" because "I found that those who addressed me so politely, and who flattered me, did not respect me."[68] Fannie Benedict, who boarded during the late 1860s, cataloged rowdyisms and eccentricities in fellow boarders which she found objectionable: the "pretty lady, who you admire, but whom you may discover some day in her room, in a beastly state of intoxication," the "light-fingered, loquacious gentlemen" with the habit of robbing fellow boarders, and the young men who went "stumbling up stairs past your door in the early hours of the morning, . . . sowing the necessary wild oats."[69]

The same close quarters of the boardinghouses that could foster supportive bonds in times of distress could also lead to less pleasant situations between roommates.[70] In 1831 a fourteen-year-old English immigrant, John Gough, following the suggestion of a friend, paid $2 a week to board in "Mrs. M——'s" establishment on William Street. For that price, he found himself sharing a bed with an Irishman, who was so "sick of fever and ague" that he died the second day after Gough's arrival.[71] Police blotters from 1856 report the case of Julius Schumacher, a German boarder in his late teens who returned from breakfast one morning to find that his roommate had broken into his trunk and taken $470 in gold.[72]

Despite its attendant aggravations, boardinghouse life in New York City was widespread enough to be an important social and city-building institution. Its chief attractions were the convenience of inexpensive housing for young men and women newly on their own and the freedom and excitement it offered. As a peer-group institution, the boardinghouse promoted collegiality among young men and women sharing the same backgrounds, trades, or interests. It is not by accident that one authority on the subject referred to himself as an "ex-member" of the "fraternity" of boarding.[73] This life offered the opportunity to strike out on one's own, free from parental authority, with the chance for exposure to a wider variety of people than otherwise would have been possible. "There is more to be learned of the world in general, from twelvemonth's residence in a boarding-house, than in five years of ordinary private life," proclaimed one young female veteran.[74] And from the boardinghouse it was only a short walk for journeymen and sailors to the tavern and other centers of lower-class leisure.[75]

A few people boarded into their late twenties and even into their thirties, but for most, boarding was simply a passing stage of the life cycle. With time would come marriage and a search for more private living arrangements—in a tenement flat, in a brownstone, or, with increasing frequency for middle-class and well-to-do boarders, in "French" apartments. Thus, even in the mid-nineteenth century, well before reformers had succeeded at branding the boardinghouse as working-class, the "extraordinary demand for individual privacy" (which some historians have blamed for the extinction of boarding) was, for most lodgers, simply a part of the aging process. In later decades, shortened periods of semiautonomy through the extension of education and longer stays with parents cut off the pool of potential boarders, and the boom of apartment house construction provided a respectable alternative to overpriced row houses and overcrowded tenements, helping to ease the housing shortage for the middle class.[76]

In its heyday boarding had been an important neighborhood-building force because young men in particular wanted little to do with family life between childhood and marriage. Boardinghouse keepers sympathetically tried to accommodate this view by discouraging families with young children. Consequently, areas in which boarders settled served as home to others much like themselves—young, transient, childless, hopeful to be upwardly mobile, and reveling in their temporary freedom. But once the transition had been made from semiautonomy into marriage, the professional boardinghouse or lodging family was invariably abandoned to set up a household of one's own prior to having children. The areas where married urbanites now settled to establish families were quite different from those where they had previously boarded, and neighborhood levels of fertility reflected this fact. Finally, variations in life-cycle transitions attributable to ethnicity indirectly imposed familial differences upon neighborhoods not easily measured by household composition. While ethnic and, to a much lesser extent, class differences in age and family composition also influenced neighborhood composition, fertility levels and boarding rates most clearly exemplified the spatial gulf between child-oriented residential neighborhoods and highly transient boardinghouse communities.

Transitions and Semiautonomy

The pattern of differences in residence actually had little to do directly with familial proclivities for certain neighborhoods. Rather, these were indirect results of important demographic differences that divided ethnic groups. New York in the 1850s had already become a city of immigrants whose extraordinary rapid population growth involving the influx of so many different cultures exceeded its ability to grow physically.

Ethnicity also shaped the timing of life-cycle transition.[77] For most New Yorkers the movement from childhood into semiautonomy as boarder, clerk, or domestic servant and, finally, into marriage was determined by ethnic and cultural factors. While some of the impact of family upon residential composition was undoubtedly a by-product of housing availability, neighborhood change, and perhaps a familial ideology that directed boarders to certain neighborhoods, much of it stemmed from ethno-cultural differences. How long an individual remained in a particular stage varied sharply between blacks and whites, between natives and immigrants of many diverse cultures, and, within all groups, between men and women.[78] This fluidity within urban households can be glimpsed in the sample of New Yorkers aged ten to forty residing in the four wards in 1855.

Ethnic difference was the strongest predictor of the timing and nature of life-cycle transition—far more so than even gender.[79] Native-whites, African-Americans, Irish, Germans, and British (English, Scottish, and Welsh) residents experienced different progressions through semiautonomy to marriage. The length of each stage, how each stage was spent, and the age at which one moved from one to another varied noticeably among groups and, to a lesser extent, between men and women (figure 4.1).[80]

In general, New York City was home to a population whose children left home earlier and remained single longer than was the case with residents of less volatile inland cities such as Buffalo.[81] But there were differences between ethnic groups, especially between natives and immigrants. On average, the Irish boarded at younger ages than members of other ethnic groups, and many continued to reside outside of nuclear families well into their thirties. The gap was especially sharp between native-born and Irish-born women, for only 28.7 percent of Irish women still resided with their parents between the ages of fifteen and nineteen, compared with 68.5 percent of native women. In addition, 23.7 percent of Irish immigrant women continued to work into their late twenties and 16.6 percent into their thirties, ages at which their sisters in other cities had abandoned domestic work.[82] German-born males also tended to leave their homes to begin apprenticeships at younger ages, striking out on their own in their late teens, whereas Buffaloans left home between the ages of twenty-one and twenty-four.[83]

The transition from childhood to adulthood, where subordination to parental control gave way to economic and familial obligations, was in its timing a product of culture rather than biology. Census data confirm, for instance, that young men born in the United States remained with their parents significantly longer than children of immigrants.[84] Between the ages of ten and fourteen, 84 percent of native males were still listed as children residing in their parents' household by census takers, compared with 78 percent for English-born, 67 percent for Germans, and 62 percent for Irish.[85] Beyond the age of fifteen, 45 percent of New York's Irish immigrant boys aged fifteen to nineteen continued to reside at home with at least one parent, compared with two out of five English and German youths and two out of three native youths.[86] Eighteen percent of Irish and 11 percent of German males remained with parents into their early

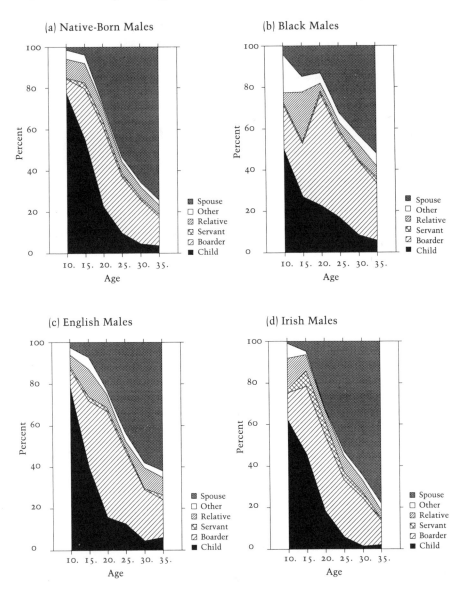

Figure 4.1 Household Status, Age, and Ethnicity by Sex, Four Sample Wards, New York City, 1855

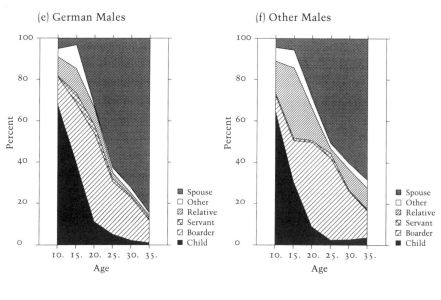

(e) German Males

(f) Other Males

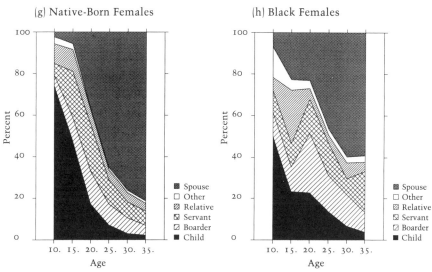

(g) Native-Born Females

(h) Black Females

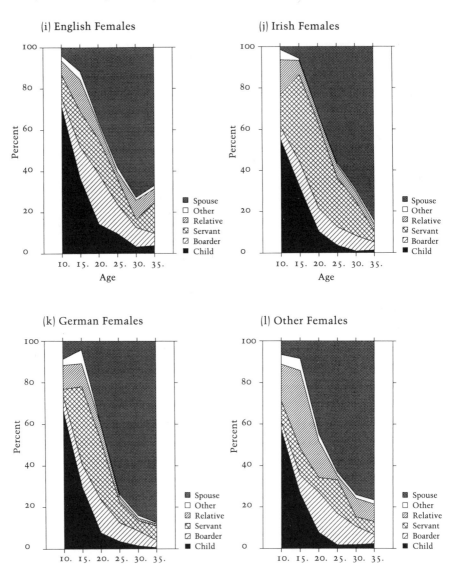

twenties, but only one in twenty remained after the age of twenty-five, by which time semiautonomy had all but ended for native-born males.[87]

In addition to ethnicity, life-cycle transitions were influenced by sex. The existence of an extensive metropolitan labor market offered young men employment opportunities outside of the city that were often unavailable to women. With the women often restricted to such trades as seamstress, bookfolder, and, in particular, domestic service, they were dependent upon a local labor market; thus the timing of their departure reflected the sexual divisions in labor. Furthermore, changes in the composition of domestic service as immigrant women supplanted children, blacks, and native-born women also intensified ethnic differences in life-cycle transitions for teenagers. Native-born women, their options now restricted—increasingly delayed their departure from parents until relatively late. By contrast, the availability of domestic employment forced immigrant daughters to leave households for which they were a burden at younger ages than sons, who often could find work while still remaining at home.[88] Thus the pattern of familial residence for native-born women paralleled that of male compatriots, and for girls through the age of nineteen it was virtually identical. What little variations existed between the sexes over the age of twenty (2–4 percent) could be attributed to a slightly younger age of marriage for women. Foreign-born women differed substantially from men of the same ethnic group in their tendency to leave home at an earlier age to work or marry. Two-thirds of British females and over 70 percent of German and Irish girls already lived away from home by their late teens. Only after the age of twenty, when the rate of male departures accelerated and young women had begun to pass the peak ages of domestic employment, did this gender-gap in parental dependency once again begin to narrow.

How young New Yorkers spent the semiautonomous period between puberty and marriage also varied among ethnic groups and, in particular, between the sexes. Young native males left their parents later than young men in other ethnic groups and were less likely to live with a relative or employer, or to board, than were members of other ethnic groups. During the primary ages of boarding (twenty to twenty-four), 33.8 percent of native men boarded, compared to 36.5 percent for Irish, 42.6 percent for Germans, and 51.2 for the English. In fact, only one in five native-born men in their late twenties boarded compared with between a quarter and a third of immigrants.[89] For many native-born young men, then, the path outside their parents' threshold—after an extended period of childhood—led almost immediately to marriage.

For young foreign-born males, on the other hand, boarding and/or living with relatives were the most favored of several alternatives available during semiautonomy.[90] From the middle-teen years through the mid-twenties, half of the Irish men, 56 percent of the German men, and between 53 and 60 percent of the English men had left home but were still not married. Many of these young men resided with relatives or apprenticed instead of boarding. Indeed, fifteen percent of the Irish boys aged ten to fourteen lived with a sibling, uncle, or cousin—more than boys from any other immigrant group of this age. Such "fostering out" to relatives was just one link of many in the chain of migration by which large numbers of Irish families sent over children as scouts to the new country before immigrating themselves. From 9 to 12 percent of German-born and from 6 to 13 percent of English boys also spent at least some part of their adolescence with a relative along with or instead of boarding. By 1855 employers housed only a small proportion of New Yorkers, mainly immigrant, who worked as clerks or apprentices (a reflection of the declining practice of apprenticeship). Fewer than 3 percent of native males in their middle teens combined residence with employment, compared with 7 percent and 4 percent of Irish and English boys, respectively. With Germans increasingly dominating baking, brewing, furrier trades, and furniture making, it is not surprising that 11.7 of teenaged German boys apprenticed or clerked as household members, a number far above that of any other group.[91]

Among teenage women—and immigrant girls in particular—occupational residence was not just a popular option; for many it came to be virtually synonymous with female semiautonomy (if that term can even be used). Like their brothers, native-born women generally followed a direct path from childhood to marriage. Fewer than 28 percent of native women between twenty and twenty-four lived with a relative or boarded and, among all age groups, domestic service for native girls was virtually nonexistent.[92] But among English, German, and Irish girls between the ages of fifteen and twenty-four, domestic service all but monopolized their adolescence. Nearly half of all Irish women in their late teens and 41 percent in their early twenties were servants at any one time, while only 11 percent boarded. Domestic service was also common among young German women, though not to the extent it was with Irish girls. Thirty-seven percent of the young women fifteen to nineteen years old and 28.9 of those in their early twenties worked as domestics (the figure dropped to only one in ten by the age of thirty). By contrast, only 17 percent of British women worked as servants during their late teens with most also remaining at home slightly longer than other foreign-born women. Like their brothers, English women also showed a strong affinity for boarding-houses upon finally leaving home. One out of four British women boarded, a figure twice that for Irish women and 9 percent higher than that for German women.

Marriage ended the period of semiautonomy and, with it, much of the limited freedom young men and women had enjoyed in their transition from youth to adulthood. Now on their own, many men could finally establish families—although it is unclear how free these men now were of familial control or obligation. For women, marriage invariably traded the restraints of domestic service or employment (which nonetheless had brought a "respite, however momentary, from familial regulation and purchased some measure of sexual and social independence, however paltry") for familial bonds and the patriarchal control of husbands.[93] Though the nature of these obligations differed little among men and women of varying ethnic groups, the timing of marriage varied considerably. One out of four native-born males married by their early twenties, half by their late twenties, and more than two-thirds by the age of thirty-five. German and Irish men generally married at younger ages than native males with nearly a third taking wives by the age of twenty-four.[94] The transition from semiautonomy to marriage progressed more rapidly for Germans than for any other ethnic group: 62 percent of German men were married by the ages of twenty-nine, compared with only half among Irish and natives.

The exodus from semiautonomy into marriage was most rapid for women, primarily because the options of boarding or residence with kin were less available.[95] For native-born women, few of whom worked as domestics, transition from parental control to married life was swift. By the age of twenty-four, 41 percent already had husbands, a number that jumped to 67 percent by age twenty-nine, and to nearly 80 percent by their early thirties. Among immigrant women, a majority had forsaken boarding or domestic service for matrimony by their late twenties. Seventy-three percent of German women between the ages of twenty-five and twenty-nine had married—a figure substantially larger than their native compatriots. Irish and British immigrant women, the former having dominated New York's antebellum pool of domestic servants while the latter spent much of their teen years and twenties away from their parents, settled down by the age of thirty-four, when 69 and 73 percent respectively had married.

For one ethnic group, African-Americans, the pattern of family transitions was sharply different from those of all others. Throughout every stage of their lives, African-American residents manifested a degree of primary-group fragmentation and nonfamily residence greater than any other group. Earlier in the nineteenth century, the numbers of urban black families with female-headed households well exceeded those of whites. In New York City it was 15–20 percent and in Philadelphia (in 1830) about

Church Street corner of Franklin Street looking north, 1861. This area of the Fifth Ward had a sizable African American population. The column on the left belongs to the Eglise du St. Espirit. Lithograph from David T. Valentine, *Manual of the Corporation of the City of New York* (New York, 1862).

25 percent. Some of this is explained by the large number of black sailors who had gone off to sea, by high levels of mortality among jobs that black males often held, and by the fact that New York was one of the few places where unattached women could earn a living, but the fragmented nature of black households was most closely linked to the migration from slave-holding areas, which presented most blacks in antebellum New York with the difficult task of reconstructing traditional families. Moving free of white households with the final elimination of slavery in New York State in 1828 or rebuilding households after the destructive effects of slavery was a painful process. Free blacks formed independent households cautiously, they married later than whites, and they joined together "to form extended or augmented households, taking in relatives and friends who had arrived recently from the countryside and were emerging from slavery with few assets and little knowledge of urban life."[96]

Compared with native- and foreign-born whites, black children struck out on their own at very tender ages. Many apparently never settled down to conventional married life. First, the number of youngsters who resided outside the traditional nuclear family was far greater for blacks than whites. Half of these children between the ages of ten and fifteen already lived away from parents, and the census classified fewer than one in four of those in their late teens as "children." Second, semiautonomy was not the transitory period between childhood and adulthood for black youngsters that it was for whites; it was rather a nearly permanent stage in itself. This is not to say that black adolescents entirely lacked a stable familial environment in which to live. Yet the role of absent or deceased parents often had to be filled by cousins, aunts, uncles, or some other family member. One quarter of the fifteen to nineteen age group resided with some relative other than their parent. The popularity of boarding among African-American men and women was a third factor that distinguished black family cycles from those of whites. More than half the males in their twenties and 28 percent of the females boarded (mainly in all-black houses). Even after the age of thirty, when marriage had sharply curtailed boarding among whites, 35.7 percent of men and 15 percent of women continued to board. And extended boarding was not the only sign of alternative family ties. Domestic service (while not as prevalent among young black women as it was among Irish girls) did not end in the late twenties as was the case for other groups, but actually increased through the late thirties.[97] A higher proportion of older black women worked as servants than was true of women from any other ethnic group. Finally, the census listed far fewer African-Americans as married than any other group, and this was especially true of those in their late twenties and early thirties. Only one out of three black males between the ages of twenty-five and twenty-nine was married, and even into their late thirties nearly half were still single. In each of these facets of family life, the pressures of widowhood and urban poverty seemed to weigh most heavily upon black New Yorkers. Extended semiautonomy, domestic service commencing at a late age, and low rates of marriage suggest a systematic pattern of family disruption that, unlike differences between Irish and native-born whites, went well beyond the dislocations of immigration.[98]

Fertility and Residence

While many of the demographic differences between neighborhoods were the indirect results of ethnicity,[99] the antagonism between semiautonomy and child-rearing was a significant spatial force as well. By the middle of the nineteenth century, buffer areas between the expanding downtown commercial areas and working-class tenement quarters had become refuges for independent singles, transients, and childless couples living in boardinghouses. As housing availability permitted, families with young children left these highly transient environs, preferring instead distant areas more welcoming to young children.[100]

Demographic patterns were largely the result of ethnicity. While it may be true, as has also been argued, that "the lower wards were disproportionately young" and had a "slight male majority"[101] such factors as age distribution or age-adjusted sex ratios were more reflections of ethnic culture that any geography of youth. Even though New Yorkers showed a weak but significant tendency to cluster in neighborhoods with other age-cohorts of the same ethnic background, the influence of age upon residence was oblique, mainly reflecting patterns of ethnic residence because of variations in age distribution between immigrant groups and natives.[102] Areas dominated by native-born New Yorkers attracted immigrants only during the peak ages of domestic employment or when they were most mobile, usually between the ages of fifteen and twenty-five. As the graphic display of modeled data makes clear (figure 4.2), the age distribution for districts that housed only a small number of immigrants was narrower than in areas that were predominantly foreign-born. Consequently, the more strongly Hibernian Fourth Ward had a slightly higher concentration of Irish residents in their thirties and forties, while compatriots in the Ninth Ward tended to cluster more narrowly in their late teens to the early twenties—peak ages for the employment of servants (a difference of nearly 6 percent during teen years). Much the same also held true for Ninth-Ward Germans when compared to their compatriots residing in the Tenth.[103]

The mutual avoidance between boarding and child-raising was a more significant predictor of neighborhood location than either age or sex (table 4.2).[104] Wards containing larger numbers of children, such as wards Nine and Ten, accommodated proportionately fewer boarders than did wards located close to commerce areas where boarders were numerous but children scarce.[105] Nearly a quarter of the Ninth Ward's population and 22.0 percent of the Tenth Ward consisted of children, while 19.0 and 11.5 percent were boarders, respectively. By contrast, in the Fourth and Fifth Wards only 17.1 and 14.1 percent were children, and 21.8 of the Fourth Ward's population and 23.3 of the Fifth Ward's were boarders. Yet the question still remains: Did family structure help to determine neighborhood *independent* of other factors or was family status as a residential force merely a by-product of other forces such as class or ethnicity?

To be sure, ethnicity, occupational difference, and the age of household head each had a considerable impact upon the composition of New York households in 1855 regardless of neighborhood, as a multivariate model clearly shows (table 4.3).[106] First, modeled data from this analysis demonstrates that the massive influx of newcomers in the late 1840s and early 1850s itself shaped the structure of immigrant households (table 4.4). Faced with tight housing, young immigrant couples delayed childbear-

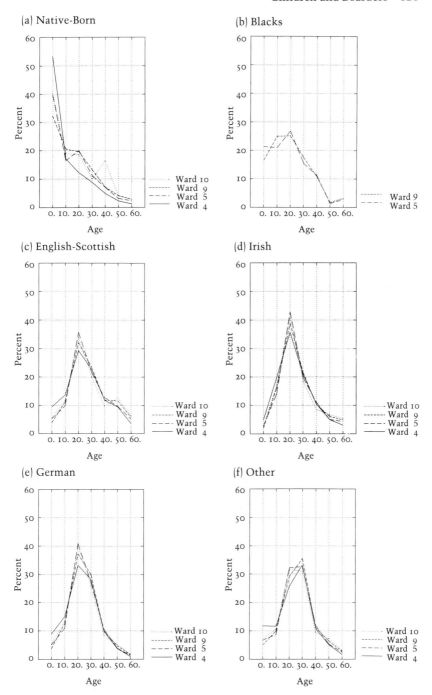

Figure 4.2 Neighborhood Age Structure and Nativity, Four Sample Wards, New York City, 1855

Table 4.2   Household Status, Age, and Residence,
Four Sample Wards, New York City, 1855

Variables: Age: 0–14, 15–19, 20–24, 25–29, 30–34, 35–39, 40+.
          Ward: 4, 5, 9, and 10.
          Household Status: child, servant, household head/spouse, parent (co-
          lateral), sibling (colateral), son/daughter-in-law, aunt/uncle, cousin/
          nephew, boarder, other.

Terms of Model (controlled for)	χ^2	χ^2 d.f.	χ^2 signif.	Difference χ^2	Diff. d.f.	Difference signif.	Coef. of determination
All 2-way associations	160.02	162	.5290	—	—	—	—
(Age, household status)	3011.34	216	.0001	2851.32	54	.0001	.9469
(Household status, ward)	351.08	189	.0001	191.06	27	.0001	.5442
(Age, ward)	200.30	180	n.s.*	—	—	—	—

*Probability over 10% (.1).

Table from modeled data: household status by age

Relation	\multicolumn{7}{Age (% down)}						
	0	15	20	25	30	35	40+
Child	79.7	52.0	19.5	7.9	3.4	2.4	2.0
Servant	2.2	13.9	13.8	6.6	3.7	2.2	2.7
Household head	0.4	2.6	33.5	59.0	72.4	79.8	72.4
Parent	0.4	0.4	0.2	0.2	0.3	0.5	8.3
Son/daughter-in-law	0.4	0.5	0.9	0.9	1.0	0.7	0.5
Brother-in-law	3.7	7.0	4.5	3.6	2.6	2.4	1.8
Aunt/uncle	0.4	0.6	0.2	0.2	0.3	0.5	0.5
Cousin/nephew	3.3	2.8	1.7	1.5	1.0	1.2	0.4
Boarder	6.3	17.5	25.1	18.9	14.3	9.4	10.0
Other	3.1	2.8	0.5	1.2	1.2	1.0	1.3
N (Column)	459.0	531.0	802.0	815.0	623.0	415.0	932.0
N (Table) = 4577.0							

Table from modeled data: household status by ward

Relation	Ward (% down)			
	4	5	9	10
Child	17.2	14.1	23.7	22.0
Servant	4.9	6.9	9.2	5.1

Table 4.2   *(continued)*

Relation	Ward (% down)			
	4	5	9	10
Household head	47.3	46.1	48.0	52.0
Parent	1.3	2.0	2.4	2.0
Son/daughter-in-law	0.4	0.7	0.9	0.7
Brother-in-law	4.0	2.9	3.3	3.9
Aunt/uncle	0.6	0.4	0.4	0.3
Cousin/nephew	1.4	1.4	2.0	1.3
Boarder	21.8	23.3	19.0	11.5
Other	1.5	2.3	1.2	1.2
N (Column)	994.0	893.0	1435.0	1244.0
N (Table) = 4577.0				

Source: New York State Census for 1855 (manuscript).

ing and often substituted boarders for kin. While some of this behavior stemmed from economic necessity, immigrants were—regardless of wealth—more likely to live as solitary individuals, childless couples, or families with boarders than were native-born New Yorkers.[107] Only 41.3 percent of Irish families sampled housed children or nonkin relatives compared with 55 percent of those headed by native-born Americans. And Irish households containing children were almost twice as likely to be headed by widows or widowers than their native counterparts (13.7 percent).

Occupational rank was a second factor that shaped household structure, although 27.5 percent of its effect was spurious (e.g., the by-product of ethnic variations rather than employment). Many New Yorkers living in poverty supplemented their incomes through the taking in of boarders. Consequently, households headed by low-status workers, widows, or retired people were more likely to take in boarders than families headed by skilled artisans, professionals, and proprietors—a pattern that intensified after their children had departed.[108] The quarter of unskilled families that took in boarders were more than twice as likely as upper-ranked households to be headed by widows (table 4.4).[109]

Finally, given the close relationship between the timing of individual life-cycle and family-cycle transitions, the age of household heads largely determined the composition of their households.[110] For young adults in their twenties, single-person households and newly married childless couples were both emblematic of the movement away from semiautonomy and toward the formation of new families. While 27 percent of families

Table 4.3   A Model of Household Structure and
Residence, Four Sample Wards, New York City, 1855

(A) An effects decomposition of a dichotomized linear
flow model measuring the impact of ethnicity, age, and
occupational rank upon familial residence (D-system).[a]

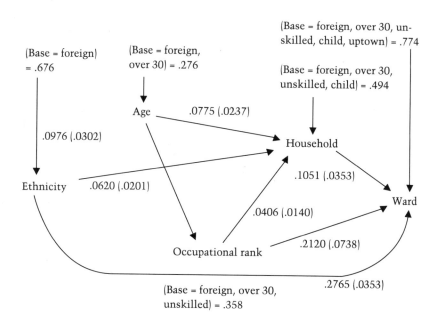

Effect[b]	Total (Raw)	Spurious	Causal (Net)	Direct	Indirect
Ethnicity-age	+.0220*	—	+.0220*	—	—
Ethnicity-occupation	+.0192*	—	+.0192*	+.0171*	+.0021*
Age-occupation	+.0981	+.0005	+.0976	—	—
Ethnicity-household	+.0620	—	+.0620	+.0644	−.0024
Age-household	+.0798	+.0023	+.0775	+.0835	−.0060
Occupation-household	+.0333	−.0073	+.0406	—	—
Ethnicity-ward	+.2765	—	+.2765	+.2837	−.0072
Age-ward	+.0343*	−.0179	+.0522*	+.0504*	+.0018*
Occupation-ward	+.2026	+.0006	+.2120	+.2079	+.0041
Household-ward	+.1290	+.0239	+.1051	—	—

[a] Numbers are d coefficients and intercept values. Values within parentheses are two-sigma confidence limits, with variances doubled to correct for multistage sampling. See James A. Davis, "Analyzing Contingency Tables with Linear Flow Graphs: D-Systems," in D. Heise, ed., *Sociological Methodology* (San Francisco: Jossey-Bass, 1976), pp. 111–45
[b] Categories: nativity—native, foreign; age—under 30, 30 and older; occupational rank— upper (professional, proprietary and skilled), lower (semiskilled, unskilled, and others);

Table 4.3 *(continued)*

household structure—urban-oriented (single/widows alone, households with boarders, and childless married couples), child-oriented (married/widowed with children,
households with relatives); ward—downtown (wards 4 and 5), uptown (wards 9 and 10).
*Pearson χ^2 not significant to the .10 level (10%).

(B) An effects decomposition of a full (nondichotomized)
linear flow model measuring the impact of ethnicity,
age, and occupational rank upon familial residence $(\chi^2)^a$

Effect	Total (Raw)	Spurious	%[b]	Causal	Direct (Net)	%[c]	Indirect	%[c]
Ethnic-age	4.79*	—		4.79*	—		—	
Ethnic-occup.	92.915	—		92.91	91.92	98.1	.98	1.1
Age-occup.	5.51	1.39	25.1	4.13	—		—	
Ethnic-house	52.00	—		52.00	43.13	82.2	8.87	17.1
Age-house	31.64	1.69	5.3	29.95	28.73	95.9	1.22	4.1
Occup.-house	52.66	14.49	27.5	28.14	—		—	
Ethnic-ward	352.04	—		352.04	307.38	87.3	44.66	12.7
Age-ward	3.84*	1.29*		2.55*	2.42*		.01*	
Occup.-ward	52.94	27.35	51.7	25.59	22.88	89.4	2.71	10.6
House-ward	38.24	13.90	36.3	24.24	—		—	

[a] Categories: ethnicity—native, English-Scottish, Irish, German, other; age—under 30,
30 and older; occupational rank—upper (professional, proprietary and skilled), lower
(semiskilled, unskilled, and others); household structure—single/widowed alone, childless married couples, couples with children or relatives, widows/widowers with children and households with boarders; ward—4, 5, 9, and 10.
[b] Figures are percentages of total (raw) χ^2 that are spurious.
[c] Figures are percentages of causal (net) χ^2 that are direct and indirect effects.
*Pearson χ^2 not significant to the .10 level (10 percent).
Source: New York State Census for 1855 (manuscript).

under the age of thirty lacked children, boarders, relatives or even spouses,
only 16.1 percent of the older households consisted of just one or two
members (table 4.4). Yet age had little impact on whether families took
in boarders. While it is commonly assumed that families took in boarders
after the departure of grown children created surplus space to rent, the
data for New York suggest that family augmentation through boarding
was as much a reflection of immediate economic pressures.[111]

But despite these patterns of interaction between ethnicity, occupational rank, age, and household structure, family still shaped where New
Yorkers chose to settle in its own right—even if the impact of "familialism" was only one third that of ethnicity and only half as strong as occu-

Table 4.4   Household Structure, Ethnicity, and
Occupation, Four Sample Wards, New York City, 1855

(A) Ethnicity and household structure controlling for age and occupational rank*

					Household Structure						
Nativity	Single/ Widow Alone	S.R.*	Child-less Parents	S.R.*	With Child/ Rela-tive	S.R.*	Wi-dowed With Child	S.R.*	With Boarder	S.R.*	N
Native	5.2		8.6	−3.1	55.3	3.5	7.8		23.1		414
England-Scotland	8.8		16.1		47.2		13.4		14.5	−2.4	138
Ireland	6.5		13.5		41.3	−3.1	13.7	2.9	25.0		365
Germany	5.6		15.0		48.0		6.9	−2.0	24.4		319
Other	11.8	2.4	15.3		46.3		8.7		17.9		117
Total	6.6		12.8		48.2		9.8		22.6		1353

(B) Age and family structure controlling for ethnicity*

					Household Structure						
Age	Single/ Widow Alone	S.R.*	Child-less Parents	S.R.*	With Child/ Rela-tive	S.R.*	Wi-dowed With Child	S.R.*	With Boarder	S.R.*	N
Under 30	9.1	2.4	17.9	3.7	46.1		5.7	−3.4	21.3		410
30 and older	5.5	−2.4	10.6	−3.7	49.1		11.6	3.4	23.2		943
Total	6.6		12.8		48.2		9.8		22.6		1353

(C) Occupational rank and family structure controlling for age and ethnicity*

					Household Structure						
Rank	Single/ Widow Alone	S.R.*	Child-less Parents	S.R.*	With Child/ Rela-tive	S.R.*	Wi-dowed With Child	S.R.*	With Boarder	S.R.*	N
Professional/ skilled	5.9		13.9		53.5	4.4	6.3	−4.8	20.4	−2.2	751.2
Unskilled/ other	7.5		11.4		41.5	−4.4	14.2	4.8	25.4	2.2	601.8
Total	6.6		12.8		48.2		9.8		22.6		1353.0

Table 4.4 *(continued)*

(D) Household structure and residence controlling
for ethnicity, age, and occupational rank*

Household Structure	Ward								Total
	4	S.R.*	5	S.R*	9	S.R.*	10	S.R.*	
Single/Widow alone	6.5		7.7		6.3		6.2		6.6
Childless parents	12.9		15.6		11.2		12.3		12.8
With child/relatives	43.4	−1.9	40.6	−2.8	55.5	3.5	49.7		48.2
Widowed with child	10.8		11.3		9.7		8.0		9.8
With boarders	26.3	1.7	24.8		17.3	−3.1	23.8		22.6
N =	304.7		273.2		400.5		374.6		1353

*Standardized Residuals: (Observed-Fitted)/SQRT(Fitted). Since standardized residuals are nor-
mally distributed, numbers greater than +/− 1.96 are significant to the .05 level. Only significant values are shown.
Source: See Table 4.3.

pational rank (controlling for downstream associations in the dichotomized model).[112]

The chief familial differences between neighborhood lay in the separation of semiautonomy from child-rearing (table 4.4).[113] All other factors
being equal, substantially fewer families with children lived in the Fourth
and Fifth Wards adjoining the commercial district than in the Ninth Ward
located further uptown. Meanwhile, boarders and lodgers were common
in strongly immigrant wards but scarce in areas dominated by native-born
residents. Only 17.3 percent of households in the Ninth Ward were augmented compared with 24.8 and 26.3 percent, respectively, for wards Four
and Five.

Several recent studies have pointed to yet another demographic variable
linked to family status: marital fertility.[114] If ethnic origin and occupational status as structural variables only "suggest" behavior differences,
marital fertility may be an even better measure of the "socio-spatial divisions of the city" because it "directly reflected fundamental behavior differences between groups in the society."[115] Variations in fertility rates
between different neighborhoods were thus not only symptoms of other
exogenous factors such as ethnicity, but also indicated that fertility acted
as a residential force in its own right. The distinct patterns of location-
related fertility show clearly the importance of family settlement in shaping neighborhood.[116]

Like household composition, fertility was also shaped by factors such as
ethno-cultural background and class—the ability of parents to afford chil-

dren. Age-adjusted fertility was highest among Irish women and lowest among British mothers, with native fertility lying somewhere in between (figure 4.3). However, interethnic differences were limited by the fact that so many New Yorkers were freshly arrived immigrants, many of whom were still too young to establish families. Characteristic surges in foreign-born fertility had yet to occur, and the very flux of the city depressed births across many groups. Ethnic differences emerge only when ages of peak fertility are compared. The high levels of domestic employment of Irish women well into their twenties made their levels of fertility the lowest for this age range, but it rose sharply after the age of twenty-five to become one of the highest for any group. By contrast, German women generally married more quickly, so their fertility rates rose gradually through the age of thirty before leveling off and declining.[117]

Family occupational status also exerted influence upon fertility, though to a much lesser extent than ethnic background. Prosperous white-collar families tended to have more children than did families headed by semi-skilled and unskilled workers. Nor did fertility levels trail off after the age of thirty for wealthy families as they did for the poor (figure 4.3).[118] Not only was fertility remarkably high for professionals, reaching 2000 per thousand in their late twenties, but for professional and business parents, the distribution of fertility peaked twice, in their late twenties and again toward their late thirties. Fertility was also high for unskilled members of the twenty-five to twenty-nine age group (1,200 per thousand), but unlike more affluent families, it fell off sharply after the age of thirty.[119] Upon closer examination, occupational variations in fertility were not the result of class but of ethno-cultural background, and these peaks vanished when the effects of ethnicity were controlled (table 4.5). For native white (and to a lesser extent British-Scottish) women whose husbands were professionals, proprietors, and skilled workers, age-adjusted fertility ranged between 811 and 1,030 per thousand. Irish families on either extreme of the occupational spectrum actually had lower fertility rates than did those in the middle. And German fertility (adjusted for occupation) ranged from an exceptionally high rate of 1,048 for proprietors and 985 for unskilled workers to a low of under 373 for professional and semiskilled ranks— although the relationship between rank and fertility followed no consistent pattern. If financial resources afforded wealthier families the "luxury" of having more children, the decision whether to have a child was most strongly mediated by cultural background.

When the effects of both nativity and occupational rank are controlled for, fertility, like household structure, produced systematic variations in residence as measured by ward (table 4.6). Some wards had higher fertility

(a) Fertility by Nativity, 1855

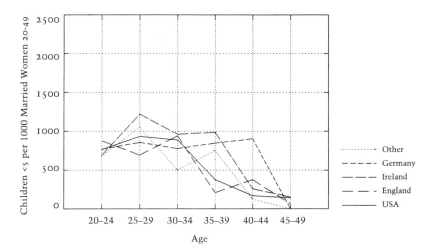

(b) Fertility by Family's Occupational Rank, 1855

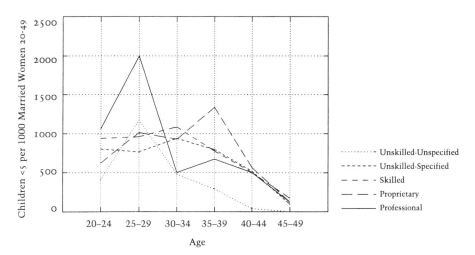

Figure 4.3 Number of Children under Five Years Old per 1000 Married Women Aged Twenty to Forty-nine, by Nativity, Four Sample Wards, New York City, 1855

Table 4.5   Number of Children Under Five Years Old per 1000
Married Women Aged Twenty to Forty-nine in Four Sample
Wards by Nativity and Occupation, New York City, 1855

Occupation	Nativity				
	Native White	England-Scotland	Ireland	Germany	Other
Professional	650	200	—	1000	1750
	811*	47*	—	315*	850*
	780**	73**	—	150**	680**
	(N = 20)	(N = 5)	(N = 0)	(N = 3)	(N = 4)
Proprietary	878	846	905	1059	667
	1030*	720*	596*	1048*	460*
	902**	545**	500**	1061**	213**
	(N = 53)	(N = 13)	(N = 21)	(N = 34)	(N = 6)
Skilled	852	986	909	840	1000
	860*	925*	926*	794*	962*
	758**	767**	866**	831**	720**
	(N = 108)	(N = 34)	(N = 6)	(N = 156)	(N = 20)
Unskilled specified	759	462	804	400	615
	730*	297*	888*	373*	594*
	630**	248**	877**	300**	550**
	(N = 58)	(N = 13)	(N = 51)	(N = 10)	(N = 13)
Unskilled unspecified	250	2000	750	1000	—
	250*	500*	753*	985*	—
	170**	340**	594**	858**	—
	(N = 4)	(N = 1)	(N = 64)	(N = 15)	(N = 0)

*Standardized for age distribution using equation:

$$Y = .21X_{20-24} + .25X_{25-29} + .22X_{30-34} + .14X_{35-39} + .10X_{40-44} + .08X_{45-49}$$

where:

Y is the age-standardized fertility ratio per 1000 married women aged 20–49 to be calculated.

X_j is the number of children under 5 per 1000 married women aged j.

The coefficients .21, .25, .22, .14, .10, and .08 are the percentages that married women of each of these age groups are of all married women aged 20–49 of the sample population in the four New York City wards.

**Standardized for age distribution as above, only using the coefficients .10, .17, .21, .22, .17, and .13 employed by Hareven and Vinovskis in their study of 1880s Boston. See Tamara Hareven and Maris Vinovskis, "Marital Fertility, Ethnicity, and Occupation in Urban Families: An Analysis of South Boston and the South End in 1880," *Journal of Social History* 9 (1974).

Source: New York State Census for 1855 (manuscript).

Table 4.6 Number of Children Under Five Years Old per 1000 Married Women Aged Twenty to Forty-nine in Four Sample Wards by Nativity, New York City, 1855

Ward	Native White	Black	English-Scottish	Irish	German	Other Foreign
			Nativity			
4	625	—	538	848	586	938
	607*	—	228*	865*	521*	860*
	467**	—	204**	859**	528**	739**
	(N = 16)	(N = 0)	(N = 12)	(N = 29)	(N = 16)	(N = 16)
5	571	353	455	647	939	500
	495*	452*	822*	649*	857*	533*
	403**	378**	678**	529**	824**	359**
	(N = 28)	(N = 17)	(N = 11)	(N = 43)	(N = 49)	(N = 18)
9	901	333	871	875	963	500
	927*	220*	964*	857*	972*	265*
	828**	210**	815**	790**	1029**	305**
	(N = 151)	(N = 3)	(N = 31)	(N = 48)	(N = 27)	(N = 4)
10	667	—	684	1000	888	917
	650*	—	573*	991*	876*	872*
	512**	—	464**	941**	819**	715**
	(N = 75)	(N = 0)	(N = 19)	(N = 24)	(N = 134)	(N = 12)

*Standardized for age distribution using coefficients .21, .25, .22, .14, .10, and .08, which are the percentages that married women of each of these age groups are of all married women aged 20–49 of the sample population in the four New York City wards.

**Standardized for age distribution as above, only using the coefficients .10, .17, .21, .22, .17, and .13 employed by Hareven and Vinovskis in their study of 1880s Boston. See Tamara Hareven and Maris Vinovskis, "Marital Fertility, Ethnicity, and Occupation in Urban Families: An Analysis of South Boston and the South End in 1880," *Journal of Social History* 9 (1974).

Source: New York State Census for 1855 (manuscript).

than others regardless of ethnic composition. Not only were age-adjusted fertility levels among native-born residents of the Ninth Ward higher than in any other area, but fertility among foreign-born residents there ranked second only to that of the strongly immigrant Fourth Ward. And while British rates paralleled those of Knickerbocker families, both dropped in predominantly foreign neighborhoods (wards Four and Ten) and rose in ostensibly native ones (wards Five and Nine). Indeed, British, and German fertility were also higher in the Ninth Ward and lowest in the Fourth Ward—an area adjoining the city's center whose overall population was declining. Only Irish fertility failed to fit this pattern, changing little from neighborhood to neighborhood. Overall, German and British rates (like those for natives) varied by as much as 50–75 percent between low- and high-fertility wards, while for Irish women the range was under 34 percent.

The downtown clustering of boarders and widows largely to the exclusion of young children suggests that by the 1850s many New Yorkers belonged to a distinctive boarding subculture. The older districts where boarders congregated had already witnessed an exodus of younger child-oriented families uptown, leaving behind long-standing residents. With the departure of younger residents and the decline of neighborhood prestige, houses were subdivided and became homes for young newcomers— many of whom were childless couples or families that took in boarders. Thus boarding and fertility became closely tied to the broader process of neighborhood transition by which demographic difference, along with the development of class-based residential patterns, the growing separation of work from residence, and ethnic affinities each emerged as fundamental residential forces.[120]

Conclusion

The emergence of family status as a determinant of neighborhood choice depended upon the evolution of residential districts that were distinct from the city's areas of commerce. Though housing for New York's transients had long clustered close to the central business district, it was not until the 1840s, with the abandonment of prime housing in the surrounding wards, that sufficient supplies of underutilized housing existed to lead to specialized boardinghouse districts. By midcentury, high rents and tight housing had led many middle-class families to sublet spaces in row houses that were being built during the building boom in the middle sections of Manhattan. In centrally located neighborhoods close to the bustle of the growing metropolitan commercial activity, middle-class boarders— most of whom were young males—spent their youthful autonomy in the boarding subculture.

Less densely populated peripheral neighborhoods, such as Greenwich Village, provided a more favorable environment for those who had married to raise their families. The fertility differences between wards underscore how even as early as the antebellum period, New Yorkers had begun to attach importance to neighborhood according to their individual and familial life cycles. Yet family status had only a weak impact upon neighborhood geography when compared with ethnicity and class. Much of the variation in fertility and age-adjusted family status stemmed from occupational and ethnic factors. Thus Irish residents of differing social statuses who lived in separate sections of the city usually had more in common with one another than did immigrants of different backgrounds who lived on the same block. Nevertheless, the significant antagonism between children and the subculture of boarding that emerges, even controlling for these variables, did presage later patterns of a familial differentiation of space.

The functioning of boarding and fertility as residential forces also has a broader significance in helping us to understand the adjustment of the family to industrialization. Family-based residence—whether it was rooted in class or ethnic background—was not destroyed by the separation of home and workplace that occurred in early industrialization. On the contrary, family neighborhoods actually emerged as a distinctive phenomenon as a result of the process of industrialization and the resulting transition from heterogeneous to homogeneous neighborhoods. The evidence presented here does not bolster the view presented by historian Richard Sennett which depicted urban life as being antithetical to family, nor does it reveal any great desire for most families to escape the city. Indeed, those who boarded reveled in the very freedom of urban life.[121] In addition, working-class families, once they had entered a stage in which family life and children meant something to them, could not flee the city—assuming they ever wanted to. They merely avoided areas in which transiency was most pronounced. For middle- and upper-class New Yorkers, the push for family privacy, when it did come, led to a flight uptown or, for a few, into other new suburbs. But the search for family privacy was a weak corollary to the forces of nativism and upper-class exclusivity that I have discussed in the preceding two chapters.

By focusing upon the evolution of four representative wards, the previous chapters have examined how massive forces of mobility typified by Moving Day operated to impose a broad pattern of social differentiation upon the spatial organization of the emerging industrial city. As New York underwent such rapid and profound changes, growing from a comparatively small seaport city to the major American metropolis in scarcely a lifetime, the informal order of undifferentiated land use gave way to a totally new pattern of well-ordered social space within the city and its metropolitan area. Yet the path of differentiation in antebellum New York was neither linear nor was it direct. The effects of ethnicity, a pervasive factor in all aspects of neighborhood development, were continually altered by the complex intermingling of diverse ethnic groups and by divisions within groups revealed in the previous analysis of variables such as the ages and timing of immigration for different arrival cohorts. The cultural cohesiveness of Americans was often as strong a residential force as ethnicity was for immigrants.[122]

In an era when many New Yorkers continued to live close to their places of work, class by itself did not yet act as the paramount determinant of urban location. In focusing on the extremes of wealth and poverty, historians have generally missed the complexity of class as a residential factor. The ethnic division of the labor force, in addition to the location of particular industries, accounted for most of the linkage between work and residence. Finally, the role of family status—still an incipient factor behind residential choice in the nineteenth century—in separating child-centered residential areas from urban-oriented enclaves of boarders and transients adjoining the central business district was complicated by variations in family practices between men and women of different classes and nativity groups. Only semiautonomy operated directly to define familial neighborhood at this early period.

Though antebellum neighborhoods failed to fit either the model of bipolar class division or ethnic insularity proffered by some historians, the ecological analysis that I have presented up to this point still falls short of comprehensively portraying the multiple dimensions that constituted the historical neighborhood. Structural variables such as social rank, ethnicity, and family status provide only partial foundations from which to explore the functioning of neighborhoods as social communities. Nor can we even begin to understand from the pattern of where people lived how participants of interneighborhood moves perceived the ritual of May Day. What importance did they attach in the change from one neighborhood to another? How did New Yorkers comprehend the transformations that their city was undergoing, or did their perceptions lag—as awareness often does—behind the changed reality? These are questions not of social structure but of subjective perception which form the basis of the relationship between neighborhood and community. The following chapter turns away from the issue of early neighborhood development to focus on the growing tension between New York's emerging spatial patterns and the way in which residents came to view urban space as symbolic community.

PART II

The Symbolic

Neighborhood

5   The Discovery of the Neighborhood—
The Symbolic Community in New York

▉▉▉▉▉▉▉▉▉ Neighborhood names are familiar, seemingly immutable aspects of urban reality for contemporary New Yorkers. In each of the five
boroughs, a myriad of smaller districts exist, each of which connotes an
individual social group or a particular quality of residential life. Not only
do names establish a cognitive image used by residents to mentally differentiate neighborhoods within each subarea of the city, they also separate
upscale from downtrodden, safe from unsafe, and in the common racially
charged language, "bad" ones from "good."[1] To a Brooklynite, Bay Ridge,
Borough Park, and Bensonhurst conjure images quite different from those
of Bedford-Stuyvesant, East New York, and Brownsville.[2] Manhattanites
make similar distinctions in their own borough, one 1969 planning survey listing no fewer than thirty-seven separate sections or subsections.
Central nodes of intersecting streets or landmarks define some of these
areas, such as Times, Herald, and Union Squares, while others consist of
bounded areas covering wide swaths of land on either side of the Island,
such as the Upper East and West Sides.[3] Only two districts are clearly identified by their names as ethnic enclaves—Chinatown and Little Italy—but
the names of others have also come to define the social status of groups
inhabiting them, particularly Harlem and the Lower East Side. Symbolic
identity is hierarchical in nature, with larger districts being composed of
telescoping subareas which the planners conveniently refer to as "neighborhoods." The Lower East Side, to cite just one example (encompassing the Two Bridges district between the Manhattan and Williamsburg
Bridges), is further divided into the Bowery, Rutgers, and Delancey areas.

Some of these names might universally be recognizable while others
would be familiar only to those who inhabit them. A cognitive aware-

ness of areas such as Washington Heights, Harlem, Yorkville, Morningside Heights, or Wall Street is no doubt more common than for such sections as St. Nicholas Terrace, Turtle Bay, Inwood, or Lenox Hill. Nor are the composition and identity of subareas fixed or immutable. For example, the less threatening appellation "Clinton" has supplanted "Hell's Kitchen." Likewise, major sections of the West Side have been transformed through the forces of urban renewal and gentrification, from "an airtight cage" or a "gilded ghetto" into the neighborhood of soaring rents and middle-class gentility known as "Lincoln Center."[4] In yet another well-known pair of examples, a shortage of space for artists' lofts followed by soaring rents recently transformed a run-down district of small industry into Soho and Tribecca.[5] Gentrification merely underscores the highly transitory nature of symbolic space, a psychosocial dimension of neighborhood that is forever changing as urban subcommunities constantly change and are redefined—even when the original buildings survive.

In both the modern and the historical city, then, neighborhoods exist not only as a physical reality, but also as a "subjective" experience derived from "mental mapping" and "cognitive mapping."[6] Roots of symbolic awareness can be traced back as far as the seventeenth century when the clustering of teamsters along Smith Street Lane led it to be known colloquially as "Cartmen's Street," much as neighboring "Brewer's Street" and "Marketfield Street" reflected the predominant occupations of their inhabitants.[7] In addition, the collective action of mobs in attacking specific churches, ethnic clusters, well-known residences, and bawdyhouses also underscores New Yorkers' awareness of key landmarks during the middle and late eighteenth century.[8] Yet the awareness of neighborhoods as *bounded* social areas often lagged behind reality because, as we have seen in the preceding chapters, the axis of spatial differentiation remained tenuous. Indeed for New Yorkers at the beginning of the nineteenth century, this process of symbolic redefinition was essentially a new one, as was the very awareness that a neighborhood could define the social characteristics of its inhabitants.[9]

It is notable that the word "suburb" was used to denote "buildings without the walls of a city; the confines, the outerpart" well before the word "neighborhood" came to describe the social order within city boundaries. The word "neighborhood" rarely referred to social space, and even when "places within New York and other cities provided a symbolic geography of urban society," the extent of such conditions as slums "was rarely specified with any precision." The well-defined residential enclaves of the affluent contrasted with "large sections of the remainder of the city" housing its "relatively heterogeneous populations."[10] Even in its common usage, "neighborhood" generally meant a "place adjoining," as in the case of a "place near to that in which one lives," to the inhabitants or neighbors taken collectively, or, simply, to the notion of nearness. Neighborhood was synonymous with vicinity, vicinage, or proximity, not with spatial community.[11] When Charles Dickens wrote about his visit to the United States in *American Notes*, he referred to the "resident gentry in Boston and its neighborhood" and to the Lowell hospital built upon the "pleasantest ground of the neighborhood," a usage more akin to "environs."[12] Only later in the century did "neighborhood" come to describe with any frequency "a district or portion in a town or country frequently considered in reference to the character or circumstances of its inhabitants."[13] Even wards, often the focus of "passionate identification" in politics,[14] seem to have evinced relatively little social commentary—with the exception of such notorious areas as "Bloody Ould Sixth" and the Fourth Ward or the upscale "Fifteenth Ward."

This evolution of an awareness of symbolic community in New York has been largely overlooked by historians, with the exception of Stuart Blumin's provocative study of how nineteenth-century writers dealt with the "new system of relations between and within its classes and subcommunities" in the emerging metropolis. How, he asked, did contemporaries perceive and interpret the metropolis "as a physical place, a more or less understandable environment within which residents and visitors must make their daily rounds"? Did New Yorkers recognize the growing gulf between rich and poor by defining "a new 'urban semiotic'"? Blumin credited one antebellum writer, George G. Foster, whom he labeled as the "neglected grandfather of urban realism," with attempting to reintegrate "the present distended urban community" by developing "a broad map of the city's social and moral life." Foster's simple map, based as it was upon "the 'shared symbolization' of the metropolitan 'social world'" focused upon "three spaces or zones" that became "the loci of upper-, middle-, and lower-class life" in the city: Broadway/Wall Street, Chatham Street/The Bowery, and Five Points. Only after the Civil War did writers come to accept the metropolis not as "a distended entity," but rather as a "collection of entities—'a little world' rather than a community."[15]

For most New Yorkers the concept of separate neighborhoods seems to have evolved only gradually from the growing complexity of the nineteenth-century city.[16] And the development of an awareness of symbolic community did not strongly develop until later, with only the very richest and very poorest areas being identifiable to contemporaries.[17] Patrician districts cultivated an image of residential exclusivity, since only the wealthy could afford the luxury of residence separate from work. (For the wealthy, spatial awareness reflected a particular class view, for the ability to view the city as a whole derived from a sense of possession and class membership.)[18] Poor neighborhoods, on the other hand, frequently had their identity imposed by outsiders—mainly reformers—who singled out these areas for their inadequate sanitation, vice, or intemperance.[19] In a study that traced how reformers came to link the idea of the "slum" with that of the immigrant "ghetto," David Ward noted how antebellum reform movements "proposed moral diagnoses of poverty" that viewed slums not only as wellsprings of virulent contagious diseases, but also as the source of "immoral contagion."[20] By the middle of the century for example, the Five Points area was so recognized that international visitors came to view its "filth and wretchedness."[21]

For the majority of inhabitants, however, blocks and streets continued to define their social world, and, with the notable exceptions of early concentrations of blacks in the Fifth and Sixth Wards and the working-class district of leisure and entertainment known as the "Bowery Republic," New Yorkers were largely unaware of the broader dimensions of ethnic or class neighborhoods until waves of immigration in the late 1840s and 1850s brought a visible German "symbolic" community to the Lower East Side. The existence of class-based symbolic communities such as the Bowery did not automatically translate into a citywide symbolic division of space.[22] The absence of "explicit commentary" on the character of most neighborhoods might indicate, as one study of nineteenth-century Leeds has suggested, that "segments of the [upper] middle class, most of the middling class and all of the diverse strata of the working class were interspersed with one another," with "only an extremely small affluent minority" living in "exclusive quarters."[23] While this was undoubtedly true for New York, the very "local consciousness" within their neighborhoods "hindered the perception among workers of the existence of huge working-class areas in the city, the reality of which was so clear to middle-class observers."[24]

Unaware of the latent development of working-class neighborhoods, working-class residents clung to an earlier, *preindustrial neighborhood mentality* that was highly localistic. Reliance upon local landmarks such as individual buildings, alleys, stores, and even private residences reflected an eighteenth-century concept of neighborhood like that of prerevolutionary Paris: "The whole system of addresses and descriptions was based on familiarity with the neighbourhood, designed for locals and not for strangers. Eighteenth-century Parisians had no use for north and south, left or right, or for numbers in order to define place. They preferred purely local landmarks: objects and very often people." The neighborhood was an "entity based on proximity but created by daily contact between neighbours: by relationships and interaction, not by simply living within certain boundaries."[25] While one might find occasional antebellum reference to Cow Bay, the Old Brewery, the "Den of Thieves," the "Gates of Hell," or "Brickbat Mansion," most local appellations were not recorded until later in the century when sociologists and the photo-exposés of Jacob Riis "discovered" this hidden world of alleys and tenements created by the "other half" of working-class New Yorkers, areas with names like Rag-Picker's Row, Blind Man's Alley, and Cat Alley.[26] Since the wealthy had more of a stake in the process of symbolic differentiation because it enhanced their status, their sentimental attachment toward their local areas was far more developed at a much earlier stage than that of the working class—perhaps as early as the 1820s.

Evidence on the perception of urban space in the nineteenth century suggests that the emerging awareness of symbolic community was as much imposed upon neighborhood by outsiders, particularly social reformers, as it was cultivated from within by local residents. First, the fascination of early epidemiologists with the ecology of contagion and the accompanying concern with dangerous miasmas believed to emanate from bad sanitation in destitute areas prompted medical authorities to investigate the social character of urban neighborhoods. The detailed reports they issued are among the earliest signs of the development of a social-spatial consciousness. The emergence of professionalized sanitation during the middle of the nineteenth century also spurred an interest in the relations between spatial and moral order. Tenement-house reformers conducted repeated ward-by-ward surveys of crowding, demographic characteristics, and sanitation which demonstrated a heightened understanding of changing community structure within Manhattan. The work of the outside reformers educated many New Yorkers, particularly those in the middle classes, to the existence of areas of poverty, disease, and, in the case of prostitution districts (carefully described by sympathetic authors in "brothel" guides), areas of vice. Only the neighborhoods of the wealthy, which assiduously sought to cultivate an image of residential exclusivity, managed to create a symbolic community of their own. Finally, the very process of urban growth itself, which absorbed preexisting suburbs and transformed the character of neighborhoods, served to educate New Yorkers about developing patterns of social geography.

Roots of Awareness

It may well be that the problem of "filth and wretchedness" uncovered by social reformers in the wake of serious epidemics first brought the existence of differentiated areas to public attention. Clear signs of an awareness of symbolic space are found not in the pre-Revolutionary period as some historians have suggested,[27] but rather several decades later in the medical literature of the late eighteenth and early nineteenth centuries. In an effort to combat the spreading Yellow Fever which afflicted New York every summer, physicians sought to document the sanitary and moral character of areas hardest hit by the disease. Following the ravages of one such epidemic in 1796, Valentine Seaman examined conditions in the Fourth Ward and found "Moore's Row," a block of tenements "the most crowded with, perhaps[,] the most dirty set of residents of all in the City, and these chiefly newly arrived Irish people," to be particularly prone to the fever. This area also contained many crowded cellar apartments. One basement alone sheltered "fourteen persons, men women and children, black and white all huddled together, having no yard at all."[28] Elsewhere in the ward, another physician observed, inhabitants lived in old, decrepit buildings on sunken lots, which were generally "below the level of the street and without drains."[29] Both of these physicians blamed much of the area's unhealthful character on poor drainage that caused water to stagnate in rutted streets and under dwellings, along the ward's many slips and docks, but they were also critical of the sanitary habits of area residents. "One's mind is struck with the ideas," noted Seaman, "that the several joint-tenants are not only determined not to clear away the other's dirt, but that each exerted himself to put, at least, his share into the noisome collection because he has as good a right to make dirt as his neighbor."[30] Thus a connection was made between the run-down character of the Fourth Ward and both the cultural background and social habits of its residents. Early epidemiologists found it hardly surprising that neighborhoods which were poor, Irish, and inadequately drained suffered the worst ravages of disease. From this naturally followed an awareness of a connection between Yellow Fever and residence and, more importantly, between neighborhood and social status.[31]

The great Yellow Fever epidemic of 1822, following nearly two decades of comparatively mild outbreaks, was the worst the city had yet experienced. The annual trickle of wealthy residents to summer homes located in the upper "rustic" sections of Manhattan quickly turned into a flood as panicked businesses and individuals fled to escape the infected lower Wards.[32] Greenwich Village, long regarded as a safe haven from disease, re-

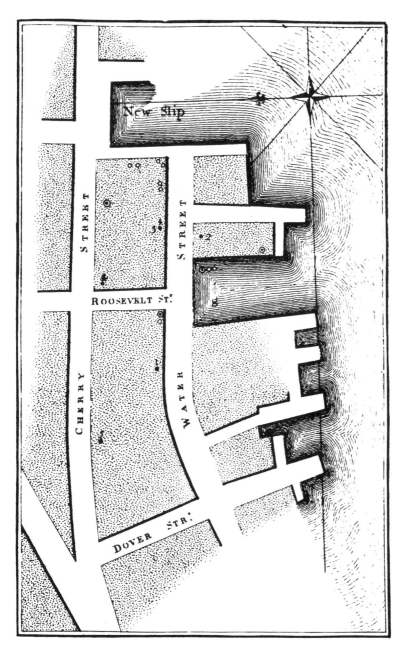

Spot map showing the spread of yellow fever in the Fourth Ward in 1798. From Valentine Seaman, "An Inquiry into the Case of the Prevalence of the Yellow Fever in New-York," *Medical Repository* I (1798), pp. 318–319. Photograph courtesy of Vanderbilt University Medical Library Special Collections.

ceived the long "line of carts, containing boxes, merchandise, and effects,"
and in general New York under evacuation presented the "appearance of
a town besieged." After a few days, "the Custom House, the Post Office,
the Banks, the Newspapers located themselves in the village or in the
upper part of Broadway, where they were free from the impending danger,"
and these places "almost instantaneously became the seat of the immense
business usually carried on, in the great metropolis."[33]

In addition to its magnitude, the 1822 epidemic also differed from those
preceding it in that affluent districts previously thought free from risk of
disease were also affected. As a result, medical examiners devoted greater
attention to the spatial aspects of contagion than ever before. Their reports
offer an especially insightful view of how contemporaries perceived differences among the emerging neighborhoods. More and more, ward names
and broad areas were employed instead of blocks and streets to describe
social areas.

Moreover, epidemiologists for the first time described fashionable districts in terms of the separation between work and residence. Peter Townsend observed that the area of the city west of Broadway ("with the exception of Washington Street") had long been "selected by wealthy merchants,
as a place of residence, rather than of resort to business," and that the
whole neighborhood was "exclusively occupied by them, without being
mingled at all with the poorer classes of the population." Along Broadway, between Rector and the Battery, the area was "entirely occupied by
superb dwellings" with yards that were "clean, airy and spacious, and
enriched and ornamented with trees and shrubbery." The inhabitants of
the thoroughfare's fashionable West Side were "all of a respectable cast,
and most of them wealthy and of the first consideration in society." To
Townsend high residential status was defined by the absence of "business
being carried out" and by the predominance of buildings which served
"exclusively" as dwelling houses.[34]

Even though contemporaries remained unsure about the boundaries between neighborhoods, they drew a sharp distinction between "the salu-
brious and cleanly neighborhood of the Bowling Green and the Battery"
on the West Side and that "very hot-bed of filth," the Fourth Ward, on the
East. And the fact that certain streets and blocks were apparently spared
the ravages of the pestilence, while others nearby suffered its full effects,
confirmed for medical investigators that some neighborhoods had a better
moral character than others. Lombard [Monroe] and Cheapside [Hamil-
ton] Streets, "a very cleanly decent place, containing not more than sixty
houses, and those not crowded," escaped major infection, while only a
few hundred feet away, on Bancker Street, a district "famous for being the

very reverse in its physical and moral characteristics" and for being the "scene of a destructive distemper of a peculiar nature three years previously," was hit hard.[35] Citing the case of an 1821 outbreak, where only such whites were afflicted as "were in extreme poverty and who led a profligate life, or associated, or lived with the worthless class of coloured persons" in the district's "filthy and confined apartments, especially in low, damp and ill ventilated cellars," the New York Board of Health emphasized that depravity, race, and disease were closely related to residence.[36] A street name alone was enough to allow epidemiologists to both describe the social character of the inhabitants in the neighborhood and to predict the likelihood of infection.

By the time New York experienced its first severe cholera outbreak in 1832, the relationship of poverty and residence to disease had become generally accepted. Again, two of the city's poorest neighborhoods suffered most from the scourge of this disease: the Five Points in the Sixth Ward, and the Riverfront in the Fourth.[37] Because the Five Points was inhabited by a "race of beings of all colours, ages, sexes, and nations, though generally of but one condition, and that . . . almost of the vilest brute," as one editorialist angrily observed, the entire area was felt to threaten respectable inhabitants who lived nearby.[38] The social character of the Points, noted a physician, was so widely known that those "who are acquainted with the city, need not be informed either of the crowded and filthy state," of "the intemperate, dissolute, and abandoned habits of the inhabitants . . . or of the proverbial filth of the streets, as well as the houses."[39] The early efforts of epidemiologists to pinpoint the cause of Yellow Fever outbreaks fostered an initial awareness of neighborhood, but with the coming of cholera in 1832, area names now actually defined the social character of the inhabitants. Thus the work of the early health reformers changed spatial awareness into an awareness of "moral areas." Even in the middle of the nineteenth century, when more distinctions were made among the poor, one scholar noted how the "fusion of environmentalism and moralism" linked the "social degeneration of the poor" to "their appalling environment" through deterministic assumptions about the "pathological social consequences of overcrowding."[40] While the extreme poverty and poor hygiene of the Fourth Ward and the Five Points marked them as New York's earliest symbolic neighborhoods, other social characteristics also shaped New Yorkers' awareness of spatial differentiation. One of the most important was prostitution.

Even before the American Revolution, the upper sections of the West Ward (south of Chambers Street adjoining the Hudson River) had become a center of prostitution. In 1774 one authority estimated that five hun-

The Five Points in 1859. The view shows the infamous crossing of Baxter (formerly Orange), Park (formerly Cross), and Worth (formerly Anthony) streets. Lithograph from David T. Valentine, *Manual of the Corporation of the City of New York* (New York, 1860).

dred women of ill repute lodged in the few short blocks between King's College (later Columbia) and St. Paul's Chapel.[41] Throughout the nineteenth century, prostitution remained one of the most visible aspects of the "moral" differentiation of land in the city. Areas of vice, with brothels, bars, and houses of assignation, functioned as peculiarly artificial communities whose location had been dictated by the need to be near busy transit junctions, the central business district, or waterfront areas (as well as by the restrictive policies of municipal authorities). These prostitution districts, similar to the diseased quarters of the Five Points and the Fourth Ward (which with Corlears Hook also had reputations for vice), had their identity imposed upon them by outsiders who defined social deviance in terms of physical space.[42]

The predominance of brothels in certain neighborhoods made the vice districts perhaps the only social areas that most middle-class contemporaries could delineate by street.[43] "On the west side of Broadway commencing at Chambers, the whole district bordering on Church Street and West Broadway with the crossing streets" (particularly at Anthony and

Leonard between Church and Hudson) contained "some of the vilest, dens of infamy to be found in the city." Many were also located on Mercer Street and in "all the streets running parallel to Broadway, between Canal and Prince, and from Broadway to Varick Street." On the east side of Broadway, on Reade and Elm Streets ("generally in all that neighborhood") existed brothels of a "very low grade." The Five Points "sink of infamy" formed a vice district that was bounded by Broadway, Reade Street, Chatham, and the Bowery. The remaining bordellos lay interspersed among the "sailors boarding houses, which skirt the East River, and end at the Hook in the Brothel dance houses of Walnut Street."[44]

During the mid-nineteenth century, publishers turned out a number of brothel "directories." These allowed one to follow the changing boundaries of the vice areas as they moved in response to commercial expansion. In 1850 the *Fast Man's Directory and Lover's Guide* located most of the older establishments in the Fifth Ward, between Broadway and West Broadway.[45] By the end of the decade, however, the conversion of homes to warehouses and stores had forced many madams to move into town houses in the vicinity of Broadway and Houston Street, a once fashionable residential neighborhood (now known as Soho). The *Directory To the Seraglios in New York, Philadelphia, Boston and All the Principal Cities in The Union By a Free Lover* noted that only a handful of establishments remained in the old location. Many brothels were now situated along Mercer, Houston, Greene, and Wooster Streets.[46] By the 1860s Broadway had become synonymous with the young, "smart, good-looking, well educated" women, "prepossessing in appearance," who were known as "Nymphes de Pace," or "Cruisers."[47] After 1870 the vice district shifted uptown again, as the encroachment of cast-iron warehouses drove the "fashionable" vice district to more elegant quarters in Chelsea and along West 25th, 26th, and 27th Streets.[48]

The deviant social community required a wide recognition in order to thrive. Despite these several moves, the prostitution districts successfully drew customers and won the tacit acceptance of the municipal police. The gaudily decorated establishments interspersed among more sedate houses of assignation left little doubt as to the neighborhood's character. The mere mention of Church Street in the 1840s and 1850s, or the corner of Broadway and Houston Street in the 1860s, was enough to conjure an image of streetwalkers and brothels. Such easy recognition, unlike that of political wards, flowed naturally from the areas' illicit function and immoral image and made these districts some of the earliest and strongest symbolic communities in New York. In point of fact, prostitutions could be found scattered throughout virtually every ward of the city, but for members of the middle class (who presumably overlooked the sexual proclivities of their neighbors), vice was an ecological phenomenon.[49]

The notoriety of these areas was generally imposed from without by reformers and moral crusaders who shared little in common with those whose neighborhoods they described. Wealthy residents, by contrast, had the luxury of cultivating their own symbolic community. Through the ostentation of their dwellings and the exclusiveness of local amenities, such as private parks and social institutions, elite residents called attention to the gentility of the areas in which they lived. For wealthy New Yorkers, the symbolic consciousness of community was a means of preserving class cohesion. "In the first decades of the nineteenth century," as one historian has noted, " 'class neighborhoods' in Manhattan emerged in the form of 'class streets' or even parts of streets divided into 'respectable' and 'non-respectable' blocks." As merchants and the middle class both demanded "living space that departed from traditional integrations housing forms" (in which work and residence were combined), the "genteel" urban dwelling with "its emphasis on convenience to a separate workplace, healthfulness, and family comfort replaced the merchant house which had often included an office or counting room and which had been situated on streets near the wharves."[50]

St. John's Park in the Fifth Ward, also known as Hudson Square, is a classic example of a self-created symbolic identity. During the late eighteenth century this area lay "vacant and unproductive" as part of Lispenard's Meadow, which belonged to Trinity Parish. In 1805 the church's vestry decided to set this land aside as "an ornamental square without any building therein" to complement St. John's Chapel, which it was constructing as part of a development project on adjacent land.[51] Lots surrounding the new square were sold to builders with ninety-nine-year leases which restricted the types of houses to be constructed and prohibited nuisance industries. In exchange, lot "owners" gained the privilege of exclusive use of the park, kept private by means of a locked gate.[52] By the early 1830s, Hudson Square and its neighborhood was "the most fashionable part of the town" with its handsome iron railing, its fancy gravel walkways, and its beautiful trees.[53] Guidebooks described the "air of elegant uniformity" which pervaded the neighborhood, with the ironwork reinforcing its "European Style and magnificence."[54] Around the park's perimeter lived the cream of the New York social elite, including Mayor William Pauling, bank president John C. Hamilton, and real estate merchant Anthony Bleecker, who together formed a tightly knit community. These people worshipped in St. John's Chapel, sent their sons to Columbia College and their daughters to Mrs. Forbes' School for Girls, and married their children to the offspring of wealthy neighbors residing close by.[55] Thus St. John's Park was a symbolic center which created "a convergence of significant functions in the lifespace of local residents."[56]

Elsewhere in Manhattan, private and semiprivate squares also served to encapsule the lives of wealthy inhabitants—and at the same time to exclude the *demi-classe.* With the construction of Gramercy Park in 1831, real-estate entrepreneur Samuel B. Ruggles expanded upon the modest plan of St. John's Park and set the pattern for exclusive residential developments to follow. Soon, the highly popular Washington Square in the Fifteenth Ward and, to a lesser extent, Union, Tompkins, Stuyvesant, and Madison Squares had all become preserves of the rich, through the successful formula of combining greenspace with elegant housing— a strategy which also raised the values of adjacent properties and reaped a substantial profit for the developer.[57] By attracting prominent residents, the distinctive neighborhoods became a means of fulfilling the aspirations of fashion-seekers who wished to share some of the prestige that their more illustrious neighbors enjoyed. A South Carolina gentleman, writing in 1852, noted that "The rage is now Stuyvesant Square immediately in the neighborhood of Hamilton Fish." Proximity to such a prominent figure was enough to label this area "all the go—the nabob street, even though the buyer never saw, and probably never will see, Mr. F., but he can say that he lives at No.—— Stuyvesant Square, *near Mr. Senator Fish of the United States Senate!*"[58] By the middle of the century, wealthy residents had developed cognitive maps that matched address with residential status. "When a person gave the number of his (house), as being on Avenue 8th or 6th, for instance, it was known (without telling) that the *informer* lived in a fine house; and another tacitly conveyed or understood was, that none but upper tens lived in these fine houses; so you see this double-entendre gave some importance to the occupant."[59]

In addition to exclusive private parks and squares, street names defined neighborhood status for the wealthy. In the modern city, thoroughfares act either as dividing lines between social areas or serve in and of themselves as linear communities.[60] But antebellum cities possessed very few identifiable boundaries that divided their social groups within residential districts. Instead, streets commonly defined the social identity of local areas, the reverse of the general pattern today. Early in the nineteenth century, Broadway served as the center of fashionable residence as well as the dividing line between rich and poor. The "West Side" of Broadway below Canal Street was known as the "Dollar Side," while the less affluent East Side was the "Shilling Side" (though New Yorkers viewed both sides north of Canal Street as equally fancy). Even as early as the mid-1830s, a for-

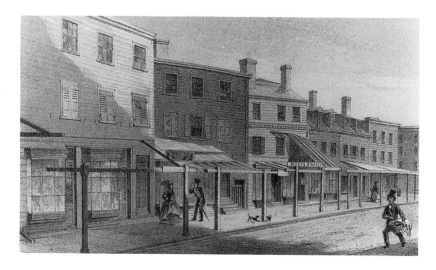

Old houses on Division Street between Eldridge and Orchard streets, 1861. Illustrations of street scenes of Lower East Side are uncommon before the Jewish influx. Lithograph from David T. Valentine, *Manual of the Corporation of the City of New York* (New York, 1861).

eign visitor could observe that "the most fashionable part of the city is that west of Broadway, the most mercantile in the opposite direction," and that the "portion east of the Bowery" comprised a "dense population of the lowest orders, and may be compared with St. Giles of London."[61] And journalist George Foster commonly used these two streets together with the Five Points to designate New York's growing social divisions.[62]

To the extent that it existed at all, awareness of social space was probably a class-related phenomenon. Lacking the cluster of affluent churches in their midst, proximity to private parks, or residence at a fashionable address on a major avenue, members of the working and crafts classes apparently possessed only the most rudimentary cognitive image of their own neighborhoods. But little substantive data exists to show how New Yorkers of different classes viewed their neighborhoods, and it could well be that high levels of mobility prevented more than a vague conception of neighborhood-as-community from arising in the minds of most residents. Major Jack Downing's inability to give his landlord a clear answer when asked if he wished to renew his lease two months before it was due to expire—"Who knows what we may all be dead before that time? . . . And besides I may have some business to do somewhere else by that time"— may reflect a footloose spirit that was common among New Yorkers. This fact might also account for the paucity of descriptive material on neighborhoods save for the very rich and the very poor.[63]

Regardless of how working-class residents actually perceived neighborhood differences, a degree of spatial identity was imposed on the city by the cholera epidemic of 1832 and by the religious revivals at the end of that decade, and this led social reformers to view the battle against poverty as essentially a moral struggle focused on the socio-spatial divisions between neighborhoods.[64] A New York Assembly Committee investigating the conditions in city tenement houses confessed: "Though expecting to look upon poverty in squalid guise, vice in repulsive aspects, and ignorance of degraded stamp, we had yet formed no adequate conception . . . of the intimate relationship existing between them and the dwellings, localities and neighborhoods where they abound." After touring many of Manhattan's and Brooklyn's worst dwellings, committee members were thoroughly convinced of the "truth of that theory which involves the health, virtue and general well-being of a people, with its methods, means and manner of living."[65]

Exposés on health and sanitation repeatedly argued that the influx of Irish and German immigrants had balkanized New York's social fabric by accentuating distinctions among areas. Middle-class residents who moved to new neighborhoods above Fourteenth Street lost touch almost totally with the changes which older wards were undergoing. At the end of the workday, a "continuous procession" of workers lost "itself gradually in the innumerable side-streets leading thence into the unknown regions of Proletaireism in the East End."[66] An inspector with the Council of Hygiene and Public Health noted how the Tenth Ward, and the east side of the city in general, had become "a 'terra *incognita*' to most of the inhabitants of the west end," who were unfamiliar with the new German quarter. But if outsiders were to go through Grand Street on a Saturday evening "they will be astonished at the immensity of the vast throngs of orderly, and cleanly, well-dressed people, and be struck with the excellent sanitary condition, as evinced by the healthful appearance, and the prevailing dialect will stamp them as coming from the land of Goethe."[67]

This inspector provides us with a valuable sense of the ethnic geography of these "unknown" areas. In the Thirteenth Sanitary District, which comprised the western half of the Seventeenth Ward, he found that the streets presented a "better key for tracing" the "peculiarities, classes, prevailing character and nationalities" than did the squares, and he was able to summarize varying social characteristics among subareas by street address. Along First Avenue south of Second Street, most inhabitants were American, while between Second and Sixth Streets, Germans predomi-

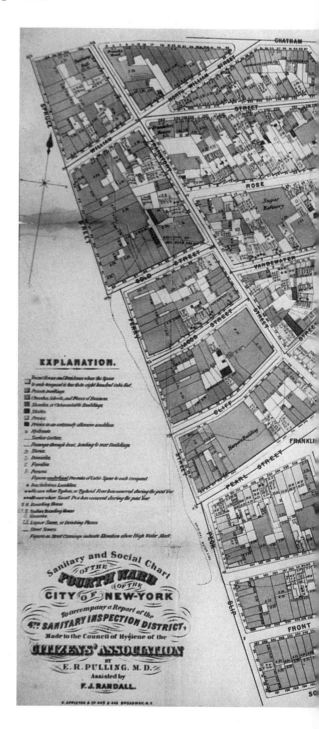

Sanitary and disease map of the Fourth Ward, 1866. From Citizens Association of New York, *Report of The Council Hygiene and Public Health Upon the Sanitary Condition of the City* (New York: Appleton and Co., 1866).

nated; Sixth to Seventh Streets had a mixed population of Americans, Irish, and Germans; Seventh to Eleventh Streets were exclusively Irish; the side streets were dominated by single ethnic groups; and blacks lived "scattered around the district in rear buildings and alleys." The Twentieth Ward, an area that would later be known as "Hell's Kitchen," also showed similar clustering by ethnicity and occupation, with residents settling in five distinct parallel bands. "The first and third belt," he noted, were "occupied principally by people of American birth, many of them engaged in commercial pursuits," a second belt was composed of a "mixed population," and a fourth and fifth belt "consisted primarily of foreign born, mostly Irish."[68]

For all the efforts such as that of the inspector, the post-1870 city was often described in terms of "a vast, unknowable 'wilderness' housing a 'mass' that threatened to engulf the remainder of urban society."[69] New Yorkers generally knew which areas were fashionable and which were to be avoided. "There are many streets and localities in New York," noted Gustav Lening, "which no resident in the city knowing the circumstances would care to pass through in the evening or night time, unless absolutely necessary."[70] But in many areas the intermingling of rich and poor on the same block created confusion and undermined the sense of residential communality. Even in the wealthy and exclusive Fifteenth Ward, with its town houses on Washington Square and along University Place, sanitary investigators discovered that "small-pox existed in a tenant-house . . . which stood at the end of the yard of one among a row of better class houses."[71] The continuing chaos of settlement in nineteenth-century New York perpetuated the mental confusion over how to define neighborhoods. For this reason, the cultural symbols of community—cultivated by wealthy residents themselves in order to foster neighborhood status— could be imposed upon the poor by zealous tenement-house reformers, sanitary inspectors, and outside missionaries.[72]

Learning Through Change

The development of cognitive community based upon cohesive identities, commonly shared names, and identifiable boundaries was also a continuing process fed by the very nature of urban change itself.[73] In antebellum New York, dynamic forces altered the symbolic character of many communities by redefining identities in the face of ecological change, by fusing identities with those of surrounding districts, or by giving rise to entirely new and distinct areas in the midst of already existing areas.[74]

During the mid-nineteenth century, wealthy and middle-class residents

Hudson Street looking north from the corner of Chambers Street, 1865. The view shows the extension of railroad tracks into the area that sped the decline of nearby St. John's Park. Photograph courtesy of the New-York Historical Society, New York City.

abandoned their ancestral homes in Lower Manhattan for formerly rustic uptown wards. With the influx of new residents, lots in the "upper reaches of the city" (above Fourteenth Street), which had sold for as little as $500 in 1834, commanded between $15,000 and $20,000 in the 1860s, and land at the junction of Fifth Avenue and Fortieth Street, once valued at only $100 or $200, now fetched $10,000 to $15,000. These sharp escalations of real-estate values were symptomatic of a more basic transformation in the social composition of New York that reversed the traditional pattern of the wealthy congregating near the city's commercial center. Reflecting back upon the 1830s, one longtime resident noted that *"Then* all the fashionable people resided down town and all the working people up town— *Now* the position of the two classes are [sic] directly reversed, or at least so near so that it is now unfashionable to live below Fourteenth Street."[75]

Once-fashionable districts such as the Fifth Ward, noted an 1859 sanitary report, have "been [so] rapidly changing in character . . . that old houses to a great extent have become occupied by many families of the poorer class."[76] With the influx of poor Germans, who worked in nearby sugar mills and garment factories, the neighborhood surrounding St. John's Park experienced a surge of crime in the late 1840s. Indeed, the crime wave became so bad that gas lights were installed along adjacent streets after local residents complained that the "neighborhood of St. John's Park" was "in night time infected with base and unprincipled persons who take advantage of the dense foliage of trees to perpetuate acts of violence" upon "unprotected individuals passing through Beach, Varick, and Laight Streets."[77]

The process of community change and decline in status which the Lower West Side underwent during the 1850s and 1860s was familiar to New Yorkers; several decades before, the eastern wards had experienced a similar transformation, and the earlier changes in Franklin Square in the Fourth Ward, and of other districts in the Lower East Side, such as East Broadway, had been no less striking. Following the American Revolution, the intersection of Pearl and William Streets had been the site of such fashionable residences as the first presidential home of George Washington and Walton Mansion. "East Broadway" served as the "Fifth Avenue of the period," and "great efforts were made to keep fashion on the east side of town." Madison, Henry, and Clinton Streets housed, according to one old New Yorker, many of "our first people" who owned nearby shipyards, while Cherry Street, between Franklin and Roosevelt Streets, "was occupied principally by doctors and lawyers."[78] However, between 1830 and 1850 most of the prominent residents had departed to newer areas such as Bond Street or Fifth Avenue, leaving "thousands of poor" to crowd in the neighborhood's "comparatively few buildings," most of which had been left in "a deplorable state" by their former tenants.[79] With this change in social composition came a corresponding redefinition of symbolic status. Now former residents seemed almost defensive about old neighborhoods, having to work hard to convince skeptical listeners that these areas had ever been nice places in which to live. In the satirical novelette *High Life in New York* (ca. 1850), a running joke involved Jonathan Slick, "Esq," a country bumpkin from Weathersfield, Connecticut, who showed his naïveté by mistaking what had already become a prostitution district for the area of fashion that it once was: " 'They talk about Cherry street not being fashionable, but I'll be darn'd if I believe there's a more genteel street in the city. It's the folks that live in a place that make it genteel or not, and if Cherry street aint at the top of the mark afore many weeks, it'll be because I move my office out on it, for there's no eend to the great shiny carriages that come down and stop afore my door, eenamost every hour

Cherry Street from the Corner of Roosevelt St., 1860. The sailor may be ca-
vorting with a prostitute. The farther barber pole stands near the entrance
of Gotham Court while the building at the end of the street was the Harper
Brothers building on Franklin Square. Lithograph from David T. Valentine,
Manual of the Corporation of the City of New York (New York, 1860).

of the day.' "[80] In reality the carriages belonged to the customers of local brothels.

The developing awareness was not limited to settled sections within the city. Many rural villages and hamlets existed beyond the bounds of Manhattan's development in the antebellum period, and a number of these had functioned as suburbs since the late eighteenth century. Many possessed either corporate or symbolic identities that managed to survive even after they had become engulfed by the swiftly moving tide of real-estate development after 1830, while others vanished entirely, losing their boundaries and their names. Dry Dock Village, along with Corlears Hook and Cherry in the Seventh Ward, were just two of the settlements adjacent to built-up areas that were totally absorbed early in the century.[81] A particularly interesting example was the area just north of the Tenth Ward, at the intersection of Bowery and St. Mark's Place, which was known to inhabitants as Bowery Village. This small enclave maintained its own local institution, a Methodist church, which fostered a feeling of tight community; Michael Floy, a young resident, noted in his diary how "all Bowery Village" turned out for an overnight prayer meeting up the Hudson River, which would suggest that most local residents felt part of a distinctive community.[82] Isolated socially from other sections of the city, Bowery Village successfully fostered a strongly localistic orientation and functioned as an inclusive solidarity community for its residents. Acceptance of neighborhood symbols (place-names and boundaries) and participation in local organizations (churches) allowed locals to socially distance themselves from "outsiders" through an informal system of community membership. Bowery Village's cohesion proved to be short-lived. With the development of the surrounding wards it rapidly broke down, and with the settlement of "newcomers" who replaced the established residents in the late 1830s, Bowery Village ceased to exist both in reality and in name.

The collective identity of another former suburb, Greenwich Village, was, by contrast, long-lasting.[83] In its early stages of development, despite large numbers of foreign squatters, the area possessed a well-defined identity of its own and "was always spoken of by persons living in that section as Greenwich."[84] Even in the 1860s and 1870s, long after the area had been engulfed by development, high levels of homeownership and the irregular street patterns preserved Greenwich Village as an island of stability in a sea of change. Despite the influx of several additional waves of Irish immigrants—some of whom rioted from time to time against older Knickerbocker residents—the "street life of Greenwich Village" remained "different from that of any other part of the City, having more of the rural atmosphere."[85] Unlike Bowery Village, whose street patterns were indistinguishable from the rest of the city, Greenwich successfully translated its distinctive rustic flavor into a sustaining symbolic identity that continued to set it apart. In this case urban change helped to impart a degree of spatial awareness in an era still marked by neighborhood heterogeneity and weak symbolic community.[86]

Conclusion

In a study of how residents of Boston, Los Angeles, and Jersey City perceived their urban environment, Kevin Lynch argued that cities were composed of a visually rich and varied fabric consisting of "edges," "districts," "nodes," and "landmarks." The contrast of these different elements enabled urbanites to visually and cognitively orient themselves and to view the city as a grouping of "very distinctive districts." As one Bostonian observed, "Each part of Boston is very different from the other. . . . You can tell pretty much what area you're in."[87] This was not necessarily the case for the average New Yorker in the mid-nineteenth century, because such elements of spatial perception were indistinct. Aside from the concentration of commerce in the vicinity of Wall Street and the working-class zone of entertainment along lower Bowery and Chatham Square, only the wealthiest and poorest residents lived in distinct and identifiable neighborhoods.[88]

Except in wealthy neighborhoods like St. John's Park, the boundaries of symbolic community were traced most clearly by streetwalkers and offal carts. Impoverished immigrant neighborhoods and vice districts became identifiable through the efforts of outside social reformers, and early efforts at disease control sought to pinpoint the spatial causes of cholera and yellow fever by highlighting areas with particularly bad housing or moral character. With the renewed interest in poverty during the middle of the century, such areas as the Five Points in the Sixth Ward and Water Street in the Fourth became synonymous with intemperance and destitution. The concentration of prostitution on several key streets produced a tangible "moral area" requiring no outsider's aid to pinpoint. Despite constant flux and change in prostitution districts, which moved several times between 1850 and 1870, they were described as having sharply defined boundaries and a distinctive symbolic identity, fixing the social reality of their existence upon urban space.

Two other factors also contributed to the development of the social-spatial awareness. First, self-contained districts that already possessed a distinctive self-image, a clear set of boundaries, and a sense of community were absorbed into the city. While some areas, such as Greenwich

Village and Chelsea, retained their unique identities among New York's neighborhoods, areas such as Bowery Village and Cherry Hill vanished entirely. Second, ethnicity played a role in the shaping of symbolic community during this period—though less than might have been expected. Although medical authorities had first noted the clustering of Irishmen and blacks late in the eighteenth century, it was not until the arrival of non-English-speaking foreign groups, such as the Germans, who settled in the "Kleindeutschland" east of the Bowery, that ethnicity emerged as a factor in the symbolic definition of neighborhoods.[89]

The creation of neighborhood identity was an ongoing, dynamic process that entailed the invention of a new vocabulary of symbolic space and an awareness of the social divisions of class. But for the most part, attachment to space remained weak throughout the period for all classes. Wealthy residents showed little psychological attachment to their old homes and few hesitated to seek quarters in new wards when the opportunity presented itself. Furthermore, spatial differentiation met a mental resistance that kept working-class community rooted in the localism of the preindustrial city.

Thus for most New Yorkers, neighborhood boundaries were as much social as they were symbolic. As we will see in the next chapter, the fundamental continuity of social networks, voluntary associations, and modes of collective action maintained some modicum of community despite the upheaval of mobility which tended to short-circuit any shared process of mental mapping. But by 1875 the process of neighborhood differentiation would be largely complete, and the West Side would be virtually unaware of how the East Side lived. "Uptown" and, "downtown" each took on a social meaning as well. With the flight of the rich and the abandonment of central wards to foreigners and the poor, the social-spatial picture of Manhattan's local areas solidified, and for the first time, the city now showed an awareness of residential differentiation as a "sovereign reality."

PART III

The Social

Neighborhood

6 Communities Out of Weak Ties

∎∎∎∎∎∎∎∎∎ During a sojourn through the northern states in 1854–1855, Jeremiah O'Donovan traveled from city to city hawking to his countrymen a poetic history of Ireland he had written. Wherever he went, O'Donovan proved the ideal salesman, whose knack for easy conversation and ability to flatter doubtless earned many sales. While O'Donovan's business acumen might be fascinating in its own right, the record he kept is of particular interest. From his home in Pittsburgh to Lynn, Massachusetts, and back, O'Donovan carefully noted not only the names of every contact and customer, but also the street addresses, occupations, and other information which he found of interest, including the person's county of birth in Ireland. Some years later, he penned another book describing his contacts with these homesick Irishmen in America and had it published at his own expense. This second book offers a treasure trove on the diffusion of contacts among working-class immigrants in mid-nineteenth-century America that helps us to better understand the functioning of social networks.[1]

O'Donovan listed the names of over 122 individuals (including addresses for 56) he met during his two visits to New York City. These were hardly representative of the city's Irish population in the 1850s, for O'Donovan's shrewd business sense led him to middle-class grocers, skilled workers, and professionals, rather than semiskilled and manual laborers. Within this range, the list does include a wide cross-section, ranging from "wealthy widow" to barkeeper, from meat dealer to market-man, and from plumber to milliner. There was even the case of Daniel J. Buckley, who despite having lived in the United States for six years remained unemployed despite his keen "mathematical abilities." (O'Donovan blamed Buckley's difficulties on his Catholicism which "nailed him to the counter" and gave "him no admittance into any institution other wise than Catholic.") But if the majority of O'Donovan's contacts were more affluent than average, virtually none seemed wealthy by native standards. Most were grocers, like Cornelius O'Sullivan who operated a store on 64 Montgomery Street with the help of his sister-in-law and who with his wife also ran a boardinghouse, in which O'Donovan lodged for a time. Another grocer named Williams also doubled as the president of the "long-shore men," the "most powerful association of the kind in New York."[2]

Few of these contacts could be considered more than acquaintances; most were probably total strangers O'Donovan approached with the sole purpose of selling his book. But the fact that customers directed him to friends and relations scattered throughout the city suggests that O'Donovan found his way into a network that ramified outward through New York's Irish community. A marketman named O'Neill directed him to three fellow produce sellers in the Washington Market. Patrick McGinn, a teacher at the Holy Cross Church on Forty-second Street, probably sent O'Donovan to John Rogers, another teacher from McGinn's home county of Louth, residing at the corner of Seventeenth Street and Tenth Avenue. In several cases the contact was made through a friend of one of O'Donovan's friends who lived outside of New York. The wife of a baker named Devlin, who resided on Frankfort Street, was the sister of a man that O'Donovan said he knew in Pittsburgh. And the letter of reference that he used to gain entrance into Mrs. Fleming's boardinghouse came from Judge McKenna, someone O'Donovan had met in Philadelphia.[3] Most of these contacts were probably members of a number of loose networks linked by shared acquaintances rather than by close sentiment.

When all the addresses are plotted on a map of Manhattan, two clear patterns emerge: geographic concentration on the West Side and Tip of Manhattan and yet within that concentration a wide diffusion north to Fourteen Street (figure 6.1). The residential enclaves where O'Donovan's contacts lived were not scattered at random. With the exception of two wards on the East River waterfront—the strongly Hibernian Fourth and the neighboring Seventh (O'Donovan boarded in the latter area during his stay)—the East Side of Manhattan was virtually devoid of socio-commercial contacts.[4] Reflecting the changing pattern of immigrant settlement away from traditional haunts in the Lower East Side to newer residential areas uptown, the majority of contacts clustered in the West Side north of Fourteenth Street, an area including Chelsea and the district later known as Hell's Kitchen. In addition, few of O'Donovan's contacts hailed from the area north of Fourteenth Street and east of Sixth Ave-

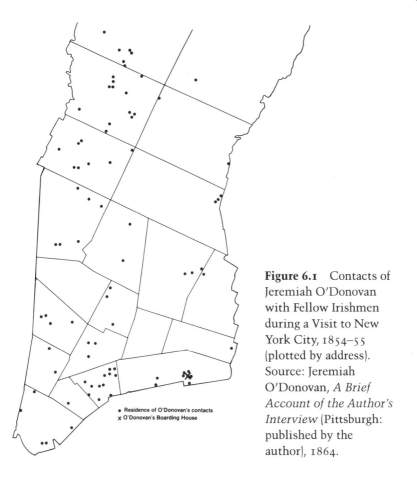

Figure 6.1 Contacts of Jeremiah O'Donovan with Fellow Irishmen during a Visit to New York City, 1854–55 (plotted by address). Source: Jeremiah O'Donovan, *A Brief Account of the Author's Interview* (Pittsburgh: published by the author), 1864.

• Residence of O'Donovan's contacts
x O'Donovan's Boarding House

nue or from the predominantly native wards Eight, Nine, and Fifteen on the Lower West Side, which suggests that associational patterns were influenced by the growing levels of ethnic and class segregation. If ethnic settlement in antebellum New York remained spatially diffuse, a clear tendency toward group cohesion and interethnic avoidance divided Manhattan socially. As scattered as New York's Irish population might have been, O'Donovan's recollections suggest that areas existed where few Irish lived or even visited—save as cooks and servants.

But the most striking feature of O'Donovan's movements was rather how widely scattered his contacts were. Irish immigrants resided and worked in numerous small, scattered enclaves rather than in any single ethnic neighborhood, so O'Donovan was able to make at least one contact in nineteen of New York's twenty-two wards. The range of such sociability—despite barriers of class, ethnicity, and association between the

East and West Sides—suggests that O'Donovan had tapped into an *aspatial* community, unbounded by the limits of neighborhood or ward. The wide distances he was able to cover (presumably on foot) as he pursued linkages between social networks of diffuse ethnic clusters thus calls into question whether physical distance actually functioned as a serious constraint upon informal association. Such a finding partially challenges the thinking of some historians who, while acknowledging the crucial role of geographical mobility in shaping community within the nineteenth-century city, nevertheless view urban sociability as if cities were a collection of urban villages in which neighborhoods functioned as quasi-exclusive social enclaves.[5]

Though residence rooted in ethnicity or class conferred a certain degree of collective identity, we have already seen not only the ambiguity of ascriptive characteristics (e.g., ethnicity) in shaping where people lived but even the tenuousness of their cognitive perceptions of urban space. Neighborhoods were stages upon which groups of players moved on and off as the location of the stage itself shifted with the changing social and spatial configuration of the city. Moreover, homogeneous "urban villages" were marginal cases occurring within narrow historical stages of urbanization and involving limited social groups, usually the very poor.[6] And with the march toward residential homogeneity partially halted in the 1850s by the flood of immigrants, it is doubtful that distinct social enclaves could have emerged at least until the 1870s if not later.[7]

Jeremiah O'Donovan's social wanderings clearly illustrate what happens when, "as the urbanite is exposed to the heterogeneity of the city and moves through contacts with various individuals and groups, he comes to accept instability and insecurity as normal."[8] Community is, then, relative, existing in "different degrees" based upon "networks of individuals, not closed and mutually exclusive, but bound together more closely than they are linked to outsiders."[9]

From other sources we know that O'Donovan's wide range of social contacts was not unusual. New Yorkers typically covered large distances by foot—a fact that should not be surprising to the modern pedestrian, who easily traverses many of the older wards in only a matter of minutes. Recreational walking imparted knowledge of the city's geography and "walking out" was a way for "single men and women to mingle."[10] If the walking city was compact because of the barrier of space on commerce, reasonable walking distances for mid-nineteenth century urbanites were long and opened up a wide range of social interaction. In the 1820s and 1830s, Rev. Henry Chase of the Mariners' Church in the Fourth Ward wrote about preaching in Greenwich Village in the morning, speaking at the Duane

Street Presbyterian Church over a mile south in the afternoon, and return-
ing to his own church in time to preside over a funeral that evening (after
numerous stops along the way)—a distance he covered entirely by foot on
a cold midwinter's day.[11] A somewhat younger New Yorker, Michael Floy,
routinely walked up to Harlem (125 Street), where his father operated
several greenhouses, a distance of over six miles from his home in Bowery
Village.[12] While Floy's employment for his father made him cover more
ground than normal, his religious fervor—which was hardly uncommon—
led him across town to Methodist churches in Greenwich Village, downtown to John Street, several times a week to Allen and Forsyth Streets a
half mile from his home, and, on one occasion, to a church bazaar up on
Forty-first Street.[13]

The recollections of O'Donovan and other contemporary observers suggest that supportive social ties had not only survived the onslaught of
urbanization, but continued to thrive as New York grew. Far from being
a forbidding place populated by isolated, antisocial "atoms,"[14] New York
City was the locus of numerous circles of friends, acquaintances, and relatives with whom one might chat on the street. As in any small town,
there was no shortage of neighbors upon whom one could call in times
of need. Scattered in almost every section of New York, wrote William
Bobo, a South Carolinian with little deep affection of his own for the city,
"you will find little knots of acquaintances, who will assist each other (of
course expecting the like favor in due time reciprocated) in many little
matters." Only in places such as Chatham Street, the working-class shopping and entertainment area known for its cold-hearted merchants, sham
auction houses, and hucksters, were the ties of friendship replaced with
the expectation that "every tub stands on its own bottom, every dog must
shake his own paw."[15]

For still other observers who believed that urban life dissolved ties between friends and family, the lack of restraints governing association loosened oppressive social strictures and came to be seen as a kind of social
liberation. The prominent editor and literary figure, N. Parker Willis, ex-
ulted that in New York City during the 1850s, with its nearly 600,000
inhabitants, "there are people enough of every kin" to satisfy virtually
everybody—without risking social embarrassment. "A hundred acquaintances may be picked from a hundred different neighborhoods, circles, or
congregations, without the selection being even known to the unselected
remainder of the neighborhood, circle, or congregation."[16]

This liberty of association held special attraction for wealthy residents.
Liberated by city life from the conventions of fashionable society, they
were free (within the restraints of class) to interact with whomever they

pleased, without having to rely exclusively upon a small circle of imposed friends. But the immigrant working class enjoyed considerably less freedom. They were bound by urban neighborliness, friendship, and preexisting kinship ties carried over from the old country. John Maguire, a nineteenth-century author writing on the Irish immigrant experience, observed how "there were old friends and former companions or acquaintances to be met with at every street corner; and there was news to give, and news to receive—too often, perhaps, in the liquor-store or dram-shop kept by a countryman—probably 'a neighbour's child,' or 'a decent boy from the next ploughland." While the English hatter James Burns focused upon social atomization and the lack of friends he claimed to have suffered, Maguire contended that immigrants actually had too many friends. Indeed, Maguire blamed excessively strong social attachments for Irish poverty, contending that such ties led the "simple, innocent countryman" to ignore the "friendly invitation" of the "virgin forest" and instead remain "the denizen of a city, for which he was unqualified by training" or habit.[17]

Whether nineteenth-century city dwellers suffered a lack of friends or possessed too many, the evidence from O'Donovan's travels suggests that the survival of social relations such as nonresident kinship, friendship, and neighbors within the urban environment requires greater historical attention. Some means is needed to better understand an unbounded urban community where residents came to accept social insecurity and instability as routine amidst a world of transience populated by a profusion of strangers. How were the day-to-day social interactions of city dwellers linked to the operation of the neighborhood community? To what extent did these interactions spill beyond neighborhood boundaries? Understanding how informal ties and social networks functioned within the context of neighborhoods for people like O'Donovan provides a starting point for answering these questions.[18]

Too little systematic attention has been paid to the historical implications of informal sociability for neighborhoods in American cities. When the ties of social community have been studied outside the immediate confines of kinship and the family, historians have tended to focus upon formal voluntary associations and churches rather than on individuals.[19] While such institutions are important building blocks of community, formal clubs and churches directly touched the lives of only a minority of New Yorkers and thus offer us no substitute for secondary relationship (although it is often impossible to separate the two).[20] Sociological findings on "the strength of weak ties" and the importance of diffuse social networks clearly demonstrate how an historical understanding of urban neighborhoods as social communities now requires an examination not only of relations embedded in formal social organizations such as churches and clubs, but of informal associations as well.[21] In point of fact, neighborhood life was characterized neither by the social atomization described by Wirth and hatter James Burns nor by the Gansian urban villages—the two rival models of urban organization mentioned most widely by historians.

First, the scope of neighborhood interaction in nineteenth-century New York was far broader than the once accepted image of the "ethnic village" would lead us to believe. As we shall see, neighborhood voluntary associations were one component of the local community, and they ranged from street gangs to crowds in saloons to church congregations. Though religious preference and the need to fraternize with fellow countrymen forced some churchgoers like the German Lutherans living in Kleindeutschland to commute across town to Greenwich Village's St. John's Church to worship, churches remained primarily neighborhood-oriented institutions (and became socially more homogeneous with the exodus of downtown Protestant churches). Churches and other voluntary associations functioned, albeit imperfectly, to intensify neighborhood identity and to homogenize the communities of association—a pattern which accelerated with the development of residential neighborhoods in the upper wards.[22]

But more importantly, much if not most meaningful social interaction was rooted in the "unbounded community": the widely dispersed network of friends and relations beyond the neighborhood or its institutions.[23] Of course, the social roles of voluntary associations focused in the local community were hard to separate from this aspatial, informal social interaction. And in everyday interaction, as well as in times of immediate crisis, face-to-face relations of neighbors did provide support and company to residents of the inner-city wards. But such outside relationships as in-laws, siblings, or friends who lived on the other side of Manhattan, in Brooklyn, or in New Jersey—although inconvenient to visit on a regular basis—acted as an even more fundamental resource for information on employment opportunities and housing in an environment characterized more by mobility and change than by stability.

There were some restraints on this aspatial community, however. New Yorkers who lived west of Broadway were far less likely to visit those on the east and, to a lesser extent, vice versa. And inhabitants of the impoverished Dry Dock wards of lower Manhattan were far less likely than residents elsewhere in New York to marry neighborhood outsiders or, for that matter, even to invite people who did not live in the immediate vicinity to witness baptisms or weddings—although even here ward boundaries were permeable to social intercourse. In the final analysis, informal and formal social interaction worked hand in hand to foster a new kind of community-neighborhood characteristic of modern city life, one not rooted in villagelike neighborhoods.

The remainder of this chapter probes the linkage of "personal communities" to "residential communities" by first discussing the function of casual contacts within neighborhood boundaries and second, examining how formal religious and voluntary organizations fostered a social-spatial identity.[24] The proximity of witnesses to those whose baptisms and marriages they solemnized serves as a rough measure of the social permeability of local boundaries, and the extent to which parishioners attended churches in the immediate local area helps to delineate the role of formal institutions in fostering a "neighborhood identity."[25]

Networks and Neighborhoods

Scholarly classification of informal social ties is easier theorized than accomplished. Social network analysis is of limited use to historians because of problems with sociological network theory and, more importantly, the lack of adequate data.[26] Diaries that dutifully note every acquaintance and illuminate aspects of the social network, such as multiplicity of linkage, content of transactions, the flow of information, frequency of contacts, and the degree of emotional attachment are rare even among wealthy New Yorkers. Their virtual absence for working-class residents makes a systematic study of social space especially difficult.[27] In addition, there are definitional problems in establishing what constituted a local "neighborhood" community. If the aspatial community of the modern city is, as many sociologists have argued, the result of technological innovation, we might expect that nineteenth-century cities, with their technological primitiveness and preindustrial character, to have shown strong tendencies toward localism in social interaction. In this view the urban neighborhoods of the past should have functioned as self-contained social areas that provided easy access to one's most cherished acquaintances. But what constitutes "easy access" and how did space delineate "neighborhood"? Should the local area be defined with reference to streets, blocks, wards, or some broader measure?[28]

In the absence of better sources, I have used the names of parties and witnesses gleaned from church marriage and baptism registries (linked with city directories to ascertain addresses) as my chief source of information on proximity of social contacts within neighborhoods and, indirectly, on the integration of friends, neighbors, and kin.

Admittedly, certain biases may undercut findings gleaned from these records. First, baptisms and marriages by definition involve individuals in a narrow stage of their life cycle. And since the number of an individual's social contacts ordinarily peaks during the early years of adulthood, the picture of sociability presented by these records may be unrepresentative. This bias might also influence one's view of the content of relations because young marrieds often relied upon nonfamily peers, while older couples relied to a greater extent upon family members.[29] A second problem is that nearly half of all witnesses were women for whom no addresses could be found. Except in the case of the few scrupulous pastors who recorded complete information for all parties, the address of each witness had to be traced in city directories, and those for whom no location could be found were discarded. Because fewer women were listed in city directories than men, this procedure risked injecting sexual bias into the sample. Still another problem was the general absence of information regarding the nature of the relationship between the witness and the parties to the ceremony. This raises questions of whether many presumed "witnesses" at weddings might have actually been strangers recruited by ministers to made the nuptials official.[30]

Serious though these biases might be, they do not entirely vitiate the usefulness of the records. While there is no easy way of controlling for life-cycle biases, neither is there any evidence that this problem significantly influences patterns of social propinquity. Indeed, given the youthful age distribution of antebellum New Yorkers (the average age was twenty-three to twenty-four years), ages at marriage were consistent with that of the general population. The problem of sex bias largely disappeared when findings from the general sample were compared with a subsample drawn from churches whose pastors were unusually thorough in noting complete addresses from all parties and witnesses.[31] The third potential bias stemming from the use of strangers as witnesses was partially controlled by deleting all cases where the names of witnesses—often the name of the church sexton—were repeated.[32]

The final problem with the data—the representativeness of church records—is the most serious and also the most difficult for which to control. Obviously many witnesses were at best only infrequent contacts for grooms, brides, or parents. But these occasional contacts served important functions which presumably more localistic, quotidian sociability did not. New York in the 1850s was a city filled with newcomers, many of whom had made significant breaks with friends and relatives as they crossed the Atlantic or arrived in the city from rural farmsteads. Under these conditions of extraordinary mobility, weak acquaintances that could easily be jettisoned during moves became important for setting up migration chains and providing intelligence on employment and housing prospects. Witnesses may well have served such a function—infrequent in contact but important at anchoring family members and friends in the informal community. The wide extent of aspatial ties is supported by the sizable number of witnesses who lived outside the immediate area. Indeed, friendship ties from militia and fire companies or from work were dependent upon broader networks that channeled individuals into the local community, providing them social linkages and easing their movement to new jobs or residences.

Nor is there any reason to believe that records of witnesses were—because of their exceptional nature—biased against usual neighborhood acquaintances. While conceding that "witnessing functions linked households in different sub-districts," one historical study that utilized marriage records nonetheless concluded that "witnesses were more likely to be drawn from households located very close by, in the same street or a few dwellings away."[33] Such was the case in nineteenth-century New York City where witnessing patterns often followed the example of future presidential candidate Alfred E. Smith, whose baptism was witnessed by a nearby friend, in this case a fellow member of his father's fire company living just around the corner.[34] Though flawed, records of witnesses nonetheless allow us to better study social propinquity for a wider range of social classes than any other sources extant. And while lists of witnesses, godparents, and wedding partners may be of limited value in the study of common daily contacts, they are among the few sources that provide information on the geography of individual association in and out of neighborhoods.

We know that local friends and neighbors were critical to day-to-day interaction, providing daily comradeship, fostering local awareness, and, in critical life situations when help from kin members was unavailable, furnishing emergency support. To be sure, residents of the same neighborhood could be total strangers to one another, as was the case when a female tenement dweller queried by a newspaper reporter in 1859 responded that no one in her building knew any fellow resident.[35] But during the Yellow Fever epidemic of 1822, it was not uncommon to find neighbors aiding one another at a risk to their own lives. When John M'Kenna, an "Irishman, and grocer aged 27" sickened, his friend Edward Arcularius (of German ancestry) came to his assistance and, as a result, contracted the disease himself. John Murphy, a six-year-old boy who lived at 51 Pearl Street, was cared for by Mrs. Hull, "an English woman, aged thirty who lived opposite, and [who] had been in to see this boy on his illness" before she too was taken sick. When Mrs. Hull and her husband, a watchman, lay dying in the same bed in their tiny room, "Mrs. Lawler and her brother-in-law, Edward Kearny, who lived in an upper apartment," took frequent care of the Hulls before they came down sick with the fever. In her illness, Eliza Fury, an Irish girl aged twelve, was aided by Catherine Dempsey, who lived in "a small dirty wooden apartment, about twelve feet square, in a back wooden building in Mrs. Fury's yard." John and Jane Wareham, an English-born bell hanger aged fifty-seven and his forty-five-year-old Irish wife, were nursed by Abraham Ball, a sixty-seven-year-old Englishman who lived in the garret of the building. When Ball was stricken, "Sarah Walker, aged 30, who lived in the room back of Mrs. Wareham, and [who] had been frequently in to assist her," also came to the aid of Ball before she died from Yellow Fever.[36] This tragic account of diseases, aid, contagion, and death described a period of uncommon danger and selfless giving at great personal risk. Nonetheless the willingness of neighbors to help one another in the midst of an epidemic would indicate that within impoverished ethnic quarters, local ties could be vitally important.

Church records largely confirm this picture and show that local neighborhoods functioned as a form of social community for many parents or marital partners who selected local witnesses. Over the period 1830–1875 for which church records were consulted, this trend intensified in predominantly native areas and diminished slightly in immigrant neighborhoods—a reflection of the growing self-segregation of native residents when confronted with the influx of newcomers.[37] An analysis of addresses for witnesses and the parties whose baptisms or marriages they witnessed (table 6.1) highlights the strong importance of residential proximity in the selection of witnesses throughout the period.[38] Residents of the Lower West Side, for example, generally invited friends and relatives from within the neighborhood rather than from other areas of the city such as the Lower East Side where nearly one half of the city's population lived.

In addition, the social contacts of New Yorkers responded to the shift of Manhattan's center of population uptown. From the 1850s onward, downtown New Yorkers had to invite more and more friends and relations from the newer wards between Fourteenth and Fortieth Streets or the suburban district to the north. More homogeneous than older districts within the city (with the possible exception of the Fifteenth Ward), these recently developed middle-class neighborhoods were ethno-cultural extensions of the Lower West Side and havens for New Yorkers of native stock who had retreated from Lower East Side neighborhoods overrun by immigrant newcomers. The proportion of Lower East Side witnesses invited to Midtown (north of Fourteenth Street) baptisms and marriages declined (from 51 to 23 percent) while the proportion of invitees from the Lower West

Table 6.1   Neighborhood Association between Grooms, Brides, and
Witnesses to Their Weddings by Date, New York City, 1830–75

Variables: Dates: 1830–39, 1840–49, 1850–59, 1860–69, 1870–75.
Groom's or bride's area of residence: groom's, bride's.
Area of residence: Lower West (wards 1, 2, 3, 5, 8, 9, 15), Lower East
(wards 4, 6, 7, 10, 11, 13, 14, 17), Middle (wards 16, 18, 20, 21), Upper
(wards 12, 19, 22).
Witness's area of residence: Lower West (wards 1, 2, 3, 5, 8, 9, 15).
Lower East (wards 4, 6, 7, 10, 11, 13, 14, 17), Middle (wards 16, 18, 20,
21), Upper (wards 12, 19, 22).

Terms of Model (controlled for)	χ^2	χ^2 d.f.	χ^2 signif.	Difference χ^2	Diff. d.f.	Difference signif.	Coef. of determination
All 2-way associations	116.63	105	.2060	—	—	—	—
(Area of residence, witness's area)	635.38	114	.0001	518.75	4	.0001	.8164
(Date, area of residence)	251.66	117	.0001	135.03	12	.0001	.5365
(Date, witness's area)	176.31	117	.0005	59.68	12	.0001	.3385
(Groom's-bride's, date)	137.28	109	.0345	20.65	4	.0006	.1504
(Groom's-bride's, area of residence)	123.88	108	n.s.*	—	—	—	—
(Groom's-bride's, witness's areas)	123.28	108	n.s.*	—	—	—	—

*Probability over 10% (.1).

Table from modeled data: area of residence by witness's area, grouped by date

Date	Area	Witness's Area (% across)								N (Row)
		Lower West	S.R.*	Lower East	S.R.*	Middle	S.R.*	Upper	S.R.*	
1830	Lower West	66.9	4.5	24.4	−4.0	6.4		2.3		33.0
1830	Lower East	19.2	−4.1	72.5	4.5	5.5		2.9		56.0
1830	Middle	35.6		36.3		22.6		5.5		6.0
1830	Upper	26.1		30.7		11.3		31.9	2.9	4.0

$\chi^2 = 33.53$ Prob. = .01

1840	Lower West	56.1	8.3	37.0	−7.8	5.6		1.3		81.0
1840	Lower East	12.1	−8.0	83.0	8.3	3.6		1.3		285.0
1840	Middle	27.6		51.0		18.5	2.5	2.9		14.0
1840	Upper	22.6		48.2		10.4		18.8	3.1	5.0

$\chi^2 = 92.11$ Prob. = .01

Table 6.1 (continued)

Date	Area	Lower West	S.R.*	Lower East	S.R.*	Middle	S.R.*	Upper	S.R.*	N (Row)
1850	Lower West	56.9	10.4	27.4	−8.1	13.6		2.1		198.0
1850	Lower East	14.5	−8.4	72.7	11.2	10.4	−4.3	2.4		344.0
1850	Middle	24.3		32.8	−4.4	38.9	7.1	4.0		113.0
1850	Upper	20.1		31.3		22.0		26.6	5.3	15.0
	$\chi^2 = 212.577$ Prob. = .01									
1860	Lower West	61.0	9.5	23.0	−4.9	14.2	−2.1	1.8	−4.5	181.0
1860	Lower East	17.4	−7.3	68.2	7.1	12.1	−4.1	2.3	5.5	159.0
1860	Middle	26.7		28.2	−2.2	41.5	6.8	3.5	−2.5	113.0
1860	Upper	23.1		28.1		24.5		24.3	2.5	25.0
	$\chi^2 = 174.40$ Prob. = .01									
1870	Lower West	64.9	7.3	18.2	−4.6	12.9	−2.2	4.0	−2.3	144.0
1870	Lower East	21.0	−4.9	61.8	2.1	12.4		5.7		86.0
1870	Middle	29.5	−2.3	23.2		39.2	4.7	8.0		59.0
1870	Upper	20.2	−2.1	18.2		18.2		43.5	6.2	20.0
	$\chi^2 = 120.41$ Prob. = .01									

N (Table) = 1941.0

*Standardized residuals: (Observed-Fitted)/SQRT(Fitted). Since standardized residuals are normally distributed, numbers greater than +/− 1.96 are significant to the .05 level. Only significant values are shown.
Source: Marriage Records Sample, 1830–75 (see appendix A).

Side—which remained ethnically stable—stayed essentially the same or rose slightly between 1840 and 1875.

The strongest social exclusivity divided the lower wards on Manhattan's Lower East Side from those on the West. After the 1840s the predominantly native West Siders became even more socially *endogamous* while ethnic East Siders became more *exogamous*. During the 1830s two-thirds of Lower West Side witnesses were also neighbors to the baptismal or marital parties, although this figure dipped to 56 percent during the 1840s and 1850s before rising once again to 65 percent by the 1870s. The proportion of Lower East Side residents invited to West Side ceremonies fell from 37 percent in the 1840s to only 18.2 percent in the 1870s. And as the spatial exclusivity of West Siders increased, the changing ethnic character of the Lower East Siders made them socially more open. In the 1840s, 83 percent of East Side witnesses came from within the wider local neighborhood and only 12.1 were invited from the West Side. By the 1870s, with the exodus of much of the area's native population to other parts of the city, the number of local witnesses dropped to 61.8 percent while the percentage of West Side invitees rose to 21 percent. New York had become a city of neighborhoods, but unlike the traditional view of the immigrant "ghetto," native working- and middle-class neighborhoods were far more socially localistic.

The social segregation which separated East Side from West would thus seem to confirm a picture of local social interaction at odds with the fluid social relations epitomized by Jeremiah O'Donovan. But the picture that these records have so far presented is a distorted one that exaggerates the importance of neighborhoods as crucibles for social interaction. Some of the "neighborhoods" of social interaction were, like the "Lower West Side," extremely large in area including numerous wards and spanning wide areas of Manhattan. (This area covered the entire district south of Fourteenth Street and west of Broadway and housed 23 percent of New York's total population in 1855. The "Lower East Side" comprised eight wards and was home to 43 percent of New Yorkers.) Despite such broad districts, between a third and half of all witnesses (depending on the decade) lived *beyond* boundaries of one-half to one mile. In light of the large sample units employed and the sizable number of witnesses who came from distant neighborhoods, we might want to look more closely at local patterns of interaction in order to understand why neighborhoods did not operate even more forcefully to constrain social interaction.

A reanalysis of the data using smaller units of geographical measurement that better approximate neighborhoods (although even here boundaries are quite broad) underscores the extent to which the social relations of residents ramified outside the local area (table 6.2). The direction of cross-town interaction followed a familiar pattern with most flowing from East Side to West. Seventeen percent of the Lower East Side residents knew at least one friend west of Broadway, compared to the 12 percent of Lower West Siders. Likewise, East Side residents tended to invite more friends and kin from the newer sections of the city north of Fourteenth Street than did West Siders, although the differences between the two were minimal (17 versus 14 percent).

But the key point is the low proportion of witnesses who hailed from within the same neighborhood. Sixty percent of residents sampled from the Lower West Side and Dry Dock districts invited witnesses from an area composed of no more than several adjoining wards, and in other areas of New York, between two-thirds and four-fifths of witnesses came from outside the local community. To the extent that localism operated, it functioned as a by-product of other factors such as ethnicity (in native areas

Table 6.2   Proximity of Neighborhood Relations:
A Comparison between Areas of Residence for Marriages and
Baptisms and Those of Witnesses, New York City, 1830–75

Variables: Source of party's address: address of parents (if baptism)/groom or
of bride.

Area of residence: Tip of Manhattan (wards 1, 2, 3). Lower West Side
(wards 5, 8, 9, 15), Dry Dock (wards 4, 7), Lower Center (wards 6,
14), Lower East Side (wards 10, 11, 13, 17), West Side (wards 16, 20),
East Side (wards 18, 21), Upper West Side (Ward 22), Upper East Side
(Ward 19), Manhattan suburb (Ward 12).

Witness's area of residence: Tip of Manhattan (wards 1, 2, 3). Lower
West Side (wards 5, 8, 9, 15), Dry Dock (wards 4, 7), Lower Center
(wards 6, 14), Lower East Side (wards 10, 11, 13, 17), West Side (wards
16, 20), East Side (wards 18, 20), Upper West Side (Ward 22), Upper
East Side (Ward 19), Manhattan Suburb (Ward 12).

Terms of Model (controlled for)	χ^2	χ^2 d.f.	χ^2 signif.	Difference χ^2	Diff. d.f.	Difference signif.	Coef. of determination
All 2-way associations	69.19	81	.8222	—	—	—	—
(Area of residence, witness's area)	1619.31	162	.0001	1550.11	81	.0001	.9573
(Source, area of residence)	87.55	90	n.s.*	—	—	—	—
(Source, witness's area)	82.83	90	n.s.*	—	—	—	—

*Probability over 10% (.1).

Table from modeled data: area of residence by witness's area

Area	Tip	L. West	Dry Dk.	Lwr. C.	L. East	West S.	East S.	Up West	Up East	Suburb	N (Row)
Tip	33.6	19.8	11.5	5.3	12.2	5.3	7.6	2.3	1.5	.8	131.0
S.R.*	*8.1*	*−2.4*			*−2.2*						
L. West	3.1	61.3	4.3	4.6	12.2	7.2	4.3	1.3	1.1	.1	829.0
S.R.*	*−2.3*	*15.1*	*−8.1*	*−2.9*	*−5.5*	*−2.0*	*−2.4*				
Dry Dk.	4.7	9.4	60.5	7.7	11.1	2.7	2.5	.7	.2	.5	405.0
S.R.*		*−8.0*	*23.3*		*−4.3*	*−4.4*	*−3.2*		*−2.4*		
Lwr. C.	5.3	14.0	14.9	35.1	16.7	3.5	5.3	2.6	1.8	.9	114.0
S.R.*		*−3.3*		*11.3*		*−2.0*					
L. East	2.0	17.0	8.4	7.2	48.0	7.2	6.8	.6	2.3	.4	512.0
S.R.*	*−2.9*	*−5.9*	*−4.0*		*13.4*			*−2.1*			

Witness's Area (% across)

Table 6.2 (*continued*)

					Witness's Area (% across)						
Area	Tip	L. West	Dry Dk.	Lwr. C.	L. East	West S.	East S.	Up West	Up East	Suburb	N (Row)
West S.	2.1	28.1	3.3	5.4	14.1	34.3	7.4	3.3	1.7	.4	242.0
S.R.*			*-4.8*		*-2.3*	*12.7*					
East S.	1.8	17.7	6.7	2.4	31.1	11.0	23.8	1.2	3.7	.6	164.0
S.R.*		*-3.2*	*-2.8*	*-2.2*	*2.9*		*8.7*				
Up West	2.1	25.5	8.5	6.4	12.8	14.9	4.3	21.3	2.1	2.1	47.0
S.R.*								*9.9*			
Up East	12.5	9.4	3.1	9.4	9.4	9.4	9.4	3.1	31.2	3.1	32.1
S.R.*	*2.0*	*2.0*	*-2.2*						*12.1*		
Suburb	7.1	7.1	7.1	7.1	7.1	21.4	14.3	7.1	7.1	14.3	14.0
S.R.*										*5.6*	
N (Table) = 2490.1											

*Standardized residuals: (Observed-Fitted)/SQRT(Fitted). Since standardized residuals are normally distributed, numbers greater than +/− 1.96 are significant to the .05 level. Only significant values are shown.
Source: Marriage and Baptism Records Sample, New York City, 1830–75 (see appendix A).

like the Lower West Side) or as a combination of ethnicity and class (in the Dry Dock wards). Nearly four-fifths of witnesses living in the Fourth and Seventh Wards—two impoverished Irish enclaves—shared the same address, block, or street as the parents, brides, and grooms who had invited them. By contrast, adjoining ethnic areas of the Lower East Side and Lower Central district (wards Six and Fourteen), which were generally less poor, invited only 48 percent and 35 percent of witnesses, respectively, from their local areas. While working-class residents undoubtedly created communities of their own, these communities were geographically compact in only the poorest of neighborhoods. Contrary to the contention of Ivar Bernstein that mid-nineteenth-century industrial workers (including highly skilled machinists) came to view "the neighborhoods where they lived and worked as a special working class place" in the same way that artisans viewed their labor organizations, the church evidence suggests that closely knit neighborhood communities might have existed chiefly for highly marginalized occupational groups.[39] Rather than functioning universally as building blocks of working-class community, intensive local ties seem to have operated most strongly for the very poor.[40]

In areas not constrained by nativistic exclusivity or grinding poverty, neighborhood boundaries proved highly permeable to social contact. On crucial family occasions New Yorkers called upon a network of relations scattered throughout the city. Two sources reveal how far-ranging these social ties could actually be: the records of the Mariner's Church in which Rev. Henry Chase devoted one page to each of the thousands of marriages that he performed among the denizens of the Fourth Ward, and those of St. John's Lutheran Church in Greenwich Village whose pastor fastidiously recorded every detail for marriages and baptisms with a minuscule Germanic penmanship (table 6.3). Although 40 to 56 percent of witnesses recorded in these records lived within the same neighborhoods as those who invited them, between 8 and 13 percent traveled from as far away as Brooklyn or New Jersey. And as the New York metropolitan area added new residential districts in Midtown Manhattan and in suburbs across the Hudson and East Rivers, the number of social contacts located in these areas increased. Having a brother in Hoboken, a sister in Williamsburg, or a friend on West Forty-sixth Street undoubtedly led newlyweds and parents to seek jobs and lodging in areas that they would never have considered had they been forced to rely entirely upon local contacts. In this way the diffuse social network probably served to complement neighborhood ties.

Nineteenth-century New Yorkers ventured outside their own neighborhoods not only to select witnesses to important ceremonies, but also to choose marital partners. Patterns of marital endogamy and exogamy paralleled those of witnesses.[41] This is significant because the earliest sociological examinations of marital endogamy suggested not only that grooms married local brides, but also that proximity was even more important in the selection of a mate than it had been in the choice of witnesses. But there is little reason offered why the pattern of spatial endogamy for married couples should have differed significantly from that for witnesses.[42] Indeed, if we examine marital propinquity using a measure based upon five discrete, mutually exclusive categories arranged in descending order of priority, we not only see that the level of marital endogamy was less than might be expected from earlier studies, but also that much of what passed as marital propinquity was actually a result of premarital cohabitation (table 6.4).[43]

Between 18 and 34 percent of men in downtown wards either married women who were listed as living at the same address or had cohabited before they married.[44] While both immigrant and native areas of Lower Manhattan showed this strong link between marriage and residence, the highest incidence of marital partners residing in the same building was found in the most strongly ethnic areas—31 percent in the Dry Dock area, and 34 percent in the Lower East Side.[45] Robert Henderson, a fireman on board the steamship "Passaic," asked Rev. Henry Chase to marry

Table 6.3   Proximity of Neighborhood Relations: A Comparison between Groom's Area of Residence and Those of Witnesses, Mariner's Church and St. John's Lutheran Church, New York City, 1830–75

Variables: Groom's Nativity: U.S.

Area of residence: Tip of Manhattan (wards 1, 2, 3). Lower West Side (wards 5, 8, 9, 15), Dry Dock (wards 4, 7), Lower Center (wards 6, 14), Lower East Side (wards 10, 11, 13, 17), West Side (wards 16, 20), East Side (wards 18, 21), Upper Manhattan (wards 12, 19, 22), Brooklyn, New Jersey.

Witness's area of residence: Tip of Manhattan (wards 1, 2, 3), Lower West Side (wards 5, 8, 9, 15), Dry Dock (wards 4, 7), Lower Center (wards 6, 14), Lower East Side (wards 10, 11, 13, 17), West Side (wards 16, 20), East Side (wards 18, 21), Upper Manhattan (wards 12, 19, 22), Brooklyn, New Jersey.

Terms of Model (controlled for)	χ^2	χ^2 d.f.	χ^2 signif.	Differ- ence χ^2	Diff. d.f.	Differ- ence signif.	Coef. of determi- nation
All 2-way associations	36.78	81	1.000	—	—	—	—
(Area of residence, witness's area)	271.11	162	.0001	234.33	81	.0001	.8643
(Nativity, area of residence)	64.81	90	n.s.*	—	—	—	—
(Nativity, witness's area)	61.21	90	n.s.*	—	—	—	—

*Probability over 10% (.1).

Table from modeled data: area of residence by witness's area

Witness's Area (% across)

Area	Tip	L. West	Dry Dk.	Lwr. C.	L. East	West S.	East S.	Upper	Brklyn	N.J.	N (Row)
Tip	12.5	21.9	9.4	3.1	6.2	6.2	21.9	6.2	6.2	6.2	32.0
S.R.*	2.5						2.8				
L. West	1.9	46.6	3.7	6.2	18.6	5.6	3.1	1.9	5.0	7.5	161.0
S.R.*		6.0	−2.3				−2.2				
Dry Dk.	3.8	11.5	55.8	7.7	5.8	1.9	1.9	3.8	1.9	5.8	52.0
S.R.*			11.2		−2.4				−2.4		
Lwr. C.	7.7	11.5	7.7	19.2	15.4	7.7	11.5	7.7	7.7	3.8	26.0
S.R.*				2.3							
L. East	1.5	13.1	2.3	8.5	40.0	8.5	10.0	5.4	5.4	5.4	130.0
S.R.*		−2.5	−2.6		4.8						
West S.	1.8	14.5	1.8	5.5	10.9	34.5	10.9	7.3	5.4	7.3	55.0
S.R.*						6.2					

Table 6.3 (continued)

					Witness's Area (% across)						
Area	Tip	L. West	Dry Dk.	Lwr. C.	L. East	West S.	East S.	Upper	Brklyn	N.J.	N (Row)
East S.	2.9	8.6	8.6	5.7	34.3	2.9	20.0	5.7	8.6	2.9	35.0
S.R.*							2.5				
Upper	5.6	19.4	8.3	8.3	16.7	13.9	5.6	13.9	2.8	5.6	36.0
S.R.*								2.2			
Brklyn	13.6	18.2	4.5	4.5	9.1	4.5	4.5	9.0	18.2	31.6	22.0
S.R.*	2.4								2.3		
N.J.	8.0	20.0	4.0	4.0	12.0	8.0	4.0	8.0	16.0	16.0	25.0
S.R.*									2.0		
N (Table) = 574.0											

*Standardized residuals: (Observed-Fitted)/SQRT(Fitted). Since standardized residuals are normally distributed, numbers greater than +/− 1.96 are significant to the .05 level. Only significant values are shown.
Source: Marriage and Baptism Records Sample, New York City, 1830–75 (see appendix A).

him to Lavinia Shephard in 1845, and when asked to explain his failure to bring witnesses, he assured Chase that it did not matter anyway, since he and Lavinia had lived together for "a number of years."[46] The marriage of Michael Griffen, a nineteen-year-old shoemaker, to Elizabeth Mary, a woman two years his elder, prompted a confession that he had known the bride for three years and had boarded with her before they formally set up house.[47] By contrast, grooms in predominantly native districts ordinarily wed brides from different buildings but from the same general area.

Most grooms and brides, however, married outside of their neighborhood altogether. This was especially true of wards in the commercial district near the Tip of Manhattan, which had experienced a population decline, and of the peripheral areas that did not yet have a large enough population to supply an adequate pool of marriage partners. Between 60 and 64 percent of couples residing in these two areas had partners who had resided in different neighborhoods. Elsewhere in New York, an average of six out of ten partners married someone for whom there was no match of address—presumably a partner living in a different ward.[48] (The main exceptions to this pattern again, were Dry Dock and the Lower West Side with between 60 and 64 percent of grooms who wed partners living in the immediate vicinity.)[49]

While face-to-face relations were an integral part of social community in nineteenth-century Manhattan neighborhoods, residents often relied

Table 6.4   Neighborhood Endogamy: Proximity and
Marriage by Area of Residence, New York City, 1830–75

Variables: Groom's or bride's address: groom's, bride's.

Relationship between groom's and bride's address: same street
address, different address but same street and ward, same ward
but different street, same section of city but different ward, no
apparent match.

Area of residence: Lower West Side (wards 1, 2, 3, 5, 8, 9, 15), Lower
East Side (wards 4, 6, 7, 10, 11, 13, 17), Middle Wards (wards 16, 18,
20, 21), Upper Manhattan (wards 12, 19, 22).

Terms of Model (controlled for)	χ^2	χ^2 d.f.	χ^2 signif.	Difference χ^2	Diff. d.f.	Difference signif.	Coef. of determination
All 2-way associations	9.70	32	.999	—	—	—	—
(Relationship of address, area of residence)	142.39	64	.0001	132.69	32	.0001	.9319
(Groom's or bride's, relationship)	28.14	36	n.s.*	—	—	—	—
(Groom's or bride's, area of residence)	18.62	40	n.s.*	—	—	—	—

*Probability over 10% (.1).

Table from modeled data: area of residence by
relationship between groom's and bride's address

Area	Relationship Between Groom's and Bride's Address (% across)										N (Row)
	Street	S.R.*	St/ Ward	S.R.*	Ward	S.R.*	Area	S.R.*	No Match	S.R.*	
Tip	18.6		5.1		8.5		5.1		62.7	2.1	59.0
L. West	23.7		3.4		16.4		20.1	6.3	36.3	−2.7	493.0
Dry Dk.	31.8		5.6		18.5	2.0	4.7	−3.1	39.5		233.0
Lwr. C.	18.5		7.7		10.8	−2.4	1.5	−2.5	61.5	2.8	65.0
L. East	33.6	2.5	4.7		9.7		17.8		44.2		321.0
West S.	17.7		4.0		13.7		10.5		54.0		124.0
East S.	30.3		3.9		11.8		21.3	−2.8	52.6		76.0
Up. W.	5.0		15.0	2.3	15.0		5.0		60.0		20.0
Up. E.	13.6		4.5		13.6		4.5		63.6	2.0	22.0

N (Table) = 1413.0

*Standardized residuals: (Observed-Fitted)/SQRT(Fitted). Since standardized residuals
are normally distributed, numbers greater than +/− 1.96 are significant to the .05 level.
Only significant values are shown.

Source: Marriage and Baptism Records Sample, New York City, 1830–75 (See appendix A).

upon friends and relatives who lived scattered throughout the city and its environs. That such a large proportion of witnesses hailed from distant neighborhoods, suburbs, or outlying cities argues for the existence of diffuse networks of friends, relatives, and acquaintances who were capable of fostering social cohesion despite geographical separation.[50] Remarkably, these diffuse social networks existed before the modern advent of improvements in communication and transportation technology deemed necessary for the formation of aspatial community. Edward E. Hale noted that many newcomers with "no special plans" and with "no relatives to provide for them" when they arrived still managed to enlist the aid of countrymen "to whom they have not the slightest ties of consanguinity or neighborhood."[51]

The existence at such an early point of diffuse social ties and network-based community should not be surprising. The roots of the unbounded community were planted with the very act of migration when individuals decided to leave traditional homes for the city. Out of necessity or choice, the mental calculus of following opportunities, taking employment risks (often out of desperation), and being prepared to move again when necessary required a social orientation best geared for collecting information, for reconnoitering old acquaintanceships or family relationships. The result was the unbounded community. But if the local neighborhood was subsumed to a broader structure of overlapping communities, what defined the local community as a social entity? And what gave neighborhoods their distinct structure? Some answers to these questions can be found in the records of neighborhood churches.

Church and Community

To many observers of antebellum New York City, religious worship was not only a demonstration of spiritual devotion, it was a social activity and popular spectacle. Protestant churches provided a strong emotional experience for young men and women, especially during the frequent revivals.[52] But the motivation of many churchgoers was not entirely religious. James Burns, the always cynical British observer, argued that the loosening of family bonds compelled men to form social circles whose "bonds of union" arose more from "matters of feeling" than they did from heartfelt "principle." American social organizations were "loose in their adhesive power," and churches proved no exception. They were like the "vast number of little human unities" which, "like the objects in a kaleidoscope, are ever changing with the evolution of time." With doctrine and devotion often playing little importance, congregations attended services to hear "dramatic ministers" who either offered "light comedy" or "strong sensational doses of oratory from men who have learned to saw the air." Although many Americans sincerely felt the "glow of true religion," Burns felt that the "vast number of the churches" were "used by the people in a theatrical manner."[53]

Contemporaries also identified another secular function of churches— as marriage markets. Baron Klinkowstrom, a Swedish visitor, chastised the practice of holding two services a day, noting that because the "lovely girls" seldom missed evensong, "subsequently the young men become quite devout, and eager to go to church." "There is only one step from emotionally demonstrative worship to love-making," he noted." After all, "A lovely woman is never so seductive as when she devoutly bows before her Maker and sends her prayers up to heaven."[54] Writing in the 1830s, another observer of the New York scene, Asa Greene, revealed somewhat less shock (despite his feigned naïveté) than Baron Klinkowstrom when he argued that churches and theaters both fulfilled a social role and that churches had certain advantages:

> Another motive for attending church, preferably to the theater, is its superior advantage for exhibiting the charms of persons and dress— fairest opportunities that could be desired for exhibiting an elegant dress or a comely person. We dare hardly ascribe it to personal vanity— because the fair sex is constitutionally devout; and yet whoever will attend church will find the balance of female beauty in proportion to the numbers attending each, immensely on the side of the church. Perhaps it is not so much their beauty that leads them to the church as the offices of devotion that contribute to their beauty.[55]

Every Sabbath, boys between the ages of fifteen and eighteen, known in the slang as "spoonies," gathered to "giggle and rudely stare at every modest girl and hang about the steps of churches, &c (as about a hundred do around the doors of Bedford-street Church every Sunday) to make impudent remarks upon every one they see." The young women were apparently eager to reciprocate. A young parishioner recorded in his diary how he "saw some ladies staring incessantly at me in Church."[56] That the latter confession appeared in the diary of a pious young Methodist suggests that the defacto sexual nature of worship (where the majority of churchgoers were female) could be reconciled to the church's role of moral stewardship despite the occasional protests that pointed to the contradiction.

To the extent that churches played the secular role of theater, marriage market, and meeting place, they can be considered as much a form of *voluntary* association as organizations whose members shared the same social background (ascriptive institutions). Despite wide fluctuations in duration of membership, churchgoing was a critical component of the neighborhood community, forming something of a subculture that combined devotion with "the opportunity to associate with co-religionists" and "formal organizational activity."[57] Thus religious institutions promoted neighborhood cohesion.

How churches functioned socially largely depended upon the religious orientation of the churchgoer. Those swayed by doctrine, usually Protestants, often attended outside their neighborhoods, while those who "valued their church for its companionship as much as for its theology" probably attended churches close to home.[58] Where church attendance was geographically circumscribed, as in Roman Catholic parishes, the parish "defined the members of the village community in opposition to those from surrounding parishes."[59] But if church parishes strengthened the ties between groups of parishioners who were already linked through family, origin, or neighborhood, churches were often physically and socially removed from neighborhoods. Catholic parishes were usually wider and more populous than the neighborhoods. Thus for many, the social function of churches was probably diffuse, cementing existing neighborhood or workplace ties through weddings, baptisms, and funerals.[60]

How relevant were churches as neighborhood institutions in mid-nineteenth-century New York? The irreligiousness of working-class residents has become something of a truism for historians.[61] While it was conceded that the Second Great Awakening had brought a sharp rise in church membership during the first quarter of the nineteenth century, most residents of poorer neighborhoods seemed immune to the message of Protestant evangelism. Sean Wilentz, who has most carefully documented the relationship between religion and the working class, contended that "while impiety and popular enthusiasm exerted their influences, most artisans" showed "a profound and shameless indifference toward any kind of organized devotion." Despite an intensified effort by middle-class reformers to foment a Finneyite revival (after Charles G. Finney, the leading evangelist) in the early 1830s, either through the opening of free churches that eliminated the pew rents or through the invitation of charismatic ministers, no effort seemed able to awaken workers from their apathy. New York produced no "shopkeeper's millennium," and Presbyterian missionaries found themselves preaching to the already converted. Episcopalians likewise failed to reach "the mass of New York workers." Methodists "barely held on to their proportional share of the city's population," while "all of the Baptist churches founded in the Bowery in the 1830s" soon disbanded. With its "immigrants, its Bowery, its tradition of popular anticlericalism, and its sheer size," Wilentz concluded, New York "lacked almost all the prerequisites for a successful revival." Thus when revivals did occur they "brought few journeymen to Jesus" and mainly provided "some craft entrepreneurs and small masters with an enhanced sense of moral purpose and righteousness."[62]

Low levels of Protestant church attendance were not entirely the result of working-class indifference or New York's own peculiarities. The strict moral standards and widespread continuance of pew rents effectively excluded many of those who wished to join. Most sects required not only proof of "personal experience and a consistent life," but attendance at numerous prayer meetings, Sunday school classes, camp and revival meetings, as well as evidence of "missionary and benevolent work." For Methodist converts there was the added burden of extended periods as "probationers" before being admitted into full communion.[63] Even the Free Church Movement that presumably opened many church doors to all comers regardless of their ability to pay often continued to enforce a profession of faith prior to granting membership. This was usually satisfied only after a long period of probation during which prospective members had their behavior scrutinized by church elders or, in the case of members in good standing relocated from other congregations, by the presentation of a letters of transference from one's previous minister.

Even the loosening of restrictive covenants that had limited membership during Protestant revivals, which periodically convulsed sections of the city in the 1830s, 1840s, and late 1850s, failed to produce many working-class converts. To be sure, accounts of successful revivals abound. During the 1844 revival spearheaded by the chiliastic Millerite sect, prophecies of impending apocalypse swept through the Lower East Side, unleashing what may well have been the "greatest plebeian revival in the city's history."[64] And across town that same year, Ezra Whitey, of the First Home Missionary Society of the Methodist Episcopal Church, "commenced to preach salvation through a crucified and risen Savior—with a Croton Pipe for my pulpit, and the blue heavens for my sounding board to a large and attentive congregation" gathered on a triangular lot between Greenwich Lane and Seventh Avenue in Greenwich Village.[65] But other supposed revivals produced less real religious excitement than met the eye. The notorious Water Street Revival of 1868 was, in retrospect, something of a sham staged more for the gratification of missionaries than the poor of the Fourth Ward.[66]

But it would be wrong to conclude from such evidence of failed revivals, restrictive membership practices, and seeming working-class indifference that religion was unimportant to the lives of large numbers of New Yorkers. The surviving membership records for churches located in four sample wards of New York City for the period 1830–1875 (see appendix A) leave no question that churchgoing was an important part of community life.[67] In 1825 the city was home to ninety-three churches with attendance on the rise and pews "regularly filled."[68] By 1855 the New York State census counted 245 churches in New York County. Of these, 86 percent were Protestant, with Episcopal congregations the most numerous (43), followed by Presbyterian and Methodist (33 each), and Baptists (26). The Roman Catholic church, which included comparatively few houses of worship, nonetheless served the largest flock; half of all worshipers on any given week were Catholics. The Episcopal church attracted 11 percent of weekly churchgoers while the Presbyterian, Methodist, and Baptist attracted 8.9, 7.6, and 6.1 percent, respectively.[69]

In response to a census question, ministers listed a combined seating capacity of 237,730 in all of the city's churches and estimated that an average of 222,250 out of a total population of 629,904 worshiped on a typical Sunday. Attendance was distributed unevenly among the different denominations. Most Protestant ministers preached to a sea of empty pews, while Catholic parishes overflowed with 100,500 worshipers often crammed into buildings capable of accommodating only 33,576.[70] If the total population of New York is divided by the average number of weekly worshipers, roughly one out of three attended church—although this number was undoubtedly higher on holidays. Assuming that the majority of these were over the age of fourteen, more than half of all adult New Yorkers might have been affiliated with some church—a figure well above the one in four previously mentioned.

Thus historians may have underestimated the importance of churches as a form of "voluntary" association. For many parishioners church membership served to structurally root newcomers in a well-defined social environment or to set the path for future moves (although many more might have attended or even received communion without being formal members). Many Protestant newcomers knew exactly which church they would be joining in their new homes and secured the necessary letter from their old ministers in New Jersey, Connecticut, upstate New York, and even Great Britain before moving to the city. And ties of formal membership, friendship, and kinship frequently overlapped as was shown by the case of John Cauldwell who, after five years, followed James Colkman from the Common Street Baptist Church in Birmingham, England, to the Oliver Street parish in New York City.[71] Indeed, churches may well have been the only formal voluntary associations available to most residents.

Factors of ethnicity and class influenced religious association (although

St. Luke's Episcopal Chapel of Trinity Parish, Hudson Street south of Christopher, 1831. Photograph courtesy of the New-York Historical Society, New York City.

socio-ethnic status and religion were not identical). The pattern of neighborhood churchgoing is best shown by focusing upon the four sample wards that have been used throughout this study. In 1855 these areas housed forty-five churches including two Catholic parishes and a Jewish synagogue. According to the New York State census of churches taken that year, 33,914 of the wards' 110,000 people attended church on an average Sunday.[72] As with other sections of the city, the small number of active Protestants probably worshiped in churches that were largely empty. This was especially true for the few Methodist churches that survived amid the changing population of the Lower East Side. The influx of large numbers of Germans and Irish in the late 1840s led to the flight of most native-born residents, so that on an average Sunday, only 60 percent of the pews in the Allen Street Methodist Church were filled, and the pastor of the old Forsyth Street congregation preached to a church that was only one-third full.[73] Only Protestant churches in Greenwich Village, which remained overwhelmingly native, saw weekly attendance levels as high as three-quarters.

At the same time, Catholic churches in predominantly foreign-born wards struggled to accommodate an ever increasing flood of worshipers—this despite the fact that only a minority of Irish immigrants ever attended church. If many of New York's Irish were only nominally Catholic, with most knowing little of church practice or dogma, they still constructed strong cultural communities focused on their church, as well as on local groceries and taverns. It was not uncommon for even unchurched Irishmen to riot in order to defend their jobs, the boundaries of their neighborhoods, and Catholic churches.[74] In addition, perhaps as many as one third of the Germans who resided in New York's Kleindeutschland were Catholic.[75] Thus it is hardly surprising that Roman Catholic parishes like St. James Church in the Fourth Ward routinely saw 8,000 worshipers in a building designed to hold scarcely one-third that number. By the late 1870s St. James had become one of the largest in the city, with a congregation numbering some 25,000, not counting the 3,000 Catholic seamen who attended when on shore.[76]

The importance that historians have placed on religion as a barometer of class affiliation is essentially correct. Church attendance reflected not only the devotional commitment and ethnic background of individual parishioners but also was strongly correlated with social rank. Whether it was the Presbyterian merchant, the Methodist cartman, or the Catholic laborer, churches united New Yorkers sharing similar occupational (and presumably ethnic) backgrounds in common organizations, and thus brought a degree of social organization to heterogeneous neighborhoods. A model comparing occupational rank, residence, and religion among a sample of Protestant and Catholic parishioners indicates a clear hierarchy of religious denominations on the basis of socioeconomic composition (table 6.5).[77] Roman Catholics were substantially poorer than Protestants, with 45 percent holding jobs that could be considered menial compared with only 24 percent among the Methodists (the Protestant denomination most likely to attract members from the working class). Only 21 percent of Catholics held jobs that could be classified as white-collar or petty-proprietary compared to 30 percent among Methodists.[78]

It should be noted that important internal variations existed among Protestant sects. Presbyterians were the wealthiest denomination with nearly half its members clustered in professional or proprietary ranks and only 10 percent situated among the semiskilled and unskilled.[79] Among Episcopal parishioners, most of whom were affluent, 17 percent belonged to the lower levels of the working class; this diversity reflected both the elite character of wealthy pewholders and the active missionary work of the downtown chapels. And while a majority of Baptists were tradesmen

Table 6.5   Religion, Residence, and Occupational Rank, New York City, 1830–75

Variables: Religion: Episcopal, Presbyterian, Methodist, Baptist, Reformed Dutch, Roman Catholic.*

Residence: Tip of Manhattan (wards 1, 2, 3). Lower West Side (wards 5, 8, 9, 15), Dry Dock (wards 4, 7), Lower Center (wards 6, 14), Lower East Side (wards 10, 11, 13, 17), West Side (wards 16, 20), East Side (wards 18, 21), Upper Wards (wards 12, 19, 22).

Occupational rank: professional, proprietary, skilled, semiskilled, unskilled.

Terms of Model (controlled for)	χ^2	χ^2 d.f.	χ^2 signif.	Differ- ence χ^2	Diff. d.f.	Differ- ence signif.	Coef. of determi- nation
All 2-way associations	95.52	140	.9991	—	—	—	—
(Religion, Residence)	303.72	175	.0001	211.20	35	.0001	.6954
(Religion, Occupation)	241.31	160	.0001	148.79	20	.0001	.6166
(Residence, Occupation)	160.17	168	n.s.**	—	—	—	—

*Probability over 10% (.1).

**Roman Catholic Church membership estimated using baptism records, n.s. = not significant

Table from modeled data: religion by occupational rank

Religion	Profes- sional	S.R.*	Proprie- tary	S.R.*	Skilled	S.R.*	Semi- skilled	S.R.*	Un- skilled	S.R.*	N (Row)
Episcopal	17.2	3.4	30.5		35.2		13.3		3.9		233.0
Presby.	17.2	3.8	31.5	2.1	41.0		8.8	−3.6	1.5	−3.8	273.0
Methodist	5.4	−4.1	24.5		46.2	2.6	22.6	4.0	1.9	−4.3	368.0
Baptist	12.3		30.2		45.3		6.6	−2.7	5.7		106.0
Reformed	9.4		31.2		37.5		15.6		6.3		64.0
Catholic	5.2	−2.9	16.0	−3.1	33.5	−2.2	20.8	2.2	24.5	11.6	212.0

Vertical Occupational Rank (% across)

N (Table) = 1256.1

*Standardized residuals: (Observed-Fitted)/SQRT(Fitted). Since standardized residuals are normally distributed, numbers greater than +/− 1.96 are significant to the .05 level. Only significant values are shown.

Source: Sample of Church Membership, New York City, 1830–75 (see appendix A).

and unskilled workers, 42 percent belonged to nonmanual classes. New York's Methodists ranked at the bottom of the Protestant occupational hierarchy. As historians have long noted, from active evangelism among the bottom ranks of the working classes. Even in such a strongly artisanal district as Greenwich Village, only a third of the Methodists were white-collar, compared to levels of between 40 and 50 percent for other denominations located in the same area. Nearly a quarter of the sampled Methodists could be classed as either semiskilled or unskilled workers.[80] The descendants of the original Dutch settlers, who maintained their collective identity largely through the Reformed Church, held a wide range of occupations which made their church perhaps the most diverse of the New York's denominations.

But the most important factor that influenced urban church membership was probably not class but transiency. The membership records of neighborhood Protestant churches—records that list dates of admission and dismissal of parishioners—suggest that churchgoers remained an extraordinarily volatile group during much of the nineteenth century despite periodic relaxations of membership requirements during revivals (table 6.6). All sects experienced considerable fluctuations in the number of new members during the period 1830–1875, and most showed an

St. James Roman Catholic Church, on James Street in the 1860s. The building is still in use. Photograph courtesy of the New-York Historical Society, New York City.

Table 6.6   Religion and Length of Church Membership among Protestants, by Date, New York City, 1830–75

Variables: Tenure (in years): 0, 1–4, 5–9, 10–14, 15+.
          Date: 1830–39, 1840–49, 1850–59, 1860–69, 1870–75.
          Religion: Episcopal, Presbyterian, Methodist, Baptist, Reformed Dutch.

Terms of Model (controlled for)	χ^2	χ^2 d.f.	χ^2 signif.	Difference χ^2	Diff. d.f.	Difference signif.	Coef. of determination
All 2-way associations	78.26	64	.1080	—	—	—	—
(Date, religion)	202.80	80	.0001	124.53	16	.0001	.6141
(Date, tenure)	169.83	80	.0001	91.57	16	.0001	.5392
(Tenure, religion)	157.72	80	.0001	79.46	16	.0001	.5038

Table from modeled data: tenure by date of membership, grouped by religion

Religion	Date	Tenure in Years (% across)					N (Row)
		0	1–4	5–9	10–14	15+	
Episc.	1830s	20.0	20.8	39.2	7.6	12.4	2.5
Episc.	1840s	10.9	69.6	10.5	2.0	7.0	22.5
Episc.	1850s	17.3	60.3	8.5	5.9	8.0	12.5
Episc.	1860s	12.2	65.6	11.7	4.5	6.0	40.5
Episc.	1870–75	17.6	49.6	14.4	10.8	7.6	2.5
Presb.	1830s	5.9	6.6	56.0	14.9	16.7	82.5
Presb.	1840s	6.0	40.8	28.0	7.7	17.6	99.5
Presb.	1850s	8.7	32.3	20.6	20.1	18.3	76.5
Presb.	1860s	6.2	35.5	28.7	15.6	14.0	62.5
Presb.	1870–75	7.0	21.1	28.2	29.5	14.2	45.5
Method.	1830s	25.3	16.9	42.3	10.8	4.7	13.5
Method.	1840s	15.9	64.6	13.0	3.4	3.1	34.6
Method.	1850s	24.1	53.2	9.9	9.4	3.3	10.5
Method.	1860s	17.2	58.8	14.0	7.4	2.6	6.5
Method.	1870–75	23.0	41.5	16.1	16.4	3.1	8.5
Baptist	1830s	4.8	6.8	67.5	10.0	10.8	2.5
Baptist	1840s	4.9	43.8	34.3	5.4	11.7	44.5
Baptist	1850s	7.6	37.2	27.1	15.0	13.0	54.5
Baptist	1860s	5.2	38.7	35.7	11.0	9.4	36.5
Baptist	1870–75	6.2	2.4	37.1	22.1	10.2	34.5
Reformed	1830s	3.9	6.7	47.9	14.1	27.5	16.5
Reformed	1840s	3.7	39.1	22.6	7.0	27.6	11.5

Table 6.6   (continued)

Religion	Date	Tenure in Years (% across)					
		0	1–4	5–9	10–14	15+	N (Row)
Reformed	1850s	5.5	31.0	16.7	18.1	28.7	17.5
Reformed	1860s	4.0	35.1	23.9	14.5	22.5	16.5
Reformed	1870–75	4.6	21.1	23.7	27.5	23.1	17.5
N (Table) = 772.5							

Source: Sample of Church Membership, New York City, 1830–75 (see appendix A).

overall drop in new conversion during the 1850s. Much of this fluctuation may have been unrelated to the dynamics of revivalism, stemming rather from variations in record-keeping procedure, the wholesale transference of membership from one assembly to another, the development of schisms, and mergers of congregations. Again, only the Dutch Reformed church seemed immune from the constant ebbs and flows in memberships that plagued other denominations.

For most churchgoers membership was short-lived; between 40 and 80 percent of new members disappeared from rosters within five years. There were, though, strong differences between Presbyterian, Episcopal, and Methodist churches involved in revivals and other Protestant denominations.[81] While 25 to 40 percent of Presbyterians and between one-third and one-half of Dutch Reformed churchgoers remained with congregations for a decade or more, fewer than 19 percent of Episcopalians and Methodists stayed within their church that long. Moreover, while the length of church affiliation generally held steady or decreased slightly between 1830 and the 1860s, those denominations that experienced surges in new members during periods of revival (e.g., the 1840s) saw particularly sharp declines in lengths of tenure.[82]

Whether church membership and attendance drew together people from throughout the city who shared the same theological outlook or, instead, functioned primarily to reinforce attachment to the local neighborhood remains an open question. It has already been suggested, at least in the case of Catholic parishes, that the sheer size of some congregations meant they were too large to represent single neighborhoods—they more often represented constellations of neighborhoods. The degree of occupational homogeneity shown by Protestant denominations, when coupled with census findings on social segregation, suggests that these churches did function chiefly as neighborhood-based institutions. Despite fluctuations over time in both residential and church addresses, an examination of the addresses of churchgoers (table 6.7) indicates that mid-nineteenth-century New Yorkers mostly lived near where they prayed.[83]

Three-quarters of the Protestants sampled attended church in the Fifth and Ninth Wards—two of the most strongly native wards in the city. Of these, 77 percent lived in the same neighborhood and an additional 7 percent commuted to church from an adjacent area. By contrast, East Side residents tended to reside in wards separate from their church; fewer than half of the parishioners who attended Dry Dock churches lived in the local area (although 30 percent commuted from adjacent wards). Indeed, while 58 percent of members in the Tenth Ward Protestant churches also resided in the Lower East Side, 40 percent traveled to church from wards outside the Lower East Side—a surprisingly long commute. Evidently ties to formal religious institutions, like informal ties to family members and kin, could be geographically diffuse, even more so when the church's neighborhood underwent ethno-cultural change. The local appeal of East Side churches diminished even further when congregations began to relocate north of Union Square, forcing long-term members who had not moved to make the long trek uptown on Sundays. One such congregation continued to list a third of its parishioners as living south of Fourteenth Street. But with the continued northward movement of Manhattan's population, these former downtown churches found fewer and fewer members willing to maintain ties over such a distance. After the mid-1850s, only 14.6 percent of the 142 members of the Duane and West Presbyterian Churches—the two sampled churches that had moved north of Fortieth Street by 1875—continued to dwell south of Fourteenth Street.

Increased residential segregation and the flight of affluent native-born Protestants north of Fourteenth Street make the uptown migration of churches an important indicator both of neighborhood change and of growing class cohesion among congregations. "Twenty-five years ago that portion of New York lying below Canal and Catherine Streets and embracing the lower six wards of the city, were the seat of church power and influence," noted one author writing in the early 1860s. "Now it is becoming a church-deserted district."[84] New Yorkers repeatedly lamented the exodus of downtown churches as morally upright native Protestants were replaced by what they considered a dangerous class of immigrants (many of whom were Catholics and Jews).[85] The blame for the "moral abandonment" of Lower Manhattan lay with a combination of factors, chief of which were the increasing property values that compelled homeowners to sell and move uptown and the changing social character of these areas as the "industrial classes" replaced the leisured class. This process was only

Table 6.7   Church Attendance and Neighborhood Among Protestants:
Residence and Membership by Decade, New York City, 1830–75

Variables: Dates: 1830–39, 1840–49, 1850–59, 1860–69, 1870–75.
Church location: Tip of Manhattan (wards 1, 2, 3), Lower West Side (wards 5,
8, 9, 10, 15), Dry Dock (wards 4, 7), Lower East Side (wards 10, 11, 13, 17),
East Side (wards 18, 21), Upper Manhattan (wards 12, 19, 22).
Area of residence: Tip of Manhattan (wards 1, 2, 3), Lower West Side (wards 5,
8, 9, 10, 15), Dry Dock (wards 4, 7), Lower Center (wards 6, 14), Lower East
Side (wards 10, 11, 13, 17), West Side (wards 16, 20), East Side (wards 18, 21),
Upper Manhattan (wards 12, 19, 22), Brooklyn, other.

Terms of Model (controlled for)	χ^2	χ^2 d.f.	χ^2 signif.	Difference χ^2	Diff. d.f.	Difference signif.	Coef. of determination
All 2-way associations	138.56	180	.9904	—	—	—	—
(Area of residence, church location)	1630.83	225	.0001	1630.83	45	.0001	.9217
(Date, church location)	341.85	200	.0001	203.28	20	.0001	.5447
(Date, area of residence)	257.56	216	.0271	119.15	36	.0001	.4623

Table from modeled data: church location by residence

Church Location by Residence (% down)

Area	Tip	S.R.*	L. West	S.R.*	Dry Dock	S.R.*	L. East	S.R.*	East	S.R.*	Upper	S.R.*
Tip	10.6	2.5	4.1		7.5	2.6	2.1		5.3		1.8	
Lower West	8.7	−4.1	77.1	13.5	8.9	−9.7	9.1	−9.4	11.7	−3.5	6.0	−7.5
Dry Dock	33.7	5.2	1.2	−10.0	46.5	18.3	16.0	2.6	5.3		1.8	−3.3
Lower Cent.	10.6	2.0	2.4	−4.1	14.1	6.6	7.7		7.4		2.5	
Lower East	4.8		3.6	−8.9	15.5		58.5	20.6	5.3		2.5	−3.5
West	4.8		7.3		1.2	−3.6	2.4	−2.7	11.7	11.3	17.3	5.1
East	4.8		2.4	−3.1	1.9	−2.1	1.3	−2.5	37.2		20.1	9.0
Upper	4.8		0.6	−5.6	0.9	−2.4	1.3	−2.3	5.3		40.5	22.1
Brooklyn	4.8		0.6		1.6		1.3		5.3	2.1	2.5	
Other	6.7	2.6	0.6	−2.4	1.9		1.3		5.3		5.3	4.1
% across	2.7		59.5		14.6		13.6		2.9		7.2	
N (Column)	52.0		1165.0		287.0		266.0		47.0		143.0	
N (Table) = 1959.0												

*Standardized residuals: (Observed-Fitted)/SQRT(Fitted). Since standardized residuals are normally distributed, numbers greater than +/− 1.96 are significant to the .05 level. Only significant values are shown.

Source: Sample of Church Membership, New York City, 1830–75 (See appendix A).

natural, given the "shape and position of Manhattan Island," noted Rev. Lewis Jackson. The "lower part of the city must necessarily be given up to business," while the "sides of the city, on the rivers, will be covered with freight depots, warehouses, factories, ship-yards, coal-yards, lumber-yards, stone-yards, etc." As a result, churches needed to seek "for their location the upper and central portions of the city, whither the population is constantly drifting; so that we may reasonably expect the church removals to go on."[86]

With this northward move, congregations that for one reason or another remained downtown found themselves depleted of active members and strapped for operating funds. Their pastors now received letters from members of long standing who declined candidacies for seats in the vestry or requested a transference of membership "owing to the great distance from the church to their present residence." Rare were churches like John Street Methodist that could resist the pressure to move without economic hardship. Many were forced to relocate not once but several times. Only fifteen years after moving to Stuyvesant Square from the Second Ward, the pastor of St. George's Church complained yet again how his church was "rapidly experiencing the results of removal to distant parts of the city and to country residences of many families of our congregation, the influence of which is painful and to a degree injurious to our work."[87] Some congregations tried without apparent success to stem the tide by loosening membership requirements. The West Presbyterian Church asked only that members "living at too great a distance to worship regularly with us" but not connected with another church, "report themselves" once a year either "in person or by letter to the pastor."[88]

The flight of lower Manhattan churches was more than a reaction to changes in the housing market and the expansion of the central business district. It was part of a broader process of adjustment though which churches came to reflect more clearly class divisions within urban society. Church migration was part of an overall withdrawal of the patrician elite that ended, as Amy Bridges has noted, the "civic leadership of the wealthy" and thereby destroyed the previous system that had made every ward a "civic community." By 1845 elite leadership had been almost entirely replaced by professionalized politics and formalized charity organizations, many of which were ostensibly geared toward social control.[89] At this same time, the churches that migrated became "purposefully exclusionary," offering wealthy membership a "surrogate community of harmony" to replace the vanished world based upon social hierarchy.[90]

To be sure, the voluntary church had long been the social institution that most clearly embodied bourgeois class consciousness and helped to define their social niche amidst the growing diversity of New York's population. But membership in many Protestant churches became even more exclusionary after the move to newer neighborhoods. The Rev. Stephan Olin, president of Wesleyan University, warned of the "anti-Christian" separation of classes which occurred when "Rich men instead of associating themselves with their more humble fellow Christians, where their money as well as their influence and counsels are so much needed," combined to "erect magnificent churches in which sittings are too expensive for any but people of fortune." Another minister echoed this sentiment: "It may be, that never again . . . will ignorant and learned, master and servant, rich and poor, feel themselves at home in the same church."[91] That such fears were not unfounded is supported by a comparison between the occupational ranks of members who joined the Duane Presbyterian, the Laight Street Baptist, and the West Presbyterian Churches when these congregations were located south of Fourteenth Street and those who joined after the move uptown (table 6.8). In each church the social composition of congregation members became more exclusive.[92] While only 16 percent of the pre-move members had been classed as professionals, 30 percent of post-move joiners belonged to this group. The proportion of proprietors showed a smaller but still significant increase, rising from 32 to 36 percent. As the ranks of white-collar members grew, the numbers of skilled laborers in each congregation fell from an average of 41 percent to 29 percent, and unskilled workers were now only half as likely to join as before.

The relocation of churches in New York City thus closely paralleled a pattern uncovered by historical geographers in studies of neighborhood church attendance in Victorian English cities. In these cities, "the proliferation of churches and church organizations" first marked "an attempt to maintain a sense of localism." But "over time, processes of selective recruitment" produced "interest groups based more in particular sectors of social or demographic space and less upon limited geographical areas."[93] New York churches that had previously oriented themselves to the local area—such as the Methodist Church which according to Michael Floy had brought a sense of community to Bowery Village—gave way to socially segregated institutions amidst the population shift uptown.[94]

Alternative Voluntary Institutions

With the withdrawal of wealthy inhabitants from neighborhood and association, the working class were left to form their own distinctive community social institutions. Churches continued to play a religious and social role for a minority of devout Protestants and for many Catholics.

Table 6.8   The Reconstitution of Church Membership after Moves: Occupation Rank before and after Relocation, Three New York City Churches, 1830–75

Variables: Pre-move: whether member joined church before or after church relocated*
Occupational rank: professional, proprietary, skilled, unskilled.
Year received into membership: 1830–39, 1840–49, 1850–59, 1860–69, 1870–75.

Terms of Model (controlled for)	χ^2	χ^2 d.f.	χ^2 signif.	Difference χ^2	Diff. d.f.	Difference signif.	Coef. of determination
All 2-way associations	13.56	12	.3293	—	—	—	—
(Pre-move, year received)	87.79	16	.0001	74.23	4	.0001	.8456
(Occupation, pre-move)	23.64	15	.0711	10.08	3	.0177	.4265
(Occupation, year received)	23.75	24	n.s.**	—	—	—	—

Table from modeled data: pre-move by occupational rank

Vertical Rank	Pre-Move (% down)			
	Before	S.R.***	After	S.R.***
Professional	16.5	−2.4	30.0	2.4
Proprietary	32.7		36.3	
Skilled	41.2		29.0	
Unskilled	9.6		4.7	
N (Columns) = 225.0				

*1852 for Duane Presbyterian Church; 1870 for Laight Baptist Church; 1865 for West Presbyterian Church.
**Probability over 10% (.1)
***Standardized residuals: (Observed-Fitted)/SQRT(Fitted). Since standardized residuals are normally distributed, numbers greater than +/− 1.96 are significant to the .05 level. Only significant values are shown.
Source: Sample of Church Membership, New York City, 1830–75 (see appendix A).

Yet these churches were now supplemented by a wide range of less structured voluntary associations ranging from clubs and volunteer fire companies to informally constituted (though structured) street gangs to the saloon, which, like the street corner, made no demands of formal membership.[95] While all of these had existed before, by the mid-nineteenth century they largely functioned independently of patrician stewardship, a fact that would ultimately produce a middle-class reformist backlash against working-class autonomy.

Also emerging was a wide array of social and fraternal clubs, patriotic societies, benevolent associations, lodges, sports clubs, singing and concert societies, and mutual aid groups. Unfortunately, the extent and the origins of their membership can only be guessed without organizational records. As one historian has noted, "The very density of associational activity renders much of that world opaque."[96] Catering to the needs of male sociability were such organizations as militia and target companies—semiofficial associations which combined elements of gangs and secret societies with military trappings. These companies brought together members of particular ethnic groups for military exercises and social "excursions to the countryside" for the benefit of "girl friends, friends, and family," who otherwise were probably more comfortable socializing at church.[97]

Indeed the proliferation of companies manned by antagonistic ethnic groups—one estimate placed the number of such companies in 1844 at fifty—often degenerated into little more than gang warfare, albeit in fancier uniforms.[98] In 1835 two clashes occurred between native-born members of the American Guard, a militia company growing out of the Native American Association, and the O'Connell Guards, an Irish group funded largely by saloon keepers. In one of these, an attack by four or five native teenagers upon the Green Dragon Tavern on the Bowery near Broome Street escalated into a small riot, with gangs of natives breaking windows of Irish-owned stores and dwellings along the Bowery and Delancey Street. When the two militia companies were called out to quell the violence, they instead turned their fists and rifles upon one another, spreading the riot up and down the length of Chatham Street.

Throughout the 1850s immigrants continued to organize their own companies. By 1852, 4,000 out of 6,000 members were foreign-born, including: 2,600 Irish in the Emmet Guard, the Irish Rifles, the Irish-American Guards, and the Ninth and Sixty-ninth Regiments; 1,700 Germans in their own regiments; the Italian Garibaldi Guard; and the French Garde Lafayette attached to the Twelfth Regiment. On the other extreme, 2,000 "American" residents of the Lower East Side joined such stoutly nativist militia companies as the American Rifles and the American Guard.[99] Like many other formal associations including street gangs, the private militia companies appealed to young journeymen and apprentice males, like Abraham Vosburgh, who joined the Native Guard. After he arrived in New York from rural Dutchess County at the age of nineteen, Vosburgh joined the newly formed company and rose through the ranks (largely because of his affability—an asset in democratic companies where leaders were popularly elected) until, at the age of twenty-seven, he became its commander.[100] Other companies included the Tomkins Blues formed from members of Engine Company Number Thirty, the Star Volunteers based in Hose Company Number Thirty-four, and the Tammany Hall Regulars consisting chiefly of Centre Market butchers.[101]

A second important locus of working-class male sociability was the neighborhood-based companies of New York City's volunteer fire department which functioned as "the premier workingmen's social clubs of the 1830's" replete with the "mottoes, insignias, and freshly minted traditions" of fraternal orders. Although their membership originally included a cross-section of their communities, the withdrawal of elite leadership made fire companies more proletarian in character. With this change, polite rivalries between once gentlemanly companies turned increasingly violent. A new determination to show pugilist prowess over a competing company at the site of a fire, rather than saving life and property, would eventually lead to the establishment of a paid, professionalized metropolitan department.[102] Until 1860 the need of firemen to live in the same neighborhood in order to respond promptly to an alarm call intensified the camaraderie of volunteer fire companies that was also rooted in shared occupations. Whether it was the Mechanics Company in the Tenth Ward, the shipwrights' Live Oak Engine Company, or the printer-dominated American Engine Company, each company built upon existing informal social networks to construct formal institutions of local solidarity. Five of the members of the Liberty Hose Company lived in the firehouse at 3 Dover Street, while another member, Alfred E. Smith (the father of the future presidential candidate) shared his residence with another fireman around the corner.[103]

For most working-class males the pubs or porterhouses and dramshops served as the principal social environment, offering a friendly opportunity to "talk about politics and expectorate tobacco-juice" or simply to "vamouse [sic] the ranch.'" If one ran into friends or acquaintances, one could not "ask his friend to drink with him without at the same time inviting all present," lest he be marked as "a mean fellow."[104] In some areas of New York, temperance reformers complained that grog shops were so common that one could be found for every forty-seven men, women, and children. The Fourth Ward alone had 465 such establishments. In two of the twenty saloons located on just one of the neighborhood's blocks, a temperance reformer counted 1,045 people going in and out on a random Sabbath; 450 men, 445 women, 82 boys, and 68 girls.[105] Notwithstanding the outrage of reformers, habitués used saloons more to socialize than to drink. One British visitor who drank in working-class bars was struck by the surprising degree of moderation shown by Americans who proved to be "decidedly more temperate in the use of intoxicating liquors than those of the same grade in Great Britain."[106]

And finally, outside tavern doors, street corners provided a gathering place for loosely organized working-class associations ranging from pugilist street gangs to the Dandies and the Bowery B'hoys. From the 1830s onward, the Fourth Ward was the home of the Buckaroos, the Hookers, the Daybreak Boys, the Short Tails, the Swamp Angels, and the Patsy Conroys. The Tenth Ward, with its many butchers, boasted the Slaughter House Gang (a group that later gained notoriety as daring waterfront thieves).[107] Many of these gangs asserted their identity through clashes with rivals for "control" over territory or settlement of feuds. The well-known clash between the largely Irish "Dead Rabbits" gang and the native Bowery B'hoys for control of the Sixth Ward, fed by popular resentment over the imposition of the newly formed Metropolitan Police, ended only after the militia had been called out. But the importance of these gangs went beyond ethnic animosity because gangs conferred on their adherents "a sense of local loyalty, while reinforcing an ethos of toughness, defense of territory, and masculine honor" that "established individual status and cemented group bonds."[108]

Those various voluntary social communities generally existed across neighborhood boundaries. A riot by members of a Hibernian "Society" in Greenwich Village in 1853 suggests that the distinction between the local social community and citywide networks was a fuzzy one indeed.[109] This particular riot began after a procession by the Hibernian Society startled several horses and escalated into a melee in which thirty-nine Irishmen were arrested. If local ties had been paramount, we would expect members of the riotous society to have inhabited the same tough neighborhood. But when the addresses of those arrested are checked in city directories, their residences turn out to be widely dispersed. For example, James Forrest lived on Delancey Street in the Lower East Side while a laborer, Charles Burns, resided totally on the other side of town on Thirty-second Street.[110] And if gangs are any measure of working-class male sociability, turf battles suggest that community was defined as much by occupation as by geography. In a study of the 1863 Draft Riots, Ivar Bernstein found that rioting manual laborers toured the entire city and demanded obeisance from business proprietors in uptown neighborhoods while the industrial workers and their families focused on "the half dozen square blocks in which these families lived and worked."[111]

The "Bowery B'hoys," although not strictly speaking a street gang, were one of the better known manifestations of a distinctive and self-sustaining youth subculture that developed during the antebellum period. Also an outgrowth of the volunteer fire department system (where many were members), most B'hoys were apprentices to butchers who during their leisure time wore a distinctive costume. This commonly consisted of a "high beaver hat with nap divided and brushed in opposite directions, hair on neck clipped close . . . front locks" which were "curled and greased" (known as "soap locks"), and "smooth face." Such bizarre tonsure was complemented by "gaudy silk neck cloth, full pantaloons turned up at the bottom over heavy fire house or slaughter house type boots and with a girl in the arms."[112] Yet as historians have recently discovered, the Bowery B'hoy was something more: an "*habitué* of . . . the theaters, a sentinel of the new army of unemployed," and "a kind of popular hero, proud of his sporting ways, willing to defend them against all comers with a punkish gaze," and one who functioned not only as a "journalistic stock figure of the late 1840s," but as the embodiment of a distinctively working-class subculture.[113]

Geographically, the milieu of the Bowery transcended local neighborhoods.[114] Because the area attracted youth from the much wider area of the Lower East Side, historians have reconstructed an entire "Republic of the Bowery." This "community" actually grew out of such fictional characters as "Mose" the Bowery B'hoy, a figure who epitomized the "traditional small town and rural virtues that the big city was supposed to have eliminated" such as "independence, spirit, honesty and directness in speech, simplicity in feeling and taste, loyalty and generosity to friends and neighbors." Yet much of the Republic's existence as a social entity seems to be based primarily upon a popular image that is "in large measure, a fiction." Although offering an alternative image to the personality type of the emerging aristocracy of the "Uppertendom" and Broadway Dandy, the Bowery B'hoy existed chiefly as an "ideal type" grounded in a particular literary genre. Few individuals were known to have actually belonged to the group nor does much evidence survive to suggest that occupation or residence was ever important in defining this group, leaving historians to infer their "ideology" from their activity. The key importance of the historian's Bowery B'hoy lies in his embodiment of "a new type from the working classes," one who is "given to leisure and who defines himself through his recreation" in the sporting life of Bowery popular entertainment, cheap dance halls, dime museums, billiard halls, and bawdy houses. The Bowery has thus become "a distinct, even oppositional milieu" to the more fashionable Broadway, and the "republicanism of the Bowery" an expression of "journeymen's fears and aspirations" that stressed "cultural autonomy and manly independence."[115] For working-class women, the Bowery came to symbolize a special milieu that attracted Bowery G'als like Liz (a metropolitan type whose character paralleled that of "Mose"), allowing them to develop their own environment in defiance of middle-class domesticity. The Bowery, it has been argued, "allowed them freedoms similar to those of the prostitute, but that nonetheless advertised their own singularity"—although unlike streetwalkers, G'als were "members of a high-spirited peer group, reveling in their associations with each other."[116] But it should be remembered that the Bowery "Republic" was more a form of sociability—a milieu—than a geographic place. Its essence was not localistic but, rather, the broader aspatial social community of which it was but another institution.

For all of these voluntary associations, then, as for churches, the relationship between sociability and neighborhood localism remains indistinct. Like church membership, association with a militia or fire company reflected factors that went well beyond locale to include not only social class, but also ethnic background, peer pressure, and existing social networks.[117] The Bowery B'hoy, whose identity was linked to locality more than any other social group in New York, was not viewed by startled reformers as "a localized danger" but as a member of a subculture unrestricted by a "single locality or class."[118]

Conclusion

To the extent that neighborhoods cohered at all, they did so through formal voluntary institutions. For the middle and upper classes, these institutions attracted members with shared interests or beliefs. Despite high levels of turnover and increasingly restrictive membership requirements, churches in particular anchored the neighborhood community, not only for the elite of Protestant parishioners but for a wide range of other New Yorkers as well. Irish and German Catholics—even those who were not ardent churchgoers—could define the wider constellation of social ties with reference to parish boundaries. However, with the migration of churches to uptown neighborhoods—an exodus that helped to render congregations socially more homogeneous—working-class residents were left to rely more than ever on informally structured neighborhood organizations. Few poor people ever joined formal organizations; proletarian interaction focused on the beer hall and the saloon, the corner grocery (which also dispensed gin), the firehouse, the contested terrain of the street corner, and, for more and more people, emerging areas of working-class leisure like the Bowery that drew together residents from a wide range of neighborhoods.

Even with the social contacts between classes growing further apart, the high levels of transiency and the operation of the aspatial community make it almost impossible to talk of New York neighborhoods in the late antebellum period as if they were self-contained social spaces. Informal social ties rooted in the unbounded community were often a more important force in shaping social contact than local neighborhoods through which most residents merely passed. The metropolitan character of many of these networks helped to channel people into available housing, churches, jobs, and even gangs through linkages with friends, relatives, and even former neighbors. Such an aspatial community—often constructed out of the flimsiest of social ties—could secure entrance into a boardinghouse or temporary quarters with a friend of a friend. (One such network probably channeled August Buffet to the Fourth Ward where he was murdered during his fateful visit.) That these densely connected networks apparently thrived only in the very poorest of neighborhoods suggests that their absence elsewhere may have been socially beneficial. Ironically, the more closed a community was socially, the more it showed signs of social pathology rather than of mutual support. By contrast, the new loosely structured community constructed out of weak ties, while rooted in the local area, was geographically unbounded and thus better suited to inure New Yorkers to the emerging world of transiency and constant neighborhood change.

7   Conclusion

▮▮▮▮▮▮▮▮ In 1904, less than two decades after the appearance of Ferdinand Tönnies's classic work on the decline of community, American sociologist Thomas Jesse Jones published a pioneering but now obscure study of the subtle interplay among family, ethnicity, and social organization on a single New York City tenement block. The argument he presented challenged the "ordinary conception of an urban population" then prevalent which had treated residents of major urban areas as if they lived "independent of one another in most respects." Jones's findings disputed the view that "the bonds of acquaintance and relationship usually found in the village are not supposed to exist in the city" (*Gesellschaft*) and suggested that "primitive" manifestations of ethnic consciousness—which he labeled "consciousness of kind"—not only survived in the city but, in fact, intensified among tenement dwellers. Indeed, the supposed indifference of urbanites could be found only among the middle and upper classes, not among the working class. Jones anticipated the later work of historian Thomas Bender when he suggested that two separate forms of community coexisted simultaneously within tenement districts: one "in which the group is limited to certain well-defined localities" and another "in which the group is independent of locality, its members being scattered in various parts of the city." If settlement patterns frequently resembled those commonly associated with ethnic villages, patterns of social interaction and local contact operated largely within the confines of the tenement buildings rather than within the broader boundaries of the neighborhood. But a nonlocal set of relations existed as well, "gathered from a wide East Side area, and to some extent from all quarters of the city," and unified by a "common interest" in the same "social organization." Whether through a voluntary institution such as a church or kinship relations or a diffused circle of friends, informal ties developed and flourished even when a family did not "have an acquaintance in the block in which it lives."[1]

These nonlocal ties emerged from residential transiency. The year following the appearance of Jones's study, another sociologist, Elsa Herzfeld, published a monograph on the lives of families living in Manhattan's "Middle West Side." After interviewing twenty-four subjects Herzfeld concluded that "tenants are nomads." The reasons for moving varied. Sometimes it was a "desire for change," sometimes "to have stationary tubs." Other times it involved problems with landlords, the housekeeper's treatment of the children, the condition of the house, the neighborhood "going 'to bad'," if the husband worked in another part of the city, or carfare that was "too great a drain on the family income." But prominent among the reasons was a desire to live "near a relative" or "to be in the same house with a friend": "They move from tenement to tenement, drifting from poorer to better quarters and back again according to the rises and falls in their fortunes. The average length of residence is about a year and a half. Sometimes the families move from house to house in the same block or, again, they change to another district. The families who have lived downtown never move back again. Occasionally, they move to a less congested quarter, to Harlem, for example. In several cases I knew of they bought a small house and lot on the installment in New Jersey."[2]

Both of these studies thus challenged the dichotomy of *Gemeinschaft und Gesellschaft* that once figured so strongly in the writings of both urban sociologists and historians. Linear assumptions about the social transformations wrought in community structure by urbanization largely fell into disfavor once scholars came to understand that these categories were not mutually exclusive. But there is more to the writing of these two turn-of-the-century social scientists than an implicit critique of modernization theory. Both challenged the sociological conception of community that then prevailed by specifically exploring social interaction in urban space. Even more importantly, both appreciated what much modern scholarship seems to have forgotten in its constant search for elements of ethnic or class-based community to fit the "neighborhood of nostalgia": that high levels of transiency modified the social structure of the urban neighborhood community to produce the two different (but often interrelated) forms of community interaction described above. Jones and Herzfeld recognized that these two levels of community imparted special flexibility to tenement dwellers even in the most squalid neighborhoods, facilitating their adjustment to pervasive transiency. This coexistence between community and change became a natural and accepted part of city life for resident and outsider alike.

More than a generation separated the tenements described by Jones and Herzfeld from the neighborhoods discussed in this book. Yet the difference seems small compared to the chasm between their vision of urban neighborhoods and the pessimistic depictions of urban life that historians and sociologists have offered in subsequent decades. As we saw at the outset, an idealized conception of neighborhood couched in terms of insular class and immigrant communities continues to shape our understanding of urban life. Some studies by labor historians have treated the evolution of working-class neighborhoods as by-products of urban industrialism and the ensuing withdrawal of social contact by the wealthy (save for their disembodied presence through the mechanisms of social control).[3] Others have focused on the formation of ethnic neighborhoods rooted in tenements or communities of immigrant homeowners.[4] But as the historical geographer Richard Dennis has noted, "too often we have studied segregation in a vacuum[,] defining groups with insufficient reference to contemporary experience, considering only *residential* segregation and concerned only with the long-term stability of the overall pattern, not with the permanence of individuals within the pattern." Indeed, residential segregation "is only significant if it is a long-term experience of individuals, and if residential segregation is matched by activity segregation." When Dennis probed the basis for residence in nineteenth-century English cities, he discovered not only that elite residents engineered their own self-segregation, but that their withdrawal had forced the poor to develop neighborhood communities of their own in the face of collapsing paternalism. Class-consciousness was thus of only secondary importance in the formation of working-class neighborhoods.[5]

In New York City the relationship between spatial neighborhood and social community—and even the extent of residential segregation—remained poorly defined until late in the nineteenth century. But it is also true that Manhattan land use evolved toward an increased degree of spatial order as the exodus of wealthy from downtown wards transformed residential address into an important badge of rank. Affluent residents followed the lead of Philip Hone in abandoning Manhattan's commercial core to move to newly constructed houses uptown or in more distant suburbs. By contrast, impoverished newcomers crowded into tenements and converted single-family homes located in established working-class areas on the Lower East Side or, as the city's population expanded, on the West Side north of Fourteenth Street. The retreat of old money to exclusive enclaves and the proclamation of newly acquired status helped to reinforce elite dominance. For middle-class New Yorkers who remained in Lower Manhattan, social status defined by occupation and by the accoutrements of wealth (such as uncrowded housing) produced an internal form of spatial differentiation between neighborhoods.

Against this growing pattern of class self-definition, the enormous tide of geographic mobility typified by May Day promoted residential homogeneity. That all classes of New Yorkers marked Moving Day with ritual attested the importance that transiency played in the lives of New Yorkers. Through this flux existing neighborhoods underwent major transformations so that by midcentury, formerly rustic wards had begun to be developed with a speed that contemporaries found amazing. Wealthy merchants, who previously clustered at the tip of Manhattan Island, abandoned their homes amidst the crush of business expansion and moved to newly fashionable districts such as Madison Square, Gramercy Park, and Fifth Avenue. In the place of high-stooped brick row houses rose fancy dry goods emporiums, workshops, or, in districts which remained primarily residential in character, tenements. And with the expansion of the central business district came highly transient neighborhoods which served as the home to an active boarding subculture.

While real-estate development was responsible for many of the changes in areas like the Fifth Ward, the Lower East Side was transformed by the arrival of new immigrants. The resulting ethnic clustering strained the available supply of housing, and the trickle of native Protestant residents uptown turned into a flood with the arrival of the Irish and Germans in the late 1840s. By the late 1850s downtown natives had been nearly overwhelmed by the tide of newcomers. By the mid-1870s, with the arrival of the Eastern European Jews, most of the single- and dual-family row homes had given way to more efficient tenements, and the once-crowded churches, such as those at Allen and Forsyth Streets, were boarded up or sold to new congregations with customs foreign to those who had once worshipped there. The Norfolk-Street Baptist and Alanson Methodist Episcopal churches were both converted into synagogues. Only Greenwich Village, with its high concentration of native residents (many of whom owned their own homes), was able to avoid major change until late in the century.

Despite the increasing segregation, residential diversity continued to characterize large parts of the area south of Fourteenth Street throughout much of the period 1830–1875. While the wealthy rebuilt the institutions of their community into socially more exclusive institutions (observed for example in the removal of churches), the withdrawal of elite stewardship from downtown wards did not leave these areas entirely bereft of upper- and middle-class residents. The older neighborhoods remained socially diverse until after the Civil War, with rich and poor often cohabiting in the same blocks—even if they increasingly inhabited different social worlds. Even with the emergence of occupation as a principal determinant of residence, industrial location and the ethnic division of the labor force ultimately proved to have a greater impact on residence than did social rank. Other measures of wealth were equally enigmatic; single- and dual-family dwellings that employed domestic servants could often be found sandwiched between tenement houses. As a determinant of residence, even ethnicity, which had long been recognized as the bedrock of neighborhood composition, defied clear explanation. An Irish immigrant who arrived in 1835 chose a very different area in which to live than did an Irish immigrant who arrived after the Potato Famine. Demographic differences involving age-at-migration and sex ratios further clouded the role of ethnicity in shaping residence. Only native-born New Yorkers showed any clear tendency toward self-segregation, as an ingrained nativism led them to avoid districts favored by immigrants. The very strength of nativism suggests that the culture of ethnicity may have cut more deeply than class culture.

If the geographical pattern of settlement was often unclear, the ongoing process that created neighborhood identity showed that New Yorkers also lacked common agreement on how the geographic boundaries of their social space were to be defined. In the midst of accelerated change, antebellum city dwellers had to invent a new vocabulary of symbolic space. Initially, they had displayed little awareness of neighborhoods. While the mention of an address might elicit recognition of a local landmark, it produced little recognition of the character of the area's inhabitants except for certain small pockets of rich and poor.

But if awareness generally lagged behind the emerging reality, there were several factors that sharpened perceptions of certain areas. The efforts of municipal government to combat the scourge of disease prompted health reformers to investigate sanitary conditions within neighborhoods, and their findings led to a classification of community by hygiene. That contagion was often linked to the moral character of the afflicted helped to establish a link between social attributes and residential location. In addition, the perceived existence of vice districts with their brazen brothels and houses of assignation, together with vast districts of crowded, malodorous tenements, etched into the minds of middle-class reformers a sharp picture of social space that sorted those living in "sunlight" from those who lurked in the "shadows." Those in the sunlight were wealthy residents who cultivated an air of residential snobbery as part of their emerging sense of class identity. The result was two opposing perceptions of urban social geography: one for the elite that divided the city into areas based on morality and wealth and the other for the working classes that reflected the highly localistic outlook of an earlier preindustrial era.

Though contemporaries' perceptions of community and neighborhood were generally not well-developed, there is evidence that helps to clarify their actual experience of social interaction, and this tends to support the views of Jones and Herzfeld on aspatial community. From charitable records, and records of witnesses to weddings and baptisms drawn from church records, we have glimpsed how urban networks might have operated in city neighborhoods. From them we can see the high degree of flexibility that New Yorkers showed in their informal sociability throughout the nineteenth century. Despite limitations in transportation and communications, residents drew upon ties scattered over a wide geographical area. Indeed, some geographic barriers may have actually aided in communication in a century when it was far easier to cross a mile of water than to navigate a mile of carriage traffic (a pattern which may still hold true in New York City today). Although cities remained essentially commercial in function and "preindustrial" in their spatial arrangement, the functional neighborhood as measured by informal ties extended to the New Jersey Meadowlands and Newark, virtually as far north as Yonkers, and, in the east, to the present-day borders of Nassau County. Only residents of the very poorest areas formed urban villages by confining social contacts to the local area—a fact suggesting that tight-knit local communities were symptomatic of the pathology of extreme poverty, not of mutual support.

While community life may have been more insular in English and American factory towns or in cities where homeownership was common, New York neighborhoods failed to fit the image commonly assigned to working-class communities until much later. The transiency and continual change that characterized neighborhoods indicate that working-class sociability was less tightly confined to the local area than previously thought. Save once again for abnormally poor areas, the workers' community grew out of networks rooted in employment, kinship, and ethnic ties rather than in geography.

Taken together the findings strongly suggest that we need to reassess the meaning of neighborhood communities for other nineteenth-century cities. Though New York City was an exceptional place with high levels of residential density and heterogeneity that may make it difficult to compare with other American cities, similarities to European industrial cities and modern urban areas point to important continuities in the pattern of residential diversity and, particularly, aspatial community over the last two centuries. Such continuities contradict the linear model of modernization theorists that attributed social dispersal to technological innovations in transportation and communication.

With researchers often unable to decide whether to treat the physical layout of towns as the result of "battles" in the transition from commercial to industrial capitalism or as static "monuments" erected by urbanites, much remains that we still do not understand about the operation of nineteenth-century urban neighborhoods.[6] The very concept of neighborhood commonly employed by historians is the product of one particular period and set of circumstances. In the narrow span between 1830 and 1875, cities like New York first witnessed the emergence of segregated areas on the basis of class, ethnicity, and family status. By the late nineteenth century, cities experienced influxes of Southern and Eastern European immigrants who created small ethnic pockets approximating European peasant villages. The self-segregation of native-born residents now turned into the first suburban flight. It was *these* specific conditions that created the spatial typology of the neighborhood immortalized by the Chicago sociologists in the 1920s.[7] After the 1920s, however, this pattern of ethnic residence had begun to fade in New York and other cities. Suburbanization and assimilation of immigrants once again returned class to the primacy it had formerly held in determining urban residence. And so by the second quarter of the twentieth century the "neighborhood of nostalgia" developed with the perceived passing of "community." Only black ghetto neighborhoods and other areas that served as short-term magnets for new immigrants seemed capable of restoring local community as a social agent in cities.

With the "passing" of the old neighborhood, new sociological definitions of community have emerged. Neighborhoods are now seen as flexible entities composed of loose networks that liberated social interaction from geographical constraints. While the "aspatial community" may be overly optimistic as a picture of social life in the industrializing cities of the past, it still has validity despite the high mortality and squalid conditions associated with widening class and ethnic divisions. Harsh conditions did not lead to social decay nor was material well-being a prerequisite for community life.

Indeed, one of the more sensational exposés on New York's seamy side in the late 1860s contained a hopeful description of city life in the midst of otherwise gloomy depictions of neighborhoods for impoverished newcomers. *Sunshine and Shadows* tells the story of a fictitious Vermonter who, before his arrival in New York, saw the new metropolis as a wicked place fraught with peril. Believing the descriptions of reformers and contemporaries who highlighted the abnormal and the grim, he supposed it to be "as wicked as Sodom and as unsafe as Gomorrah in the time of Lot," and he "had prayers offered in the church" to preserve him from sin before he traveled to the city. Although the teller of this story may exaggerate the ease with which strangers adapted to city life, the parable suggests that city life was seldom as bad as the newspapers would have led one to believe and that the openness of informal sociability eased the newcomer's adjustment into neighborhood life:

> As a home it has few attractions to a stranger. Its babel and confusion distract and almost craze. Its solitude is distressing, in the midst of a crowd the stranger is alone. He might live or die without any one's knowing or caring. The distinguished man, or well-to-do merchant from the country has not deference paid to him. He is jostled by the crowd, trampled down by the omnibus, or run over by the market vans. He stands in the vestibule of a fashionable church till his legs tire and his lady faints from indignation, and when he has a seat, it probably is a back one. A short residence in New York changes things wonderfully. Order and harmony seem to come out of confusion. Families find themselves as well protected and as comfortable as in a small town. The loneliness and solitude find a compensation in the independence which each family and person secures. . . . No one will meddle with or trouble him unless he undertakes to make great display. On change, in business, in the social circle, or at church, the style of a man's living and doing harms him not. There is a warm, Christian, benevolent heart in New York, a frank and generous sociability, when one can command it, that is delightful. The family who "would not live in New York if you would give them the best house of Fifth Avenue," after a year's residence are seldom willing to live anywhere else.[8]

Appendix A   A Note on the Method
and Sources Employed in Data Selection

The manuscript census—the bones and sinew of any statistical recon-
struction of life in nineteenth-century cities and towns—has not entirely
freed historians limitations of elite descriptive sources. Nor does census
data, despite its presumed inclusion of every man, woman, and child offer
much freedom, for the scholar becomes a captive to the caprice of legisla-
tors and statisticians who formulated questions over a century ago. Moreover, as sources for community structure, these censuses are singularly
unproductive, serving mainly to reinforce traditional ecological views of
neighborhood that have equated residential proximity with social contact,
and community with the local area. Yet census data provide a valuable
supplement to qualitative sources in the statistical study of ecological
and social aspects of neighborhood if augmented by other, albeit limited,
quantifiable sources.

The 1855 Census

New York State is blessed with a wealth of detailed censuses information
lacking for other states. While the federal canvass only started recording
the occupations, age, names, and ethnicity of every resident in 1850, the
1855 New York schedules already asked for information on the material
of construction and value of each dwelling, the name of each occupant,
the age, birthplace, length of residence in the country, the exact relationship of that individual to the head of the household, the marital status
(including widows), whether the person was a citizen, alien or naturalized,
and miscellaneous information on schooling and handicaps. Furthermore,
unlike the federal canvass, the birthplace data gathered by the state in-

Table A1.1   Population of New York City, Sample Wards, 1830–75

Ward	1830	1835	1840	1845
4	12,705	11,439	15,770	21,000
5	17,722	18,495	19,159	20,362
9	17,333*	20,618	24,795	30,907
10	16,438	20,929	29,026	20,993
Total City	197,112	268,089	312,710	371,223

*Including Ward 15.

cluded counties for those born in New York, the state for those born in the United States but outside of New York, and the countries of birth for the foreign-born. The 1865 and 1875 canvasses requested even more detailed information, but, unfortunately, no copies survive of the schedules for New York County, which included the city of New York.[1]

The sheer numbers of people living in the four wards that provided the basis of this study—wards Four, Five, Nine, and Ten—made sampling essential. In 1855 these areas contained a combined population of 110,846 residents which would have produced a core sample of 11,000 cases at a sampling ratio of one in ten.[2] Yet even this provided more cases than statistically necessary, which led to the selection of clustered random sampling by electoral district within wards. Using these smaller sampling units not only facilitated the factor analysis presented in chapter 2 but also reduced the number of cases in the sample by nearly half. While the selection of clusters selected was not, strictly speaking, a random process, the electoral districts that were chosen formed a "checkerboard" pattern representative of the diversity of each ward. Out of five electoral districts for the Fourth Ward, E.D. 1, 3, and 5 were selected; for the Fifth Ward, E.D. 1, 2, and 5 out of six; for the Ninth Ward, E.D. 1, 2, 5, 7, and 9 out of a total of nine; and for Ward Ten, E.D. 1, 3, and 5 out of five. In several districts where state marshals had divided districts into two parts, only one of these subdistricts was utilized. This included the first part for Ward Nine, E.D. 9; and the second parts for Ward 4, E.D. 1, Ward 9, E.D. 5, and Ward 10, E.D. 1.

The actual sampling was taken at the household level by using random number tables. First, the last numbered household was examined to determine the total number in the sample area. The total number of households to be sampled was determined by multiplying this number by the sample ratio. Once this number was known, random number tables were used to select the desired sample by household without replacement. This yielded

1850	1855	1860	1865	1870	1875
23,250	22,869	21,994	17,352	23,748	20,828
22,686	21,617	22,337	18,205	17,150	15,951
40,657	39,982	44,385	38,504	47,609	49,403
23,316	26,378	29,004	31,537	41,431	41,757
515,547	629,904	805,358	726,389	942,292	1,041,886

a sample consisting of 1,255 households or roughly one in ten.[3] In the case of the fifth electoral district of the Tenth Ward, the sampling ratio was one in five due to unusually rich information on the length of marriage and widowhood from a marshal who had obviously exceeded his instruction.

The procedure for coding the census data was relatively straightforward, but the manipulation of the data sets required a more elaborate procedure. Instead of coding only by head of household, as is frequently done in historical studies, I felt that the greatest flexibility could be gained without sacrificing the integrity of the original data by preparing two separate data sets; one organized by individual for every person living in the sample households and a second "hierarchical" data set arranged by household with each family member listed as a separate variable under a single family identification code.[4] The former sample numbered 5,816 cases while the latter came to 1,255 households.

Hierarchical data sets have the advantage of preserving all individual level variables, while at the same time permitting analysis of patterns of family behavior and household composition. Normally, households are classified by composition when first coded, but this technique is inflexible and freezes the researcher to his initial coding scheme. A hierarchical structure, on the other hand, preserves all the detail of the original data while still permitting not only regrouping and recoding of original data, but also the generation of totally new variables. Since earlier versions of SPSS lacked the capacity to reformat data, the array generating capacity of SAS was employed to generate the hierarchical data set. After first ascertaining the maximum number of individuals per household in the sample districts, the program prepared an array with thirty-five empty slots for each variable, which were filled with information from individuals within the household (for households with fewer than thirty-five members, corresponding slots were left empty). The household number served to tag cases, and after each individual containing that number had been pro-

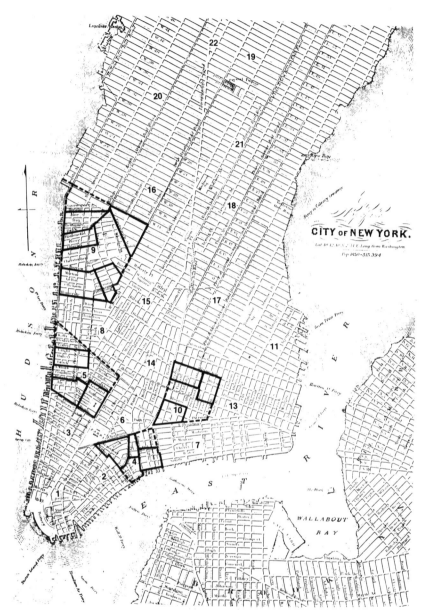

Figure A1.1   Sample Wards and Enumeration Districts, New York City, 1855

cessed the program moved on to the next household. Other information was also added to the household tag including house number, electoral district, and ward, together with information on the type and density of the residential dwelling. By making comparisons between household members within each array, it was possible to study such issues as how age-adjusted fertility differed between ethnic groups or whether immigrant families added new members after leaving their country of origin but before reaching New York. Additional variables recorded the number of nuclear family members, boarders, children, and servants. Dummy variables signaled the presence of parents, grandparents, in-laws, grandchildren, siblings, uncles, aunts, cousins, nieces, nephews, boarders, and outside employees.

Most of the recoding and transformation of variables entailed sorting values by newly defined categories. Length of residence was calculated by subtracting length of residence from the year of the census (1855). Age of arrival was determined by subtracting length of arrival from the individual's age. Birthplace was classified in three different ways: (1) by recorded county of birth for those born in New York State, (2) by state of birth for native-born Americans, and (3) by country of birth. Occupational information, which was the most complicated and confusing variable, was coded according to several different classifications derived from the Philadelphia Social History Project (PSHP): vertical rank, functional category, and industry. While any occupational scheme is far from perfect, coding of the New York data followed the Philadelphia scheme as closely as possible for the sake of consistency. When New York occupations could not be located in the code books of the PSHP, estimates of vertical rank, function, and industry were made by interpolation. Rather than list my entire scheme, interested readers are referred to the published occupational listing of the PSHP.[5]

The 1865 census

While the 1865 state census has long since vanished, published material provided data for a citywide factor analysis sampled at the ward level. Tabularized results offer breakdowns by ward of ethnicity, age, marital status, naturalization, population density, and housing values. Furthermore, other published information lists occupational information for 310 different trades for each of the twenty-two wards which could then be collapsed and reclassified according to the occupational scheme employed with the 1855 census data. These wards were then collapsed into ten broad

Figure A1.2 Broad Sample Areas in New York City, 1855 and 1865. I. Tip of Manhattan, II. Lower West Side, III. Dry Dock, IV. Lower Center, V. Lower East Side, VI. West Side, VII. East Side, VIII. Upper West Side, IX. Upper East Side.

sample areas. This allowed the study of the spatial clustering of industrial employment in New York City at the close of the Civil War.[6]

Vagrants from 1855 to 1856

In addition to reports of crime and police procedure, the two surviving police blotters from antebellum New York City also listed the names of all persons who sought lodging in the Tenth District Police Station during several months for the period 1855–1856. These ledgers contain information on birthplace, occupation, citizenship, race, sex, age, occupation, and literacy. Instead of sampling randomly or by interval, I decided to only select every tenth *day* and record every lodger staying in the station that night. This procedure sought to avoid oversampling "rounders"—those who sought lodging on consecutive nights. Sometime between 1855 and 1856, the Tenth District Station ceased lodging (or recording) men and more than half of the 183 lodgers in the sample were women.

Witnesses and Endogamy

The associational patterns of residents of the four sample wards were studied by comparing the occupations and addresses of witnesses with those whose baptisms and marriages they solemnized. This data was also supplemented with data on endogamy-exogamy derived by comparing the backgrounds of prospective spouses gathered from marriage records. The complex and haphazard nature of most marriage and baptism records made them exceedingly difficult to standardize and code. Many ministers kept track only of the names of the parties, with no additional information save for the date of the ceremony, rendering them useless for the study of neighborhood social relations. The study of proximity of witnesses required address information for both the parents or wedding parties and those who solemnized the ceremonies. Since few ministers recorded much of this information, most cases had to be discarded even after efforts at data linkage through city directories.

The sampling ratio was calculated by surveying every surviving record that could be located for churches located in the four sample wards during the period 1830–1875 and then estimating the total number of baptisms and marriages. Records for Protestant congregations listed approximately 19,635 marriages and 26,220 baptisms while the two Roman Catholic churches located in the area listed an estimated 22,700 marriages and nearly as many baptisms. Differential sample ratios were utilized for Protestant and Catholic ratios. Where one in five marriages and one in forty baptisms were selected for Protestant records, the ratio for Roman Catholics was one in thirty and one in eighty, respectively. These ratios and interval sampling produced a sample of 3,017 cases which were then laboriously checked in city directories when no other addresses or occupations could be found. Even with the use of directories for several successive years, 1,384 cases had to be discarded because of an absence of information on the address of either witness or participant. Furthermore, the witnesses listed in the sample are almost exclusively male due to the absence of residential information for female witnesses.

Nonetheless, the number of marriages and baptisms included in the final sample still tends to exaggerate the level of successful linkages. Some ministers routinely kept careful records of the ethnic backgrounds, ages, addresses, occupations, and previous marital statuses of marriage partners. Furthermore, New York State temporarily required churches to record detailed information in 1854, although this requirement was never fully followed before it was dropped after two years. Only the establishment of a state-administered Board of Health in 1866 standardized and consolidated vital records-keeping. Whenever more detailed records appeared, I tended to oversample. For example, the marriage volumes of Rev. Henry Chase, who was pastor of the Mariner's Church in the Fourth Ward, encompassed thirteen volumes for the period 1830 through Chase's death in 1853 and provided exceptionally detailed data on both endogamy and association.[7] These records were examined at five-year intervals and sampled by taking every tenth entry. Similarly, St. John's Lutheran Church in Greenwich Village—a German congregation—contained detailed records, many of which listed occupations and addresses for multiple witnesses. Here an interval sample was generated by estimating the total number of marriages on each page and then selecting every *n*th page. Then the first marriage on the page was selected where two or more witnesses were present and where at least one of the marriage partners or parents lived in New York City. A similar technique was also applied to the voluminous records of the two Roman Catholic churches. Since most of the names were of Irish extraction that could not be traced in city directories, the first entry was selected where groom or parent seemed to have the least common *first* name in order to maximize the potential for successful links. Although this procedure also ran the risk of biasing the sample, I felt that the risk was still justified and that the biases would be less severe than with the use of uncommon *last* names.[8] Still many of the 1,637 cases in the marriage and baptism sample produced no linked witness.

Church Membership

Formal associations through neighborhood institutions was studied through the quantitative analysis of Protestant church membership lists. An estimated 38,590 New Yorkers belonged to churches that were, at one time or another, located in the sample wards during the period 1830–1875. Interval techniques were used to sample one out of twenty Protestant church members. When churches recorded the origin or destinations of members who were admitted or dismissed through letters of transference, a sampling ratio of one in ten was used. All records—including women— were also checked in several consecutive directories for the dates closest to the date of admission. Although only a fraction of this churchgoing population could be located in city directories (and virtually none of the women were located), the sample included all these members whether linked or not. Among Protestant churchgoers, the sample contained 2,598 individuals. No formal records of Roman Catholic membership were kept because receiving communion was equivalent to membership under the laws of the church. For the sake of comparison, I supplemented Protestant membership records with a sample of Catholic baptisms for which the address of at least one parent was known—although this risked introducing age bias into Catholic membership. The addition of these 223 cases brought the total number of persons in the sample of church members up to 2,821.

Appendix B   A Note on the Presentation and Analysis of Contingency Tables

The use of samples is a necessary practice with large populations, but also one which is fraught with danger; the researcher is never fully sure whether the cases that she selects truly represent the group she wishes to describe. Furthermore, for most social historians and sociologists, data from records such as manuscript censuses is categorical in nature, which precludes conventional analysis through linear statistical techniques, including regression. At best, the fortunate researcher may be able to apply techniques such as Multiple Classification Analysis (a relative of analysis of variance), which requires that the independent variable at least be integral (ordered and scaled). But when available data consists only of variables grouped by discrete categories lacking either a clear order or integral level of measurement, such as ethnicity, religion, family relation, or industrial employment (other than occupational rank), there was until recently little that could be done other than to test for significance in tables. This also meant that only two variables were handled at a time, making it virtually impossible to study the multiple interaction among a number of variables. The advent of multivariate techniques in social statistics and their application to categorical data have opened up a wide range of opportunities for the historian and the sociologist alike. Now it is possible to analyze data in contingency tables through methods which examine the proportional or odds ratios between different cells and which allow the study of interactions involving four, five, or more variables—depending on the total number of cells and programming limitations.

Log-linear analysis and iterative proportional fitting are two of the most commonly used techniques, although one is simply a variant of the other. Both use odds-ratios or, in other words, the odds of having a specific cell frequency in a contingency table given another cell frequency in that table. Thus odds-ratios produce a multiplicative model of the table consisting of the overall level of the table (the total cell frequencies), the odds of being in one category of a variable given another category, the odds of being in a category given the values of an additional variable, the odds of being in a given category given the odds of two additional variables, and so forth. If natural logs are taken of both sides of the resulting equation of effects, we get an additive model of effects resembling equations in analysis of variance (hence "log-linear analysis").[1]

Most computer packages that perform either of these techniques are designed to be interactive allowing the user to methodically investigate groups of associations within the table, testing each effect for significance as one proceeds. With Loglin (from the Harvard School of Public Health), Bigleo (from the Harvard University Sociology Department), or MICLOG (the data matrix—usually the numbers output by a cross-tabular program of a standard statistical package—is fed into the program and checked to insure that no cells have zero values (division by zero is mathematically undefined and many tabular analysis programs like SYSTAT can add small decimal values directly to each cell as a correction). The adjusted table is then examined for the interaction of individual effects. For example, a three-variable table comparing religion, ethnicity, and sex would be scrutinized by testing each combination of relations for statistical significance: sex-religion-ethnicity, sex-religion, sex-ethnicity, ethnicity-religion, sex, religion, and religion. Since this model is *hierarchical*, which means that three-way interactions automatically contain the two-way and one-variable effects, one can experiment with constructing modeled tables that leave out insignificant effects with the goal of producing as parsimonious an approximation of the original table's effects as possible with statistical significance to the 5 or 10 percent level of confidence.

With a few simple commands, the computer program creates a modeled table which includes only the effects requested, and this table can, then, be tested for significance and/or percentaged. When these steps are repeated systematically—comparing each individual paired association with a model containing all the paired associations possible in the table—one can see whether an effect is significant or not. As is the case with the use of chi-square, the determination of significance is actually a negative test of a "null hypothesis" which assumes that a particular effect is superfluous to the overall model and tests if a significant model can be produced without it. A low probability for the chi-square indicates that the probability of creating a viable approximation of the original contingency table without the effect is statistically unlikely.

Using the above example, if one wants to test the significance of the effect sex-religion, one specifies a model which includes associations for sex-ethnicity and religion-ethnicity and tests for significance. Assuming that all second-order effects contained in the original model tested positively to the specified confidence level, one can accept or reject the null hypothesis that sex-religion has no bearing upon sex, religion, and ethnicity. Ranking the chi-square statistics for significant effects allows us to assess the relative importance of each effect compared to others. One can also calculate a coefficient of determination based upon chi-square differences. However this particular statistic is highly susceptible to variations in degrees of freedom between effects and, for this reason, must be interpreted with caution.

Nearly all of the tables in the study have been modeled through log-linear analysis using Bigleo, Loglin, or the "Tables" routine of the microcomputer statistical package SYSTAT. After testing for all the paired associations, a final parsimonious model was produced containing only significant effects. Percentage tables in the text use data from this final model. Tables showing percentaged output together with standardized residuals were computed using either the "hierarchical log-linear" module of SPSS-X or, more commonly, the log-linear routine in the microcomputer version of SYSTAT. Standardized residuals larger than ± 1.96 are normally distributed and, therefore, significant to the 5 percent level of confidence.

In the case of two-variable tables, the values displayed are often unstandardized residuals (e.g., the differences between observed and the modeled data). These residuals were obtained by subtracting modeled data from the original table and the table of residuals which resulted sums to zero across each row and column.

Lastly, when no significant associations emerged in my initial analysis of the tables, which was usually the case when there were a large number of cells for the sample size (the chi-square significance tests presume an average of five observations per cell) I collapsed the table by combining related values. This explains why some tables divide Manhattan into ten areas while others use only four. The collapsing of tables was done in a manner consistent with the overall classification used in coding the data.[2]

Notes

1 Toward an Historical Understanding of Neighborhood

1 Morris Dickstein, "Neighborhoods," *Dissent* 34 (Fall 1987), pp. 602–607.

2 Dickstein, "Neighborhoods," pp. 606, 603. Also Irving How, *World of Our Fathers: The Journey of the East European Jews to America and the Life They Found and Made* (New York: Simon and Schuster, 1976), chap. 6; and Deborah Dash Moore, *At Home in America: Second Generation New York Jews* (New York: Columbia University Press, 1981), pp. 61–87.

3 Jonathan Rieder, *Canarsie: The Jews and Italians of Brooklyn Against Liberalism* (Cambridge: Harvard University Press, 1985), pp. 13–26, 57–94.

4 Kenneth T. Jackson, *Crabgrass Frontier: The Suburbanization of the United States* (New York: Oxford University Press, 1985), pp. 272–282, 289–290.

5 Robert Lekachman, "The West Side of My Youth," *Dissent* 34 (Fall 1987), p. 611.

6 Robert A. Caro, *The Power Broker: Robert Moses and the Fall of New York* (New York: Vintage Books, 1974), pp. 850–856.

7 Dickstein, "Neighborhoods," p. 607.

8 "Text of Speech by President On Plan to Seek Re-election," *New York Times*, Jan. 30, 1984, p. A10:6.

9 "Jesse Jackson: A Clash Within," *Los Angeles Times*, December 16, 1987, p. I:16.

10 For a discussion of the subjectivity of urban structure, see T. R. Lee, "Cities in the Mind," in D. T. Herbert and R. J. Johnston, *Spatial Perspectives on Problems and Policies* (London: John Wiley & Sons, 1976), vol. 2, pp. 159–187.

11 Louis Hartz, *The Liberal Tradition in America: An Interpretation of American Political Thought Since the Revolution* (New York: Harcourt Brace, 1955); David Potter, *People of Plenty: Economic Abundance and the American Character* (Chicago: University of Chicago Press, 1954); Daniel Bell, *Marxian Socialism in the United States* (Princeton: Princeton University Press, 1967), and *The End of Ideology* (Glencoe, Il.: Free Press, 1960); Daniel Boorstin, *The Genius of American Politics* (Chicago: University of Chicago Press, 1953). The significance of consensus theory to labor history is discussed in Marie Jo Buhle and Paul Buhle, "The New

Labor History at the Cultural Crossroads," *Journal of American History* 75 (June 1988), pp. 151–161.

12 Sean Wilentz, *Chants Democratic: New York City & the Rise of the American Working Class, 1788–1850* (New York: Oxford University Press, 1984), p. 10.

13 John P. Diggins, "The Misuses of Gramsci," *Journal of American History* 75, no. 1 (1988), p. 143.

14 Peter George Buckley, "To the Opera House: Culture and Society in New York City, 1820–1860" (Ph.D. Diss., SUNY Stony Brook, 1984), pp. 221–222.

15 See Sam Bass Warner, *The Private City: Philadelphia in Three Periods of Its Growth* (Philadelphia: University of Pennsylvania Press, 1968).

16 Betsy Blackmar, "Re-walking the 'Walking City': Housing and Property Relations in New York City, 1780–1840," *Radical History Review* 21 (Fall 1979), pp. 131–148.

17 Elizabeth Blackmar, *Manhattan for Rent, 1785–1850* (Ithaca: Cornell University Press, 1989), pp. 11–12, 82–86, 89–92, 100–108, 250. Blackmar's arguments have also influenced the writings of other historians on this key aspect of early neighborhood formation. See Buckley, "To the Opera House: Culture and Society in New York City, 1820–1860," p. 225; and Gary Nash, "The Social Evolution of Preindustrial American Cities, 1700–1820," in Raymond A. Mohl, ed., *The Making of Urban America* (Wilmington, Del.: Scholarly Resources, 1988), pp. 24–44.

18 Wilentz, *Chants Democratic*, pp. 26–27. An almost identical description is given in Christine Stansell, *City of Women: Sex and Class in New York, 1789–1860* (New York: Alfred A. Knopf, 1986), pp. 41–46. Both works erroneously locate Bancker Street in the Fifth Ward. To be sure, the Fifth did have a significant black enclave, but New York City at different times had two Bancker Streets, one which became Duane Street in the 1790s and another that was renamed Madison Street in the late 1820s. Kenneth H. Dunshee, *As You Pass By* (New York: Hastings House, 1952), p. 272. This latter area in the Seventh Ward near the intersection with Cheapside [Hamilton] and Lombard [Monroe] Streets became the subject of several epidemiological studies. See John H. Griscom, *A History, Chronology and Circumstantial, of the Visitation of Yellow Fever at New York* (New York: Hall, Clayton, 1858), p. 17; and New York City Board of Health, *Statement of Facts Relative to the Late Fever Which Appeared in Bancker-street and Its Vicinity* (New York: Elam Bliss, 1821), p. 5.

19 Stansell, *City of Women*, pp. xi–xii, 3–10, 41, 202–203.

20 Stansell, *City of Women*, pp. 41, 55–62, 62–69, 100, 202–203.

21 For a discussion of findings and meaning of the new urban history, see Stephan Thernstrom and Richard Sennett, eds., *Nineteenth-Century Cities: Essays in the New Urban History* (New Haven: Yale University Press, 1969). Also see Thernstrom, "Reflections on the New Urban History," in Alexander B. Callow, ed., *American Urban History*, 2d ed. (New York: Oxford University Press, 1973), pp. 672–684, and "The New Urban History," in Charles F. Delzell, ed., *The Future of History* (Nashville: Vanderbilt University Press, 1977), pp. 43–52.

22 Eric H. Monkkonen, *America Becomes Urban: The Development of U.S. Cities and Towns, 1780–1980* (Berkeley: University of California Press, 1988), pp. 24–30.

23 Charles Tilly, "What is Good Urban History?" New School for Social Research Center for Studies of Social Change, Working Paper no. 99 (July 1990), p. 3. Monkkonen contends that the new urban history was less flawed than its critics contended.

To be sure it ran out of enthusiasm when it began to run out of new questions. But important implications have not been followed such as "What does the concept of community designate when only a handful of people remain over a long period of time?" The new urban history, according to Monkkonen, prematurely caved in to criticism "that should have sharpened the researchers, not terrified them." In sum the critics "threw out the baby with the bathwater, and the great pity is that the baby's parents stood by and watched passively." Monkkonen, *America Becomes Urban*, pp. 26–30. Tilly countered by attributing its decline to "a wider disillusionment with formalization."

24   Stephan Thernstrom notes that much of his early work wished to "illuminate the Hartzian question, the question of American exceptionalism." Bruce M. Stave, *The Making of Urban History: Historiography Through Oral History* (Beverly Hills: Sage Publications, 1977), p. 224. See also Peter R. Knight, *The Plain People of Boston, 1830–1860* (New York: Oxford University Press, 1971).

25   Stephan Thernstrom, *The Other Bostonians, Poverty and Progress in the American Metropolis, 1880–1970* (Cambridge: Harvard University Press, 1973), p. 258.

26   Persistence rates for urban communities range from a low of 30 percent per decade in antebellum Philadelphia, to a high of 64 percent in Boston during the 1880s. For a detailed discussion of variations in migration levels, see Thernstrom, *The Other Bostonians*, pp. 221–232. The life cycle and occupational dimensions of transiency are explored in Michael Katz, *The People of Hamilton, Canada West: Family and Class in a Mid-Nineteenth Century City* (Cambridge: Harvard University Press, 1975), pp. 94–134. For Poughkeepsie the rate among male workers ranged between 20 to 40 percent depending upon occupational status. Clyde Griffen and Sally Griffen, *Natives and Newcomers: The Ordering of Opportunity in Mid-Nineteenth-Century Poughkeepsie* (Cambridge: Harvard University Press, 1978), pp. 15–22. One of the more detailed studies of residential mobility is Howard P. Chudacoff, *Mobile Americans: Residential and Social Mobility in Omaha, Nebraska, 1880–1920* (New York: Oxford University Press, 1972). Length of residence has also been probed for Buffalo and surrounding counties in two papers by the York Social History Project. Michael B. Katz and Michael Doucet, "The Determinants of Length of Residence in Buffalo, N.Y., 1855," and "The Determinants of Residential Persistence in Rural Erie County, New York, 1855," Working Papers nos. 10 and 11, in Michael B. Katz, *York Social History Project*, Second Report, November 1976 (Toronto: York University Institute of Behavioral Research, 1976). For persistence among Italians and Jews in late-century New York City, see Thomas Kessner, *The Golden Door: Italian and Jewish Immigrant Mobility in New York City, 1880–1915* (New York: Oxford University Press, 1977), pp. 139–160. All of the above works rely either on manuscript census or city directories for their data. For a qualitative, nonstatistical discussion of English transiency, see Raphael Samuel, "Comers and Goers," in H. J. Dyos and Michael J. Wolff, eds., *The Victorian City: Images and Realities*, vol. 1 (London:Routledge & Kegan Paul, 1977), pp. 123–160.

27   Thernstrom, *The Other Bostonians*, pp. 18–19. These high levels of mobility have been questioned by Richard Jensen, who has noted that such high levels of mobility may be the result of the inadequacy of existing data and the failures of historians to account for immigration outside the country and mortality. See his "Found: Fifty Million Missing Americans" (Paper presented at the Social Science History

Association Meeting, Rochester, New York: November 1980). Also see Donald H. Parkenson, "How Mobile Were Nineteenth-Century Americans?" *Historical Methods* 15 (Summer 1982), pp. 99–109.

28 Stephan Thernstrom and Peter R. Knights, "Men in Motion: Some Data and Speculations about Urban Population Mobility in Nineteenth-Century America," *Journal of Interdisciplinary History* 1 (1970), p. 34.

29 Michael Katz, Michael J. Doucet, and Mark J. Stern, "Migration and Social Order in Erie County, New York: 1855," *Journal of Interdisciplinary History* 8 (Spring 1978), p. 701. A revised version of this essay appears in Michael B. Katz, Michael J. Doucet, and Mark J. Stern, *The Social Organization of Early Industrial Capitalism* (Cambridge: Harvard University Press, 1982), pp. 102–130.

30 For a discussion of high mobility or "tramping" to the disruptive effects of unemployment, see Alexander Kayssar, *Out of Work: The First Century of Unemployment in Massachusetts* (New York: Cambridge University Press, 1986), pp. 111–142.

31 Olivier Zunz, *The Changing Face of Inequality: Urbanization, Industrial Development, and Immigrants in Detroit, 1880–1920* (Chicago: University of Chicago Press, 1982), p. 44. The most prominent historian with the view has been Oscar Handlin. See his *Boston's Immigrants: A Study of Acculturation*, rev. ed. (New York: Atheneum, 1972), pp. 88–101, and *The Uprooted* (Boston: Little, Brown, 1951).

32 Zunz, *The Changing Face of Inequality*, p. 44. For a discussion of urban community and ethnic adjustment, see John Bodnar, Roger Simon, and Michael P. Weber, *Lives of Their Own: Blacks, Italians, and Poles in Pittsburgh, 1900–1960* (Urbana: University of Illinois Press, 1982), pp. 72–73.

33 Stephan Thernstrom, "Reflections of the New Urban History," in Alexander B. Callow Jr., ed., *American Urban History*, 2d ed. (New York: Oxford University Press, 1973), pp. 672–684. For a discussion of immigrant settlement patterns, see Kathleen N. Conzen, "Immigrants, Immigrant Neighborhoods, and Ethnic Identity: Historical Issues," *Journal of American History* 66 (December 1979), pp. 603–615. Also David Ward, *Cities and Immigrants: A Geography of Change in Nineteenth Century America* (New York: Oxford University Press, 1971), pp. 105–123; and Sam Bass Warner, Jr., and Colin B. Burke, "Cultural Change and the Ghetto," *Journal of Contemporary History* 4 (October 1969), pp. 173–187.

34 Conzen, "Immigrants," pp. 603–615. Even when clearly defined immigrant neighborhoods did exist with their assortment of supportive local institutions, the revisionists argued, the high levels of geographic mobility indicated that only a minority of the inhabitants could have remained in such "ghettos" long enough to have benefited from its "institutional completeness." For a discussion of the debate between the rival constructs of the "ghetto" and the "residential melting pot," see Zunz, *The Changing Face of Inequality*, pp. 41–47.

35 An especially sophisticated treatment is offered in Bodnar, Simon, and Weber, *Lives of Their Own*, and John Bodnar, *The Transplanted: A History of Immigrants in Urban America* (Bloomington: University of Indiana Press, 1985), chap. 6. Also Alan Kraut, *The Huddled Masses: The Immigrant in American Society, 1880–1921* (Arlington Heights, Il.: Harlan Davidson, 1982), chap. 4.

36 Lizabeth Cohen, *Making a New Deal: Industrial Workers in Chicago, 1919–1939* (New York: Cambridge University Press, 1990), pp. 30, 51.

37 See Stanley Nadel, *Little Germany: Ethnicity, Religion and Class in New York City, 1845–80* (Urbana: University of Illinois Press, 1990), pp. 60–61, 153–162, on the ambiguous relationship between homogeneity and community.

38 Nash, "The Social Evolution of Preindustrial American Cities, 1700–1820," p. 27.

39 "The question of differences—ethnic and economic—*within* neighborhoods is," Stansell concedes, "difficult to answer" given the lack of ethnic homogeneity. Thus "Economic differences within the working class manifested themselves within buildings and blocks rather than *between* neighborhoods, with the very poorest residents living in sunless rear buildings, cellars and attics and the more prosperous house in apartment on the lower floors." Stansell, *City of Women*, pp. 245–250. Elizabeth Blackmar, who is frequently cited on growing class specificity of neighborhoods, relies primarily upon descriptive sources and early city directories. Blackmar, "Housing and Property Relations in New York City 1785–1850," pp. 260–265, 291, and *Manhattan for Rent*, chap. 3. The little work that has been done on the actual residential composition of New York neighborhoods in the nineteenth century relies mainly upon ward-level aggregate data. See also Paul O. Weinbaum, *Mobs and Demagogues: The New York Response to Collective Violence in the Early Nineteenth Century* (Ann Arbor: UMI Research Press, 1979), p. 137; Robert Ernst, *Immigrant Life In New York City, 1825–1863* (New York: Octagon Press, 1979; reprint of 1949 ed.), chap. 4. Edward Spann's assertion that New York was "crudely organized on the basis of economic class" is tempered by this additional acknowledgment: "segregation by zones was both imprecise and unstable; the expansion of commerce and the growth in the number of poor people was too rapid for either to be contained within an established zone." His evidence is also drawn from either descriptive sources or ward-based analysis of flawed published *personal* property data. Edward K. Spann, *The New Metropolis: New York City, 1840–1857* (New York: Columbia University Press, 1981), pp. 106–109, 456n37. The best systematic, multivariate analysis by Richard Stott warns against the excessive reliance upon class in studying neighborhood development. Richard B. Stott, *Workers in the Metropolis: Class, Ethnicity, and Youth in Antebellum New York City* (Ithaca: Cornell University Press, 1990), pp. 201–211.

40 Jeremy Boulton, *Neighbourhood and Society: A London Suburb in the Seventeenth Century* (Cambridge: Cambridge University Press, 1987), pp. 229–230. Another historian concluded: "one to some extent finds the sort of community that one is looking for or that the records available dictate." David Garrioch, *Neighborhood & Community in Paris, 1740–1790* (Cambridge: Cambridge University Press, 1986), p. 3.

41 Richard Dennis and Stephen Daniels, " 'Community' and the Social Geography of Victorian Cities," *Urban History Yearbook* (1981), p. 21.

42 The wide gradations and complexity of neighborhoods is discussed in Stott, *Workers in the Metropolis*, pp. 202–203.

43 Dennis and Daniels, " 'Community' and the Social Geography of Victorian Cities," pp. 7–23. They note that the concept of community has evolved with both descriptive meaning, indicating a particular social group living in a certain area, and an evaluative meaning, indicating a positive neighbourly quality of social relations and "seems never to be used unfavorably."

44 David Ward, "Environs and Neighbours in the 'Two Nations': Residential Differentiation in Mid-Nineteenth-Century Leeds," *Journal of Historical Geography* 6

(1980), pp. 134–135. See also Frederich Engels, *The Conditions of the Working Class in England* (Stanford: Stanford University Press, 1968), pp. 30–87. This question of perceptions and biases by contemporaries is discussed for New York City in Stuart Blumin, "Explaining the New Metropolis: Perception, Depiction, and Analysis in Mid-Nineteenth-Century New York City," *Journal of Urban History* 11 (November 1984), pp. 9–38.

45   Ward, "Environs and Neighbours in the 'Two Nations': Residential Differentiation in Mid-Nineteenth-Century Leeds," pp. 157–161. Even cities like nineteenth-century Odessa failed to have "neighborhoods in the sense of ethnic and social self-segregated residential areas." Patricia Herlihy, *Odessa: A History, 1794–1914* (Cambridge: Harvard University Press, 1986), p. 272.

46   Paul E. Johnson, *A Shopkeeper's Millennium: Society and Revival in Rochester, New York, 1815–1837* (New York: Hill and Wang, 1978), pp. 48, 52–53.

47   Paul G. Faler, *Mechanics and Manufacturers in the Early Industrial Revolution: Lynn, Massachusetts, 1780–1860* (Albany: State University of New York Press, 1981), pp. 50–56, 221. Faler notes "The composition of neighborhoods" did not come to closely "reflect class" until the 1860s and the 1870s by which time "certain social institutions were more clearly the domain of a single class."

48   Thomas Bender, *Community and Social Change in America* (New Brunswick, N.J.: Rutgers University Press, 1978), pp. 49–52.

49   While mentions of Tönnies and Wirth have faded, the work of Park and Burgess with its ecological underpinning related to class continues to enjoy some degree of popularity. Indeed, it can be wondered whether some of the current interest in the deskilling of urban artisans is an update of older arguments with industrial capitalism replacing segmentation of roles. Robert E. Park, *Human Communities* (Glencoe, Ill.: Free Press, 1952), pp. 18–29, 32–34. For a discussion of Park's writings, see Charles Tilly and C. Harold Brown, "On Uprooting, Kinship, and the Auspices of Migration," in Charles Tilly, *An Urban World* (Boston: Little, Brown, 1974), pp. 108–114. See also Albert Hunter, *Symbolic Communities: The Persistence and Change of Chicago's Local Community* (Chicago: University of Chicago Press, 1974), pp. xi, 5; and John D. Kassarda and Morris Janowitz, "Community Attachment in Mass Society," *American Sociological Review* 39 (June 1974), pp. 328–329. Yet the view of the Chicago school was complex and hardly monolithic. See Leonard S. Cottrell, Jr., et al., eds., *Ernest W. Burgess On Community, Family, and Delinquency: Selected Writings* (Chicago: University of Chicago Press, 1973), pp. 48–49. For a criticism of community decline, see Barrett A. Lee, R.S. Oropese, Barbara J. Metch, and Avery M. Guest, "Testing the Decline-of-Community Thesis: Neighborhood Organization in Seattle, 1929 and 1979," *American Journal of Sociology* 89 (1984), pp. 1161–1188.

50   Louis Wirth, "Urbanism as a Way of Life," *American Journal of Sociology* 44 (July 1938), p. 23. Industrial capitalism was blamed for the destruction of organic community life, as well as the supportive structure of family, village, and neighbors, although other, more sophisticated studies have stressed a dialectical struggle between working-class families and both industrial capitalism and its middle-class reform allies. Ivar Bernstein, *The New York City Draft Riots: Their Significance for American Society and Politics in the Age of the Civil War* (New York: Oxford University Press, 1990); Daniel J. Walkowitz, *Worker City, Company Town: Iron and Cotton-Worker Protest in Troy and Cohoes, New York, 1855–84* (Urbana: Uni-

versity of Illinois Press, 1978); Stott, *Workers in the Metropolis*; and Steven J. Ross, *Workers on the Edge: Work, Leisure, and Politics in Industrializing Cincinnati, 1788–1890* (New York: Columbia University Press, 1985). Such a view demonstrates a tendency to conflate Laslett's picture of family, household, and neighborhood life in preindustrial era with the harsh effects of newly emerged industrial capitalism. Peter Laslett, *The World We Have Lost* (London: Methuen, 1971), pp. 55–58.

51 Herbert J. Gans, *The Urban Villagers: Group and Class in the Life of Italian-Americans* (New York: Free Press, 1965). See also Herbert J. Gans, "Urbanism and Suburbanism as Ways of Life: A Re-Evaluation of Definitions," in Robert Gutman and David Poponoe, eds., *Neighborhood, City and Metropolis* (New York: Random House, 1970), pp. 70–84; John J. Macionis, "The Search for Community in Modern Society: An Interpretation," *Qualitative Sociology* 1 (1978), pp. 130–143; Claude S. Fischer et al., *Networks and Places: Social Relations in the Urban Setting* (New York: Basic Books, 1976), pp. 47–48; Robert Nisbet, *The Sociological Tradition* (New York: Basic Books, 1966), p. 47; and Albert Hunter, "The Loss of Community: An Empirical Test Through Replication," *American Sociological Review* 40 (October 1975), p. 537. Historical and anthropological scholarship after Park and Burgess questions whether preindustrial societies ever truly possessed pure *Gemeinschaft* because of their "internal discontinuities, complexity, and especially because of their dependence on some variant of bureaucratic or associational institutions." Kassarda and Janowitz, "Community Attachment in Mass Society," p. 329.

52 Barry Wellman and Barry Leighton, "Networks, Neighborhoods, and Communities: Approaches to the Study of the Community Question," *Urban Affairs Quarterly* 54 (March 1979), pp. 363–390; Eugene Litwak and Ivan Szelenyi, "Primary Group Structures and Their Functions: Kin, Neighbors, and Friends," *American Sociological Review* 35 (August 1969), pp. 465–480; and Harvey M. Choldin, "Kinship and Networks in the Migration Process," *International Migration Review* 7 (February 1973), pp. 163–175.

53 Ulf Hannerz, *Exploring the City: Inquiries Toward an Urban Anthropology* (New York: Columbia University Press, 1980), p. 261. See also Gerald D. Suttles, *The Social Construction of Community* (Chicago: University of Chicago Press, 1972), p. 46.

54 Lilly and Brown, "On Uprooting," p. 130. See also John S. MacDonald and Leatrice D. MacDonald, "Chain Migration, Ethnic Neighborhood Formation, and Social Networks," in Tilly, *The Urban World*, pp. 226–236. The use of social networks in examining urban neighborhoods originated in anthropology; see J. Clyde Mitchell, "Networks, Norms and Institutions," in Jeremy Boissevain and J. Clyde Mitchell, eds., *Network Analysis: Studies in Human Interaction* (The Hague: Mouton, 1973), pp. 15–35. For other anthropological work on network analysis, see both J. Clyde Mitchell, "The Concept and Use of Social Networks," in J. Clyde Mitchell, ed., *Social Networks in Urban Situations: Analysis of Personal Relationships in Central African Towns* (Manchester, Eng.: Manchester University Press, 1969), pp. 1–50; and Jeremy Boissevain, *Friends of Friends: Networks, Manipulators and Coalitions* (New York: St. Martin's Press, 1974), pp. 24–48. Much of the impetus for network analysis comes from the pioneering study by Elizabeth Bott, *Family and Social Network: Roles, Norms, and External Relationships in Ordinary Urban Families*, 2d ed. (New York: Free Press, 1971). Two useful anthologies, both strong in sociometry, are Samuel Leinhardt, ed., *Social Networks: A Developing Para-*

digm (New York: Academic Press, 1977); and Barry Wellman and S. D. Berkowitz, eds., *Social Structures: A Network Approach* (Cambridge: Cambridge University Press, 1988). For an historical appraisal of the potential of social network theory, see Charles Wetherell, "Network Analysis Comes of Age," *Journal of Interdisciplinary History* 19 (Spring 1989), pp. 645–651.

55 Paul Craven and Barry Wellman, "The Network City," *Sociological Inquiry* 93 (December 1973), pp. 80–84; Barry Wellman, "The Community Question: The Intimate Networks of East Yorkers," *American Journal of Sociology* 134 (1979), pp. 1201–1231; Wellman and Leighton, "Networks, Neighborhoods, and Communities: Approaches to the Study of the Community Question"; Claude S. Fischer et al., *Networks and Places: Social Relations in the Urban Setting* (New York: Basic Books, 1976), p. 32; and Donald E. Strickland, "The Social Structure of Urban Neighborhoods," *Urban Affairs Quarterly* 14 (March 1979), pp. 391–400; R. Robert Huckfeldt, "Social Contexts, Social Networks, and Urban Neighborhoods: Environmental Constraints on Friendship Choice," *American Journal of Sociology* 89 (1983), pp. 651–669; Roger S. Ahlbrandt, *Neighborhoods, People, and Community* (New York: Plenum Press, 1984); and Peggy Wireman, *Urban Neighborhoods, Networks, and Families: New Forms for Old Values* (Lexington, Mass: Lexington Books, 1984), Chapter 3; and Howard W. Hallman, *Neighborhoods: Their Place in Urban Life* (Beverly Hills: Sage Publications, 1984), Chapters 3 and 4. For historical findings on intimate ties preserved over long distances, see Bender, *Community and Social Change in America*, pp. 132–135.

56 "The possibility of a non-territorial community based either on religion or ethnic origin" has become an integral part of recent European urban historical scholarship. Garrioch, *Neighborhood & Community in Paris, 1740–1790*, p. 3. One study of German community in mid-nineteenth-century New York also found that community is "subject to numerous and inconsistent formulations" and that different levels of community can exist. Nadel, *Little Germany*, p. 3. In an analysis of New York bawdyhouse riots, Paul Gilje also noted in passing that: "A sense of community existed that knew no neighborhood boundaries." Paul A. Gilje, *The Road to Mobocracy: Popular Disorder in New York City, 1763–1834* (Chapel Hill: Institute of Early American History and Culture and University of North Carolina Press, 1987), p. 90.

57 Even with the renewed interest of many American historians in the survival of ethnic community, their social theory, terminology, and assumptions remain mired in the sociology of the 1920s and 1930s, not the "new" urban sociology. Olivier Zunz, who recently tried to bridge the gap between the "ghetto" theorists and their critics arguing for the "residential melting pot," still grounded his new concept of "dominance" in the work of the same classical urban theorists who had first equated social cohesion with geographic proximity more than a half century before. Zunz, *The Changing Face of Inequality*, pp. 41–47, 59, 178–195. For earlier reflections of sociological writing on historians, see Oscar Handlin, "The Modern City as a Field of Historical Study," in Oscar Handlin, and John Burchard, eds., *The Historian and the City* (Cambridge, 1963) p. 18.

58 "Mysterious Murder in the Fourth Ward," *New York Times*, September 23, 1853, p.8:3.

59 Garrioch, *Neighborhood & Community in Paris, 1740–1790*, p. 258.

60   Robert A. Slayton, *Back of the Yards: The Making of a Local Democracy* (Chicago: University of Chicago Press, 1986), pp. 8–9.

61   Hunter, "The Loss of Community," p. 538. Also Albert Hunter, "The Urban Neighborhood: Analytical and Social Contexts," *Urban Affairs Quarterly* 14 (March 1979), pp. 267–289. For a more detailed discussion, see his *Symbolic Communities*, pp. 3–16 and 173–197. To some extent, Hunter's formulation also approximates Brian J. L. Berry's "mosaic culture," since both have roots in the work of the Chicago sociologists of the 1920s. Berry, *The Human Consequences of Urbanization* (New York: St. Martin's Press, 1973), pp. 64–66.

62   Ties to the outside enabled these formal organizations "to maintain and enhance local orientation while at the same time integrating 'the periphery' with 'the center,' " so as to form a hierarchy of groups. Hunter, *Symbolic Communities*, p. 189. In this manner, Hunter could accept the existence of neighborhoods as a "social fact" posed by classical urban sociology, while, at the same time, he anticipated the view later popularized by Wellman of urban communities as ordered social interaction, independent of space, which provided urbanites "limited involvement" through ramified social networks. Wellman and Leighton, "Networks," p. 376.

While such interdisciplinary borrowing is not without dangers, Hunter offers a coherent framework for the historical study of neighborhoods as physical, symbolic-cultural, and social entities. The theoretical questions raised by urban sociologists also combats historical particularism, which has frequently produced a body of studies, in the words of one historian, "filled with the stuff of history but so idiosyncratic as to defy comparison or generalization." If sociological theory fails to offer convincing answers to historians, it still can provide the proper questions and techniques for historical sleuthing. Darrett B. Rutman, "Community Study," *Historical Methods* 13 (Winter 1980), p. 30. See also Alan Macfarlane, "History, Anthropology, and the Study of Communities," *Social History* 4 (May 1977), pp. 631–652, and the critique by C. J. Calhoun, "History, Anthropology, and the Study of Communities: Some Problems in Macfarlane's Proposal," *Social History* 3 (October 1978), pp. 363–373. For another effort to apply network analysis to colonial American history, see Linda A. Bissell, "Family, Friends, and Neighbors: Social Interaction in Seventeenth-Century Windsor, Connecticut" (Ph.D. diss., Brandeis, 1973).

63   Hunter, *Symbolic Communities*, pp. 136–139, 67–70.

64   Don H. Doyle, "The Social Functions of Voluntary Associations in a Nineteenth-Century American Town," *Social Science History* 1 (Spring 1977), pp. 333–355, and his book, *The Social Order of a Frontier Community: Jacksonville, Illinois, 1825–1870* (Urbana: University of Illinois Press, 1978), pp. 93–97. Also Walter S. Glazer, "Participation and Power: Voluntary Associations and the Functional Organization of Cincinnati in 1840," *Historical Methods Newsletter* 5 (Fall 1972), pp. 151–168. While this framework of consensual social control has some use in explaining the cohesion of social order, it fails to incorporate primary group action, since a minority of Americans joined such organizations—at least in larger cities.

65   I deviate from his scheme only with regards to the use of voluntary associations as the exclusive "embodiment of local community solidarity," which strikes me as being too narrow a measure of the social community; I supplement this with the informal ties between neighbors, friends, and kin. See Hunter, *Symbolic Communities*, p. 143.

2   Moving Day

1   Remarks of M. Thresher, Marshall, July 5, 1855, Statistics of Marriages and Deaths, Ward 7, Electoral District 6, Manuscript State Census for New York City, 1855.

2   Lawrence Goulding, comp., *Goulding's New York City Directory*, 1875–1876 (New York: Lawrence G. Goulding, 1875), p. iv.

3   Asa Greene, *A Glance at New York* (New York: A. Greene, 1837), p. 13.

4   Only 43 percent of the 626,225 immigrants who landed at Castle Garden, the point of arrival from its opening in mid-1855 until 1865, listed New York as their final destination. New York State Commissioners of Emigration, *Annual Reports of 1847–1860* (New York: John F. Trow, 1861), pp. 288, 240. See also Kate H. Claghorn, "The Foreign Immigrant in New York City," in U.S. Industrial Commission, *Reports on Immigration and on Education*, vol. 15 (Washington, 1901), pp. 449–492. Also Robert Ernst, *Immigrant Life in New York City, 1825–1863* (New York: Octagon Books, 1979), pp. 25–36, 187–190.

5   Graham Russell Hodges, *New York Cartman, 1667–1850* (New York: New York University Press, 1986), pp. 160–163, and "May Day in Manhattan" *Seaport* 21, no. 4 (Spring 1988), pp. 29–33.

6   James Boardman cited in Bayard Still, *Mirror for Gotham As Seen by Contemporaries from Dutch Days to the Present* (New York: New York University Press, 1956), p. 114.

7   Mrs. Felton, *American Life: A Narrative of Two Years' City and Country Residence in the United States* (London: Simpkin, Marshall, 1842), p. 54.

8   Elizabeth Blackmar, *Manhattan for Rent, 1785–1850* (Ithaca: Cornell University Press, 1989), pp. 213–219.

9   Gary Nash, "The Social Evolution of Preindustrial American Cities, 1700–1820," in Raymond A. Mohl, ed., *The Making of Urban America* (Wilmington, Del.: Scholarly Resources, 1988), p. 31. Also Stuart M. Blumin, *The Urban Threshold: Growth and Change in a Nineteenth-Century American Community* (Chicago: University of Chicago Press, 1976), p. 46.

10   Howard B. Rock, *Artisans of the New Republic: The Tradesmen of New York City in the Age of Jefferson* (New York: New York University Press, 1979), pp. 242–247. See also Sean Wilentz, *Chants Democratic: New York City & the Rise of the American Working Class, 1788–1850* (New York: Oxford University Press, 1984), pp. 35, 52–53.

11   Edward K. Spann, *The New Metropolis: New York City, 1840–1857* (New York: Columbia University Press, 1981), pp. 18–19. Spann's view largely anticipates that of David Garrioch on local community in eighteenth-century Paris. Garrioch argued that while the rapid influx of newcomers "changed the patterns of sociability, particularly in the central districts," it was the "growth in residential mobility and in the quantity of traffic, both pedestrian and vehicular," which spread "new individualistic ideals of privacy and delicacy in family and social behaviour" that relegated the once dominant "collective values of the local community" to that of a " 'sub-culture." The rediscovery of "working-class communities of the nineteenth and twentieth centuries" was merely a rediscovery of the "heirs" to these local communities. David Garrioch, *Neighborhood & Community in Paris, 1740–1790* (Cambridge: Cambridge University Press, 1986), p. 254.

12   This was also the case in European cities where "migration could be an admission

of failure" or "also provide a new start." Garrioch, *Neighborhood & Community in Paris, 1740–1790*, p. 228.

13   Allan Nevins, ed., *The Diary of Philip Hone* (New York: Dodd, Mead 1927) vol. 1, pp. 201–202.

14   Nevins, *The Diary of Philip Hone*, vol. 2, p. 703.

15   Peter George Buckley, "To the Opera House: Culture and Society in New York City, 1820–1860" (Ph.D. diss., SUNY Stony Brook, 1984), pp. 224–225.

16   The same process of neighborhood change that enhanced consciousness of community also pointed to the relatively low levels of attachment which many residents felt toward the areas in which they lived. Local attachment can be used to measure the extent of community. The nature of these local bonds was, in itself, complex and multidimensional. Claude Fischer, *Networks and Places: Social Relations in the Urban Setting* (New York: Free Press, 1977), pp. 155–158.

17   Allan Nevins and Milton Halsy Thomas, eds., *The Diary of George Templeton Strong* (New York: Octagon Press, 1974), vol. 1, p. 321. Community attachments, of course, occurs at different levels and at different strengths. See Jeffrey S. Slovak, "Attachments in the Nested Community: Evidence from a Case Study," *Urban Affairs Quarterly* 21 (1986), pp. 575–597, and Roger S. Ahlbrandt, *Neighborhoods, People, and Community* (New York: Plenum Press, 1984) pp. 39–54.

18   Edward Lubitz, "The Tenement House Problem in New York City and the Movement for Its Reform, 1856–1867" (Ph.D. diss., New York University, 1970), p. 135.

19   [Seba Smith], *May-Day in New York: Or House Hunting and Moving* (New York: Burgess, Stringer, 1845), p. 48. Graham Hodges suggests that this tableau occurred in Greenwich Village, although Seba Smith is unclear about the particular location. Hodges, *New York Cartman, 1667–1850*, p. 163.

20   Susan G. Davis, *Parades and Power: Street Theater in Nineteenth-Century Philadelphia* (Philadelphia: Temple University Press, 1986), pp. 35, 42.

21   Hodges, *New York Cartman, 1667–1850*, pp. 161–163.

22   Blumin also cautions that such information "only suggests whether a particular cluster of families and individuals actually functioned as a real and significant social group." Blumin, *The Urban Threshold*, pp. 108–109. David Ward similarly warns that high levels of mobility might also serve to undercut spatial differentiation. David Ward, "Environs and Neighbours in the 'Two Nations' Residential Differentiation in Mid-Nineteenth-Century Leeds," *Journal of Historical Geography* 6 (1980), p. 147.

23   New York Association for Improving the Condition of the Poor, *Twenty-Second Annual Report* (New York, 1865), p. 80.

24   Sam Bass Warner, Jr., *The Private City: Philadelphia in Three Periods of its Growth* (Philadelphia: University of Pennsylvania Press, 1973), p. 50. Although Warner's description of Philadelphia describes a city whose crisscrossing alleyways precluded the formation of areas set aside exclusively for the wealthy, a situation distinct from that of New York where wealthy clusters had already begun to form west of Broadway in the late eighteenth century, wealthy and middle-class residents continued to commingle with residents of lesser means well into the nineteenth century. Stuart M. Blumin, *The Emergence of the Middle Class: Social Experience in the American City, 1760–1900* (Cambridge: Cambridge University Press, 1989), p. 46.

25   W. Frothingham, "Stewart, and the Dry Goods Trade in New York," *Continental*

Monthly 2 (1862), p. 528. For an historical discussion of commercial segregation in Jacksonian cities, see Blumin, *The Emergence of the Middle Class*, pp. 85–87.

26 Floyd M. Shumway, *Seaport City: New York in 1775* (New York: South Street Seaport Museum, 1975), p. 5.

27 Martyn J. Bowden, "The Growth of the Central Business Districts in Large Cities," in Schnore and Lampard, *The New Urban History*, pp. 83–85.

28 Allan Pred, *The Spatial Dynamics of U.S. Urban-Industrial Growth, 1800–1914* (Cambridge: MIT Press, 1966), p. 197.

29 Nan A. Rothschild, *New York City Neighborhoods: The 18th Century* (San Diego: Academic Press, 1990), pp. 3–4, 8, 18–21, 89–90, 102, 126, 130–133, 182–183.

30 Bruce M. Wilkenfeld, "New York City Neighborhoods, 1730," *New York History* 57 (1976), pp. 165–182.

31 Carl Abbott, "The Neighborhoods of New York, 1760–1775," *New York History* 55 (1974), p. 51.

32 Blackmar, *Manhattan for Rent*, chap. 3.

33 Pred, *The Spatial Dynamics of U.S. Urban-Industrial Growth*, pp. 207, 211. For a discussion of intra-urban transportation conditions at this time, see Glen E. Holt, "The Changing Perceptions of Urban Pathology: An Essay on the Development of Mass Transit in the United States," in Kenneth T. Jackson and Stanley K. Schultz, eds., *Cities in American History* (New York: Alfred A. Knopf, 1972), pp. 324–343.

34 New York City Common Council, *Report of a Special Committee, Appointed on Greenwich Village in Common Council, September 7, 1818* (New York: Thomas P. Low, 1818), p. 1. For a discussion of the city's role in street paving, see Jon C. Teaford, *The Municipal Revolution in America: Origins of Modern Urban Government, 1650–1825* (Chicago: University of Chicago Press, 1975). Not all Greenwich residents approved of the growth. See Hendrik Hartog, *Public Property and Private Power: The Corporation of the City of New York in American Law, 1730–1830* (Chapel Hill: University of North Carolina Press, 1983), p. 163.

35 Lindsay Denison and Max Fischell, *Villages and Hamlets Within New York City* (New York: New York Evening World, 1925), p. 18.

36 Smith, *May Day*, p. 40.

37 Kenneth T. Jackson, "Urban Deconcentration in the Nineteenth Century: A Statistical Inquiry," in Leo F. Schnore and Eric E. Lampard, *The New Urban History: Quantitative Explorations by American Historians* (Princeton: Princeton University Press, 1975), p. 120.

38 Jackson, "Urban Decentralization," pp. 135–138.

39 The very effort of interpolating changes in urban social structure from patterns of residential location may be reductionist and therefore misleading. Apparent shifts in the land use may actually mask more subtle shifts in social relations apparent only upon closer examination of changes in the rental housing market. Betsy Blackmar, "Re-walking the 'Walking City': Housing and Property Relations in New York City, 1780–1840," *Radical History Review* 21 (Fall 1979), p. 132.

40 Charles Lockwood, *Manhattan Moves Uptown: An Illustrated History* (Boston: Houghton Mifflin, 1976), pp. xvii–xxi.

41 Richard Dennis and Stephen Daniels, " 'Community' and the Social Geography of Victorian Cities," *Urban History Yearbook* (1981), p. 8.

42 Olivier Zunz, *The Changing Face of Inequality: Urbanization, Industrial Development, and Immigrants in Detroit, 1880–1920* (Chicago: University of Chicago

Press, 1982), pp. 57, 81. In his use of the concept of "dominance" Zunz, like other urban historians, merely follows in the footsteps of social scientists who have long sought to establish the universality of "physical isolation of differing populations" as an "inevitable concomitant" to urbanism that "characterizes both the pre-industrial and the industrial city, both the laissez-faire and the planned, both the capitalist and the socialist." D. W. G. Timms, *The Urban Mosaic: Towards a Theory of Residential Differentiation* (Cambridge: Cambridge University Press, 1971), p. 2.

43   See R. L. Johnston, *Urban Residential Patterns: An Introductory Review* (New York: Prager Publishers, 1972), p. 24. Also Walter Firey, "Sentiment and Symbolism as Ecological Variables," in Scott and Ann L. Greer, eds., *Neighborhood and Ghetto* (New York: Basic Books, 1974), pp. 269–283; Carl-Gunnar Janson, "Factorial Social Ecology: An Attempt at Summary and Evaluation," *Annual Review of Sociology* 6 (1980), p. 436; Michael J. White, *American Neighborhoods and Residential Differentiation* (New York: Russell Sage Foundation, 1987), pp. 64–81; and B. T. Robson, *Urban Analysis: A Study of City Structure with Special Reference to Sunderland* (Cambridge: Cambridge University Press, 1969), pp. 46–47. The use of factorial ecology to trace the transition from preindustrial to modern has been criticized as tautological. See three articles by David Ward: "The Internal Spatial Differentiation of Immigrant Residential Districts," in Northwestern University, Department of Geography, *Special Publication Number 3* (1970), pp. 24–42; *Cities and Immigrants: A Geography of Change in Nineteenth Century America* (New York: Oxford University Press, 1971), pp. 105–121; "Victorian Cities: How Modern?" *Journal of Historical Geography* 1 (1975), p. 151. For historical uses of factorial ecology, see Kathleen Neils Conzen, "Patterns of Residence in Early Milwaukee," in Leo F. Schnore and Eric E. Lampard, *The New Urban History: Quantitative Explorations by American Historians* (Princeton: Princeton University Press, 1975), pp. 148–150; and Peter G. Goheen, *Victorian Toronto, 1850 to 1900: Patterns and Process of Growth* (Chicago: University of Chicago Press, 1970), pp. 31–43, 109–114.

44   In contemporary society, three basic factors were presumed to operate independently of one another (orthogonal in their relationship), reflecting the bureaucratic social order imposed by industrialization and urban growth. Their relative presence and absence in different neighborhoods, by comparing one with another, could thus be used to study urban spatial order and, more importantly, as a crucial measure of modernization in cities. Timms, *The Urban Mosaic*, pp. 146–149. For an excellent and cogent discussion of the use of factor analysis in the historical study of cities, see Richard Dennis, *English Industrial Cities of the Nineteenth Century* (Cambridge: Cambridge University Press, 1984), pp. 3, 208–210, 240–249.

45   Goheen, *Victorian Toronto, 1850 to 1900*, pp. 31–43, 109–114. Garrioch, however, argues "social area analysis" is "unsatisfactory" because the "extent and the nature of the 'community' thus mapped depend very much on predetermined categories, and will vary according to the specific criteria chosen. In other words, one to some extent finds the sort of community that one is looking for or that the records available dictate." While this may be true, an approach that accepts overlapping definitions of community still allows "social area analysis" a useful role in examining the ecological dimension of community, perhaps even challenging spatially based definitions of community. Garrioch, *Neighborhood & Community in Paris, 1740–1790*, p. 3.

46   D. W. G. Timms, *The Urban Mosaic*, pp. 133–136. See also David Ward, "Immigration: Settlement Patterns and Spatial Distribution," in Stephan Thernstrom, *Harvard Encyclopedia of American Ethnic Groups* (Cambridge: Harvard University Press, 1980), pp. 496–508. Since factor analysis is capable of reducing a confusing array of variables (indicants) into a smaller and more manageable number of descriptive factors, practitioners of social area analysis have utilized this statistical tool to explore the role of family, ethnicity, and class in residential decision-making (despite its complexity and the difficulty in interpretation which its findings commonly present). Janson, "Factorial Social Ecology," p. 439; and Albert Hunter, *Symbolic Communities: The Persistence and Change of Chicago's Local Community* (Chicago: University of Chicago Press, 1974), p. 24.

47   Konrad H. Jarausch and Kenneth A. Hardy, *Quantitative Methods for Historians: A Guide to Research, Data, and Statistics* (Chapel Hill: University of North Carolina Press, 1991), pp. 176–178. Loadings of factor analysis can be rendered as graphs whose axes represent multiple factors. One can maximize the portion of available variance accounted for by these factors by rotating the axis to remove negligible factors—in effect, fine-tuning the analysis to simplify the results. The popular rotation known as "VARIMAX" is used in the analysis presented here. Leland Wilkinson, *SYSTAT: The System for Statistics*, Statistics Volume (Evanston, Ill.: Systat, 1990), pp. 68–79.

48   My concerns were to describe the nature of social interaction, cognitive awareness, and, in the bulk of the quantitative analysis, to chart the transition from the heterogeneity of a walking city to the higher degree of differentiation which ecologists theorized occurred during the mid-nineteenth century. The analysis relies upon four areas cluster-sampled by political ward. The ward is admittedly an imprecise unit of measurement which, as an artificial political entity, need not bear any resemblance to a "natural" area or neighborhood which it might overlap. And while it is doubtful that any of the wards in the sample constituted a socially complete "neighborhood," with some probably containing only small clusters of community, the extent to which one area differed from another—even with such a broad unit of analysis—should indicate an overall pattern of social differentiation. The four wards that were chosen all lay in the city south of Fourteenth Street, a section that had already been developed by the 1830s. Together, these areas housed 32 percent of New York's inhabitants in 1830, although this figure would drop to 12 percent by 1875, as the center of population moved north. For a discussion of sampling and the difficulty in using ward boundaries for the study of urban neighborhoods, see Zunz, *The Changing Face of Inequality*, pp. 21–27.

49   In this regard the high degree of linkage across the constructs for each of the remaining factors suggests that in 1855, New York City's spatial evolution had reached only an intermediate stage in its development. Timms, *The Urban Mosaic*, p. 146.

50   We could speculate that the subdivision of row houses, the sprouting of scores of new tenements, and the encroachment of warehouses in New York's densely populated lower wards during the 1840s and 1850s made residence in a single-family dwelling a luxury enjoyed only by the stable, native inhabitants who remained—or were trapped—in these changing neighborhoods. Furthermore, given Manhattan's chronic housing shortage, the private home told more about status and wealth than about occupational rank. Thus white-collar employment and the ability to afford servants might have functioned to internally differentiate residence by dividing

rich from poor *within* socially diverse districts such as the Lower East Side. But the presence of other apparently unrelated indicants (including high levels of fertility, property ownership, residential stability, and single men and women) make such speculation risky.

51 The measures of class used in the factor analysis are, it should be pointed out, structural rather than cultural. They partially overlap the bases for class distinction offered by Blackmar, which included property ownership, the employment of servants, the condition and quality of housing, ideology of domestic respectability, and the ability to use housing for profit. Blackmar, *Manhattan for Rent*, chap. 4, conclusion. While my data does not dispute either the changing nature of property relations as class differences widened or cultural distinctions between class, it nonetheless questions its ecological importance. Individual decision on the basis of ethnic preference, social networks, and familial preference often served to smooth the harsh edges of class residence. The restriction of housing supply to enhance profits and the proliferation of tenements, in other words, did not automatically lead to greater residential homogeneity. For further cultural discussions of class, see Christine Stansell, *City of Women: Sex and Class in New York, 1789–1860* (New York: Alfred A. Knopf, 1986), chaps. 3 and 4; and Wilentz, *Chants Democratic*, pp. 10, 14–17, 25–27, 48–55. See also Spann, *The New Metropolis*, pp. 108–109.

52 This principal-component factor analysis with presumed orthogonal factor solutions (independence between factors) rotated by the varimax criteria produced seven factors accounting for over 90 percent of the explained variance.

53 The manuscript schedules for Manhattan have been lost, but ward-level aggregate data found in unusually detailed published tables for New York County still produced twenty-three indicants for a citywide factor analysis of residence; Franklin B. Hough, *Statistics of Population of the City and County of New York as Shown by the State Census of 1865* (New York: New York Printing, 1866). The census of 1865 may well have been the least accurate one ever taken for New York City, missing an estimated 15 percent of the population who continued to hide from draft boards and tax collectors in the months following the end of the Civil War. Contemporaries were well aware of this wartime census's phenomenal undercount, which showed an actual drop in the city's population of nearly 80,000. A recount of the Seventeenth Ward taken just two years later by the Metropolitan Police showed a population of 95,091 compared with 79,563 for the state canvas, or an improbable increase of 15,528. If the remaining wards had experienced the same proportion of uncounted, then the entire population should have been 865,000 instead of 726,389. See New York Association for Improving the Condition of the Poor, *Twenty-Third Annual Report* (1867), p. 26.

54 Historical studies of other antebellum cities like Hamilton, Canada West, have suggested that "residential patterns blurred the otherwise sharp divisions among social groups," leaving boundaries between such groups "surprisingly ambiguous." Ian Davey and Michael Doucet, "The Social Geography of a Commercial City, ca. 1853," in Michael Katz, *The People of Hamilton, Canada West: Family and Class in a Mid-Nineteenth Century City* (Cambridge: Harvard University Press, 1975), p. 334.

55 Zunz notes at the onset that "most of our understanding of the urban past and many generalizations about it come from . . . the commercial walking city of the early nineteenth-century Eastern Seaboard or the crowded giant industrial metropolis of

the twentieth century" that were quite different from Detroit. Zunz, *The Changing Face of Inequality*, p. 41.

56   Evidence from Philadelphia also suggests that the placement of industry and the socioeconomic division of land served to very forcefully shape residential location even *after* the arrival of Germans and Irish, leading to clustering by employment rather than by "ethnic dominance." Stephanie W. Greenberg, "Industrial Location and Ethnic Patterns in an Industrializing City: Philadelphia, 1880," in Hershberg, ed., *Philadelphia*, pp. 204–229.

57   Katz, *The People of Hamilton*, p. 119. The sociological study of geographical mobility has commended considerably more attention. See P. Neal Ritchie, "Explanations of Migration," *Annual Review of Sociology* 2 (1976), pp. 363–404; John S. and Leatrice D. MacDonald, "Chain Migration, Ethnic Neighborhood Formation, and Social Networks," in Charles Tilly, *An Urban World* (Boston: Little, Brown, 1974), pp. 226–236; and in the same volume, Charles Tilly and C. Harold Brown, "On Uprooting, Kinship, and the Auspices of Migration," pp. 108–133. Also Harvey M. Choldin, "Kinship and Networks in the Migration Process," *International Migration Review* 7 (February 1973), pp. 163–175.

58   Historians have recognized the existence of regional chains of geographical mobility in which labor exchanges, tramping, and trade ticketing directed workers to jobs in surrounding communities and regional industries. Wilentz, *Chants Democratic*, pp. 52–53. On the metropolitan development of industry within the vicinity of New York City, see Richard Stott, *Workers in the Metropolis: Class, Ethnicity, and Youth in Antebellum New York City* (Ithaca: Cornell University Press, 1990), pp. 24–33.

59   Christine Stansell, *City of Women: Sex and Class in New York, 1789–1860* (New York: Alfred A. Knopf, 1986), pp. 55–56, 242n12, 245–250. Wilentz noted that one half of masters stayed in the city from one decade to the next and one out of six at the same address. Wilentz, *Chants Democratic*, p. 35. Stott cites somewhat lower figures of 38 percent for Germans and 43 percent for Irish between 1850 and 1859. Jay P. Dolan, *The Immigrant Church: New York's Irish and German Catholics, 1815–1865* (Baltimore: Johns Hopkins University Press, 1975), pp. 39–41. See also Thomas Dublin, "Rural-Urban Migrants in Industrial New England: The Case of Lynn, Massachusetts, in the Mid-Nineteenth Century," *Journal of American History* 73 (1986), pp. 623–644.

60   John Bodnar, Roger Simon, and Michael P. Weber, *Lives of Their Own: Blacks, Italians, and Poles in Pittsburgh, 1900–1960* (Urbana: University of Illinois Press, 1982), pp. 216–217.

61   Historians have tried to study mobility through the use of city directories and census, these sources have presented enormous difficulties in terms of linkage. A growing amount of literature exists on how to link records, with E. A. Wrigley, ed., *Identifying People in the Past* (London: Arnold, 1973) standing as a basic work. See also Dennis Kelly, "Linking Nineteenth-Century Manuscript Census Records: A Computer Strategy," *Historical Methods Newsletter* 7 (March 1974), pp. 72–82; and Charles Stephenson, "Tracing Those Who Left: Mobility Studies and the Soundex Indexes to the U.S. Census," *Journal of Urban History* 1 (1974), pp. 73–84. A pioneering mobility study employing extensive linkage was Howard Chudacoff, *Mobile Americans: Residential and Social Mobility in Omaha, 1880–1920* (New York: Oxford University Press, 1972). In the last decade record linkage has been refined

by elaborate and well-funded social history projects, most notably for Hamilton, Ontario, and Philadelphia. See Michael Katz and John Tiller, "Record Linkage for Everyman: A Semi-Automated Process," *Historical Methods Newsletter* 5 (Sept. 1972), pp. 114–150; and Michael B. Katz, *The People of Hamilton*, pp. 349–352. An even more ambitious effort was conducted by a team led by Theodore Hershberg for Philadelphia. See Theodore Hershberg, Alan Burstein, and Robert Dockhorn, "Record Linkage," *Historical Methods Newsletter* 9, nos. 2–3 (1976), pp. 99–137. For the use of city directories, see Sidney Goldstein, *Patterns of Mobility, 1910–1950: The Norristown Study* (Philadelphia: University of Pennsylvania Press, 1971). For historical use of city directories, see Peter R. Knights, *The Plain People of Boston, 1830–1860: A Study in City Growth* (New York: Oxford University Press, 1971), pp. 127–131; Stephan Thernstrom, *The Other Bostonians: Poverty and Progress in the American Metropolis, 1880–1970* (Cambridge: Harvard University Press, 1973), pp. 280–288; Richard Jensen, "Found: Fifty Million Missing Americans" (Paper Presented at the Social Science History Association Meeting, Rochester, New York, November 1980); John Modell, "The People of a Working-Class Ward: Reading, Pennsylvania, 1850," *Journal of Social History* 5 (1971), p. 81; and John Bodnar, Roger Simon, and Michael P. Weber, *Lives of Their Own: Blacks, Italians, and Poles in Pittsburgh, 1900–1960* (Urbana: University of Illinois Press, 1982), pp. 216–220, 119–129.

62 Dolan, *The Immigrant Church*, pp. 39–41.

63 For other uses of church records, see Robert E. Bieder, "Kinship as a Factor in Migration," *Journal of Marriage and Family* 35 (1973), pp. 429–438.

64 The strength of metropolitan ties is not surprising given Howard Rock's findings that out of 132 mechanics on watch lists, 21 percent had been born in New York City, 35 percent in New York State, 30 percent in New Jersey, 9 percent in New England, 1 percent in Pennsylvania and Virginia, and 7 percent abroad. Howard B. Rock, *Artisans of the New Republic: The Tradesmen of New York City in the Age of Jefferson* (New York: New York University Press, 1979), pp. 242–247.

65 The sample size was too small to permit analysis of the impact of employment in different industries upon destination.

66 Previous membership in other congregations also affected the direction of move. For those for whom both a place of origin and a destination are known, many merely transferred to another congregation in their same neighborhood or returned to their old churches in their previous neighborhood or town. Suburbanites were most likely to move back to their church of origin.

67 Jackson, "Urban Decentralization," pp. 114–115, 134, and his *Crabgrass Frontier: The Suburbanization of the United States* (New York: Oxford University Press, 1985), pp. 25–33. That such suburban trends were linked to emerging middle-class self-definition is discussed in Blumin, *The Emergence of the Middle Class*, pp. 149–150, 275–285.

68 Franklin D. Scott, trans. and ed., *Baron Klinkowstrom's America 1818–1820* (Evanston, Ill.: Northwestern University Press, 1952), p. 75.

69 Greene, *A Glance at New York*, p. 260; and Jackson, *Crabgrass Frontier*, pp. 32–33.

70 J. S. Buckingham, *America: Historical, Statistic, and Descriptive*, vol. 1 (London: Fisher, Sons 1841), p. 250.

71 Mrs. Felton, *American Life*, p. 41.

72 Still, *Mirror for Gotham*, p. 128.

73 This phenomenon also led to the impoverishment of many a downtown congregation. Rev. S. D. Burchard, *The Centennial Historical Discourse Preached in the Thirteenth Street Presbyterian Church, July 1876* (New York: Arthur & Bonnel, 1877).

74 Henry Theodore Lutz, "Reminiscences of the Fifth Ward," in Henry Collins Brown, ed., *Valentine's Manual of Old New York* 1 (New York: Valentine, 1916), p. 85. Thomas Picton, *Rose Street: Its Past Present and Future* (New York: Russell Brow, 1873), p. 11.

75 *London v. New York by an English Workman* (London: Bosworth & Harrison, 1859), p. 3.

76 Samuel B. Halliday, *The Lost and Found or Life Among the Poor* (New York: Blakeman and Mason, 1859), p. 222.

77 Ernst, *Immigrant Life*, p. 42.

78 Alan Nevins, *The Evening Post: A Century of Journalism* (New York: Bonnie and Liveright, 1922), p. 366.

79 Edward Crapsey, *The Neither Side of New York or, the Vice, Crime, and Poverty of the Great Metropolis* (Montclair, N.J.: Patterson Smith, 1969 [1872]), p. 8.

3   Patterns of Neighborhood Change

1 New York Association for Improving the Condition of the Poor, *Twenty-Fourth Annual Report* (1867), p. 25.

2 "New York Daguerreotyped," *Putnam's Monthly* 1 (1858), p. 126.

3 Asa Greene, *A Glance at New York* (New York: Asa Greene, 1837), pp. 17–18.

4 [Isaac S. Lyon], *Recollection of an Ex Carter* (Newark, N.J.: 1872), pp. 8–9.

5 Emory Holloway and Ralph Adimain, eds., *New York Dissected by Walt Whitman* (New York: Rufus Rockwell & Wilson, 1936), p. 93.

6 Elizabeth Blackmar, *Manhattan for Rent, 1785–1850* (Ithaca: Cornell University Press, 1989), p. 76.

7 Duncan Timms, *The Urban Mosaic: Towards a Theory of Residential Differentiation* (Cambridge: Cambridge University Press, 1971), pp. 99–100.

8 Amy Bridges, *A City In the Republic* (New York: Cambridge University Press, 1984), pp. 43–44; Edward Pessen, *Riches, Class, and Power* (Boston: D. C. Heath, 1973), p. 179. Nonetheless, many historians have come to define urban residence largely in terms of class-based segregation. Edward Spann cited river fronts "taken up for business purposes," adjoining areas populated by "the workmen and laboring classes," and "the center of the island" where the residences of "the wealthier classes" could be found. Edward K. Spann, *The New Metropolis: New York City, 1840–1857* (New York: Columbia University Press, 1981), p. 109. Another scholar attributed the emergence of Boss Tweed's political organization to an attempt to bridge the fragmentation of adjacent neighborhoods that were "so near, and yet so far." Seymour J. Mandelbaum, *Boss Tweed's New York* (New York: John Wiley & Sons, 1965), pp. 7–18.

9 Sean Wilentz, *Chants Democratic: New York City & the Rise of the American Working Class, 1788–1850* (New York: Oxford University Press, 1984), pp. 25–27, 52–53; Christine Stansell, *City of Women: Sex and Class in New York, 1789–1860* (New York: Alfred A. Knopf, 1986), pp. 9, 44–45; and Steven J. Ross, *Workers on the*

Edge: Work, Leisure, and Politics in Industrializing Cincinnati, 1788–1890 (New York: Columbia University Press, 1985), pp. 196, 237–239.

10   Spann, *The New Metropolis*, p. 109.

11   Stansell, *City of Women*, p. 245–250. A similar pattern is described for blacks in Shane White, " 'We Dwell in Safety and Pursue Our Honest Callings': Free Blacks in New York City, 1783–1810," *Journal of American History* 75 (1988), p. 466, and *Somewhat More Independent: The End of Slavery in New York City, 1770–1810* (Athens: University of Georgia Press, 1991), pp. 171–179.

12   David Ward, "Victorian Cities: How Modern?" *Journal of Historical Geography* 1 (1975), pp. 142, 145. Such a complex picture also resembles that of late-eighteenth-century London where class mixing was common due to the spread of manufacturing. L. D. Schwarz, "Social Class and Social Geography: The Middle Classes in London at the End of the Eighteenth Century," *Social History* 7, no. 1 (May 1982), p. 178. See also David Ward, "Environs and Neighbours in the 'Two Nations' Residential Differentiation in Mid-Nineteenth-Century Leeds," *Journal of Historical Geography* 6 (1980), pp. 159, 161. See also Richard Dennis and Stephen Daniels, " 'Community' and the Social Geography of Victorian Cities," *Urban History Yearbook* (1981), pp. 7–23. The ethnic mix of the labor force and the persistence of small workshop organization amidst industrialized trades may have initially served to delay differentiation. Indeed, the degradation of crafts through industrialization and the emergence of "sweated trades," while "reducing the range of social differentiation" that had previously divided neighborhoods into "well defined craft groups," failed to alter the diverse socioeconomic character of New York's older wards.

13   Pessen, *Riches, Class and Power*, p. 179.

14   Immigrant quarters determined by employment, housing availability, and group consciousness have been traced back to before the great waves of migration in the late 1840s. See Robert Ernst, *Immigrant Life in New York City, 1825–1863* (New York: Octagon Books, 1979 [1949]), p. 37.

15   Nadel's study of German segregation concluded that Germans were moderately segregated with a segregation index of 29 (35 correcting for American-born children) versus 17 for Irish when any index under 25 was taken to indicate little segregation. My interpretation of these figures compared with those of other groups suggests that the German figures were not particularly high. Stanley Nadel, *Little Germany: Ethnicity, Religion, and Class in New York City, 1845–80* (Urbana: University of Illinois Press, 1990), p. 39.

16   David Ward, "The Internal Spatial Differentiation of Immigrant Residential Districts," in Northwestern University, Dept. of Geography, *Special Publications Number 3* (1970), pp. 24–42. See also Citizens Association of New York, *Report of the Council of Hygiene and Public Health Upon the Sanitary Condition of the City* (New York: D. Appleton, 1866), pp. 300–303, for a description of outlying shanties. However, once ethnic segregation occurred, it remained a strong force through the 1960s and beyond. See N. Kantrowitz, "Ethnic and Racial Segregation in the New York Metropolis," in Ceri Peach, ed., *Urban Social Segregation* (London: Longman, 1975), pp. 135–149.

17   Richard Dennis and Stephen Daniels, " 'Community' and the Social Geography of Victorian Cities," *Urban History Yearbook* (1981), p. 16. The very tenuousness of the relationship between residence and community should hardly be surpris-

ing. Ghetto theorists overlooked a fundamental flaw with their analogy to plant ecology: "People, unlike plants, move around. Not all their relationships are based on enduring territorial sharing or on competition for land." Ulf Hannerz, *Exploring the City: Inquiries Toward an Urban Anthropology* (New York: Columbia University Press, 1980), p. 57. In addition, the study of ethnic segregation in New York is complicated by regional differences even within established immigrant clusters. Richard Stott, *Workers in the Metropolis: Class, Ethnicity, and Youth in Antebellum New York City* (Ithaca: Cornell University Press, 1990), pp. 203–204; Nadel, *Little Germany*, pp. 37–42; Carol Groneman Pernicone, "The 'Bloody Ould Sixth': A Social Analysis of A New York City Working-Class Community in the Mid-Nineteenth Century" (Ph.D. diss., University of Rochester, 1973), pp. 63–65.

18 Moses Rischin, *The Promised City: New York's Jews, 1870–1914* (Cambridge: Harvard University Press, 1977), p. 76. Studies focusing on the settlement patterns of second-wave immigrants in other cities during the late nineteenth and early twentieth centuries, including one work on Poles in Philadelphia, another examination of the relationship between ethnicity, employment, and residence in Detroit, and a third on the residence of Poles, Italians, and blacks in twentieth-century Pittsburgh, each stressed the process of "community building" through ethnic cohesion where neighborhoods were "institutionally complete and self-contained" entities. And two underscored the importance of ethnically determined rates of homeownership and job stability in the establishment of "functional neighborhoods"—both of which were foreign to most nineteenth-century Manhattanites. Caroline Golab's study of Philadelphia challenges one important aspect of the traditional ghetto stereotype by showing how residential patterns were "decentralized but highly clustered," while still accepting the definition of the immigrant neighborhood as an "institutionally complete and self-contained entity." Caroline Golab, *Immigrant Destinations* (Philadelphia: Temple University Press, 1977), pp. 113–117, 120, 154–156. Also Olivier Zunz, *The Changing Face of Inequality: Urbanization, Industrial Development, and Immigrants in Detroit, 1880–1920* (Chicago: University of Chicago Press, 1982), pp. 57, 81–88, 399–403. Bodnar, Simon, and Weber's sophisticated comparative study of Poles, blacks, and Italians in twentieth-century Pittsburgh employs the concept of "networks of contact" and views "different patterns of community-building" as the consequence of the "interaction between urban forces and tradition." John Bodnar, Roger Simon, and Michael Weber, *Lives of Their Own: Blacks, Italians, and Poles in Pittsburgh, 1900–1960* (Urbana: University of Illinois Press, 1982), pp. 263–266.

19 For a detailed discussion of the social implications and meaning of residential rental market, see Blackmar, *Manhattan for Rent, 1785–1850*, pp. 100–106 and chap. 4; and Betsy Blackmar, "Re-walking the 'Walking City': Housing and Property Relations in New York City, 1780–1840," *Radical History Review* 21 (Fall 1979), pp. 131–148. Blackmar also links tenancy to the emergence of homogeneous industrial neighborhoods like the Tenth Ward.

20 This compares with levels of between 26 and 41 percent for Detroit and between 8 and 26 percent for Pittsburgh in 1900. Calculated from Manuscript N.Y. State Census for 1855. Using aggregate property ownership data for each ward gathered from the 1855 published census, the proportion of households which were owners (when adjusted for variations in household size for different wards) had a median of 11.5 percent, with a low of 3.5 percent in Ward Four and a high of 24.8 percent for

the affluent Fifteenth Ward. The majority of wards ranged between 7.0 and 16.5 percent. These figures undoubtedly overstate levels of homeownership greatly because they also include declarations of personal property. Secretary of State, *Census of the State of New York for 1855* (Albany, 1857), p. 8. Citizens Association of New York, *Council of Hygiene and Public Health, Report on the Sanitary Condition of the City* (New York: Appleton, 1866), p. 120. Zunz, *the Changing Face of Inequality*, p. 156; and Bodnar et al., *Lives of Their Own*, p. 156. The level of Italian homeownership in Pittsburgh of 8.1 percent, which was the lowest of any group, still far exceeded the level for New York. For a discussion of the Ninth Ward, see also several of the reminiscences on this area: Charles T. Harris, *Memories of Manhattan in the Sixties and Seventies* (New York: Derrydale Press, 1928), pp. 43–46; Frank Moss, *The American Metropolis* (New York: Peter Fenelon Collier, 1897), vol. 3, pp. 282–286; and Thomas J. Barton, "Greenwich Village and its Vicinity," clippings in the New York Historical Society [New York: 1897]. For a discussion of Greenwich Village residential development, see New York City Landmarks Preservation Commission, *Greenwich Village Historic District Designation Report* (New York: City Record, 1969), 2 vols.

21   Computed from the Communication of the New York City Superintendent of Buildings (New York Building Department), *Annual Report of Superintendents* (New York: 1863–1873). In 1835, only 274 out of 1259 (22 percent) buildings constructed in New York City were erected north of Fourteenth Street. In 1847, 820 out of 1846 (44 percent) of new constructions occurred in the city's northern sections, although this dropped to 31 percent in 1848, which was a slow building year. New York City Inspector of New Buildings, *Annual Report*, in Aldermanic Documents (1836-no. 119; 1840-no. 63; 1841-no. 64; 1844-no. 67; 1849-no. 60).

22   A retired merchant called upon "every capitalist" to "benefit the poor while he enriches himself" by buying "anywhere on the island" and erecting rental units on "any spot of good grade," which, he predicted, could produce a return that would exceed other investments at "two per cent per month." *The Value of Real Estate in the City of New York, Past, Present, and Prospective By a Retired Merchant* (New York: J. W. Orr, 1860), p. 3.

23   Thomas Jesse Jones, *The Sociology of a New York City Block* (New York: Printed by the author, 1904), pp. 98–117.

24   For a discussion of this concept, see Robert A. Woods and Albert J. Kennedy, *Zones of Emergence: Observations of the Lower Middle and Upper Working Class Communities of Boston, 1905–1914* (Cambridge: MIT Press, 1969). Stanley Nadel noted that "New York's German-Americans were integrated by numerous overlapping affiliations and associations into a common ethnic metropolis" constructed out of "many smaller and more cohesive geographic and social German-American communities." Nadel, *Little Germany*, pp. 2–3.

25   For a discussion of Park's definition of dominance, see Timms, *The Urban Mosaic*, pp. 85–89. The concept of dominance has found recent use in trying to measure the "complex interplay of the variables which causes geographic concentration and dispersion" and which produces a "threshold at which geographic concentration is significant for a given group." See Zunz, *The Changing Face of Inequality*, p. 47. In the competition for housing in mid-nineteenth-century New York City, where no abundant supply of underused or unwanted land existed, dominance operated through the common choices exercised within a given cohort group. Unlike other

cities studied at later periods in their history, Manhattan's neighborhoods were in such a high state of flux that only predominantly native areas could be said to have shown ethnic dominance (notwithstanding the clustering of other earlier groups). The existence of social network ties almost overnight helped to steer groups to particular areas, producing residential change. Yet, even here dominance must be seen more as a factor in the competition for housing than as a force behind residential homogeneity in itself.

26 Immigrant minorities were not uncommon in other wards even before the late 1840s. The Tenth Ward, with nearly as high a proportion of native-born as the "American" Ninth (72.1 versus 77.7 percent), was already 10.9 percent German. Following the great migration between 1845 and 1855, the Irish population in the Fourth Ward peaked at 45.6 percent and then dropped to 32.1 percent in 1875, with the birth of first generation children and the diffusion of residents to other parts of this city.

27 For a discussion of racial segregation see Ivar Bernstein, *The New York City Draft Riots: Their Significance for American Society and Politics in the Age of the Civil War* (New York: Oxford University Press, 1990), pp. 25–28; Paul A. Gilje, *The Road to Mobocracy: Popular Disorder in New York City, 1763–1834* (Chapel Hill: Institute of Early American History and Culture and University of North Carolina Press, 1987), pp. 160–161; Graham Russell Hodges, *New York Cartman, 1667–1850* (New York: New York University Press, 1986), p. 110. In 1855 the Fifth and the Eighth Wards had the largest concentration of blacks with 9.6 and 7.3 percent respectively. Other wards averaged under 1 percent black, and for the Fourth Ward the figure was only .4 percent. Overall, 1.9 percent of New York's population was black in 1855. Secretary of State, *Census of the State of New York for 1855* (Albany, 1857), p. 8. Yet, such levels of segregation were probably new in the nineteenth century. According to one study, free blacks and whites in the late eighteenth and early nineteenth centuries, "far from being separated, lived in one another's pocket." Thus free blacks "were not segregated in black enclaves" but lived instead in basement residences. White, *Somewhat More Independent*, p. 178. White, "'We Dwell in Safety and Pursue Our Honest Callings'," pp. 445–470. For a general discussion of the emerging racial segregation in relationship, early nineteenth-century cities, see Gary Nash, "The Social Evolution of Preindustrial American Cities, 1700–1820," in Raymond A. Mohl, ed., *The Making of Urban America* (Wilmington, Del.: Scholarly Resources, 1988), p. 35.

28 This pattern would have appeared even more clearly had it been possible to separate children of immigrants from native stock in the category "New York City-Born," which showed a significantly lower level of concentration for the tip of Manhattan but only a marginally larger concentration for the Lower West and Middle West Sides, which included the Ninth Ward.

29 Sociologists have long employed two different sets of indices to measure residential clustering: (1) an index of dissimilarity to measure avoidance between a pair of ethnic groups and (2) a segregation index to measure the hypothetical proportion of a single subgroup having to move in order to ensure a uniform distribution vis-à-vis the remaining population who were not members of that group. This technique is sensitive to the levels of measurement used. See Beverly and Otis D. Duncan, "Residential and Occupational Stratification," in Robert Gutman and David Poponoe, eds., *Neighborhood, City and Metropolis* (New York: Random House, 1970),

pp. 70–84, and Michael J. White, *American Neighborhoods and Residential Differentiation* (New York: Russell Sage Foundation, 1987), pp. 83–87. See also Nathan Kantrowitz, "The Index of Dissimilarity: A Measurement of Residential Segregation for Historical Analysis," *Historical Methods Newsletter* 7 (1974), pp. 285–289; Janet Rothenberg Pack, "The Transformation of Urban Neighborhoods, 1850–1880 Philadelphia: Heterogeneity to Homogeneity?" Paper Presented at American Historical Association Meeting, Washington, D.C. (December 1982), pp. 12–16; and Ceri Peach, "Conflicting Interpretations of Segregation," in Peter Jackson and Susan J. Smith, eds., *Social Interaction And Ethnic Segregation*, Institute of British Geographers Special Publication, no. 12 (London: Academic Press, 1981), pp. 19–33.

30 For a discussion of nativism as it related to competition for employment, religion, and politics, see Ernst, *Immigrant Life in New York City*, pp. 101–104, 135–136; Wilentz, *Chants Democratic*, pp. 315–324; Bridges, *A City in the Republic*, pp. 83–98; Spann, *The New Metropolis*, pp. 36–41, 335–340. The pervasive nature of interethnic animosity among the working class is detailed in Gilje, *The Road to Mobocracy*, pp. 123–42.

31 This technique employing conditional odds, based on one developed by Leo Goodman, is designed to test for multiple associations for categorical data in *n*-way tables, proceeding hierarchically from higher to lower orders of relationships using Goodman's chi-square likelihood ratio to test for significance. A 4-way table composed of variables *a, b, c,* and *d* contains the following possible associations: *abcd, abc, abd, acd, bcd, ab, ac, ad, bc, bd, cd,* along with the random effects for each variable taken by itself. By the rules of hierarchical associations, *abc* is a higher-order of relation than *ab, ac,* or *bc*. In other words, *abc* can be significant with or without any of these three pairs testing positively, but none of these three pairs can be significant without a significant relationship for their corresponding higher-order triplet (*abc*). The same rule would apply between *abcd* and associations *abc, abd, acd,* and *bcd*.

32 Among the second-order (three-way) models including the variables residence, nativity, year of arrival, and age at arrival, only that model of the effect "residence-nativity-year of arrival" was significant (.10 level). Age-at-arrival, although also strongly related to ethnicity, had little direct impact on residence.

33 The coefficient of determination is computed by dividing the difference between the chi-squared likelihood ratio for the base model and the data leaving out a given association by the chi-square for that given association. For a more detailed description, see James A. Davis, "Hierarchical Models for Significance Tests in Multivariate Contingency Tables: An Exegesis of Goodman's Recent Paper," in H. L. Coster, ed., *Sociological Methodology* (San Francisco: Jossey-Bass, 1974), pp. 189–231, and his "Analyzing Contingency Tables with Linear Flow Graphs: D Systems," in D. R. Heise, ed., *Sociological Methodology* (San Francisco: Jossey-Bass, 1976), pp. 111–145. Also, William F. Page, "Interpretation of Goodman's Log-Linear Model Effects: An Odds Approach," *Social Methods and Research* 5 (1977), pp. 419–435; and for a more detailed description, see David Knoke and Peter J. Burke, *Log-Linear Models*, Sage University Paper Series on Quantitative Approaches in the Social Sciences, 07-020 (Beverly Hills: Sage Publications, 1980). The merits of conventional log-linear analysis are compared with those of its variants, conditional odds (iterative proportional fitting), conditional proportions, and a hybrid technique combining conditional odds and log-linear models in Marshall I. Pomer,

"Demystifying Log-Linear Analysis: Four Ways to Assess Interaction in a $2 \times 2 \times 2$ Table," *Sociological Perspectives* 27 (1984), pp. 111–135. For an historical application, see Mark J. Stern, "Homeownership: A Multivariate Analysis," in Michael Katz, ed., *York Social History Project Second Research Report* (Toronto: York University Institute of Behavioral Research, 1976), pp. 177–213. Two recent and particularly thorough discussions of log-linear analysis can be found in J. Morgan Kousser, Gary W. Cox, and David W. Galenson, "Log-linear Analysis of Contingency, Tables: An Introduction for Historians with an Application to Thernstrom on the 'Floating Proletariat'," *Historical Methods* 15 (1982), pp. 152–169, and Marco H. D. van Leeuwen and Ineke Maas, "Log-linear Analysis of Changes in Mobility Patterns: Some Models with an Application to the Amsterdam Upper Classes in the Second Half of the Nineteenth Century," *Historical Methods* 24 (1991), pp. 66–79.

34 See Joseph Levenson, "History of the Lower East Side of Manhattan and Grand Street, Its Leading Thoroughfare," in *Souvenir Journal of the Grand Street Boys Association of New York* (New York: 1921), pp. 9–16. For a description of dwindling native congregations in Lower East Side Churches, see Samuel Seaman, *Annals of New York Methodism: A History of the Methodist Episcopal Church of New York from A.D. 1766 to A.D. 1890* (New York: Hunt and Eaton, 1892), pp. 181, 285–287, 296; and Rev. Joseph H. Price, *An Historical Sketch Delivered at the Closing Service in St. Stephen's Church, New York* (New York: 1866), pp. 10, 19.

35 Its class composition might have changed with public improvements raising rents that forced weavers to move. Blackmar, *Manhattan for Rent*, p. 162.

36 If it had been possible to know the length of residence in the ward of native New York-born inhabitants, the level of stability would have been even higher. In addition, many of the post-1850 Irish settlers were not residents in the conventional sense, but, rather, servants to native-headed families. A third of the Irish living in the ward for whom occupations were known were females employed as domestics.

37 The analysis presented here does not fully support Richard Stott's contention of the importance of divisions in working-class neighborhoods by age and sex. Stott, *Workers in the Metropolis*, pp. 204–210. Much of the apparent difference in age and sex vanishes when controlling for ethnicity. Weak but significant relations between sex and arrival age, sex and nativity, and sex and residence show that variations existed in migration patterns between men and women, but that sex only operated as a secondary factor in determining residence. However, Stott does correctly tie these differences to the distinction between boarding and child-rearing, a point that I will discuss in chapter 4.

38 The relationship between female employment and ethnicity also produced variations in sex ratios for particular ethnic groups depending upon residence. In the Fourth Ward, with its assortment of chandlers, shipbuilders, and rowdy sailors, men outnumbered women by margins of 3:2 and in some cases by nearly 3:1. In other areas of the city, the ratio of women to men fluctuated, although the margin of difference was narrow. Among native-born migrants in Ward Five, men exceeded women by 52.7 to 48.3 percent, while in the Ninth and Tenth Wards, women slightly outnumbered men. Irish immigrants, however, present a clear exception to the pattern of sex distribution found among other migrant groups. In the Fourth Ward, where Irish immigrants comprised the dominant group, daughters of Erin outnumbered sons, although by a small margin. In other areas, however, where Irish were not as numerous, women outnumbered men by 3:2. Irish residing in

poor areas such as Ward Four frequently lived in family groups with balanced sex ratios.

39   The complex operation of marriage patterns among young women and the higher earning potential of young men, many of whom had already learned a trade as adolescents, contributed to differences in migration age for young men and women. Without local marital prospects or sources of employment, migrant teenage girls may have been "burdens" to their families because of the lower earning potentials of daughters than sons, and for this reason fewer ties bound young women to home. But there is little evidence that these women migrated unwillingly; the opportunity and freedom for late adolescents was unique to this stage of the life cycle before most assumed the role of wives and mothers. For a description of the role of children in supporting parents and the sex-specific timing of departure, see Michael B. Katz and Ian E. Dewey, "Youth and Early Industrialization in a Canadian City," *American Journal of Sociology* 84 (suppl.), pp. S81–S119; and Laurence Glasco, "The Life Cycles and Household Structure of American Ethnic Grouped: Irish, Germans, and Native-born Whites in Buffalo, New York, 1855," in Tamara K. Hareven, ed., *Family and Kin in Urban Communities, 1700–1930* (New York: New Viewpoints, 1977), pp. 122–143. The question of timing and kin support by industrially employed young women of their rural parents is discussed in Thomas Dublin, *Women At Work: The Transformation of Work and Community in Lowell, Massachusetts, 1826–1860* (New York: Columbia University Press, 1979).

40   Oscar Handlin makes the distinction between such casual and forced immigration in *Boston's Immigrants: A Study in Acculturation*, 2d rev. ed. (Cambridge: Harvard University Press, 1959). For a discussion of families and immigration, see Kathleen Neils Conzen, *Immigrant Milwaukee* (Cambridge: Harvard University Press, 1976). For New York Germans, see Nadel, *Little Germany*, pp. 47–61. For a discussion of Irish families and migration in New York, see Pernicone, "The 'Bloody Ould Sixth'," pp. 53–89. Still, the interrelationship among demographic variations, immigrant culture, and settlement patterns needs more concrete analysis, especially for the nineteenth century. For suggestive examples of how such work might be accomplished, see Lynn H. Lees, *Exiles of Erin: Irish Migrants to Victorian London* (Ithaca: Cornell University Press, 1979); and Dino Cinel, *From Italy to San Francisco: The Immigrant Experience* (Stanford: Stanford University Press, 1983). For a discussion of the roots of domestic migration particular among shoeworkers, see Thomas Dublin, "Rural-Urban Migrants in Industrial New England: The Case of Lynn, Massachusetts, in the Mid-Nineteenth Century," *Journal of American History* 73 (1986), pp. 623–644. Dublin found that one quarter of women migrated as wives or widows.

41   Robert E. Park, Ernest W. Burgess, and Roderick D. McKenzie, *The City* (Chicago: University of Chicago Press, 1925), pp. 1–79. Their literature is discussed in light of more recent developments in urban sociology in Mark Baldassare, "Urban Change and Continuity," in Baldassare, ed., *Cities and Urban Living* (New York: Columbia University Press, 1983), pp. 1–39. Oscar Handlin, *The Uprooted: The Epic Story of the Great Migrations that Made the American People* (New York: Grosset and Dunlap, 1951), pp. 144–160. Rischin, *The Promised City* (Cambridge: Harvard University Press, 1977 edition), pp. 76–94. David Ward, *Cities and Immigrants: A Geography of Change in Nineteenth Century America* (New York: Oxford University Press, 1971), pp. 105–124. Josef J. Barton, *Peasants and Strangers: Italians,*

Rumanians, and Slovaks in an American City, 1890–1950 (Cambridge: Harvard University Press, 1975), pp. 48–63.

42 Kathleen Conzen noted that "economic distinctions" were "insufficient" explanations of residential segregation because "German areas in effect" presented "a microcosm of the economic differentiation of the city as a whole, with internal economic differentiation." Kathleen Neils Conzen, "Patterns of Residence in Early Milwaukee," in Leo F. Schnore, ed., *The New Urban History: Quantitative Explorations by American Historians* (Princeton: Princeton University Press, 1975), pp. 178, 182. Zunz likewise suggested that "Detroit was made up largely of cross-class ethnic communities" which "kept many of their upwardly mobile members within their boundaries" before the coming of the modern industrial corporation in the early twentieth century. Zunz, *The Changing Face of Inequality*, pp. 50–59.

43 Caroline Golab's study of the immigrants in Philadelphia argued that even in strongly ethnic areas work "was the original impetus for the creation and location of the neighborhood." Golab, *Immigrant Destinations*, pp. 6, 111–120, 154, 164–166. See also Stephanie Greenberg, "Industrial Location and Ethnic Residential Patterns in an Industrializing City: Philadelphia, 1880," in Theodore Hershberg, ed., *Philadelphia: Work, Space, Family, and Group Experience in the 19th Century* (New York: Oxford University Press, 1981), pp. 204–229.

44 Paul E. Johnson, *A Shopkeeper's Millennium: Society and Revivalism in Rochester, New York, 1815–1837* (New York: Hill & Wang, 1978), pp. 48–55. Daniel J. Walkowitz noted that workers in Troy and Cohoes "tended to reside in clusters with common ethnic, socioeconomic, and skills levels. Such clusters usually gave character to a particular section . . . of the city." *Worker City, Company Town: Iron and Cotton-Worker Protest in Troy and Cohoes, New York, 1855–84* (Urbana: University of Illinois Press, 1978), pp. 110–112. Paul Faler discusses neighborhood as self-contained communities based upon, although not strictly segregated by, class in *Mechanics and Manufacturers in the Early Industrial Revolution: Lynn, Massachusetts, 1780–1860* (Albany: SUNY Press, 1981), pp. 51–56. In a study of the effects of industrialization in nineteenth-century Cincinnati, Steven J. Ross also briefly discusses residential segregation as a concomitant to class formation and concludes that by the late 1860s "the growing separations between the worlds of employers and employees engendered by change at the workplace" was reflected in and "further exacerbated by the growing geographical isolation between the city's classes." Ross, *Workers on the Edge*, pp. 18, 237. These arguments find theoretical expression in Marxist urban analysis that holds that "there is no cultural system linked to a given form of spatial organization." Consequently, "the social history of humanity is not determined by the type of development of territorial collectivity" nor is "the spatial environment . . . the root of a specificity of behavior and representation." Rather, the spatial concentration of social characteristics is predicated upon "the social production of a certain cultural autonomy" which in turn is dependent upon "the place occupied in the relations of production and "the institutional system and the system of social stratification." Manuel Castells, *The Urban Question: A Marxist Approach* (Cambridge: MIT Press, 1977), pp. 108–112. This view is disputed in Peach, "Conflicting Interpretations of Segregation," pp. 31–32.

45 Stott, *Workers in the Metropolis*, pp. 24–33, 193–201. Sean Wilentz also ties neighborhood formation to widening inequality between the rich and workers and views the influx of immigrants in midcentury as being ancillary to the broader process

of class formation. Wilentz, *Chants Democratic*, pp. 25–28, 108–112. However, Paul O. Weinbaum cautions that "overemphasizing middle and upper class segregation would be a mistake" and that even "judging by twentieth century residential patterns, the poor too were relatively unsegregated." Paul O. Weinbaum, *Mobs and Demagogues: The New York Response to Collective Violence in the Early Nineteenth Century* (Ann Arbor: UMI Research Press, 1979), p. 134.

46   Cited in Richard Briggs Stott, "The Worker in the Metropolis: New York City, 1820–1860" (Ph.D. diss., Cornell University, 1983), pp. 36–38. Stott nevertheless acknowledges that clustering by craft seems "to have been more the exception than the rule, and less significant than the general geographical distinction between the three types" of industrial land use. See also Stuart M. Blumin, *The Emergence of the Middle Class: Social Experience in the American City, 1760–1900* (Cambridge: Cambridge University Press, 1989), pp. 85–86.

47   For a discussion of trade neighborhoods, see Blackmar, *Manhattan for Rent*, pp. 88–91, 100–104.

48   Matthew Hale Smith, *Sunshine and Shadow in New York* (Hartford: J. B. Burr, 1868), pp. 226–234, and "A Guide to the Mission Station for the Use of the Director," *City Mission Document No. 7* (New York: City Mission Society, n.d.), p. 6. The Fourth Ward was a center of cardboard production, printing, and bookbinding, with some establishments, such as that of Jarvis and Hands, employing as many as 145 workers. Manuscript Schedules of the New York Industrial Census of 1855, Ward 4. The industrial censuses only recorded the names of large industrial employers, thus omitting the workplaces of the majority of workers who labored under the system of sweating in small workshops or, as was widely the case for seamstresses, dressmakers, and tailoresses, in home employment.

49   The Ninth Ward, because of its location close to New York's outskirts, served as a center for building construction-related and land-intensive "nuisance" industries. While local workers turned out everything from coffins to straw hats, most employees found work in the area's bleacheries, alcohol distilleries, iron foundries, and sawmills. Manuscript Schedules of the New York Manufacturing Census of 1855, Ward 9, E.D. 9, County Clerk's Office, New York City. A fire in this section of Greenwich Village in 1853 left between 800 and 1000 mechanics without work when it destroyed Selden's Paint Factory, a "mechanical factory," Philander Griffen's Chocolate manufactory, Abbott and Willcomb's clothes finishing establishment, the Marsten Fire Arm works, several other workshops, and a score of houses that together covered an entire block. *New York Times*, "A Night of Disaster," November 18, 1853, 1:3.

50   Even though the Tenth Ward lacked industrial manufacturers of this magnitude, it contained a number of smaller shops, tallow boilers, and breweries which turned out soap, tinware, lager beer, shoes, and artificial flowers. Only one employer—a large chair factory—employed more than 100 workers. Manuscript Schedules of the New York Industrial Census of 1855, Ward 10.

51   For a description of Washington Market, see Thomas Farrington Devoe, *The Market Book* (New York: Printed by the Author, 1862). Immigrant employment in sugar refining is discussed in Ernst, *Immigrant Life in New York*, pp. 79–80. For a description of Thompson's Saloon, see "The Palaces of Trade," *The International Magazine* 5 (1852), pp. 436–441. Some of lower Manhattan's largest industrial employers were also located on the Lower West Side including a railroad yard and the bulk of the

city's sugar refining industry, with two factories alone employing over 330 sugar boilers and helpers. In other workshops, 300 women stitched ladies' and children's clothing or manufactured mantillas for monthly wages that ranged from $12 to $25 or worked in scattered businesses assembling sewing machines, constructing fire engines, and producing daguerreotypes, jewelry, and silver plate. Manuscript Schedules of the New York Industrial Census of 1855, Ward 5.

52 These findings approximate those of Stott who noted that "The East Side was becoming a domain of workers no matter what their nationality." Stott, *Workers in the Metropolis*, p. 204.

53 For a description of fashionable residential areas, see Theodore S. Fay, *Views of New York City and Its Environs* (New York: Peabody, 1831), p. 16. Also, Charles Lockwood, "The Bond Street Area," *New York Historical Society Quarterly* 56 (1972), pp. 309–320, and his *Bricks and Brownstones: The New York Row House, 1783–1929—An Architectural and Social History* (New York: McGraw-Hill, 1972). For information on the real-estate pressures that forced the elite to flee their downtown homes, see W. Frothingham, "Stewart and the Dry Goods Trade in New York," *Continental Monthly* 2 (1862), p. 529, and, "The Palaces of Trade," *New York Times*, September 1, 1854, p. 8. Within two short decades, even these newer areas had begun to lose their luster, as the wealthy moved once again to Murray Hill and Gramercy Park on the East Side. The stretch of Fifth Avenue south of Fortieth Street emerged as New York's prime residential address, though many a merchant preferred to live the life of a country squire in the suburban Twelfth Ward. "New York—Private Residences," *Putnam's Monthly* 3 (1854), pp. 233–248; and William M. Bobo, *Glimpses of New York City by a South Carolinian* (New York: J. J. McCarter, 1852), pp. 168–177. Also Pessen, *Riches, Class and Power*, pp. 170–179. Not surprisingly, the pattern of residence for "unskilled specified" workers also coincided with that of the wealthy, since this category was composed mainly (but not exclusively) of servants.

54 See "Visits to the Homes of the Poor in the First and Fourth Wards," *New York Times*, June 20, 1859, p. 8:1.

55 Blackmar, *Manhattan for Rent*, p. 102.

56 Georg Techla, *Drei Jahre in New York, Eine Skizze für das Volk nach der Natur gezeichnet* (Zwickau: Verein zur Verbreitung Volkschriften, 1862), p. 33.

57 One former retailer enumerated their diverse stock listing such items as "splendid streamers of sanguinary, golden-hued, and verdant flannels, the checkered surfaces of gorgeous tartan shawls, the interminable strings of flighty, sky-seeking hats, the fluttering cloaks well off the way to heaven, . . . the long lines of aspiring hams broiling and dripping from the awning beams, the glistening panoply of tinners wares, the titan boots, the patagonian shirts and pantaloons, the scores of lambs and turkeys, stove-pipes and brooms, [and] carpet-bags and gridirons that fringe the sidewalk from one end to the other." *A Peep Into Catherine Street or the Mysteries of Shopping by a Late Retailer* (New York: John Slater, 1846), p. 1.

58 Blumin, *The Emergence of the Middle Class*, pp. 134–135.

59 It should be noted that professionals and businessmen often cluster in separate areas. The West Side and the sections north of Fortieth Street housed proportionately more lawyers, doctors, and dentists but fewer businessmen, while men of commerce favored the East Side.

60 Ward, "Victorian Cities," pp. 140–141; and Timms, *The Urban Mosaic*, pp. 211–

249. Also Alan N. Burstein, "Immigrant Residential Mobility: The Irish and Germans in Philadelphia, 1850–1880," in Theodore Hershberg, ed., *Philadelphia: Work, Space, Family, and Group Experience in the Nineteenth Century: Essays Toward an Interdisciplinary History of the City* (New York: Oxford University Press, 1981), pp. 199–200.

61   See Olivier Zunz, "Technology and Society in an Urban Environment: The Case of the Third Avenue Elevated Railway," *Journal of Interdisciplinary History* 3 (1972), pp. 89–102. In fact, heavy industry was usually located in satellite cities within the New York metropolitan area, but outside the city's boundaries. For a discussion of industrial location within the metropolitan area, see Stott, *Workers in the Metropolis*, chap. 1. Spann, *The New Metropolis*, pp. 401–411.

62   Contrary to the assertion by David Ward that an "ethnic division of labor capable of influencing the location of different immigrant groups had not developed before the Civil War," such an ethnic division of the labor force profoundly influenced where workers lived and was a more powerful force behind residential location than industrial location alone. See Ward, "The Internal Differentiation of Immigrant Residential Districts," pp. 24–42.

63   The correlations between the ethnic backgrounds of workers and their industrial employment (coefficient of determination of .6963 on chi-square of 953.37) and between ethnicity and residence (coefficient of determination of .6182 on chi-square of 758.43) were both substantially stronger for industrial location and residence alone when controlling for ethnicity (coefficient of determination of .4741 on chi-square of 550.58). This was largely because "prior experience in the Old World" shaped the skills level of newly arrived immigrants thus compounding the impact of ethnicity upon residence. "Native-white and German immigrants dominated the most desirable skilled occupations," while Irish workers clung precariously to the lowest levels of the job force. Stansell, *City of Women*, pp. 44–45. Bruce Laurie, George Alter, and Theodore Hershberg, "Immigrants and Industry: The Philadelphia Experience, 1850–1880," in *Philadelphia*, p. 109.

64   For licensure of cartmen see [Lyon], *Recollection of an Ex-Cartman*, pp. 3–4; Graham R. Hodges, *New York City Cartmen, 1667–1850* (New York: New York University Press, 1986); Wilentz, *Chants Democratic*, p. 26; and Howard B. Rock, *Artisans of the New Republic: The Tradesmen of New York City in the Age of Jefferson* (New York: New York University Press, 1979), pp. 205–234.

65   For a discussion of ethnic division of industrial employment in New York for this period, see Ernst, *Immigrant Life in New York City*, pp. 61–98; and Stott, *Workers in The Metropolis*, chap. 2, passim. For Irish workers, see Pernicone, "The 'Bloody Ould Sixth'," pp. 90–138, while Germans are discussed in Stanley Nadel, *Little Germany*, pp. 62–90. The ethnic composition of the work force in New York City was further complicated by the sexual division of labor, which confined women to a narrow range of employment. While male workers were scattered throughout a number of industries, clustering in commerce, transportation, clothing, food, building, and manual labor, three quarters of the working women held jobs in just two areas: apparel and domestic services. The garment industry, which was the largest employer of skilled New Yorkers before the Civil War, was strongly female, although many women could also be found selling dry goods and notions, hand coloring daguerreotypes, making playing cards, and binding books. Those not employed as servants who held manufacturing jobs or turned out goods through the

sweat system earned salaries that averaged only half those of their male counterparts. Salaries in the factories of the Fourth and Fifth Wards ranged from $12 to
$25 a month for women as compared to $25 to $45 or higher for men. Manuscript
Schedules of the New York Industrial Census of 1855, Ward 5, E.D. 1. However, employment frequently offered freedom to single women prior to marriage. "A good
book-sewer," noted one observer, "may pay three dollars a week for her board, fifty
cents to her washerwoman and have a hundred dollars a year for clothes. . . . That
is she can earn from five to five dollars and a half a week by her labors." William
Burns, *Life in New-York: Indoors and Outdoors* (New York: Bunce and Bros., 1851).
For a detailed discussion of the sexual division of labor in nineteenth-century New
York, see Stansell, *City of Women*, chap. 6.

66   Theodore Hershberg and Robert Dockhorn, "Occupational Classification," *Historical Methods Newsletter* 9 (March–June 1976), pp. 59–98; and Theodore Hershberg,
Michael Katz, Stuart Blumin, Laurence Glasco, and Clyde Griffen, "Occupation
and Ethnicity in Five Nineteenth-Century Cities: A Collaborative Inquiry," *Historical Methods Newsletter* 7 (June 1974), pp. 174–216. For a discussion of servants
as symbols of wealth, see Michael B. Katz, *The People of Hamilton, Canada West*
(Cambridge: Harvard University Press, 1975), pp. 27–28; and Conzen, *Immigrant
Milwaukee, 1836–1860*, pp. 81–82. Occupation was the most complex measure
of status differentiation and required two subvariables to encompass its different
dimensions reflecting both the "individual life experiences of ordinary persons"
and the "changing nature of the economy as a whole." Hershberg and Dockhorn,
"Occupational Classification," pp. 59–62.

67   For an overview of the debate between opposing schemes of measuring class, see
Olivier Zunz, "The Synthesis of Social Change: Reflections on American Social
History," in Olivier Zunz, ed., *Reliving the Past: The Worlds of Social History*
(Chapel Hill: University of North Carolina Press, 1985), pp. 86–92.

68   Since effects in an ordered causal system (such as path analysis) are recursive,
causal and partial paths measuring relations between a pair of variables can be
calculated controlling for prior-effects factors. Thus, the use of flow graphs in
d-systems analysis of contingency tables produces effect coefficients that make
possible statistical inference for nominal data in a manner roughly comparable
to regression, although, for practical reasons, the results are difficult to interpret
for polytomous (e.g., nondichotomous) variables. The related procedure of "direct
standardization"—a multivariate technique that modifies data by resetting percentages in rows—produces simulations in an n-variable model that controls for
the contribution of earlier (or lower-order) variables upon later ones, thus producing modeled tables for dichotomous and polytomous variables. In tandem, both
techniques allow the analysis of partials, causal effects, spurious portions, and indirect portions for associations within an ordered system of variables. James A.
Davis, "Analyzing Contingency Tables with Linear Flow Graphs: D System," in
David R. Heise, ed., *Sociological Methodology 1976* (San Francisco: Jossey-Bass,
1975), pp. 111–145. Problems with d-system analysis assuming that the "effects of
the independent variable being constant over the entire (0,1) range of the dependent
variable" are discussed by Christopher Winship and Robert D. Mare, "Structural
Equations and Path Analysis for Discrete Data," *American Journal of Sociology* 89,
no. 1 (1983), pp. 54–110, esp. note 2. D-system also has a problem summarizing

relations among polytomous variables. Not only are the values of coefficients predicated upon which value is selected as a basing criterion, but also upon the causal order of variables within the system. Indeed, multivariate d-system analysis for polytomous variables produces as many causal paths as the degree of freedom (the number of rows minus one times the number or columns minus one). For "direct standardization," see James A. Davis, "Extending Rosenberg's Technique for Standardizing Percentage Tables," *Social Forces* 62, no. 3 (1984) pp. 679–708; John S. Reed, *The Enduring South* (Chapel Hill: University of North Carolina Press, 1972), pp. 96–103; and Kent W. Smith, "Test-Factor Standardization and Marginal Standardization," *Social Forces* 56, no. 1 (1977), pp. 240–249.

69   For convenience, the variables used in the five-variable causal system were dichotomized. The categories were divided between native and foreign; male and female; under and over 30; upper and lower status (with skilled combined with white-collar); and "downtown" and "uptown" wards. Each of these in turn helped to shape the level of employment for New Yorkers. Even discounting intervening patterns such as the strong reluctance (or lack of need) for native women to work and age differences between working men and women in different ethnic groups, foreign-born were strongly overrepresented in lower-level jobs. Age, which at first glance seemed to shape employment level, proved to be insignificant when controlling for spurious effects of nativity and gender.

70   This fact is also supported by the cruder effects decomposition for the nondichotomized model where a comparison of the relative size of chi-squares also reveals the continued importance of occupational status, although at a much lower level than nativity and the ethnic division of labor.

71   Patterns of occupational distribution are not easily interpreted. The high concentration of wealthy professionals in the Fifth Ward was paradoxically accompanied by a significant level of unskilled laborers (12.8 percent). Furthermore, even if the large number of semiskilled workers in the Fourth Ward—many of whom were sailors or longshoremen—underscored the neighborhood's poverty, the substantial number of semiskilled workers in the Ninth Ward actually indicated affluence. Many of the semiskilled workers in the Ninth Ward were also cartmen, a group of a higher occupational status than their job title would indicate. The tough municipal regulation of cartmen fixing rates for cartage and forbidding their employment to others or the sale of shares of their business—regulations that dated from the late eighteenth century—still remained in force into the 1850s. Consequently, municipal regulations turned this class of semiskilled workers into petty-proprietors. See Rock, *Artisans of the New Republic*, pp. 29, 205–234. In the mid-eighteenth century, cartmen had formed neighborhoods apart from their masters on Church's Farm. By the early nineteenth century, they had begun to shift away from the Sixty and Seventh Wards toward the Eighth and Eleventh, abandoning the trade in older neighborhoods to Irish dirt carters. Hodges, *New York City Cartmen, 1667–1850*, pp. 47–48, 130.

72   The dearth of professionals and skilled workers (3.5 and 35.8 percent) and surplus of semiskilled workers (34.4 percent) would have occurred even had the number of Irishmen been far smaller. Controlling for ethnicity may have cut the percentage of skilled workers from 57.2 to 54.1 percent and boosted the number of laborers from 4.8 to 6.5 percent, but the basic character of this area remained little changed.

73 This finding is not consistent with Richard Stott's contention that ethnic variation lessened while class variation widened in the 1850s. Stott, *Workers in the
Metropolis*, p. 204.

74 Occupational rank is often an imprecise measure at best of the impact of social
status upon residence. As a yardstick for stratification (independent of class), vertical status is flawed by its arbitrary classification scheme that imposes an artifice
of twentieth-century social science upon a time to which it might not apply. As
a measure of class consciousness, it is even a poorer proxy which fails to describe
with any precision whether occupational clustering translated into an awareness
of social space—although this is commonly presumed. And as a factor designed
to tap a number of other components of residential status for which data might
be lacking such as wealth, income, and rental cost, it all too often presumes what
in fact needs to be investigated. Conceptual criticisms of arguments on class relations from quantitative evidence are presented in James A. Henretta, "The Study of
Social Mobility: Ideological Assumptions and Conceptual Bias," *Labor History* 18
(Spring 1977), pp. 165–178; and Nancy Fitch, "Statistical Fantasies and Historical
Facts: History in Crisis and Its *Methodological Implications*," *Historical Methods*
17 (Fall 1984), pp. 239–254.

75 Without detailed labor statistics that were later compiled by state labor departments
it is often difficult to evaluate such harsh criticism of proletarian consumption on
the part of antebellum social reformers. See John Modell, "Patterns of Consumption, Acculturation, and Family Income Strategies in Late Nineteenth-Century
America," in Tamara K. Hareven and Maris Vinovskis, eds., *Family and Population
in Nineteenth-Century America* (Princeton: Princeton University Press, 1978), pp.
206–240. Ohio labor statistics are also employed by Steven Ross, in *Workers on
the Edge*, pp. 241–245. Nor do other figures—like those from Civil War income tax
levies which showed only one family in eight of the city's 160,000 households to
have a taxable income that exceeded $600 plus the cost of rent—indicate whether
most families were as destitute of material goods as they were in taxable income.
Only one family in sixteen had a taxable income in excess of $1,000. *The Income
Record: A List Giving the Taxable Income for the Year 1863, of Every Resident in
New York* (New York: American News, 1865), pp. ii–vii. For information on the tax
regulations, see George Boutwell, *Manual of the Direct and Excise Tax System of
the United States* (Boston: Little, Brown, 1863), p. 155; and James Ritchie, *The Tax-
Payer's Guide* (Boston: William H. Forbes, 1864), p. 33. The actual assessments for
the sample areas, an underused source, still survive as well. Manuscript Assessment Lists for New York, 1862–1866, Reels T56-8, 62-3, 67A, and 216-7 for Tax
Districts 4, 5, 6, 32, National Archives, Washington, D.C..

76 [James D. Burns], *Three Years Among the Working-Classes in the United States
During the War* (London: Smith, Elder, 1865), p. 85. For a detailed discussion of
working-class consumption, see Richard Stott, *Workers in the Metropolis: Class,
Ethnicity and Youth in Antebellum New York City* (Ithaca: Cornell University
Press, 1990), pp. 168–181. Consumption for middle-class counterparts and its impact on class formation is discussed in Blumin, *The Emergence of the Middle Class*,
pp. 158–163. *London v. New York by an English Workman* (London: Bosworth &
Harrison, 1859), p. 67. Sympathetic observers noted how Irish and German immigrants frequently saved their money in order to help relatives afford the arduous
transatlantic passage—though for many Germans this favor was extended "on the

understanding that one day or another it will be refunded—that it will become a matter of account." John F. Maguire, *The Irish in America* (London: Longmans Green, 1868), p. 320.

77 For a discussion of property ownership, wealth, and status among Newburyport laborers, see Stephan Thernstrom, *Poverty and Progress: Social Mobility in a Nineteenth Century City* (New York: Atheneum, 1969), pp. 115–122. See also Bodnar, Simon, and Webber, *Lives of Their Own*, pp. 154–155; and Zunz, *The Changing Face of Inequality*, pp. 171–176. It should be noted, however, that status from ownership of homes or other durable goods was susceptible to slippage as the extent of ownership expanded. For a critical evaluation of this phenomenon in light of social mobility, see Matthew Edel, Elliott D. Sclar, and Daniel Luria, *Shaky Palaces: Homeownership and Social Mobility in Boston's Suburbanization* (New York: Columbia University Press, 1984), pp. 11–35. Blackmar noted (without much evidence) that poor families exercise "little control over property," with possessions gaining value from "their ability to be traded, pawned, or sold." Likewise, household furnishings were eschewed for clothing which provided "more efficient heating that fuel and a more readily visible expression of self-esteem." Blackmar, *Manhattan for Rent*, p. 146.

78 Unfortunately, municipal tax assessments, which were unreliable in measuring personal wealth, are of little value in determining the direction of family expenditures. Probate records are of limited use in helping us to understand the consumption of people who lay outside the reach of legal authority and whose members transferred goods informally and privately. Sean Wilentz, "Crime, Poverty and the Streets of New York City: The Diary of William H. Bell 1850–51," in *History Workshop*, no. 7 (Spring 1979), pp. 128–129.

79 New York Association for Improving the Condition of the Poor, *Twenty-Third Annual Report* (New York: 1866), p. 25.

80 New York Police Dept., Manuscript Tenth Ward Police Blotters for May 25–Aug. 27, 1855, and July 7–Nov. 29, 1856, Box 4063, New York City Municipal Archives.

81 Manuscript Tenth Ward Police Blotters. Stott suggests that possessions such as watches and clothing may have diminished class differences as housing differences between the working and middle classes were growing. Stott, *Workers in the Metropolis*, pp. 174–176.

82 While it is difficult to know whether these Tenth Ward residents were victimized because they were wealthier or more ostentatious than their neighbors, it was not uncommon for a single item to represent several weeks of its owner's wages. Once these goods were stolen, they became part of a "contraband economy of the New York poor," for the Lower East Side abounded with secondhand dealers, junk shops, and pawnbrokers. Wilentz, "Crime, Poverty and the Streets of New York City," p. 128. For values of consumer goods in the mid-nineteenth century, see Edgar W. Martin, *The Standard of Living in 1860* (Chicago: University of Chicago Press, 1942), pp. 181–197 and 210–215. Ninety-four of the city's 118 secondhand dealers were located in this section of New York, with eleven in the Tenth Ward alone. The Sixth and Fourth Wards boasted the largest concentration, where Irish and Jewish sellers, some of whom, such as Jane Devine and Henrietta Cohen, were women, divided up the Chatham Square trade. Computed from the Bonds of Second-Hand Dealers 1840–1858, City Clerk Filed Papers, Box 3072, New York City Municipal Archives. Also on file are the Bonds of Keepers of Junk Shops 1844–1855 in Box

3074 and the Bonds of Second Hand Dealers for 1859–1863 in Box 4063. Though the municipal government imposed stiff regulations upon dealers in an effort to keep them honest, including a $250 bond and annual licenses, fences were still common. See Ernst, *Immigrant Life in New York City*, p. 96. For a description of a junk shop, see Theodore Griesinger, *Lebende Bilder aus America* (Stuttgart: Wilh Ritzschke, 1858), pp. 129–135. Before he was finally arrested, Ephraim Snow carried a "complete assortment of every variety of stolen goods" from a store at the corner of Allen and Grand Street in the Tenth Ward. Edward Crapsey, *The Neither Side of New York or, the Vice, Crime and Poverty of the Great Metropolis* (Montclair, N.J.: Patterson Smith, 1969; reprint of 1872 ed.), p. 84. Also, for a warning against such establishments, see *Tricks and Traps of New York City* (Boston: C. H. Brainard, 1857), part 1.

83 Ernst, *Immigrant Life in New York City*, p. 132.

84 Computed from Emerson W. Keyes, *A History of Savings Banks in the State of New York* (Albany, 1870), pp. 276–279. Many of these institutions were opened with the intention, as articulated by trustees and presidents, of providing a safe investment with a ready rate of return for New York's working population—to give the poor man "a bank he can call his own." Bowery Savings Bank President Thomas Jeremiah cited in Keyes, *A History of Savings Banks*, p. 164. However, in his study of the early history of New York savings banks, Alan Olmstead found that even though "the majority of mutual customers were domestics, unskilled laborers, or semi-skilled persons of small means for whom the first mutuals were intended," these institutions were also a "haven for the savings of many middle- and upper-class individuals whose accounts composed a sizable proportion of all mutual funds." Alan L. Olmstead, *New York City Mutual Savings Banks, 1819–1861* (Chapel Hill: University of North Carolina Press, 1976), p. 71. A more in-depth discussion of savings patterns and motivation can be found in Kenneth Alan Scherzer, "The Unbounded Community: Neighborhood Life and Social Structure in New York City, 1830–1875" (Ph.D. diss., Harvard University, 1982), pp. 176–204.

85 Pessen, *Riches, Class, and Power Before the Civil War*, pp. 172–179.

86 Manuscript schedules of the New York State Census of 1855, Tenth Ward, E.D. 5, County Clerk's Office, New York City.

87 Low levels of home ownership did not by themselves produce discomfort and crowding, for even well-to-do families rented their luxurious accommodations. Philip Hone, a wealthy merchant and famous diarist, "hired" his home in 1836 for $1600 per year. Alan Nevins, ed., *The Diary of Philip Hone* (New York: Dodd, Mead, 1928), vol. 1, p. 207. Contemporaries commonly defined the difference between poverty and comfort with regard to housing quality, not in terms of title. Thus Samuel Halliday, a prominent social reformer of the 1850s, could attack what he called the "barbarism of living two, three, or four families in the house," citing for support the adage that "no house was ever yet built large enough for two families who have correct ideas of independency and comfort." Samuel B. Halliday, *The Lost and Found or Life Among the Poor* (New York: Blakeman and Mason, 1859), p. 120. Given the high population density in Lower Manhattan, it is not surprising that rent levels and residence in single- and dual-family dwelling houses separated the "better classes," who could afford between $600 and $800 annually for rent in "respectable quarters," from the "great mass of the poor," who paid $10 per month for tenement flats. Holoway and Adimain, *New York Dissected*, p. 93.

88 The figure of 64.2 percent for the Tenth Ward was not significantly above the standard distribution to the .1 level.

89 Controlling for variations in occupational rank between ethnic groups made little difference, save for German families whose percentage in multifamily houses dropped from 73.1 to 69.9 percent.

90 New York City Common Council, "Report of the Special Committee in Relation to a Reorganization of the Police Department," *Board of Aldermen Document No. 53* (1844), p. 690. For a discussion of the growing intolerance of vagrancy, see Blackmar, *Manhattan for Rent,* pp. 169–170.

91 [Edward Crapsey], "Public Lodgers," *Harpers New Monthly Magazine* 39 (1869), p. 754.

92 New York City Chief of Police, *Semi-Annual Report, January 1–June 30, 1853,* Board of Alderman Document 50 (1853), p. 1153.

93 Lubitz, "The Tenement House Problem," p. 142.

94 New York Metropolitan Police Board of Commissioners, *Annual Report for 1867* (New York: Bergen & Tripp, 1868), p. 11. Also James F. Richardson, *The New York Police: Colonial Times to 1901* (New York: Oxford University Press, 1970), p. 152.

95 [Crapsey], "Public Lodgers," p. 754.

96 Samples drawn from savings records and the inventoried losses of crime victims for stolen clothing and jewelry in one working-class ward indicated how New Yorkers saved and spent their money—two aspects of wealth not available through the census which only show occupational rank. When linked with city directories, savings accounts also indicate the local orientation of depositors and the function of savings banks within the community. Hunter, "The Loss of Community," pp. 540–541; and also Richard P. Taub et al., "Urban Voluntary Associations, Locally Based and Externally Induced," *American Journal of Sociology* 133 (1978), pp. 425–442. For my discussion of neighborhood savings patterns, see Scherzer, "The Unbounded Community," chap. 3.

97 Inadequate record-keeping led one contemporary to surmise that the proportion of native vagrants nearly equaled that of those born abroad. [Crapsey], "Public Lodgers," pp. 757–758. For a later description of public lodgers, see Edward T. Devine, "The Shiftless and Floating City Population," *Annals of the American Academy of Political Science* 10 (1897), pp. 149–164. Manuscript censuses invariably missed the most transient strata of society, and lodgers in police stations comprised a sizable proportion of the Tenth Ward's population. During the first six months of 1853, the local police station accommodated 2,158 of these vagrants, though many of these were undoubtedly "rounders" or repeaters. With the total population of 25,000 in the surrounding neighborhood, as many as 15 percent might have been lodgers (doubling the six-month figure and assuming no repeaters). Since many lodgers clearly did repeat, a more likely estimate of homeless in the wards runs between 5 and 10 percent.

These blotters do not record lengths of residence for native-born lodgers, making it impossible to study arrival cohorting for anyone but foreign-born lodgers. Manuscript State Census, Tenth Ward, New York County, 1855 in the County Clerk's Office, New York County and Manuscript Police Blotters (2), Tenth District, New York City, 1855–1856, in the New York Municipal Archives.

98 Many arrived past the age of twenty (often in their middle age). A sex comparison between the two groups is not possible because the Tenth District station house

seemed to have started accommodating women exclusively in 1856.

99 The link between sex and vagrancy may also be the result of biases in the police blotters, since the Tenth Precinct ceased to accommodate men sometime between 1855 and 1856. For an account of intelligence offices, see Joel H. Ross, *What I Saw in New-York; Or a Bird's Eye View of City Life* (Auburn, N. Y.: Dervy and Miller, 1851), p. 145; and Edward E. Hale, *Letters on Irish Emigration* (Freeport, N. Y.: Books for Libraries Press, 1972; reprint of 1852 ed.), p. 34. For more on servants in New York City, see Ernst, *Immigrant Life in New York City,* pp. 65–67.

100 Stansell, *City of Women,* pp. 245–250. This finding of a temporary increase in heterogeneity following the first 1850s surge in immigration also agrees with that of Pack, "The Transformation of Urban Neighborhoods," p. 32.

4   Children and Boarders

1 Percy Townsend, *Appleton's Dictionary of New York City* (New York: D. Appleton, 1880), pp. 5–6. For a discussion of the replacement of boardinghouses by apartment houses, see Elizabeth Collins Cromley, *Alone Together: A History of New York's Early Apartments* (Ithaca: Cornell University Press, 1990), chap. 1.

2 The role of boarding in the formation of neighborhoods is often overlooked—a surprising oversight given the importance urban sociologists have attached to family status—or "familialism"—in shaping modern cities and suburbs. The universality of "familialism" in urban residential selection has been widely documented by ecologists and sociologists in cities throughout the world. Raymond Hoover and Edgar Vernon, *Anatomy of a Metropolis* (Garden City, N. Y.: Doubleday Anchor, 1962), pp. 168–169; Duncan Timms, *The Urban Mosaic: Towards a Theory of Residential Differentiation* (Cambridge: Cambridge University Press, 1971), p. 107. Unlike either ethnicity or occupation, familialism presumes individual choice. It assumes the operation of an ideology of family which forms a social consensus among residents of different urban zones. The association of low density settlement with the life stage of child-raising, best seen in the importance recent suburbanites attach to single-family housing, suggests an ideology of familial orientation that views the spatial organization of the metropolis in terms of needs of families with children as opposed to those without. Herbert Gans, "Urbanism and Suburbanism as Ways of Life: A Re-evaluation of Definitions," in Robert Gutman and David Poponoe, eds., *Neighborhood and Metropolis* (New York: Random House, 1970), pp. 71–72, 81. Albert Hunter's work on Chicago revealed that family status influenced the formation of neighborhoods in a way that paralleled the life cycles of the families who inhabited them. Albert Hunter, *Symbolic Communities: The Persistence and Change of Chicago's Local Communities* (Chicago: University of Chicago Press, 1974), p. 61. Family status continued to differentiate neighborhoods in American cities into the 1980s, with certain neighborhoods forming "distinct child-rearing (childbearing) communities." See Michael J. White, *American Neighborhoods and Residential Differentiation* (New York: Russell Sage Foundation, 1987), pp. 73–74.

3 Whether household structure played such a role in shaping nineteenth-century neighborhoods has scarcely been addressed, even with the recent upsurge of interest in family history, and the geography of urban family life remains "one of the most

neglected aspects" in the study of the "family's interaction with urban life." These
include efforts of historians such as Tamara Hareven, Maris Vinovskis, and Olivier
Zunz to analyze the age-adjusted fertility levels, nuclear family size, and house-
hold composition in Boston's central wards and South End, as well as in Detroit.
Tamara K. Hareven, ed., *Family and Kin in Urban Communities, 1700–1930* (New
York: New Viewpoints, 1977), p. 10. See also Hareven and Maris Vinovskis, "Mari-
tal Fertility, Ethnicity and Occupation in Urban Families: An Analysis of the South
End in 1880," *Journal of Social History* 3 (March 1975), pp. 69–93; and Olivier Zunz,
*The Changing Face of Inequality: Urbanization, Industrial Development, and Im-
migrants in Detroit, 1880–1920* (Chicago: University of Chicago Press, 1982), pp.
67–79. For notable exceptions, see Donna R. Gabaccia, *From Sicily to Elizabeth
Street: Housing and Social Change Among Italian Immigrants, 1880–1930* (Albany:
SUNY Press, 1984), pp. 65–85; and Judith E. Smith, *Family Connections: A History
of Italian and Jewish Immigrant Lives in Providence, Rhode Island, 1900–1940*
(Albany: SUNY Press, 1985), pp. 82–123.

4   Various studies on the history of the family have suggested that the residential
function of family status was tied to the development of a conception of familial
privacy during the first half of the nineteenth century. Family history has focused
upon transitional stages of individual and family cycles, the role of children in the
family economy, and the discovery of schooling as an accepted component of urban
family life—largely to the exclusion of its impact upon the city. Finally, respectable
home life suggested a "person's capacity to enter into obligations within the community." By contrast, boarding and tenant houses "appeared socially promiscuous,
and immediately vulnerable to market determinations." Thus boarding might have
represented a "condition of social immaturity that rejected principles of family
duty and selective obligation." Elizabeth Blackmar, *Manhattan for Rent, 1785–1850*
(Ithaca: Cornell University Press, 1989), pp. 128–129. However, the discussion that I
present in this chapter suggests wider acceptance. Studies of Chicago, Los Angeles,
Philadelphia, Hamilton, Buffalo, and Providence, completed during the last two
decades, have sought to examine the importance of family structure in coping
with the pressures of urban life, such as the demands of job-seeking and migration,
and have also sought to examine critical life situations such as sickness and widowhood. For Chicago, see Richard Sennett, *Families Against the City: Middle Class
Homes of Industrial Chicago, 1872–1890* (New York: Vintage Books, 1974), which
uses cross-sectional data to paint a frequently misleading portrait of family isolation. Also, Barbara Laslett's "Household Structure on an American Frontier: Los
Angeles, California, in 1850," *American Journal of Sociology* 81 (1976), pp. 109–
128. For Philadelphia, see several articles in Theodore Hershberg, ed., *Philadelphia: Work, Space, Family, and Group Experience in the Nineteenth Century* (New
York: Oxford University Press, 1981), including: John Modell, Theodore Hershberg,
and Frank F. Furstenberg, Jr., "Social Change and Transition to Adulthood in Historical Perspective," pp. 311–341; Michael R. Haines, "Poverty, Economic Stress,
and the Family in a Late Nineteenth-Century American City: Whites in Philadelphia, 1880," pp. 240–276; and Claudia Goldin, "Family Strategies and the Family
Economy in the Late Nineteenth Century: The Role of Secondary Workers," pp.
277–310. For Hamilton, Ontario, see Michael B. Katz, *The People of Hamilton,
Canada West: Family and Class in a Mid-Nineteenth-Century City* (Cambridge:
Harvard University Press, 1975). Laurence A. Glasco has done considerable work

on Buffalo, including his "The Life Cycles and Household Structure of American Ethnic Groups: Irish, Germans, and Native-born Whites in Buffalo, New York, 1855," in Hareven, ed., *Family and Kin in Urban Communities*, pp. 122–143; and "Migration and Adjustment in the Nineteenth-Century City: Occupation, Property, and Household Structure of Native-born Whites, Buffalo, New York, 1855," in Tamara K. Hareven and Maris A. Vinovskis, eds., *Family and Population in Nineteenth-Century America* (Princeton: Princeton University Press, 1978), pp. 154–178. This latter volume also contains the results on Providence, Rhode Island. See Howard P. Chudacoff, "Newlyweds and Family Extension: The First Stage of the Family Cycle in Providence, Rhode Island, 1864–1865 and 1879–1880," pp. 179–205. Hareven and John Modell, "Urbanization and the Malleable Household: An Examination of Boarding and Lodging in American Families," *Journal of Marriage and the Family* 35 (August 1973), pp. 467–479. For the relationship between sexual divisions of roles and the changing role of domesticity, see Christine Stansell, *City of Women: Sex and Class in New York, 1789–1860* (New York: Alfred A. Knopf, 1986), p. 41; Kenneth T. Jackson, *Crabgrass Frontier: The Suburbanization of the United States* (New York: Oxford University Press, 1985), pp. 47–49; and Mary P. Ryan, *Cradle of the Middle Class: The Family in Oneida County, New York, 1780–1865* (Cambridge: Cambridge University Press, 1981), pp. 167–168, 184–185, 150. Whether a wide enough cross-section of residents accepted domesticity to make it a city-building force remains an open question. Immigrants commonly recreated old-world kinship and familial institutions and had little use for domesticity—at least before the assimilation of the second generation. See, for example, Donna Gabaccia, "Sicilians in Space: Environmental Change and Family Geography," *Journal of Social History* 16 (Winter 1982), pp. 53–65; and Smith, *Family Connections*, chap. 3.

5   Peel notes that "Social history needs to probe" the "middle ground between urban working class and the elites and should reach beyond the family and familistic values as the only molders of responses to urban environments." Mark Peel, "On the Margins: Lodgers and Boarders in Boston, 1860–1900," *Journal of American History* 72 (1986), p. 834.

6   Joseph F. Kett, *Rites of Passage: Adolescence in America 1790 to the Present* (New York: Basic Books, 1977), pp. 11–37. Katz, Douchet, and Stern contend that capitalism radically transformed family life in nineteenth-century cities by imposing a prolonged period of institutional dependency upon youth, of which prolonged residence with parents and extended schooling were but two features. Michael B. Katz, Michael J. Doucet, and Mark J. Stern, *The Social Organization of Early Industrial Capitalism* (Cambridge: Harvard University Press, 1982), pp. 241–244, 281–284.

7   Semiautonomy is commonly associated with the decay of household production. Betsy Blackmar, "Re-walking the 'Walking City': Housing and Property Relations in New York City, 1780–1840," *Radical History Review* 21 (Fall 1979), p. 136.

8   Peter Laslett, *The World We Have Lost* (London: Methuen, 1971), chap. 1; Alice Kessler-Harris, *Out to Work: A History of Wage-Earning Women in the United States* (New York: Oxford University Press, 1982), pp. 20–33; Stansell, *City of Women*, pp. 11–12, 157–158; Nancy F. Cott, *The Bonds of Womanhood: "Women's Sphere" in New England, 1780–1835* (New Haven: Yale University Press, 1977), pp. 36–44. Semiautonomy was particularly well-suited to the high levels of transiency at a time when the dynamic environment of urban neighborhoods, immigration,

changing patterns of work, and housing shortages all served to alter the operation the individual and family life-cycles for urbanites.

9   For a satirical description of New York boardinghouses, see Thomas B. Gunn, *The Physiology of New York Boarding-Houses* (New York: Mason Brothers, 1857). For an account of the Bohemian area that had developed along Bleeker Street by the early 1870s, see James D. McCabe, Jr., *Lights and Shadows of New York Life: Or, the Sights and Sensations of the Great City* (Philadelphia: National Publication, 1872), pp. 386–389.

10   *British Mechanic's and Labourer's Hand Book*, quoted in Richard Stott, *Workers in the Metropolis: Class, Ethnicity, and Youth in Antebellum New York City* (Ithaca: Cornell University Press, 1990), p. 205.

11   Hareven and Modell, "Urbanization and the Malleable Household," p. 470.

12   Sociologists have labeled this lifestyle "urbanism." Louis Wirth, "Urbanism and Suburbanism as a Way of Life," *American Journal of Sociology* 44 (July 1938), pp. 1–24; and Gans, "Urbanism and Suburbanism," pp. 70–84. But historians have also attached a similar importance to boarding as a distinct subculture. See James Sterling Young, *The Washington Community: 1800–1828* (New York: Harcourt, Brace, World, 1966), p. 98. For boardinghouses as instruments for industrial social control, see Thomas Dublin, *Women at Work: The Transformation of Work and Community in Lowell, Massachusetts, 1826–1860* (New York: Columbia University Press, 1979), pp. 75–85. While it is doubtful that the New York boarding community possessed quite the cohesiveness of "segmented social structure of face-to-face peer groups" that Young uncovered in early nineteenth-century Washington's congressional houses, it still can be viewed as a system of "mutually exclusive, closely-knit voluntary associations." Semiautonomy nonetheless represented greater freedom even to those who boarded only with private families. Life with an uncle, a cousin, a friend, or even a stranger was often less constraining than the earlier subservience to a parent or the responsibilities of marriage that followed. Even for the small number of women who did not move directly into domestic service or marriage, life in a boardinghouse (particularly a coeducational one) loosened the shackles of family obligation while also teaching much about the world.

13   Claude S. Fischer, *To Dwell Among Friends: Personal Networks in Town and City* (Chicago: University of Chicago Press, 1982), pp. 194–197. Fischer points out that "subcultures and membership in them are matters of degree," such that not all of these criteria fit equally well. See also his "Toward a Subcultural Theory of Urbanism," in Mark Baldassare, ed., *Cities and Urban Living* (New York: Columbia University Press, 1983), pp. 84–114. The notion of social world as a spatial entity is described in its earliest form by Robert E. Park in "The City: Suggestions for the Investigation of Human Behavior in the Urban Environment," in Robert Park, Ernest Burgess, and Roderick McKenzie, *The City* (Chicago: University of Chicago Press, 1925), pp. 1–46; and "The Urban Community as a Spatial Pattern and a Moral Order," in Ralph Turner, ed., *Robert E. Park on Social Control and Collective Behavior* (Chicago: University of Chicago Press, 1967), pp. 55–68.

14   Blackmar, "Re-walking the 'Walking City,'" pp. 134, 136, 140; and Blackmar, *Manhattan for Rent*, pp. 62–68. For a discussion of boarding as familial income, also see Stansell, *City of Women*, pp. 13, 234–229. The rise of lodging-house districts in Boston's South and West Ends after 1870 has also been linked to a "downward shift in economic status" produced by the exodus of middle-class residents to sub-

urbs and the "encroachment of light industry and commerce." See Peel, "On the Margins," pp. 819–820.

15 Stansell, *City of Women*, p. 9.

16 McCabe, *Light and Shadows of New York Life*, p. 503; *New York in a Nutshell* (New York: J. W. Strong, 1853), p. 102. Scholars of the city have long recognized the importance of boarding in helping to effect the process of neighborhood change. Writing in the 1920s and 1930s, Chicago ecologists viewed the concentration of boardinghouses as an indicator of social decline. For a good description and critique of Burgess' work on zones of transition, see Timms, *The Urban Mosaic*, pp. 211–214.

17 Emory Holloway and Ralph Adimain, eds., *New York Dissected by Walt Whitman* (New York: Rufus Rockwell & Wilson, 1936), p. 96. For a discussion of boarding as a response to housing shortages, see Gunther Barth, *City People: The Rise of Modern City Culture in Nineteenth-Century America* (New York: Oxford University Press, 1980), pp. 42–43.

18 *Trow's New York City Business Directory, 1854–1855* (New York: John F. Trow, 1854), pp. 10–13. The table presents the differences between observed and modeled data in a two-variable comparison.

19 Glasco, "Migration and Adjustment in the City," p. 170; and Hareven and Modell, "Urbanization and the Malleable Household," p. 472.

20 Some of the boarding families may have operated in a manner that differed little from professional establishments. The instructions to marshals conducting the canvass required them to record only the first occupation provided by an individual, causing them to overlook boarding as a secondary source of income. Thus, the observation of Hareven and Modell that boarding was often a form of woman's work "performed by the wife within the home" cannot be tested with the New York data. New York Secretary of State, *Instructions for Taking the Census of the State of New York in the Year 1855* (Albany: Weed Parsons, 1855), pp. 12–17. Hareven and Modell, "Urbanization and the Malleable Household," p. 473.

21 The size and structure of boarding was frequently determined by the ethnic background of the household's head. A comparison among nativity, the number of boarders, and the presence of children found little evidence of boarders serving as a replacement for children who had departed. However, the census could only tell whether the family had any children present, not whether any had left. Relatively few Native and British families took in boarders, while for other groups, familial augmentation was common. Germans housed only one boarder at a time, while Irish were more likely to include several. Black New Yorkers showed perhaps the strongest propensity to take in boarders, a fact that is consistent with the earlier findings on the importance of boarding for the sampled Afro-Americans. For a discussion elsewhere of high levels of Afro-American boarding, see Weber, Bodnar, and Simon, *Lives of Their Own*, pp. 102–106.

22 The "malleable household" represented the formalized relationship between "distant relatives," former neighbors and friends, or "young men sharing a trade with the household head." Hareven and Modell, "Urbanization and the Malleable Household," pp. 467–468. For a discussion of boarding, household structure, and familial economics, see Katz, Doucet, and Stern, *The Social Organization of Early Industrial Capitalism*, pp. 296–307.

23 The formal boardinghouse was a place in which inhabitants—particularly young

males—received food, laundry, and upkeep like they had in the preindustrial systems of apprenticeship but with the crucial difference that boarders were free from
the authority and constraints of parent or master. While one scholar has stressed
their function as a "surrogate for the family" that guided "the young migrant from
the family home to marriage while keeping ties to family and community intact,"
evidence for New York City suggests that the environment of the boardinghouse
was far more fluid than traditional family life and, despite the occasional paternal
control of proprietors, socially liberating. Peel, "On the Margins," pp. 813–814; and
Paul Boyer, *Urban Masses and Moral Order in America, 1820–1920* (Cambridge:
Harvard University Press, 1978), p. 110. Blackmar also links boarding to transiency
and youth but stressed the negative stigma with which reformers viewed the practice. The liberty of female boardinghouses which suggested prostitution and the
alleged corruption of wealthy sons is tied to a growing domestic ethos in the early
1830s that "framed the perception of the private home as a distinct arena apart from
'public' workshops, boardinghouses, and institutions of workers' leisure." Blackmar, *Manhattan for Rent*, pp. 127–128, 134–137. Yet such social promiscuity seems
to have been tolerated as a stage of youth, and census evidence shows little drop in
the popularity of boarding despite such protests until the 1860s. Often the comfort
and sociability of boardinghouse life was enough to create a sense of loyalty and
conviviality among inmates.

24 Hareven and Modell, "Urbanization and the Malleable Household," pp. 467–479.

25 Gunn, *The Physiology of the New York Boarding-Houses*. This little volume was
especially popular in its day, and George Templeton Strong referred to it in his
diary, calling it "one of the most genuine attempts of humor I've seen lately." Allan
Nevins and Milton H. Thomas, eds., *The Diary of George Templeton Strong: The
Turbulent Fifties 1850–1859* (New York: Octagon Books, 1974), vol. 2, p. 349. A decade later the work was still held to be the authoritative work on its subject. See
Edward W. Martin, *The Secrets of the Great City* (Philadelphia: Jones, Brothers,
1868), pp. 211–214.

26 Gunn, *The Physiology of the New York Boarding-Houses*, pp. 21–22.

27 J. S. Buckingham, *America, Historical, Statistic and Descriptive*, vol. 1 (London:
Fisher, Son, 1841), p. 233. See also Blackmar, *Manhattan for Rent*, pp. 134–135.

28 Holloway and Adimain, eds., *New York Dissected by Walt Whitman*, p. 96.

29 Edgar W. Martin, *The Standard of Living in 1860: American Consumption Levels
on the Eve of the Civil War* (Chicago: University of Chicago Press, 1942), p. 168;
and James D. Burns, *Three Years Among the Working-Class in the United States
During the War* (London: Smith, Elder, 1865), p. 7. Among their principal residents, Blackmar listed mariners, laborers, widows, unmarried journeymen. Blackmar, "Re-walking the 'Walking City'," p. 134. Also Howard B. Rock, *Artisans of
the New Republic: The Tradesmen of New York City in the Age of Jefferson* (New
York: New York University Press, 1979), p. 3; Gary Nash, "The Social Evolution of
Preindustrial American Cities, 1700–1820," in Raymond A. Mohl, ed., *The Making
of Urban America* (Wilmington, Del.: Scholarly Resources, 1988), p. 31.

30 Such a meal consisted of a breakfast of leftover hash and hot vegetables with the
first and third meals—although the author told of how one morning he and his
housemates gave a "funeral" to an unusually stale mackerel. *The British Mechanic's
and Labourer's Hand Book and True Guide to the United States* (London: Chas.
Knight, 1840), pp. 48, 56–57.

31 Henry Taylor, *New York as It Was Sixty Years Ago* (Brooklyn: Nolan, 1894), p. 16; Fannie Benedict, "Boarding-House Experience in New York," *Packard's Monthly* (1869), p. 101; Burns, *Three Years Among the Working-Class in the United States During the War*, p. 8; Mrs. Felton, *American Life: A Narrative of Two Years' Life and Country Residence in the United States* (London: Simpkin Marshall, 1842), p. 72; Buckingham, *America*, vol. 1, p. 232; and John F. Maguire, *The Irish in America* (London: 1868), pp. 26–29, 194. A figure of $4–$6 was given by William Hancock, *An Emigrant's Five Years in the Free States of America* (London: T. Cautley, 1860), p. 83.

32 Buckingham, *America*, vol. 1, p. 232.

33 Stanley Nadel, *Little Germany: Ethnicity, Religion, and Class in New York City, 1845–80* (Urbana: University of Illinois Press, 1990), p. 47. Nadel based this argument upon the assumption that "networks of friends were rarely as reliable as those of kin."

34 Franklin D. Scott, trans. and ed., *Baron Klinkowstrom's America 1818–1820* (Evanston: Northwestern University Press, 1952), p. 87.

35 Felton, *American Life*, p. 73.

36 Benedict, "Boarding-House Experience in New York," p. 103.

37 Jeremiah O'Donovan, *A Brief Account of the Author's Interview with His Countrymen, and the Parts of the Emerald Isle Whence They Emigrated Together with a Direct Reference to Their Present Location in the Land of Their Adoption, During the Travels Through Various States of the Union in 1854 and 1855* (Pittsburgh: Published by the Author, 1864), p. 92.

38 Kathleen Conzen, *Immigrant Milwaukee 1836–1860: Accommodation and Community in a Frontier City* (Cambridge: Harvard University Press, 1976), pp. 57–58.

39 Hareven and Modell, "Urbanization and the Malleable Household," pp. 472–473. The acculturative value of boarding often came from the mixing of cultures between newcomer and experienced household head. The pattern by which boarders found a house or family could be complicated, reflecting not only ethnic ties, but also a particular "avoidance pattern" among the foreign-born, as Hareven and Modell have noted. Ironically, immigrants mingled more often with New England-born Bostonians than with foreigners from ethnic groups other than their own. Another study of Boston boarding found that in 1860, 89 percent of tenants lodged with individuals of similar national background and occupation. Peel, "On the Margins," pp. 823–829.

40 Wilentz, *Chants Democratic*, pp. 52–53, 55.

41 See chapters from Gunn's *The Physiology of New York Boarding-Houses* on each respective group. For a discussion of Jewish boardinghouses in New York City, see Hyman B. Grinstein, *The Rise of the Jewish Community of New York 1654–1860* (Philadelphia: Jewish Publication Society of America, 1945), pp. 299–300.

42 Nearly 57 percent of native-born New Yorkers also resided with fellow natives. Furthermore, certain groups also demonstrated patterns of mutual avoidance. Native-born boarders were commonly found in the homes of English families but spurned Irish and German households. English boarders showed no particular tendency toward ethnic exclusivity but avoided boarding with Germans. Hibernians generally shunned other ethnic groups. This strong pattern of segregation among ethnic groups in their boarding habits runs counter to the findings of other histori-

ans who argued that boarding was a phenomenon limited to native migrants who "were newest to the city" and to immigrants who "resorted to boarding as a temporary measure until they settled in their own households in other parts of the city or in other towns." In New York, boarding was as much a life-style for those already knowledgeable with the ways of the city as it was an institution for socializing newcomers. Hareven and Modell, "Urbanization and the Malleable Household," p. 471. See also Glasco, "Migration and Adjustment in the City," pp. 170–173.

43   The occupational data suggests that professional boardinghouses appealed largely to a middle-class audience. Many of those who chose not to live with private families were probably petty-proprietary workers, mainly clerks, who found the close proximity of boarding establishments to their places of work to be especially attractive. One such house from the 1820s, which was "looked upon as somwhat superior to the common; it being an established rule of the house for not more than six gentlemen to sleep in one room," boarded "principally young men, mostly clerk," who worked in nearby dry goods stores. Cited in Alvin Harlow, *Old Bowery Days* (New York: D. Appleton, 1931), pp. 170–171.

44   O'Donovan, *A Brief Account of the Author's Interview with His Countrymen*, p. 92.

45   For a description of the process, see Gunn, *The Physiology of New York Boarding-Houses*, pp. 15–20.

46   Barbara J. Berg, *The Remembered Gate: Origins of American Feminism—The Woman and the City 1800–1860* (New York: Oxford University Press, 1978), p. 97.

47   McCabe, *Light and Shadows*, p. 215.

48   Hancock, *An Emigrant's Five Years in the Free States of America*, pp. 81–83. For a lurid description of vice and crime in boardinghouses, see Martin, *The Secrets of the Great City*, pp. 214–222, 300–303. Also Smith, *Sunshine and Shadow in New York*, pp. 431–434; McCabe, *Light and Shadows*, pp. 505–507. For a listing of boardinghouses used as brothels or houses of assignation, see [H. D. Eastman], *Fast Man's Directory and Lover's Guide by the Ladies' Man* (New York: n.p., 1853), and *Directory To the Seraglios in New York, Philadelphia, Boston and All the Principal Cities in The Union By a Free Lover* (New York: 1859).

49   Townsend, *Appleton's Dictionary of New York City*, p. 32.

50   Felton, *American Life*, p. 61.

51   Halliday, *The Lost and Found or Life Among the Poor*, p. 48.

52   Rev. Henry Chase, Manuscript Marriage Records, 1830–1853 (fifteen volumes), at the New York Historical Society. Record for January 22, 1850.

53   Burns, *Three Years Among the Working-Class*, p. 7.

54   Benedict, "Boarding-House Experience in New York," p. 103.

55   Fenton, *American Life*, p. 74.

56   McCabe, *Lights and Shadows*, p. 503. While it was not uncommon to find married boarders residing in New York houses, families with children over the age of ten were a rarity. Since boarding was much more commonly a part of semiautonomy for men than it was for women, only 10 to 14 percent of male boarders over the age of ten were married. Native-born white males, however, were exceptions since only one-fifth were married. With males outnumbering female boarders in most cases by two to one, and, in the case of German-born boarders, by better than five to one, it is not surprising that a substantially larger proportion of women were married

than men (assuming that married boarders lived as couples). If children were ever present in boardinghouses, virtually all their parents very quickly moved to more private accommodations.

57 Gunn, *The Physiology of New York Boarding-Houses*, p. 36; Burns, *Three Years Among the Working-Class*, p. 8.

58 New York City Common Council, *Minutes 1789–1831*, vol. 2 (New York: 1911), p. 496.

59 Samuel Latham Mitchell, *The Picture of New York or the Traveler's Guide* (New York: I. Riley, 1807), p. 210. Also John Duffy, *A History of Public Health in New York City 1725–1866* (New York: Russell Sage Foundation, 1971), p. 228.

60 New York City Common Council, *Minutes 1789–1831*, vol. 3, p. 677.

61 Peter Townsend, *An Account of the Yellow Fever as it Prevailed in the City of New York in Summer and Autumn 1822* (New York: O. Halstead, 1823), p. 254.

62 Hareven and Modell, "Urbanization and the Malleable Household," pp. 468–469.

63 Charles Mackay, *Life and Liberty in America*, vol. 1 (London: Smith, Elder, 1859), p. 44.

64 Buckingham, *America*, vol. 1, p. 234.

65 Burns, *Three Years Life Among the Working-Class*, p. 69.

66 Burns, *Three Years Life Among the Working-Class*, p. 9.

67 Stansell, *City of Women*, pp. 185–186.

68 William Burns, *Life in New York* (New York: 1853), [p. 2].

69 Benedict, "Boarding-House Experience in New York," p. 103.

70 Townsend, *An Account of the Yellow Fever*, p. 57.

71 John B. Gough, *Autobiography and Personal Recollections* (Springfield, Mass.: Bill, Nichols, 1870), pp. 63–64.

72 New York City Police Department, Manuscript Tenth District Police Blotter, July 7, 1856–November 29, 1856, New York City Municipal Archives, Box 4063. Entry from p. 196. The roommate was arrested.

73 Gunn, *The Physiology of New York Boarding-Houses*, dedication. Peel attributes the rise of tenant subculture to the transition from boarding to lodging. Since boarding maintained a "disciplinary and explicit social-control function," the rise of a distinct group of lodgers composed of "immigrants, Americans, middle-rank workers, and working women," who had moved away from "family surrogates and segregation and toward independence and greater integration," promoted "marginality" rather than semiautonomy. Peel may be correct in challenging the reform view of the lodging-house as a social evil. But he makes too great a distinction between the familial control of the boardinghouse and the freedom of the new institution of lodging. In antebellum New York City—despite the social control exercised by boardinghouse keepers—tenants clearly saw their lives as less restrictive than they are portrayed as being by Peel. "On the Margins," pp. 833–834.

74 Many boarders in downtown wards might have been the children of the middle classes, a fact which suggested that boarders, like members of other urban subcultures, were more than representatives of class, ethnicity, or trade; they also constituted the nineteenth-century equivalents of the modern pleasure-seeking "cosmopolitanite." Benedict, "Boarding-House Experience in New York," p. 103. Such cosmopolitanism placed boardinghouse life in league with other urban subculture described (and frequently satirized) by contemporaries such as the Broadway Dandy and the Bohemian (not to mention the Bowery Boy). Broadway Dandies were

young single men of the middle and upper classes who chose city life because of the excitement that it presented. See John D. Vose, *Fresh Leaves from the Diary of a Broadway Dandy* (New York: Bunnell & Price, 1852); and John F. Kasson, *Rudeness & Civility: Manners in Nineteenth-Century Urban America* (New York: Hill and Wang, 1990), pp. 118–119, 127–128.

75 Wilentz, *Chants Democratic*, p. 53; Stansell, *City of Women*, pp. 86–93; Peter George Buckley, "To the Opera House: Culture and Society in New York City, 1820–1860" (Ph.D. diss., SUNY Stony Brook, 1984), pp. 323–325.

76 For a discussion of boarding and apartment buildings as middle- and upper-class urban phenomena, see Barth, *City People*, pp. 45, 51–52. The increasing importance of privacy in nineteenth-century family life is covered in Barbara Laslett, "The Family as a Public and Private Institution: An Historical Perspective," *Journal of Marriage and the Family* 35 (1973), pp. 480–491. The attenuation of semiautonomy in the maturing urban-industrial society is described in Katz, Doucet, and Stern, *The Social Organization of Early Industrial Society*, pp. 242–285. For the decline of boarding and its replacement by lodging, which was less segregated by occupation and ethnicity, see Peel, "On the Margins," pp. 813–834.

77 The household was more than a familial institution in which individuals performed some substantive roles, be it as "head," spouse, child, some other resident relative, or coresident outsider such as boarder or servant. Yet it is necessary to go beyond static pictures of the family frozen at a single point in time to the study of the "cycle of individual families over time." Hareven, "The Family as Process: The Historical Study of the Family Cycle," pp. 322–329. Though schemes vary among historians, three schemes are generally employed to study household structure: nuclearity, extension, and augmentation. See also Katz, *The People of Hamilton, Canada West*, pp. 213–240; and Stuart M. Blumin, "Rip Van Winkle's Grandchildren: Family and Household in the Hudson Valley, 1800–1860," in Tamara Hareven, ed., *Family and Kin in Urban Communities, 1700–1930*, pp. 100–121. The most important recent application of these classifications can be found in Hareven's *Family Time & Industry Time: The Relationship between the Family and Work in a New England Industrial Community* (Cambridge: Cambridge University Press, 1982), pp. 154–188. The changing nature of household organization over the course of the familial life cycle makes familialism important in understanding the development of neighborhoods. By studying the multiple interaction among the age of household heads, the site of neighborhoods, and the roominess of housing in Cleveland, Avery Guest concluded that "most neighborhoods are apt to have a relatively wide range of family types." Avery M. Guest, "Patterns of Family Location," *Demography* 9, no. 1 (February 1972), pp. 159–171. Still, among even those most critical of efforts to study neighborhood morphology in terms of "family status," there is agreement that "familialism and urbanism" exist, in the words of Duncan Timms, as "virtually incompatible lifestyles." Timms, *The Urban Mosaic*, p. 107.

78 The extent of ethnic variation in life-cycle transition remains a question of some disagreement. While some have argued for an ethnic patterning of such transitions, others have argued that "the most consistent differences in life cycle" occurred between men and women of the same ethnic group. Even though immigrant girls were more likely to spend their adolescence working as domestic servants than those born in America, the gap between the cosmopolitan Irish servant girls who had been exposed to "an intimate living situation with persons of another ethnic

group" and her Irish brothers may have been *wider* than it was with a native-born Buffaloan of the same age. Glasco, "The Life Cycles and Household Structure of American Ethnic Groups," pp. 122–143. However, Zunz discounted any ability of household organization to show "cultural and behavior differences among groups." Zunz, *The Changing Face of Inequality*, pp. 67–73.

79 Household composition was studied by grouping residents listed in the census both by household and individually. Similar methodology is described in Michael Anderson, "Family and Class in Nineteenth-Century Cities," *Journal of Family History* 2 (1977), p. 145. Unfortunately, the 1855 census is the only surviving source containing exact information on family relationships before 1880. Consequently, the picture that the following quantitative analysis presents is a static one that tells little about the overlap between family and neighborhood life cycles. Nonetheless, an awareness of life courses in the process of residential transition does provide a useful framework for examining the role of demography in promoting neighborhood change, much as Tamara Hareven's concept of the personal and family life course can aid in understanding the process of change for the individual. Tamara Hareven, "The Family as Process: The Historical Study of the Family Cycle," *Journal of Social History* 7 (Spring 1974), pp. 322–329. Also, her "Cycles, Courses and Cohorts: Reflections on the Theoretical and Methodological Approaches to the Historical Study of Family Development," *Journal of Interdisciplinary History* 11 (1978), pp. 79–109. For an early application of life-cycle analysis, see Peter R. Uhlenberg, "A Study of Cohort Life Cycles: Cohorts of Native-Born Massachusetts Women, 1830–1920," *Population Studies* 23 (November 1969), pp. 407–420.

80 I have drawn heavily upon Glasco's methodology, which uses the 1855 New York manuscript census for Buffalo. However, my methodology differs from Glasco's in its use of five-year intervals. My feeling was that the loss in precision was more than made up for by the benefits of the multivariate analysis that fewer categories allowed me to use. But I have followed his lead in excluding individuals under the age of ten or older than thirty-nine, which controlled for error stemming from the failure of the census to differentiate children of native parents from native-born children of foreign parents. Glasco, "The Life Cycles and Household Structure of American Ethnic Groups," pp. 122–143, and "Migration and Adjustment in the Nineteenth-Century City," pp. 154–178. The modeled data is the product of a four-variable analysis of relationship to the head-of-household from the 1855 manuscript census including as additional variables, ethnicity, age, and sex. The material presented in the graphs consist of the significant third-order effect "nativity-age-household status" and the second-order association "sex-household status."

81 In Buffalo most residents had already been filtered through the selective sieve of a seaport community as immigrants or through the countryside as migrants. Glasco, "The Life Cycles and Household Structure of American Ethnic Groups," pp. 122–143.

82 The long periods of domestic service also delayed marriage for the daughters of Erin. According to the 1855 state census, only one in three Irish-born women aged twenty to twenty-four living in New York was married, compared with the four-fifths of women who were already married by the age of twenty-two in Buffalo.

83 The data fails to resolve whether apprenticeship existed as "an additional intermediate step between childhood and boarding or marriage," as Glasco had argued, since the proportion of Germans boarding between the ages of fifteen and nine-

teen equals that of similarly aged Irish youth—even when excluding apprentices. Glasco, "The Life Cycles and Household Structure of American Ethnic Groups," pp. 135–138. Michael Katz, Michael Doucet, and Mark Stern used multivariate analysis to reestimate the probability of different ethnic group members residing with their parents, boarding, and being married at a given age; see their *The Social Organization of Early Industrial Capitalism*, pp. 261–264.

84   What determined the timing of the departure of children from parental control has been a source for considerable historical debate. Michael Katz argued that the expansion of capitalism replaced extended periods of semiautonomy and fostering out to other families with extended periods at home, schooling, and delayed marriage. Class differences influenced levels of youth employment, producing a bifurcation of school attendance and early employment between middle-class children, who remained at home and attended school, and working-class children—many of whom were impoverished—who departed home for work. However, Michael Anderson contended that the death of one or both parents must have been the main reason why many teenagers went into lodging or to live with kin, "largely because kinship ties provided a way of caring for orphans," forced outside the home by the "critical life situation" of a parent's death. See Katz, *The People of Hamilton, Canada West*, pp. 54–55; more detailed multivariate analysis in Katz, Doucet, and Stern, *The Social Organization of Early Industrial Capitalism*, pp. 264–278; and also Michael Anderson, *Family Structure in Nineteenth-Century Lancashire* (Cambridge: Cambridge University Press, 1971), pp. 54–55. While many of these contentions cannot be tested for New York City, the North River Savings Bank, which asked new depositors to provide information on their ethnic background together with the names of surviving parents, largely supports Anderson's findings on the relationship between boarding and the loss of a parent. Half of those depositors in their early teens had lost at least one parent, 27.8 percent lacked a father, and 13 percent were already orphans by the age of fifteen. By the age of twenty-four, half were without fathers. These figures, which did not vary significantly by ethnic group, can only suggest the relationship between the loss of earnings from a deceased parent and the need to strike out on one's own—assuming depositors are representative of the broader population. North River Savings Bank Signature Book, New York City, vol. 1, 1866–1869.

85   The small proportion of Irish teenagers who resided with their parents, coupled with the data on the age of migration presented in the second chapter, raises questions with Carol Groneman Pernicone's conclusion that New York's Irish came over in family groups rather than as individuals. Pernicone, "The 'Bloody Ould Sixth': A Social Analysis of a New York City Working-Class Community in the Mid-Nineteenth Century" (Ph.D. diss., University of Rochester, 1973), p. 55. However, the manuscript state census data does not show the operation of chain migration—whether immigrants reformed families once they arrived or whether they migrated in family groups.

86   Whether this pattern was a continuation of traditional Irish rural family-rearing patterns where patriarchal dominance governed the family is unclear, although family ties of affection and obligation in Ireland often delayed marriage so that parents could extract the unpaid labor of sons and partible inheritance. Kerby A. Miller, *Emigrants and Exiles: Ireland and the Irish Exodus to North America* (New York: Oxford University Press, 1985), pp. 54–60. For another discussion of Irish family

life, see Hasia R. Diner, *Erin's Daughters in America: Irish Immigrant Women in the Nineteenth Century* (Baltimore: Johns Hopkins University Press, 1983), pp. 53–60.

87 Despite the late departure of children among native-born and Irish adolescent males, there is little sign in New York City that such an extended period of adolescent dependency was the result of a prolongation of schooling, as some have argued. The extension of adolescent dependency for schooling described by Katz, Doucet, and Stern failed to apply to foreign-born, for all but a few of the remaining males had left home by their early twenties. In Hamilton, Ontario, the proportion of young men living with their parents rose from 24 percent in 1851 to 54 percent in 1861, while, in New York City, one-third of the native-born men twenty to twenty-four years of age and 18 percent of those in the twenty-five to twenty-nine age range still resided at home. Katz, Doucet, and Stern, *The Social Organization of Early Industrial Capitalism,* pp. 244–252.

88 The out-migration of young men in search of employment also produced a bulge in the demographic balance of New York neighborhoods favoring women. Stott, *Workers in the Metropolis,* pp. 72–74, 102–108; Stansell, *City of Women,* pp. 83–85, 105–125, 155–157; Pernicone, "The 'Bloody Ould Sixth'," pp. 157–160; Kessler-Harris, *Out to Work,* pp. 46–47, 55.

89 Although native women were slightly more likely to board than were their Irish counterparts, in almost all categories, native boarding was substantially below that of other nativity groups. This runs counter to the findings of other historians in one crucial regard: native-born city dwellers were not more likely to board than other groups—indeed, proportionally fewer American males in the sample wards boarded with families or in houses than males from other groups. Glasco, "Migration and Adjustment in the City," pp. 170–175; and Hareven and Modell, "Urbanization and the Malleable Household," pp. 471–473.

90 The option of boarding enhanced opportunities by forming acquaintances that promoted new social bridges for jobs. While evidence does not specifically exist for New York, David Garrioch's study of Paris argued that increased residence in lodging-houses of young unmarried journeymen led these men to live and eat together with other journeymen of different trades. In the short run, this might have strengthened local community and produced a "city-wide solidarity among journeymen of many trades." Garrioch, *Neighborhood & Community in Paris, 1740–1790* (Cambridge: Cambridge University Press, 1986), p. 111.

91 Other trades dominated by Germans included tailoring and shoemaking. One historian found that of twelve- and thirteen-year-old German boys, a third worked as apprentices and the majority as store clerks. Among fourteen and fifteen year olds, 60 percent were learning trades. Nadel, *Little Germany,* pp. 62–64, 78–81. Since Germans were the only group with a substantial number of apprentices, this would suggest that this form of apprenticeship was a peculiarly ethnic arrangement. This assumption is supported by the general decline of the practice of formalized apprenticeship and the loosening of the requirements (and benefits) of indenture. See Sean Wilentz, *Chants Democratic: New York City & the Rise of the American Working Class, 1788–1850* (New York: Oxford University Press, 1984), pp. 28, 33; and Stansell, *City of Women,* p. 203. For a discussion of the broader decline of this practice and its relationship to schooling, see Katz, Doucet, and Stern, *The Social Organization of Early Industrial Capitalism,* p. 255. Yet, despite decline, "apprenticeship

before 1860 never completely degenerated into wage work; instruction, albeit increasingly shallow, continued to play a role." Immigrants still wondered at the ease at which boys could find productive work. Stott, *Workers in the Metropolis*, pp. 96–102.

92   Michael Katz has suggested that such a period of extended childhood might have led to affluent daughters spending "several years in what only can be described as a state of semi-idleness"—a circumstance that he blamed for the high levels of "nervous disease" reported among well-to-do Victorian women. Whether this was the case for young native women in New York is unclear, and much evidence exists of highly structured social lives for adolescents, including schooling in female academies, religious activities, and a myriad of social occasions. Katz, *The People of Hamilton, Canada West*, p. 322. For a discussion of fancy balls, see *The Fancy Ball Given by Mrs SXXXX: A Description of the Characters, Dresses &c, Assumed on the Occasion* (New York: Morning Courier, 1829). For a description of one woman's growing up, see Marian Gouverneur, *As I Remember: Recollections of American Society During the Nineteenth Century* (New York: D. Appleton, 1911).

93   Stansell, *City of Women*, pp. 100, 77–80.

94   After the age of twenty-four marriage patterns among Irish and native males were largely identical with the small exception of Irishmen, who in their late thirties were even *more* likely to be married than their American counterparts (78 compared to 71 percent). By the age of thirty-five, 72 percent of Germans had taken wives (5 percent above other groups), and by the age of forty, this figure had jumped to nearly 85 percent. English men, however, were reluctant husbands; nearly one in four continued to board well into their thirties, and 38 percent over the age of thirty-five still lived outside nuclear families.

95   Stott, *Workers in the Metropolis*, pp. 207–208; Stansell, *City of Women*, pp. 84–85.

96   Shane White, " 'We Dwell in Safety and Pursue Our Honest Calling': Free Blacks in New York City, 1783–1810," *Journal of American History* 75 (September 1988), pp. 457–458, and *Somewhat More Independent: The End of Slavery in New York City, 1770–1810* (Athens: University of Georgia Press, 1991), pp. 166–171. While similar late-marriage, matrifocal households, and even nonmarriage have also been described for Irish households, the phased manumission in New York and the higher employment opportunities in New York than other cities, which drew in immigrants, added a "fragility" to black family life that well exceeded that for the Irish. Finding of high degrees of family fragmentation strongly contradicts the discovery of significant nuclearity in early nineteenth-century Philadelphia and among Boston blacks for a later period. See Gary B. Nash, *Forging Freedom: The Formation of Philadelphia's Black Community, 1720–1840* (Cambridge: Harvard University Press, 1988), pp. 136, 158–159, 161–164; and Elizabeth Pleck "The Two-Parent Household: Black Family Structure in Late Nineteenth Century Boston," *Journal of Social History* 6, no. 1 (Fall 1972), pp. 3–31. Modell, Furstenberg, and Hershberg documented a proportion of female-headed black households that was twice that of other groups in nineteenth-century Philadelphia, but attribute this entirely to higher mortality rates from poverty to be found in cities. Frank K. Furstenberg, Jr., John Modell, and Theodore Hershberg, "The Origin of the Female-Headed Black Family: The Impact of the Urban Experience," in Theodore Hershberg, ed., *Philadelphia: Work, Space, Family, and Group Experience in the 19th Century* (New York: Oxford University Press, 1981), pp. 434–454. However, both studies

employ only the vague yardstick of household "nuclearity" suggested by the long-simmering historical controversy over fatherless black families. The timing of life cycle, when studied using multivariate techniques, offers a more detailed mode analysis that catches differences which household structure misses—not only for blacks but for other ethnic groups as well. The New York data suggests that there is more to black differences in family structure during the nineteenth century than just the matrifocal household. This finding is supported by twentieth-century data for Pittsburgh. See John Bodnar, Roger Simon, and Michael P. Weber, *Lives of Their Own: Blacks, Italians, and Poles in Pittsburgh, 1900–1960* (Urbana: University of Illinois Press, 1982), p. 108. Anthro-historical studies of the adjustment of black families to urban life reveal similar patterns of differences between the main-stream (white) model of sex-roles, legitimacy, and marriage and that of blacks, but deny this necessarily resulted in "broken families." See James Borchert, *Alley Life in Washington: Family, Community, Religion, and Folklife in the City, 1850–1970* (Urbana: University of Illinois Press, 1980) pp. 57–99; and Carol B. Stack, *All Our Kin: Strategies for Survival in a Black Community* (New York: Harper & Row, 1974), pp. 90–129.

97   Black women were pushed out of general household service into "specialized situations in the retinues of the wealthy and in brothels as laundresses, charwomen, and maids." Stansell, *City of Women*, pp. 156–157.

98   The high number of boardinghouses in the Fifth Ward may have biased the findings by exaggerating the rootlessness of its population.

99   Stott, *Workers in the Metropolis*, pp. 210, 244. Stott also contends that this movement "did much to further the development of a strong neighborhood localism in the city."

100   For an historical discussion of suburbs as family-based enclaves, see John Modell, "An Ecology of Family Decisions: Suburbanization, Schooling, and Fertility in Philadelphia, 1860–1920," *Journal of Urban History* 6 (August 1980), pp. 397–477. For an early assessment of suburbs as an ideal place in which to raise children compared to central city slums, see Samuel B. Halliday, *The Lost and Found or Life Among the Poor* (New York: Blakeman & Mason, 1859), pp. 221–223.

101   Stott, *Workers in the Metropolis*, pp. 207–210.

102   A comparison of the impact of age, sex, and nativity upon residential selection showed that while sex and age did not influence where New Yorkers settled independent of ethnicity, a third-order association for the effect "age-nativity-ward" was significant (chi-square reduction = 175.67).

103   This pattern is complicated by the fact that the category native-born encompassed both those born of American parents and second generation immigrants. Thus the level of native-born children was actually higher in predominantly German or Irish wards. In addition, because the 1855 census came at the close of a major period of immigration, the age distribution is essentially that of a highly volatile population of newcomers. In addition, ethnic groups showed significant variations in sex-ratio. Irish-born, and, to a lesser extent, blacks showed a surplus of women (57.5 and 52.8 percent, respectively), while German-, English-Scottish-, and "Other Foreign-born" had a deficit of females (44.8, 46.6, and 41.1 percent). The proportion of females equaled that of males only for native-born whites. In neither case were these differences large enough to be reflected either directly or indirectly in residential choice. See also Pernicone, in "The 'Bloody Ould Sixth'," p. 71.

104   Tamara Hareven, in her major study of family structure and industrialization in Manchester, New Hampshire, has observed that "Households are like a revolving stage on which different members appeared and disappeared, under their own momentum or under the impact of external conditions." As with the movement of individuals through different roles in the family, households themselves exhibited changes which can be measured through the movement of kin, relatives, and strangers in and out of its boundaries. Hareven, *Family Time & Industrial Time*, pp. 154–156, 163–164. For other cities, see Conzen, *Immigrant Milwaukee*, p. 55. By contrast, Lynn Lees's study of Irish families in Victorian London discovered that recently arrived settlers "adjusted their household composition to fit family and communal needs," despite the dominance of nuclear families. Lynn H. Lees, *Exiles of Erin: Irish Migrants in Victorian London* (Ithaca: Cornell University Press, 1979), pp. 134–135.

105   The weak relationship found between age and ward in the model controlling for ethnicity disappeared once ethnicity was replaced by family status. The categories employed to study family status correspond to the scheme widely used by family historians to measure life-cycle transition: (1) a state of full dependency as a child, progressing through (2) an adolescent stage of semiautonomy, to (3) a stage of obligation as parent, and, finally, to (4) a new stage of dependency upon children or other relatives.

106   If we construct an ordered causal system (path model) on the basis of what has already been learned about ethnic differences in ages-at-arrival, settlement of different arrival cohorts, and the occupational basis of residence, the resulting model presumes that the ethnic background of household heads influenced their age distribution, job status, and the composition of the households they headed. In turn, each of these factors acted singly or in concert with other variables to influence where families chose to settle. Because polytomous variables add considerable complexity to the effects models, two analyses were conducted: one using a model computed for dichotomized variables that produces "coefficients as slopes for the change in Y per unit change in X" (Panel A) and a second model employing polytomous variables that, while only showing effects through reductions in chi-square (which do not produce cross-sectional slopes), yield standardized tables showing relationships among categories within variables controlling for prior variables (Panel B). Davis, "Extending Rosenberg's Technique for Standardizing Percentage Tables," p. 694.

107   Occupational rank masked the fact that significantly fewer native households were headed by widows. Controlling for prior associations, the chief ethnic differences in household composition lay with widowhood and the inclusion of children and/ or relatives.

108   This pattern differed from what Katz found for Hamilton, Ontario, where professional and petty-proprietary families were considerably more likely to take in boarders than either skilled workers or laborers. Katz, *The People of Hamilton, Canada West*, pp. 75–77. As often as not, the ability to care for relatives was related to the family's available resources for feeding and housing kin. Stansell, *City of Women*, p. 13.

109   Among Kleindeutschland Germans, "family formation and childbearing" were "affected more by occupational and economic factors than by the mother's place of origin in Germany." Thus men without skills or property married later and had children at later ages than others. Nadel, *Little Germany*, pp. 53, 56–58.

110 The impact of age upon household structure was nonspurious and direct. While 27.5 percent of the relationship between occupational rank and household was the spurious result of prior factors, only 5.3 percent of the age-based variation was spurious. And while 17.1 percent of ethnic variations in households was the indirect product of intervening variables, only 4.1 percent of the causal (net) effect of age upon family was indirect.

111 Hareven and Modell, "Urbanization and the Malleable Household," pp. 472–475. Other analysis on New York data found that the propensity to incorporate relatives into the family also did not alter with age—although which relatives were included varied with age. Young families tended to take in parents or siblings, while older ones (after the death of parents and the maturing of siblings) housed cousins, nieces, and nephews. For a discussion of the role of urban households in providing housing, employment, and other aid to migrant siblings, cousins, nieces, and nephews, see Anderson, *Family Structure in Nineteenth-Century Lancashire*, pp. 43–46, 155–156.

112 In the polytomous model, more than a third of the chi-square variation was the spurious result of associations discussed above. Nonetheless, dichotomized data suggests that for every ten points' change in the proportion of families with boarders, the proportion of those living in "downtown" neighborhoods rose one point—a substantial relationship that existed independent of other variables.

113 Some of the apparent influence of family was spurious: a seeming concentration of childless parents in the Fifth Ward and widow-headed families in the Tenth disappeared when controlling for prior effects of ethnicity and age. Furthermore, adjusting for occupational rank also removed much of the Fourth Ward's importance as a magnet for boarders.

114 Tamara Hareven and Maris Vinovskis were the first historians to employ an age-adjusted fertility technique for married women aged twenty to twenty-nine to measure fertility in two neighborhoods in late-nineteenth-century Boston. Their comparison of Irish fertility in the South End with that in South Boston led them to conclude that historians could no longer "treat urban areas as homogeneous entities." Hareven and Vinovskis, "Marital Fertility and Occupation in Urban Families," pp. 75–76, 84–85.

115 Olivier Zunz, "The Organization of the American City in the Late Nineteenth Century: Ethnic Structure and Spatial Arrangement in Detroit," *Journal of Urban History* 3 (August 1977), p. 457. Zunz is essentially correct in arguing fertility rates combine "many immeasurable factors," including: the "opportunity structure" of education and career, the cultural attitudes of parents regarding contraception and children, mortality rates, and the "relative cost of children weighed against their usefulness in the context of the family economy." Zunz, *The Changing Face of Inequality*, p. 73.

116 John Modell, "An Ecology of Family Decisions: Suburbanization, Schooling, and Fertility in Philadelphia, 1860–1920," *Journal of Urban History* 6 (August 1980), pp. 397–477. Striking ethnic differences could be found in unstandardized marital fertility levels (children younger than five per woman aged between twenty and forty-nine years) of different ethnic groups of New Yorkers comparable to those found by other historians studying Boston, Detroit, and Hamilton, Ontario. See Tamara Hareven and Maris Vinovskis, "Patterns of Childbearing in Late Nineteenth-Century America: The Determinants of Marital Fertility in Five Mas-

sachusetts Towns in 1880," in Hareven and Vinovskis, eds., *Family and Population in Nineteenth-Century America*, p. 85–125; and Michael R. Haines, "Fertility, Marriage, and Occupation in the Pennsylvania Anthracite Region, 1850–1880," *Journal of Family History* 2 (Spring 1977), pp. 28–55. Neighborhood fertility levels are presented in Hareven and Vinovskis, "Marital Fertility and Occupation in Urban Families," pp. 76–78, 84. For Detroit, see Zunz, *The Changing Face of Inequality*, pp. 74–78; and for Hamilton, Ontario, see Katz, Doucet, and Stern, *The Social Organization of Early Industrial Capitalism*, pp. 336–340.

117 English childbearing rose briefly in the early forties after a sharp decline. After age forty-five, no married German or "Other" women in the sample had children under five years of age. Because of the smallness of sample size for this group, no fertility ratios were calculated for black women.

118 For New York women, unlike their counterparts in other cities, the relationship was neither "curvilinear" nor "inversely proportional" to occupational rank, but instead direct. Hareven and Vinovskis, "Marital Fertility and Occupation in Urban Families," p. 79. Zunz, *The Changing Face of Inequality*, p. 74. Katz, Doucet, and Stern find that working-class fertility increased between 1851 and 1871, while that for the business class fell, suggesting a need to depend more upon children for the family economy; however, the gap between classes at no point approaches that observed for Boston, Detroit, or here for New York. See their *The Social Organization of Early Industrial Capitalism*, pp. 336–338.

119 The pattern of descending rates of fertility as one moved from business to working classes was primarily a reflection of an ethnic division in the labor force rather than class-based differences in the value of children. While fewer children were born to native semiskilled and unskilled households than to skilled, professionals, and proprietors, the pattern was not conclusive among foreign-born women. However, these tables must be interpreted with some care due to the fact that age-standardized marital fertility is susceptible to wide fluctuations due to small sample sizes. This problem has been largely overlooked by proponents of this technique. See, for example, Zunz's occupational breakdown of Poles, which included only forty-eight women, while many of his cells contain under ten. Zunz, *The Changing Face of Inequality*, p. 74. The same caveat of small sample size applies to the New York data.

120 The close associations between urban subcultures and particular subareas of the city have been interpreted as evidence that neighborhoods possessed life cycles of their own, paralleling those of families. Hoover and Vernon described five separate stages in urban evolution for New York City based upon the response of the housing market to family demography: (1) the construction of new single-family subdivisions, (2) apartment development, (3) downgrading associated with conversion, (4) thinning-out, and (5) renewal. Hoover and Vernon, *The Anatomy of a Metropolis*, p. 198, and White, *American Neighborhoods and Residential Differentiation* pp. 200–202.

121 Sennett, *Families Against the City*. See also Neil J. Smelser, *Social Change and the Industrial Revolution* (Chicago: University of Chicago Press, 1959).

122 The result was a complex and, at times, blurred picture of neighborhood structure that failed to conform to either the model of the spatial ecologists or to that of the ethnically divided industrializing city sketched out by Zunz in his study of Detroit. See Zunz, *The Changing Face of Inequality*, part 1.

5 The Discovery of Neighborhood

1 Sociologists have noted that the neighborhood is as much a creation of the mind as it is a concrete entity traceable on a map, by which they mean, urban space must first be translated into a significant and distinctive cognitive force capable of shaping the social world before it can have meaning to the city dweller. Local areas gain their distinctive psycho-spatial identity from four different factors: a well-defined set of geographic boundaries, the shared "ethnic or cultural characteristics of the inhabitants," "the psychological unity of people who feel that they belong together," and the "concentrated use of an area's facilities" for activities such as shopping or leisure. Through a sharing of background in a common environment, neighborhood residents are "marked by a particular pattern of life" which, in turn, is itself shaped by where they live—a distinctive "subculture of their district"— with norms reflecting "the type of terrain occupied, the dominant type of land usage, the social traditions, and the general socio-economic structure of the area." Suzanne Keller, *The Urban Neighborhood: A Sociological Perspective* (New York: Random House, 1968), pp. 87–88. The evolution of neighborhood awareness—what might be called a sense of "symbolic community"—is seen as the result of either an ongoing process of neighborhood change or from the imposition of an identity by outsiders to the community over time to local areas. Walter Firey, "Sentiment and Symbolism as Ecological Variables," in Scott and Ann L. Greer, eds., *Neighborhood and Ghetto: The Local Area in Large-Scale Society* (New York: Basic Books, 1974), pp. 275, 281; and Albert Hunter, *Symbolic Communities: The Persistence and Change of Chicago's Local Communities* (Chicago: University of Chicago Press, 1974), pp. 67–72, 117, 139, 179. See also Hunter, "The Urban Neighborhood: Its Analytical and Social Contexts," in *Urban Affairs Quarterly* 14 (1979), p. 283; Hunter, "The Loss of Community: An Empirical Test Through Replication," in *American Sociological Review* 40 (1975), p. 537; Gerald Suttles, *The Social Construction of Communities* (Chicago: University of Chicago Press, 1972), pp. 8, 15, 35, 50–52; and Avery M. Guest, Barrett A. Lee, and Lynn Staeheli, "Changing Locality Identification in the Metropolis: Seattle, 1920–1978," *American Sociological Review* 42 (1982), pp. 543–549.

2 New York City Planning Commission, *A Plan for New York City*, vol. 3, Brooklyn (Cambridge: MIT Press, 1969).

3 New York City Planning Commission, *A Plan for New York City*, vol. 4, Manhattan, pp. 4, 42–45.

4 Norval White and Eliot Willensky, *AIA Guide to New York City*, third edition (New York: Harcourt Brace Jovanovich, 1988), pp. 287–289. See also Paul Goldberger, *The City Observed: New York City* (New York: Vintage Books, 1979), pp. 198–199. For a description of the social character of this area, ostensibly before its recent gentrification, see Joseph P. Lyford, *The Airtight Cage: A Study of New York's West Side* (New York: Harper & Row, 1968).

5 New York City Landmarks Preservation Commission, *Soho Cast Iron Historical District Designation Report* (New York: 1973), pp. 4–8; and Alexandra Anderson and B. J. Archer, *Anderson & Archer's Soho: The Essential Guide to Art and Life in Lower Manhattan* (New York: Simon and Schuster, 1979). See also White and Willensky, *AIA Guide to New York City*, pp. 45–49. Yet another new district, Noho ("North of Houston"), may also be in the offing.

6   T. R. Lee, "Cities in the Mind," in D. T. Herbert and R. J. Johnston, *Spatial Perspectives on Problems and Policies* (London: John Wiley & Sons, 1976), vol. 2, pp. 159–187, and Tridib Banerjee and William C. Baer, *Beyond the Neighborhood Unit: Residential Environments and Public Policy* (New York: Plenum Press, 1984), chapter 4. The evolution of neighborhood awareness—what might be called a sense of "symbolic community" is essentially an historical process, reflecting both the emergence of class and ethnic variations in settlement and the development of an awareness of social differences capable of translating such divisions into social action. Local areas gain symbolic identity chiefly through an ongoing process of neighborhood change or from the imposition of an identity by outsiders to the community over time to local areas. In the nineteenth century, with the emergence of major seaboard cities for the first time, this process was novel. The entire historical process of residential identity needs to be studied to see exactly *when* the "organic solidarity" of the whole city-community gave way to an awareness of subareas. The importance of streets, blocks, and political divisions, such as wards, in helping to orient urbanites toward their urban environment comes into play here. For an historical discussion of symbolic space, see Francois Bedarida and Anthony Sutcliffe, "The Street in the Structure and Life of the City: Reflections on Nineteenth-Century London and Paris," *Journal of Urban History* 6 (1980), pp. 379–396.

7   Graham Russell Hodges, *New York Cartman, 1667–1850* (New York: New York University Press, 1986), pp. 28, 39. Cartmen in 1733 also lived in what contemporaries referred to as the "now downtrodden East Ward."

8   Paul A. Gilje, *The Road to Mobocracy: Popular Disorder in New York City, 1763–1834* (Chapel Hill: Institute of Early American History and Culture and University of North Carolina Press, 1987), pp. 90, 127–135, 160–161, 207–209, 239–241.

9   Given the relatively small population size before the nineteenth century, little opportunity existed for distinct enclaves to emerge. A number of historians have argued that "neighborhoods in fact existed" before 1820 that "were much larger than the city's political wards." Stuart Blumin, "Mobility and Change in Ante-Bellum Philadelphia," in Stephan Thernstrom and Richard Sennett, eds., *Nineteenth-Century Cities: Essays in the New Urban History* (New Haven: Yale University Press, 1970), p. 186. Carl Abbott found evidence suggesting that New York neighborhoods predated the coming of the American Revolution, and Bruce Wilkenfeld argued that clearly defined areas based upon "socio-economic distinctions" existed as early as 1730. While the compactness of Colonial New York precluded a "complete segregation of land uses and activities," residential patterns of the 22,000 people crowded into a "triangle 4000 feet wide and 6000 feet from apex to base" in the early 1770s still, it was argued, allowed one to "roughly block out a division of New York" on the basis of economic and social status. Whether such vaguely defined spatial patterns of settlement ever actually translated themselves into a systematic awareness of neighborhood is unclear. Carl Abbott, "The Neighborhoods of New York, 1760–1775," in *New York History* 60 (1974), p. 51; and Bruce M. Wilkenfeld, "New York City Neighborhoods, 1730," *New York History* 57 (1976), pp. 165–182.

10 David Ward, *Poverty, Ethnicity, and the American City, 1840–1925* (New York: Cambridge University Press, 1989), p. 19.

11 John Walker, *A Special Pronouncing Dictionary and Exposition of the English*

Dictionary (New York: Collins & Hanney, 1828), p. 355, 520; *Walker's Critical Pronouncing Dictionary* (Cooperstown: H & E Phinney, 1825); Samuel Johnson, *Johnson's and Walker's English Dictionary* (Boston: Charles Even & T. Harrington Carter, 1828), pp. 629, 893; N. Bailey, *A Universal Etymological English Dictionary* (London: P. Ogilvie, 1783); James Buchanan, *A New English Dictionary* (London: A. Lillar, 1757); Noah Webster, *An American Dictionary of the English Language* (Springfield, Mass.: G & G Merrian, 1880), vol. 2, p. 881.

12 Charles Dickens, *American Notes for General Circulation* (London: Penguin Books, 1972), pp. 77, 116. In a parallel study of the terminology of symbolic space focusing on eighteenth-century Paris, David Garrioch found that "the spatial term in which the identification of people and place was most complete was *le voisinage* (the neighborhood)." This word was of particular significance because, "unlike *la maison, la rue*, or *le quartier*, it never applied to a clearly defined object or space." Derived from the word *voisin* (neighbor), "it could be used ambiguously to mean both place and a group of people." Unlike New York, where the relationship between social, symbolic, and ecological space were often ambiguous, the French *le voisinage* differed from other spatial terms because it "could refer explicitly to the people who lived there." Ultimately *le quartier* "retained something of its physical reference" while *le voisinage* became a "social description," like community, that referred not to an area but a "group of people who acted and reacted as one, a single social unit." David Garrioch, *Neighborhood & Community in Paris, 1740–1790* (Cambridge: Cambridge University Press, 1986), pp. 30–31.

13 James A. H. Murray, *A New English Dictionary on Historical Principles* (Oxford: Clarendon Press, 1908), vol. 6, part 2. Despite several early uses of neighborhood to describe the quality of an area, one going back as far as 1697, the only examples which refer to a "low neighborhood" of "black slums" of a "ferocious neighborhood" come from Dickens in 1838 and Disraeli in 1880.

14 Richard Stott, *Workers in the Metropolis: Class, Ethnicity, and Youth in Antebellum New York City* (Ithaca: Cornell University Press, 1990), p. 210.

15 Stuart Blumin, "Explaining the New Metropolis: Perception, Depiction, and Analysis in Mid-Nineteenth-Century New York City," *Journal of Urban History* 11 (November, 1984), pp. 9–38. Blumin notes that "the scale of Foster's New York still seems small, and each symbolic zone continues to represent the same aspect of the urban social world." Consequently "the various zones, though collectively representing a dangerously attenuated society, are remarkably close to one another in space." Yet Foster's eagerness to heighten "the irony and the tragedy of social polarization" in the metropolis, coupled with his unwillingness to admit that "rapid growth has made the metropolis illegible" led him to ignore "the massive spread of the wealthy to the north and the poor to the east of these traditional symbolic loci of New York's social extremes." Even after the Civil War, Blumin continues, writers still continued to describe New York's social organization "by reference to a small number of symbolic zones."

16 Only with growing spatial differentiation did artificial boundaries, including political wards, come to demarcate socioeconomic divisions in New York. Amy Bridges notes, although without mentioning documentation, that "Even in the antebellum period contemporary descriptions attributed certain kinds of character to particular wards: One was the seat of Quaker respectability, another the home of temperance, another German, another Irish, and so on. At the same time, the city retained a

kind of social wholeness that was both symbolic and real." It is telling that she also found that when Germans organized politically "it was not as representatives of the seventeenth ward, but in the citywide German League or German Democracy." Amy Bridges, *A City In the Republic* (New York: Cambridge University Press, 1984), pp. 43–44.

17   A similar argument concerning the weakness of spatial identity has also been made for the contemporary city. See Suzanne Keller, *The Urban Neighborhood: A Sociological Perspective* (New York: Random House, 1968), pp. 87–88.

18   Elizabeth Blackmar, *Manhattan for Rent, 1785–1850* (Ithaca: Cornell University Press, 1989), pp. 109–110.

19   In Philadelphia, "back alleys and working-class blocks" came to be seen "as 'regions' populated by 'demons' who menaced peace and morality," prompting affluent residents to police "accessible and symbolic spaces" and later "central streets." Susan G. Davis, *Parades and Power: Street Theatre in Nineteenth-Century Philadelphia* (Philadelphia: Temple University Press, 1986), pp. 30–31.

20   With the exodus of affluent residents, "the poor had been left to the contagious influences of the most depraved amongst them." Ward, *Poverty, Ethnicity, and the American City*, pp. 3–4, 13–28. See also Christine Stansell, *City of Women: Sex and Class in New York, 1789–1860* (New York: Alfred A. Knopf, 1986), pp. 63–68.

21   For an account by its most famous visitor, see Dickens, *American Notes*, pp. 128, 136–140.

22   The extent to which working-class New Yorkers demonstrated the same spatial consciousness as the wealthy is an important question but extremely difficult to answer given the highly circumstantial nature of evidence. Sean Wilentz described a "Republic of the Bowery" in which workers built a social community revolving around mass entertainment and working-class social organizations, something that Christine Stansell expanded to encompass a sexual subculture of working women. See Sean Wilentz, *Chants Democratic: New York City & the Rise of the American Working Class, 1788–1850* (New York: Oxford University Press, 1984), pp. 257–271; Stansell, *City of Women*, pp. 90–91; and Peter George Buckley, "To the Opera House: Culture and Society in New York City, 1820–1860" (Ph.D. diss, SUNY Stony Brook, 1984), pp. 294–353. While the Bowery with its concentration of working-class entertainment was emblematic of an emerging class-based culture, its importance can also be overstated. Symbolic identity is hierarchical, which means spatial identity (regardless of class) does not focus upon a single space but encompasses a wide range of areas from the East Side/West Side dichotomy down to corner saloon. The Bowery was only one element in a wider system that ranged from streets, parks, and squares to wider areas for which contemporaries were able to name boundaries. Furthermore, it must be remembered that the seven or eight wards (4, 6, 7, 10, 11, 13, 14, 17) presumably served by the Bowery Republic housed nearly half of New York's population. Can an area several square miles in size, housing more than a quarter of a million people, be expected to focus on one relatively small area? Even if the "Bowery Republic" possessed the importance ascribed to it by scholars, historians should still wonder why such a large urban area contained only a handful of subareas for which names survive (e.g., such notorious symbolic areas as Five Points, Corlears Hook, and the Fourth Ward). In other words, why was there only one Bowery and not several? The answer may well be that most areas housing working-class and artisanal New Yorkers lacked anything but the

most rudimentary, localistic, social-spatial identity. For a theoretical discussion of community based upon residence in a given locality but unified by common interest, see Lee, "Cities in the Mind," p. 170.

23   Ward, "Environs and Neighbours in the 'Two Nations'," p. 135.

24   Richard Stott, "The Worker in the Metropolis: New York 1820–1860" (Ph.D. diss., Cornell University, 1983), p. 366. In his subsequent book, Stott noted that while "many workers did have a fair knowledge of the city's geography" from recreational walks, workers generally "lived, labored, shopped, and were entertained on the lower East Side." Stott, *Workers in the Metropolis*, p. 210.

25   Garrioch, *Neighborhood & Community in Paris*, pp. 29–31.

26   The small scale of working-class urban imagery and the frequent lack of boundaries makes their features opaque to historical study and this probably accounts for the lack of detailed description for all but the wealthiest or most notorious residential areas of the city. Carol Groneman Pernicone, "The 'Bloody Ould Sixth': A Social Analysis of A New York City Working-Class Community in the Mid-Nineteenth Century" (Ph.D. diss., University of Rochester, 1973), p. 40; "Rebecca," *Tramps in New York* (New York: American Tract Society, 1863), pp. 45–56; Robert Ernst, *Immigrant Life in New York City 1825–1863* (New York: Kings Crown Press, 1949), pp. 39–40; [Five Points Mission], *The Old Brewery and the New Mission House at the Five Points* (New York: Stringer & Townsend, 1854); Jacob A. Riis, *How the Other Half Lives* (New York: Charles Scribner's Sons, 1890, 1900). By the time Riis wrote *Other Half*, spatial differentiation had progressed far enough for these little landmarks to fit well into an ascending system of spatial symbols. It may also be that the ethnic and social character of the Lower East Side was far too heterogeneous to support such symbolic mapping until the mid-1850s. However, one must be careful to separate local names that may have been created by Riis from those employed by the residents themselves.

27   Carl Abbott, "The Neighborhoods of New York, 1760–1775," in *New York History* 60 (1974), p. 51; and Bruce M. Wilkenfeld, "New York City Neighborhoods, 1730," *New York History* 57 (1976), pp. 165–182.

28   Valentine Seaman, "An Inquiry into the Cause of the Prevalence of the Yellow Fever in New-York," in *Medical Repository* 1 (1798), pp. 329–330. For a discussion of the early cartography of epidemics, see Lloyd G. Stevenson, "Putting Disease on the Map: The Early Use of Spot Maps in the Study of Yellow Fever," *Journal of the History of Medicine* 39 (July 1965), pp. 226–261. For a discussion of the use of epidemiological spot maps to measure the location of working-class neighborhoods in nineteenth-century Leeds, see also Ward, "Environs and Neighbours in the 'Two Nations'," pp. 140–141.

29   James Hardie, *An Account of the Malignant Fever Lately Prevalent in the City of New-York* (New York: Hurtin & M'Farline, 1799), pp. 28–29.

30   Seaman, "An Inquiry into the Case of the Prevalence of the Yellow Fever in New York," p. 323. For a discussion of riots in the area involving prostitution, see Gilje, *The Road to Mobocracy*, p. 240. Gilje cites one account which described the area as "a motley mixture of whites, yellows, and blacks, from all ends of the earth."

31   In other regards, medical authorities retained an older strongly localistic view of urban space which divided the city not by area, but by street and block frontage. Instead of referring to any wider district or neighborhood, James Callander, a laborer who "was employed towards the lower end of town," was described in characteris-

tic fashion as residing in the "vicinity of Roosevelt Street and Water." Seaman, "An Inquiry Into the Case of the Prevalence of the Yellow Fever in New York," p. 327. In most early accounts of residence, "vicinity" was synonymous with what is now commonly referred to as "neighborhood." Albert Hunter makes the distinction between two kinds of symbolic state with larger bounded districts postdating small nodes such as the intersection of streets. Hunter, *Symbolic Communities*, p. 186, and his "The Urban Neighborhood: Its Analytical and Social Contexts," in *Urban Affairs Quarterly* 14 (1979), p. 283. For a description of the discovery and awareness of poverty in late eighteenth century, see Raymond Mohl, *Poverty in New York 1783–1823* (New York: Oxford University Press, 1971), p. 20. The role of epidemics in reorienting wealthy New Yorkers away from waterfront areas is discussed in Blackmar, *Manhattan for Rent*, p. 86.

32   These areas were commonly referred to as "places of retreat in the event of pestilence." New York City Board of Health, *A History of the Proceeding of the Board of Health of the City of New-York in the Summer and Fall of 1822; Together with an Account of the Rise and Progress of the Yellow Fever, Which Appeared During that Season* (New York: P & H Van Pelt, 1823), p. 3. The inability to flee pestilence in summers also separated working-class areas from those of wealth. Howard B. Rock, *Artisans of the New Republic: The Tradesmen of New York City in the Age of Jefferson* (New York: New York University Press, 1979), pp. 2–3.

33   James Hardie, *An Account of the Yellow Fever As It Prevailed in the City of New York, in the Year 1822* (New York: Samuel Marks, 1822), p. 42.

34   P. S. Townsend, *An Account of the Yellow Fever as It Prevailed in the City of New York in Summer and Autumn 1822* (New York: O. Halstead, 1823), pp. 18–21.

35   John H. Griscom, *A History, Chronology and Circumstantial, of the Visitation of Yellow Fever at New York* (New York: Hall, Clayton, 1858), p. 17.

36   New York City Board of Health, *Statement of Facts Relative to the Late Fever Which Appeared in Bancker-Street and Its Vicinity* (New York: Elam Bliss, 1821), p. 5.

37   For a compelling description of the epidemic in the Fourth Ward, see Henry Chase, Manuscript Diary, vol. 3, entries for July 25 and July 29, 1832, New–York Historical Society.

38   With "such a crew, inhabiting the most populous and central portion of the city," be "the air pure from Heaven, their breath would contaminate it." Cited in Charles Rosenberg, *The Cholera Years: The United States in 1832, 1849, and 1866* (Chicago: University of Chicago Press, 1971), pp. 33–34.

39   David Reese, *A Plain and Practical Treatise on the Epidemic Cholera As It Prevailed in the City of New York in the Summer of 1832* (New York: Conner & Cooke, 1833), frontispiece.

40   Ward, *Poverty, Ethnicity, and the American City*, pp. 28–31.

41   Carl Abbott, "The Neighborhoods of New York, 1760–1775," pp. 49–50, and Bayard Still, *Mirror for Gotham: New York As Seen by Contemporaries from Dutch Days to the Present* (New York: New York University Press, 1956), p. 25.

42   For a description of how reformers in other antebellum cities viewed these areas, see Paul Boyer, *Urban Masses and Moral Order in America, 1820–1920* (Cambridge: Harvard University Press, 1978), pp. 17–21, and Roger Lane, *Policing the City: Boston 1822–1885* (Cambridge: Harvard University Press, 1967), pp. 114–117, 174–175.

43   The Fifth Ward was one center of New York City's prostitution throughout much of the antebellum period. This area witnessed bawdyhouse riots in 1793 and 1799, and twenty public disturbances occurred between 1805 and 1834, consisting largely of attacks upon prostitutes. In 1839 a major fire destroyed several important churches, a theater, and a number of houses of ill repute, sending "the unfortunate inmates of these dwellings" rushing "frantically out in the attire in which the alarms found them." Gilje, *The Road to Mobocracy*, p. 239. Augustine E. Costello, *Our Firemen: A History of the New York Fire Department Volunteer and Paid* (New York: Augustine Costello, 1887), p. 231. Also "Fire on Cor of Church and Leonard," *New York Evening Post*, September 24, 1839. Even when a police report in 1846 found brothels scattered throughout almost every ward, the Fifth, Sixth, Eighth, and Fourteenth Wards were still cited as the areas with the largest concentrations. The First, Second, and Third Wards also had brothels on side streets, though they were usually less well-known. New York City Common Council, *Report of Special Committee in Relation To a Re-organization of the Police Department*, Board of Alderman Document 53 (New York: 1846), p. 693.

44   *Madame Restell, An Account of Her Life and Horrible Practice Together With Prostitution In New York, By a Physician of New York* (New York: Proprietor—Charles Smith, 1847), p. 29. See also William M. Bobo, *Glimpses of New-York City By a South Carolinian* (Charleston: J. J. McCarter, 1852), pp. 123–130.

45   [H. D. Eastman], *Fast Man's Directory and Lover's Guide by the Ladies' Man* (New York: n.p., 1853).

46   *Directory To the Seraglios in New York, Philadelphia, Boston and All the Principal Cities in The Union By a Free Lover* (New York: 1859), p. 13.

47   *The Gentleman's Directory [The Gentleman's Companion]* (New York: John F. Murray, 1870), pp. 9–10. For an illustration of Broadway streetwalkers in the late 1840s, see John A. Kouwenhoven, *The Columbia Historical Portrait of New York* (New York: Harper and Row, 1972), p. 226.

48   *The Gentleman's Guide*, pp. 34–50.

49   These areas of vice also help to underscore the subjectivity of symbolic space. Where contemporary descriptions clearly describe well-defined vice districts, a recent effort to pinpoint the actual geographical location of prostitution in New York City actually discovered that commercialized sex was diffused throughout the city. While prostitution had been "confined and well ordered" in the Third Ward and along the East River prior to 1820, between 1820 and 1850 prostitutes could be found in most city neighborhoods, reflecting an overall pattern of urban decentralized. Only after 1850 did the actual patterns of vice once again come to reflect perceptions, when Soho emerged as a new primary center. Timothy J. Gilfoyle, "The Urban Geography of Commercial Sex: Prostitution in New York City, 1790–1860," *Journal of Urban History* 13 (1987), pp. 371–393. The interior and functions of the houses are described (although no locations are given) in William W. Sanger, *The History of Prostitution: Its Extent, Causes and Effects Throughout the World* (New York: Eugenics Publishing House, 1937, reprint of 1859 ed.), pp. 549–574.

50   Betsy Blackmar, "Re-walking the 'Walking City': Housing and Property Relations in New York City, 1780–1840" *Radical History Review* 21 (Fall 1979), p. 143.

51   New York City Board of Health, *A History of the Proceedings*, p. 3.

52   John A. Dix, *A History of the Parish of Trinity Church in the City of New York* (New York: Columbia University Press, 1950), vol. 5, pp. 65–67. Also I. N. Phelps

Stokes, *The Iconography of Manhattan Island 1498–1909* (New York: Robert H. Dodd, 1915–1928), vol. 3, pp. 607–609.

53   Mrs. Francis Trollope, *Domestic Manners in the Americas* (London: Whittaker, Treacher, 1832), p. 270.

54   O. L. Holley, *A Description of the City of New York* (New York: J. Disturnell, 1847), p. 15; E. Porter Belden, *New York As It Is, Being a Counterpart of the Metropolis of America* (New York: John P. Proll, 1849), p. 11; and James G. Wilson, *The Memorial History of the City of New York* (New York: New York History, 1893), vol. 3, pp. 367–368.

55   R. W. Newman, "Old New York: The City in '32: Its People and Public Institutions" (New York: Evening Mail, 1873), clipping book in the New York Historical Society Library, pp. 50–52; and Marian Gouveneur, *As I Remember: Recollections of American Society During the Nineteenth Century* (New York: D. Appleton, 1911), pp. 21–25, 47.

56   Hunter, *Symbolic Communities*, p. 89.

57   Edward K. Spann, *The New Metropolis: New York City, 1840–1857* (New York: Columbia University Press, 1981), pp. 103–104. Also see *Miller's New York As It Is: or Stranger's Guide-Book to the Cities of New York, Brooklyn and Adjacent Places* (New York: James Miller, 1864), pp. 73–74; and "New York—Private Residences," *Putnam's Monthly* 3 (1854), pp. 333–348.

58   Bobo, *Glimpses of New-York City By A South Carolinian*, pp. 169–171.

59   Bobo, *Glimpses of New York-City*, p. 169. Just as vice areas shifted from one area to another, the fashion of particular streets changed over time. Broadway, Park Place, Bleecker, and Bond Streets had epitomized wealth in the 1830s, but the many affluent residents shifted to newer districts uptown after 1840, establishing new areas of high status. Fifth Avenue had been known as the "nabob" street from early in its history, but the erection of "splendid mansions" during the middle of the century reinforced its reputation as perhaps the city's most fashionable residential thoroughfare. Charles Lockwood, *Bricks and Brownstones: The New York Row House 1783–1929—An Architectural and Social History* (New York: McGraw-Hill, 1972), pp. 40–49.

60   "Strips" only rarely function as the sole "basis of symbolic community" in contemporary urban America. Hunter, *Symbolic Communities*, pp. 89–92.

61   Robert Burford, *Description of A View of the City of New York* (London: T. Brettell, 1834), p. 4.

62   Stuart M. Blumin, ed., *New York by Gas-Light and Other Urban Sketches by George G. Foster* (Berkeley: University of California Press, 1990).

63   [Seba Smith], *May-Day in New York: Or House Hunting and Moving* (New York: Burgess, Stringer, 1845), p. 32.

64   Paul Boyer has noted that cities appeared to a middle class less and less familiar with the lives of the lower classes to be increasingly a moral "abstraction: a problem to be dealt with in isolation from the economic transformations of which even so sweeping a process as urbanization was merely a side effect." The search for moral order on the part of reformers helped to schematize and define neighborhoods by connecting social status and moral depravity with location. Boyer, *Urban Masses and Moral Order in America, 1820–1920*, p. 75.

65   New York State Assembly, *Report of the Special Committee on Tenement Houses in New-York and Brooklyn*, Documents of the Assembly of the State of New York

(79th session, 1856), vol. 3, Doc. 199 (Albany: C. Van Benthuyser, 1856), p. 8.

66 George G. Foster cited in Stansell, *City of Women*, p. 92.

67 Citizens Association of New York, *Report of the Council of Hygiene and Public Health Upon the Sanitary Condition of the City* (New York: Appleton, 1866), p. 93. Conditions were in reality much less flattering. See Stanley Nadel, *Little Germany: Ethnicity, Religion, and Class in New York City, 1845–80* (Urbana: University of Illinois Press, 1990), pp. 34–36, 104–106.

68 Citizens Association, *Report of the Council of Hygiene and Public Health*, pp. 148, 240.

69 Ward, *Poverty, Ethnicity, and the American City, 1840–1925*, p. 43.

70 Gustav Lening, *The Dark Side of New York Life and Its Criminal Classes from Fifth Avenue Down to the Five Points* (New York: Fred'k Oerhard, 1873), p. 165.

71 Citizens Association of New York, *Report of the Council of Hygiene and Public Health*, p. 131.

72 The reputation for bad health seemed to have predated that of immorality. The Fourth Ward, which had "long been noted as one of the principal 'nests' for fever, cholera, and other deadly malaria on the island," had only developed its strong moral stigma as the home of drunk and depraved Irish immigrants and sailors in the 1850s, and interest in the area accelerated only late in the 1860s, with an offensive by missionaries to save the ward known as the "Water Street Revival." Rev. J. F. Richmond, *New York and Its Institutions 1609–1873* (New York: E. B. Treat, 1872), p. 474. See also Oliver Dyer, *"The Wickedest Man" in New York or the Great Awakening in Water Street* (New York: P. Dwight, 1868), reprinted from *Packard's Monthly*.

73 The birth and death of neighborhoods enhances both local consciousness and the awareness of spatial divisions in a way which identity imposed from without cannot. One study of seventeenth-century London dates the awareness of spatial status to the early eighteenth century when Chequer Alley came to serve as a "superior 'social enclave'." Yet as cities grew following the Restoration, "their residents arguably found it harder to comprehend their totality and were increasingly absorbed into local cultures generated by the emergence of distinct functional and social areas." Jeremy Boulton, *Neighbourhood and Society: A London Suburb in the Seventeenth Century* (Cambridge: Cambridge University Press, 1987), pp. 175, 294.

74 Hunter, *Symbolic Communities*, p. 93.

75 Lyon, *Recollections of an Ex Cartman*, p. 7.

76 New York State Senate, *Report on the Sanitary Condition of the City of New York*, Senate Documents 49 (1859), p. 186.

77 Stokes, *The Iconography of Manhattan Island*, vol. 5, p. 1812.

78 Silvanus J. Macy, *Memories of Old New York* (Rochester, 1899), scrapbook of newspaper clippings at the New York Historical Society, clipping no. 1. See also *A History of Real Estate, Building and Architecture in New York City During the Last Quarter Century* (New York: Arno Press, 1967; reprint of 1898 ed.), p. 51; and Newman, *Old New York: The City of New York in '32*, pp. 104–112.

79 New York Association for Improving the Condition of the Poor, *First Report of a Committee on the Sanitary Condition of the Laboring Class in the City of New York with Remedial Suggestions* (New York: John F. Trow, 1853), p. 7.

80 *High Life in New York By Jonathan Slick Esq.* (New York: Burgess, Stringer, ca 1850), p. 32. A cartman argued that Oak Street in the area "is a *very respectable*

street, at least that part of it in which we reside." Lyon, *Recollections of an Ex Cartman*, pp. 79–80.

81   Lindsay Denison and Max Fischell, *Villages and Hamlets Within New York City* (New York: New York Evening World, 1925), p. 13.

82   Richard A. E. Brooks, ed., *The Diary of Michael Floy Jr., Bowery Village 1833–1837* (New Haven: Yale University Press, 1941), p. 180; and also Samuel Seaman, *Annals of New York Methodism: A History of the Methodist Episcopal Church in the City of New York From A.D. 1766 to A.D. 1890* (New York: Hunt & Eaton, 1892), p. 181.

83   Once the location for country residences of wealthy New Yorkers, such as the Van Nest Estate, Aaron Burr's Richmond Hill, and Rose Hill, Greenwich, was also the northern terminus of intracity stage routes and, after 1797, the site of a state penitentiary. Despite a sharp surge in development following the Yellow Fever Epidemic of 1822, this area differed little from other squatters' settlements surrounding the built-up parts of New York early in its history. After a great fire consumed the three-block area bounded by Bank, Greenwich, Hudson, and Hammond Streets in 1833, destroying seventy buildings, it was noted that most were "mere shanties" of "little value," inhabited primarily by foreigners, few of whom lived "above comfortable circumstances," forced by their poverty to occupy "frail wooden tenements" easily destroyed by fire. For a discussion of the early estates, see Mrs. Ann VanNest Bussing, *Reminiscences of the Van Nest Homestead* (New York: Privately Printed, 1867), pp. [1–2]. Also William A. Duer, *Reminiscences of an Old New Yorker* (New York: W. C. Andrews, 1867), p. 18; and Charles Lockwood, *Manhattan Moves Uptown: An Illustrated History* (Boston: Houghton Mifflin, 1976), pp. 66–69. For a detailed but antiquarian description of Greenwich Village history, see Ann Alice Chapin, *Greenwich Village* (New York: Dodd, Meade, 1917). For information on the fire, see: "Destroyed in Fire April 30, 1833," *New York Evening Post*, May 2, 1833, p. 2. Prominent citizens held a benefit at the Richmond Hill Theater to raise funds to care for the 1000–1200 individuals left homeless. See *New York Evening Post* for May 2, 1833. In 1838 another fire devastated an entire block in the same vicinity. See Costello, *Our Firemen*, pp. 218, 230.

84   Macy, *Memories of Old New York*, p. [xvi]; and Frank Moss, *The American Metropolis: New York City Life* (New York: Peter Fenelon Collier, 1897), vol. 3, pp. 286–292.

85   Charles T. Harris, *Memories of Manhattan in the Sixties and Seventies* (New York: Derrydale Press, 1928), pp. 44–46. For a description of one such clash, see "Terrible Riot in the Ninth Ward," *New York Times*, July 6, 1853. Interethnic tension was recorded in the area as early as the 1820s. See Thomas A. Emmet, *Memoir of Thomas Addis and Robert Emmet with Their Ancestors and Immediate Family* (New York: The Emmet Press, 1915), vol. 1, pp. 464–465.

86   The western section of Greenwich Village was held up as the ideal form of community diversity and urban scale in the 1960s by critics of urban planning such as Jane Jacobs. See her *The Death and Life of the Great American City* (New York: Vintage Books, 1961). In mid-nineteenth-century New York City the same process of neighborhood change that enhanced consciousness of community also pointed to the relatively low levels of attachment which many residents felt toward the areas in which they lived. For a contemporary study of neighborhood attachment, see Claude Fischer, *Networks and Places: Social Relations in the Urban Setting* (New York: Free Press, 1977), pp. 155–158. Undoubtedly many downtown residents

were reluctant to abandon their old neighborhoods, despite changes in the status and population of Lower Manhattan. Yet departing patricians seemed to show little remorse in their change of address, and, for the regretful few, their optimism at the time of their move more than made up for the reluctance to leave the old. Given the high population turnover in the lower wards and the rapid expansion of the once-suburban sections of Manhattan—offering grander quarters in less crowded surroundings—it is not surprising that old attachments could so easily be broken. Mid-nineteenth-century New Yorkers apparently possessed only the weakest image of spatially oriented community and felt little constrained by the boundaries of the neighborhood. Allan Nevins, ed., *The Diary of Philip Hone* (New York: Dodd, Mead, 1927), vol. 1, pp. 201–202; Allan Nevins and Milton Halsy Thomas, eds., *The Diary of George Templeton Strong* (New York: Octagon Press, 1974), vol. 1, p. 321.

87   Kevin Lynch, *The Image of the City* (Cambridge: M.I.T. Press, 1960), pp. 17, 66.

88   Early in the century, areas such as lower Broadway, Park Place, and St. John's Park "were almost exclusively the neighborhoods of the elite rather than the 'common man'," and their status was commonly known. Rich merchants sought not only to gain an "exalted status" by living together in exclusive areas, but in so doing, they conferred an air of gentility upon these neighborhoods. Edward Pessen, *Riches, Class, and Power Before the Civil War* (Lexington, Mass.: D. C. Heath, 1973), pp. 172–179, 201.

89   For a brief description of the German center, see Still, *Mirror for Gotham*, pp. 160–163.

6 Communities Out of Weak Ties

1   Jeremiah O'Donovan, *A Brief Account of the Author's Interviews with His Countrymen, and the Parts of the Emerald Isle Whence They Emigrated Together with a Direct Reference to their Present Location in the Land of Their Adoption, During Travels Through Various States of the Union in 1854 and 1855* (Pittsburgh: Published by author, 1864). The book that he hawked was *A History of Ireland, Containing a Compendious Account of Her Woes, Affliction and Suffering, . . . in Epic Verse* (Pittsburgh: Published by the author, 1854).

2   O'Donovan, *A Brief Account of the Author's Interviews with His Countrymen*, pp. 149, 161, 173, 174.

3   O'Donovan, *A Brief Account of the Author's Interviews with His Countrymen*, pp. 169, 170, 92.

4   Many of O'Donovan's contacts were undoubtedly the result of chance from particular social networks with which he happened to connect. But the avoidance of the East Side, where the proportion of Irish residents was equal to many other areas of the city, suggests an additional propensity for visiting Irish countrymen who were not domestic servants. If most domestics were in fact Irish, as many as one out of three Irish residents of the East Side's Irish population in the Eighteenth and Twenty-first Wards might have been servants in 1865. For the West Side's Sixteenth and Twentieth Wards, the ratio of servants to total Irish population was 27.7 and 16.9 percent, respectively. Calculated from Franklin B. Hough, *Statistics of Population of the City and County of New York as Shown by the State Census of 1865*

(New York: N.Y. Printing, 1866), p. 273; and Secretary of State, *Census of the State of New York for 1865* (Albany, 1867).

5 Writing about antebellum working-class neighborhoods of New York, Stansell noted how "strands of family, regional and village loyalties" were supplemented by a form of community created by the poor themselves from "traditions of cooperation and mutual aid reminiscent of life in poor neighborhoods in early modern London or even Paris." Christine Stansell, *City of Women: Sex and Class in New York, 1789–1860* (New York: Alfred A. Knopf, 1986), pp. 55–62, 246n52ff. Stansell's interpretation is shaped by the sources which she used: assault cases recorded in the papers of the New York Court of General Sessions and in County Coroner's reports. As my own earlier use of the case of August Buffet makes clear, these records of atypical outbursts of violence or sudden death are better suited for recording internal linkages among witnesses than they are for pursuing social networks outside community boundaries, nor do they shed much light upon the density, intensity, or multiplicity of such ties. For other discussions of urban village communitarianism, see Judith Smith, *Family Connections: A History of Italian & Jewish Immigrant Lives in Providence, Rhode Island, 1900–1940* (Albany: SUNY Press, 1985); Olivier Zunz, *The Changing Face of Inequality: Urbanization, Industrial Development, and Immigrants in Detroit, 1880–1920* (Chicago: University of Chicago Press, 1982), chap. 7; and Dino Cinel, *From Italy to San Francisco: The Immigrant Experience* (Stanford: Stanford University Press, 1982), chap. 5.

6 John Connell, "Social Networks in Urban Society," in B. D. Clark and M. B. Gleave, eds., *Social Patterns in Cities, Institute of British Geographers Special Publication*, London, March 1973 (no. 5), pp. 41–52.

7 Historical examinations of Victorian British cities concluded that "the close-knit community structure of working-class urban villages from the late nineteenth century onwards was a consequence of modern urban structure, not an anachronistic survival from pre-industrial or early industrial 'workplace communities'." Richard Dennis and Stephen Daniels, " 'Community' and the Social Geography of Victorian Cities," *Urban History Yearbook* (1981), p. 17.

8 The excessive attention paid to neighborhood communities is therefore—to use the words of anthropologist Ulf Hannerz—something of an "evasion." It may be true that some urban neighborhoods *were* places where residents, if they did not know everyone else, at least knew "something about everyone else." But the city is in actuality "a place where people do not know one another too well." Ulf Hannerz, *Exploring the City: Inquiries Toward an Urban Anthropology* (New York: Columbia University Press, 1980), pp. 5, 63. Historian Gary Nash echoes this sentiment by extending Thomas Bender's question of "Why cannot *Gemeinschaft* and *Gesellschaft* simultaneously shape social life," to ask whether "homogeneity and smallness are the indispensable elements of community and viable social relations"? Gary Nash, "The Social Evolution of Preindustrial American Cities, 1700–1820," in Raymond A. Mohl, ed., *The Making of Urban America* (Wilmington, Del.: Scholarly Resources, 1988), p. 26. Stuart Blumin also confronted the paradox of community among strangers when he noted that while village growth in Kingston, New York, certainly "reduced the proportion of townsmen each resident could personally know," it was never clear "that town wide acquaintance" was ever "automatically translated into 'community.' " The creation of new subcommunities

built upon local organization actually increased the "feeling of belonging" as village grew into town. Stuart M. Blumin, *The Urban Threshold: Growth and Change in a Nineteenth-Century American Community* (Chicago: University of Chicago Press, 1976), pp. 220–222.

9   Any historical definition of neighborhood community should recognize that neither "social homogeneity" nor "living and working in the same area with similar socioeconomic status, or with family ties"—factors which may lay the basis for social interaction and promote a "sense of belonging and of collective identity"—are "necessarily concomitant with any of these." David Garrioch, *Neighborhood & Community in Paris, 1740–1790* (Cambridge: Cambridge University Press, 1986), p. 3. Another study focusing on seventeenth-century London found the opposite, arguing for the existence of "geographically restricted social horizons." This finding would suggest that multiplexity of social networks is a function of developing commercial capitalism. Jeremy Boulton, *Neighbourhood and Society: A London Suburb in the Seventeenth Century* (Cambridge: Cambridge University Press, 1987), pp. 260–261, 292. For an anthropological discussion of multiplicity within the modern city, see also Hannerz, *Exploring the City*, p. 267.

10   Richard Stott, *Workers in the Metropolis: Class, Ethnicity, and Youth in Antebellum New York City* (Ithaca: Cornell University Press, 1990), p. 210; and Stansell, *City of Women*, p. 86. Walking is examined under the concept of "time-geography" in Allan Pred, *Making Histories and Constructing Human Geographies: The Local Transformation of Practice, Power Relations, and Consciousness* (Boulder: Westview Press, 1990), pp. 48–49, 60–63.

11   Henry Chase, Manuscript Diary, vol. 2, entry for January 16, 1825. Located at the New-York Historical Society.

12   Richard A. E. Brooks, ed., *The Diary of Michael Floy Jr, Bowery Village 1833–37* (New Haven: Yale University Press, 1941), p. 3.

13   Brooks, *The Diary of Michael Floy*, pp. 44, 69, 126.

14   Some contemporary observers argued that mobile ties were symptomatic of the darker force of anomie and dislocation rather than social liberation. The English immigrant hatter James Burns argued that American workers lived lives of painful social "isolation," members of a proletarian lonely crowd. "Men here," he complained upon his return to England, "form so many atoms in a mass, in which all individuality (with few exceptions) is swallowed up. . . . I have conversed with men who have been in the country for several years, and who avowed that they never knew what it was to have a friend in the proper acceptation [sic] of the term, since they landed," and he confessed to not remembering "a single being (if I leave my shopmates out of the question during the hours of labour) beyond my own family" during his three years in America. [James D. Burns], *Three Years Among the Working-Classes in the United States During the War* (London: Smith, Elder, 1865), p. 24. For an extensive discussion of nineteenth-century crowds and the uncertainties they presented, see John F. Kasson, *Rudeness and Civility: Manners in Nineteenth-Century Urban America* (New York: Hill and Wang, 1990), pp. 80–86.

15   William M. Bobo, *Glimpses of New York City By A South Carolinian* (New York: J. J. McCaster, 1852), p. 117.

16   N. Parker Willis, *The Rag-Bag: A Collection of Ephemera* (New York: Charles Scribner, 1855), p. 259.

17   John F. Maguire, *The Irish in America* (New York: 1887), p. 215.

18   These questions have been vitally important to recent urban sociology. See Mirra
     Komarovsky, "The Voluntary Associations of Urban Dwellers," *American Socio-
     logical Review* 11 (1946), pp. 687, 698; Wendell Bell and Marion Boat, "Urban
     Neighborhoods and Informal Social Relations," *American Journal of Sociology* 62
     (1956), pp. 391–398; Michael Young and Peter Wilmott, *Family and Kinship in
     East London* (London: Routledge & Kegan Paul, 1957); Nicholas Babchuk and Alan
     Booth, "Voluntary Association Membership: A Longitudinal Analysis," *American
     Sociological Review* 34 (1969), pp. 31–45; Herbert J. Gans, *The Urban Villagers:
     Group and Class in the Life of Italian-Americans* (New York: Free Press, 1962),
     pp. 109–113; Harvey M. Choldin, "Kinship and Networks in the Migration Pro-
     cess," *International Migration Review* 7 (February 1973), pp. 163–175; John D.
     Kasarda and Morris Janowitz, "Community Attachment in Mass Society," *Ameri-
     can Sociological Review* 39 (June 1974), pp. 328–329; Raymond Breton, "Institu-
     tional Completeness of Ethnic Communities and the Personal Relations of Immi-
     grants," *American Journal of Sociology* 70 (1964), pp. 193–205; Richard P. Taub,
     George P. Surgeon, Sarah Lindhol, Phylis B. Otti, and Ann Bridges, "Urban Vol-
     untary Associations, Locally Based and Externally Induced," *American Journal of
     Sociology* 83 (1977), pp. 425–442; Albert Hunter, *Symbolic Communities: The Per-
     sistence and Change of Chicago's Local Community* (Chicago: University of Chi-
     cago Press, 1974), pp. 151–152; Claude S. Fischer et al., *Networks and Places: Social
     Relations in the Urban Setting* (New York: Basic Books, 1976), p. 173; Claude S.
     Fischer, *To Dwell Among Friends: Personal Networks in Town and City* (Chi-
     cago: University of Chicago Press, 1982), p. 103; Paul Craven and Barry Wellman,
     "The Network City," *Sociological Inquiry* 93 (December 1973), pp. 57–88; Peter
     McGahan, "The Neighbor Role and Neighboring in a Highly Urban Area," *The
     Sociological Quarterly* 13 (1972), p. 397–408; Martin Bulmer, *Neighbours: The
     Work of Philip Abrams* (Cambridge: Cambridge University Press, 1986); Peggy
     Wireman, *Urban Neighborhoods, Networks, and Families: New Forms for Old
     Values* (Lexington, Mass: Lexington Books, 1984). pp. 29–37; Roger S. Ahlbrandt,
     Neighborhoods, People, and Community (New York: Plenum Press, 1984) pp. 13–
     27, 108–114, 189–194. Judith Shuval, "Class and Ethnic Correlates of Casual Neigh-
     boring," *American Sociological Review* 21 (1956), pp. 453–458; and Henry W.
     Irving, "Social Networks in the Modern City," *Social Forces* 55 (June 1977), pp.
     867–880.

19   For a discussion of the relationship between churchgoing as "special interest" ac-
     tivity and community relations within the local area, see Dennis and Daniels,
     " 'Community' and the Social Geography of Victorian Cities," pp. 18–19.

20   Don H. Doyle, *The Social Order of a Frontier Community: Jacksonville, Illinois
     1825–1870* (Urbana: University of Illinois Press, 1978). Also see the study of "leader-
     ship structure" and "power elites" for Cincinnati in the following two works by
     Walter S. Glazer, "Cincinnati in 1840: A Community Profile" (Ph.D. diss., Univer-
     sity of Michigan, 1968), and "Participation and Power: Voluntary Associations and
     the Functional Organization of Cincinnati in 1840," *Historical Methods Newsletter*
     5 (1972), pp. 151–168. For another detailed description of religious membership, see
     Paul E. Johnson, *A Shopkeeper's Millennium: Society and Revivals in Rochester,
     New York 1815–1837* (New York: Hill and Wang, 1978). German voluntary asso-
     ciations are discussed in Kathleen N. Conzen, *Immigrant Milwaukee, 1836–1860*
     (Cambridge: Harvard University Press, 1976).

21 Although ethnic historians still frequently define ethnic communities in terms of
    "institutional completeness" measured by stores, churches, clubs, and societies,
    it is not clear that such institutions are even necessary to socially rooting urban
    individuals. Furthermore, the theoretical work of sociologist Mark Granovetter on
    the "strength of weak ties" implies that close-knit social ties as might be found
    in ethnic neighborhoods not only were poor defenses against social alienation, but
    were actually detrimental to an adaptation to urban life. Where strong ties straight-
    jacketed residents by cutting them off from leads on jobs or housing, weak loosely
    connected ties that extended well beyond the boundaries of the local neighborhood
    offered greater support and information for urbanites. As Granovetter noted, "weak
    ties, often denounced as generative of alienation," are in reality "indispensable to
    individuals' opportunities and their integration into communities" while "strong
    ties, breeding local cohesion lead to overall fragmentation." Mark S. Granovetter,
    "The Strength of Weak Ties," *American Journal of Sociology* 78 (1973), p. 1378, and
    "The Strength of Weak Ties: A Network Theory Revisited," in Peter V. Marsden and
    Nan Lin, eds., *Social Structure and Network Analysis* (Beverly Hills: Sage Publica-
    tions, 1982) pp. 105–130. For a debate between Gans and Granovetter on this point,
    see "Commentary and Debate: Gans on Granovetter's 'Strength of Weak Ties';
    Granovetter Replies to Gans; Gans Responds to Granovetter," *American Journal of
    Sociology* 80 (1974), pp. 524–532. Granovetter's theory is also applied to neighbor-
    hood political participation in Matthew A. Crenson, "Social Networks and Politi-
    cal Processes in Urban Neighborhoods," *American Journal of Political Science* 22
    (August 1978), pp. 578–594. For an application of Granovetter to network analy-
    sis in a historical context, see Naomi Rosenthal, Meryl Fingrutd, Michele Ethier,
    Roberta Karant, and David McDonald, "Social Movements and Network Analy-
    sis: A Case Study of Nineteenth-Century Women's Reform in New York State,"
    American Journal of Sociology 90 (1985), pp. 1022–1054. Granovetter's relevance to
    neighborhood structure is disputed in Susan D. Greenbaum and Paul E. Greenbaum,
    "The Ecology of Social Networks in Four Urban Neighborhoods," *Social Networks*
    7 (1985), pp. 47–76; and Susan D. Greenbaum, "Bridging Ties at the Neighborhood
    Level," *Social Networks* 4 (1982), pp. 367–384.
22 For a discussion of the social roles of religion in determining associations, see
    Edward O. Laumann, "The Social Structure of Religion," *American Sociological
    Review* 34 (1969), pp. 182–197; Gerhard Lenski, *The Religious Factor: A Sociologi-
    cal Study of Religion's Impact on Politics, Economics, and Family Life* (New York:
    Doubleday, 1961); and Fischer, *To Dwell Among Friends,* chap. 16. The location
    of churches readily "identified the 'moral character' of the new residential areas
    that sprang up around them." Elizabeth Blackmar, *Manhattan for Rent, 1785–1850*
    (Ithaca: Cornell University Press, 1989), p. 131.
23 Unlike the neighborhood organization that fostered local orientation primarily for
    the elite members of the community, these informal ties were truly democratic—
    extending the social circles of all classes of individuals well beyond the boundaries
    of the neighborhood.
24 This relationship has become an important underpinning of modern revisionism
    within urban sociology. See Fischer, *To Dwell Among Friends,* pp. 8–9.
25 Church membership records are used in lieu of missing membership list for other
    local voluntary organizations. For a discussion of the integrative role of churches,
    see Blumin, *The Urban Threshold,* pp. 28–29.

26 For a discussion of the difficulties of applying network analysis to urban communities, see Norman Shulman, "Network Analysis: A New Addition to an Old Bag of Tricks," *Acta Sociologica* 19 (December 1976), pp. 307–323; Jeremy Boissevain, *Friends of Friends: Networks, Manipulators and Coalitions* (New York: St. Martin's Press, 1974), p. 36. The full range of primary-order ties of Pietru Cardona of Malta would require, in theory, a 1,750 by 1,750 matrix to calculate while a second-order network would consist of 875,000 for an island with only 314,000 inhabitants. See also Thomas Bender, *Community and Social Change in America* (New Brunswick, N.J.: Rutgers University Press, 1978), pp. 125–128.

27 For a discussion of the use of diaries in the historical study of social networks, see Bender, *Community and Social Change in America*, pp. 125–128. The extralocal aspects of community ties have received some attention in historical research, although hardly the attention which they deserve. Michael Anderson, in his study of family structure in nineteenth-century Lancashire, noted that kinship "does not stop at the front door." See Michael Anderson, *Family Structure in Nineteenth-Century Lancashire* (Cambridge: Cambridge University Press, 1971), p. 61. Some of the same assumptions seem to be made by Donna R. Gabaccia in her study of Italians in New York's Lower East Side, "Sicilians in Space: Environmental Change and Family Geography," *Journal of Social History* 16 (Winter 1982), pp. 53–66. Also Howard P. Chudacoff, "Newlyweds and Family Extension: The First Stage of Family Cycle in Providence, Rhode Island, 1864–1865 and 1879–1880," in Tamara Hareven and Maris Vinovskis, eds., *Family and Population in Nineteenth-Century America* (Princeton: Princeton University Press, 1978), pp. 179–205; Tamara Hareven, *Family Time and Industrial Time* (Cambridge: Cambridge University Press, 1982), pp. 114–116; Ralph Janis, "The Brave New World That Failed: Patterns of Parish Social Structure in Detroit, 1880–1940" (Ph.D. diss., University of Michigan, 1972), p. 40; and Margaret E. Connor, "Their Own Kind: Family and Community in Albany New York 1850–1915" (Ph.D. diss., Harvard University, 1975), pp. 230–243. For other works examining neighboring and social networks, see also Linda Bissell, "Family, Friends, and Neighbors: Social Interaction in Seventeenth-Century Windsor, Connecticut" (Ph.D. diss., Brandeis University, 1973), pp. 139–147; and R. M. Smith, "Kin and Neighbors in a Thirteenth-Century Suffolk Community," *Journal of Family History* 4 (Fall 1979), pp. 219–256.

28 Given the tight antebellum housing market which well may have made associational proximity largely a function of available vacancies, the following analysis employs only a very coarse measure based upon *clusters* of wards in broad districts. Witnesses who lived within, approximately, a fifteen-minutes walk of a couple were considered to inhabit the same "local area."

29 Very few cases actually listed the relation of the witnesses. For a sociological study of the changing content of social relations, see Norma Shulman, "Life-Cycle Variations in Patterns of Close Relationships," *Journal of Marriage and the Family* 37 (1975), pp. 813–821.

30 This also makes social propinquity especially difficult to study because it is often unclear whose address to use in the case of a marriage.

31 See tables 6.2 and 6.3.

32 Witnesses by law and custom could not be closer than siblings to the parties and usually were cousins or friends.

33 Boulton, *Neighbourhood and Society*, p. 240.

34   Baptism Records, St. James Roman Catholic Church, January 25, 1874.

35   "Cellars and Attics of the Fourth Ward," *New York Times*, July 1, 1859, 2:1.

36   Peter Townsend, *An Account of the Yellow Fever as It Prevailed in the City of New York in Summer and Autumn 1822* (New York: O. Halstead, 1823), pp. 137–139.

37   Even before comparing residences, it was clear that witnesses had much in common with the backgrounds of those whose ceremonies they solemnized. Although a lack of data makes a comparison on the basis of ethnicity virtually impossible, linkage with city directories provided information for a study of the impact of occupational rank upon association. Not surprisingly, people were most likely to draw associates from the same occupational category as themselves or from an adjacent category. In terms of choice and avoidance, the sampled New Yorkers formed three separate classes: white-collar, skilled, and unskilled. Professionals and proprietors freely chose associates from one another's group while avoiding contact with skilled or unskilled workers. Skilled workers generally invited their fellow tradesmen. And unskilled workers either chose other laborers or, lacking in friends and relations, seem to have relied upon boardinghouse proprietors, barkeepers, or other local proprietors (classified as "site-only" because only the place of business rather than the job itself was listed) as witnesses. The data indicates a hardening of class boundaries, particularly between white-collar on the one hand and artisans or unskilled workers on the other. Marriage Records Sample, New York City, 1830–1875 (see appendix A).

38   Proximity produced the strongest second-order association with a chi-square likelihood statistic of 635.38 (d.f. of 114) compared to other interactions such as that between the date of the ceremony and either the address of the party (likelihood of 251.66 with d.f. of 117) or the witness (likelihood of 176.31 with d.f. of 117). This model, which included a fourth variable that controlled for the lack of information on the relationship of witnesses to bride or groom in church records (and the corresponding confusion over which marital partner's address to use), produced a second-order base model significant to the .2060 level. Which spouse's address was used in the comparison was not a significant predictor of associational proximity for the witness. The number listed in the percentaged output from the modeled data is almost twice the real sample size, and the results are a *composite* of both grooms' and brides' addresses.

39   The case of working-class localism is raised in a creative and telling manner by Ivar Bernstein's study of the 1863 Draft Riots. By studying their behavior during the riots, Bernstein engages in rudimentary network analysis using court records. Ivar Bernstein, *The New York City Draft Riots: Their Significance for American Society and Politics in the Age of the Civil War* (New York: Oxford University Press, 1990), pp. 105–106, 114–123. Lack of adequate data makes this thorny problem virtual impossible to resolve, but in either case the complexity of working-class social networks makes any single model difficult to apply.

40   Granovetter has noted, "in lower socioeconomic groups, weak ties are often not bridges, but rather represent friends' or relatives' acquaintances; the information they provide would not constitute a real broadening of opportunity, reflected in the fact that the net effect on income of using such ties is actually negative." "The Strength of Weak Ties: A Network Theory Revisited," p. 112.

41   For historians and sociologists, marital endogamy has served as the conventional measure of social cohesion. In the early 1930s, James Bossard first sought to study

marital propinquity within the city as a way of testing then current scholarship on the "passing of the neighborhood in the larger city." Through the use of 5,000 consecutive Philadelphia marriage licenses, Bossard found that, controlling for other variables such as race, economic status, "culture," or employment, men usually tended to marry the girl next door. As he put it, "Cupid may have wings, but apparently they are not adapted for long flights." Similar conclusions concerning the constraints of neighborhood marriage were reached as other researchers replicated these findings in one form or another over the next thirty years. James H. S. Bossard, "Residential Propinquity As a Factor in Marriage Selection," *American Journal of Sociology* 38 (1932), pp. 219–224. Other studies conducted in the 1930s, 1940s, and the early 1950s, consisting principally of Ruby Jo Reeves Kennedy's research on New Haven, which replicated Bossard's research and confirmed repeatedly the importance of residential proximity upon the selection of a marital partner. Ruby Jo Reeves Kennedy, "Premarital Residential Propinquity and Ethnic Endogamy," *American Journal of Sociology* 48 (1943), pp. 580–584; Maurice Davie and Ruby Jo Reeves, "Propinquity of Residence Before Marriage," *American Journal of Sociology* 54 (1939), pp. 510–517; and Kennedy's "Single or Triple Melting Pot? Inter Marriage in New Haven," *American Journal of Sociology* 58 (1952), pp. 56–59. In the early 1950s, the use of marital propinquity to measure social cohesion came under increasing fire. It was now argued that marital endogamy too easily overlooked the existence of multiple communities shared by residents of the same urban locale. Gerald Schnepp and Louis Roberts, "Residential Propinquity and Mate Selection on a Parish Basis," *American Journal of Sociology* 58 (1952), pp. 45–50. Only with the emergence of social network analysis in the 1960s, and the use of more sophisticated measures of social cohesion, did interest in urban marital propinquity begin to fade. A number of historians, however, continue to use marital endogamy as a barometer of "social cohesion" and community. See Bissell, "Family, Friends, and Neighbors," pp. 139–143; Janis, "The Brave New World That Failed."

42   The sparseness of information on anything other than the premarital addresses prevented me from conducting a multivariate analysis of the effects of other variables such as age, ethnicity, and residential propinquity. Historical studies of other cities have found that the majority of marriage partners were selected within local parishes, although some have pointed up the difficulty in interpreting address at time of marriage. Boulton, *Neighbourhood and Society*, p. 235, and Dennis and Daniels, " 'Community' and the Social Geography of Victorian Cities," p. 19.

43   The categories were: same address, a different address on the same street and ward, on a different street in the same ward, in an adjacent ward (same area), or in an area that failed to match at all.

44   These levels were twice as high as those found in a study of Philadelphia marital geography focusing on the years 1885–1886. Ray H. Abrams, "Residential Propinquity as a Factor in Marriage Selection: Fifty Year Trends in Philadelphia," *American Sociological Review* 8 (1953), pp. 288–294. However, the actual levels of propinquity, as Abrams noted, were somewhat lower. The figure was inflated by those husbands who married their housekeepers, by common-law marriages that were finally solemnized, and by an out-of-town partner who stayed with a prospective in-law while in the city (with both giving the same address). Some may have also been marriages where the minister listed the partners' intended address after marriage.

45 The issue of geographic proximity is separate from that of ethnic endogamy. Not only did immigrants marry within their own ethnic group, but among such groups as Germans, according to regional differences within their country of origin. Stanley Nadel, *Little Germany: Ethnicity, Religion, and Class in New York City, 1845–80* (Urbana: University of Illinois Press, 1990), pp. 22–24, 48–51, 155. The pattern of high regional endogamy went beyond religious similarities to insure that Prussians married Prussians, Bavarians married Bavarians—a pattern which was repeated "for each of the 'nationalities' that made up Kleindeutschland's population."

46 Rev. Henry Chase, Manuscript Marriages for the Mariner's Church, located at the New-York Historical Society. Entry for June 9, 1845. Henderson was unable to produce any witnesses because his friends refused to help solemnize a wedding not performed by a priest.

47 Chase, Manuscript Marriage, entry for August 4, 1845.

48 For a discussion of "two Irish districts geographically separated by the town centre," forming "one 'marriage community'," see Dennis and Daniels, " 'Community' and the Social Geography," p. 17.

49 When the addresses of grooms and brides were compared directly in virtually all areas of the city, grooms tended to marry women residing in their general area, including adjacent districts. Thus, grooms from the Upper East Side took wives from their own neighborhood or from the Upper West Side, Suburban Manhattan, Brooklyn, or New Jersey. Once again, residents of immigrant areas tended to be slightly less localistically rooted in marital propinquity, choosing spouses from farther away, while native residents were slightly more likely to rely upon a neighborhood community.

50 For a sociological critique of local friendship, see Carol J. Silverman, "Neighboring and Urbanism: Commonality Versus Friendship," *Urban Affairs Quarterly* 22 (1986), pp. 312–328.

51 Edward E. Hale, *Letters on Irish Emigration* (Freeport, N. Y.: Books for Libraries Press, 1972; reprint of 1852 ed.), p. 33.

52 Baptists and Methodists were not the only denominations to exercise high levels of moral oversight. Parish minutes from Presbyterian (including one black congregation) and, on occasion, Dutch Reformed churches contain mentions of ecclesiastic trials and expulsions of members. Episcopalians and Catholics were the only obvious groups for which such coercion seemed minimal. However, very few of the Episcopal churches were "free" of pew rents keeping the number of full communicants small compared to other denominations. See for example records of Shiloh Presbyterian Church 1857–1869, Presbyterian Historical Society, Philadelphia, and of the West Presbyterian Church 1831–1875, West-Park Presbyterian Church, New York City.

53 [Burns], *Three Years Among the Working-Classes in the United States During the War*, pp. 42–43.

54 Franklin D. Scott, ed., *Baron Klinkowstrom's America 1818–1820* (Evanston, Ill.: Northwestern University Press, 1952), p. 107.

55 Asa Greene, *A Glance at New York* (New York: A. Greene, 1837), p. 20.

56 John D. Vose, *Fresh Leaves from the Diary of a Broadway Dandy* (New York: Bunnel & Price, 1852), p. 30. Brooks, *The Diary of Michael Floy*, p. 116.

57 Fischer, *To Dwell Among Friends*, pp. 212–214. Fischer's main concern is to study whether, as Gerhard Lenski had claimed, urbanism decreased church attendance.

He found that churches filled the role of "communal institutions for religious fellowship" such as social circles and clubs in small towns which lacked these institutions. The abundance of associational activities in the city tended to replace the social church.

58 Dennis and Daniels, " 'Community' and the Social Geography of Victorian Cities," p. 18.

59 The New York Diocese usually established Roman Catholic parishes with clearly defined geographical boundaries. See manuscript map of church boundaries in manuscript records of St. James Roman Catholic Church, St. James Church, New York City.

60 Garrioch, *Neighborhood & Community in Paris, 1740–1790*, pp. 149, 157, 161, 167. Another study noted that while churches might have been an "important component of a true local social system" by creating "a gathering of neighbours" to counteract "the dislocating influences of heavy immigration by acting as a 'home-from-home for first generation immigrants'," the extent of membership and church attendance was unclear. In the case of one parish that was studied, it was clear that "the church was *not* a significant social force." Boulton, *Neighbourhood and Society*, p. 275.

61 Despite Timothy Dwight's remark that "everything of a religious nature" was treated with "reverence by the great proportion of the citizens" of New York, churches clearly held no monopoly on Sunday amusements. Cited in Rock, *Artisans of the New Republic*, p. 316. In addition to spending time with one's family, there was shopping, drinking in porterhouses and saloons, visiting candy stores, or, perhaps, having one's picture taken at a daguerreotype gallery—all of which frequently stayed open on Sundays in violation of state blue laws. These examples were drawn from the list of establishments accused of violating Sunday closure laws by police in the Tenth Ward during one brief period of 1855. See New York Police Department, Manuscript "List of Saloons Open on Sunday, January 13, 1855," Box 4063, New York City Municipal Archives.

62 Sean Wilentz, *Chants Democratic: New York City & the Rise of the American Working Class, 1788–1850* (New York: Oxford University Press, 1984), pp. 80–81, 83, 277–281. Wilentz bases these conclusions largely on an analysis of the records of the Brainerd Presbyterian church supplemented by records of the parish register of the Church of the Epiphany. See also Richard Stott, *Workers in the Metropolis: Class, Ethnicity, and Youth in Antebellum New York City*, pp. 240–242; and Stansell, *City of Women*, pp. 66, 87.

63 Timothy Smith, *Revivalism and Social Reform in Mid-Nineteenth-Century America* (New York: Abington Press, 1957), p. 18. Examples of church discipline and moral control of established members in a black congregation can be found in the manuscript minutes of the Shiloh Presbyterian Church for the years 1857–1869, located at the Presbyterian Historical Society, Philadelphia. For a description of revivalism among working-class New Yorkers in the 1830s, see Wilentz, *Chants Democratic*, pp. 277–281. The young Methodist Michael Floy wrote of twice-weekly choral practices, prayer meetings, and classes that finally culminated in his own religious transformation when he found himself at the altar "trembling all over; my teeth chattering" in a fashion that was "so violent that it was noticed by all who were in the pew." Brooks, *The Diary of Michael Floy*, p. 16.

64 Wilentz, *Chants Democratic*, p. 300. No evidence is offered on this revival's actual

magnitude. See also Stansell, *City of Women*, p. 66. Lydia Child told of one unfortunate shoemaker who gave away his stock before his son arrived and "caused him
to be sent to an asylum, till the excitement of his mind abated," while at another
shop on the Bowery, the enterprising owner had hung a sign advertising "MUSLIN
FOR ASCENSION ROBES!" L[ydia] Maria Child, *Letters from New York* (New York:
C. S. Francis, 1846), pp. 235–236.

65 Manuscript history of the Jane Street Methodist Church, dated December 25, 1844,
in the Records of the Jane Street Methodist Church, 1844–1870, at the New York
Annual Conference Center, Rye, New York. For a discussion of similar outdoor
evangelism in the early nineteenth century, see the discussion of Domanic Van
Velsor, Amos Broad, and Jonny Edwards in Wilentz, *Chants Democratic*, pp. 80–
81. Evangelical Methodists were also harassed by traditionalists in their revival
efforts. In 1830 the Bedford Street Methodist Church, the Mariner's Church on
Roosevelt Street, the Forsyth Street Methodist Church, and the Allen Street Meth-
odist Church were each attacked by mobs in separate incidents. Paul A. Gilje, *The
Road to Mobocracy: Popular Disorder in New York City, 1763–1834* (Chapel Hill:
Institute of Early American History and Culture and University of North Carolina
Press, 1987), pp. 207–209.

66 In this revival, dance hall owner John Allen offered to rent his establishment to several clergymen to be used as the site for a prayer meeting attracting 1,500, mostly
"well-dressed, respectable looking class of people." After the forces of righteousness scored a further victory by persuading Kit Burns to lease his saloon and "rat
pit" at 273 Water Street for meetings, the revival quickly lost its steam and Burns
soon reopened his dive. Oliver Dyer, *The 'Wickedest Man' in New York or the
Great Awakening in Water Street* (New York: P. Dwight, 1868), pp. 22, 27; and Rev.
J. F. Richmond, *New York and Its Institutions 1609–1873* (New York: E. B. Treat,
1872), p. 27. In the wake of this abortive "Great Awakening," the Metropolitan
Board of Health could only conclude that the whole affair was the product of a
group of "badly-advised, but very benevolent and religious men," in which "little
was accomplished towards reform" save for bringing the district's already notorious brothels and dance halls into "a clear light." Metropolitan Board of Health of
the State of New York, *Third Annual Report* (Albany, 1868), p. 501.

67 Church members who joined before 1876 were traced in subsequent records. It
should be kept in mind that inconsistencies in record-keeping from church to
church, as well as doctrinal differences in membership requirements between various denominations, influenced the sample. Because Roman Catholic parishes did
not generally keep membership lists, a rough estimate of communicants had to be
compiled using a procedure similar to one employed by Jay Dolan in his study of an
Upper West Side parish during the late nineteenth century. Dolan used baptismal
records as a proxy for Irish membership and divided the total number of cases by
the birthrate in the surrounding ward to estimate a net attendance rate. Since I was
mainly interested in producing a sample that could be used for comparison with
Protestant membership (not the size of the congregation), I did not adjust for fertility. See Jay Dolan, *Catholic Revivalism in the United States 1830–1900* (South
Bend, Ind.: University of Notre Dame Press, 1978), pp. 121–127.

68 Howard B. Rock, *Artisans of the New Republic: The Tradesmen of New York City
in the Age of Jefferson* (New York: NYU Press, 1979), p. 316.

69 Computed from the Secretary of State, *Census of the State of New York for 1855*

(Albany, 1857), pp. 447–479. Roman Catholic churches lacked either these strict tests of membership or formalized record-keeping to ensure the purity of their flock. Compared with Protestant sects, Catholic communion was open to all, and attendance at Mass was not a privilege but a "necessary duty" for "to be absent without strong reason" was a "mortal sin." Still, despite open communion and the strict requirement to attend, Jay Dolan found that a majority of Catholics were not religiously observant, with only between 40 and 60 percent attending on a typical Sunday in the 1860s. Jay Dolan, *The Immigrant Church: New York's Irish and German Catholics, 1815–1865* (Baltimore: Johns Hopkins University Press, 1975), p. 56. The variable attendance rates and conflicts within congregations between Irish, Germans, and natives apparently did not detract from the church's role as a local institutional anchor for a highly mobile immigrant community.

70   Computed from the Secretary of State, *Census of the State of New York for 1855*, pp. 447–479.

71   Manuscript Letters of Admission, Oliver Street (Epiphany) Baptist Church, letters from May 24, 1798, and January 28, 1793, in New–York Historical Society. Most of the 136 certificates of transference received by the Oliver Street Baptist Church between 1790 and 1821 were addressed specifically to that church. This pattern conflicts with that found in a study of Jacksonville, Illinois, where ministers routinely recommended in a blanket fashion that an individual be granted "Christian friendship and affection of those among who his lot may be cast." Doyle, *The Social Order of a Frontier Community: Jacksonville, Illinois, 1825–1870*, p. 165.

72   Computed from the Manuscript Census of Churches for New York City, 1855. Located in the County Clerk's Office, New York City. The average attendance for the tiny French Church of St. Espirit in Fifth Ward was read as 400. The recording figure of 4,000 was obviously in error.

73   The Fifth Ward was also experiencing a general decline in population, though in its case, the drop came because of the encroachment of the central business district. In this ward the Duane Street Methodist Church saw only 300 communicants in a building designed to hold 1000.

74   Wilentz, *Chants Democratic*, pp. 85, 252–253. Wilentz cites one outbreak of sectarian violence on the part of Greenwich Village weavers that disrupted a celebration by Orangemen in 1824. Gilje, *The Road to Mobocracy*, p. 128.

75   Nadel, *Little Germany*, p. 91.

76   John Gilmary Shea, *The Catholic Churches of New York City* (New York: Lawrence G. Goulding, 1878), p. 398.

77   Since none of the Roman Catholic churches sampled maintained lists of members, this analysis relies upon an estimate derived from baptismal records.

78   The low occupational rank of Catholics might have been inflated due to age-induced biases stemming from the use of baptismal records that tended to capture parents in the early stages of their occupational careers.

79   If Protestant churches often had a decidedly bourgeois cast to them, their middle-class appeal can easily be exaggerated given the wide appeal they also had for artisans and small tradesmen. Dennis and Daniels, " 'Community' and the Social Geography of Victorian Cities," p. 18.

80   These figures might slightly overstate the proletarian nature of Methodists because many of the semiskilled workers were native cartmen who attended the Bedford, Jane, and Perry Street Churches. Isaac S. Lyon's memoir raises doubt as to whether

cartmen should be classified as semiskilled workers, as is the case with the Philadelphia Social History Project employed in this analysis, or as skilled workers because of the artisanal nature of their trade. See his *Recollection of an Ex Carter* (Newark, N.J.: Daily Journal, 1872). For a more detailed discussion of this trade, also see Graham R. Hodges, *New York City Cartmen, 1667–1850* (New York: New York University Press, 1986).

81 Many of the fashionable churches uptown, ran the downtown churches as missionary chapels. The high turnover of evangelical converts was especially obvious to the pastors. Rev. S. D. Burchard of the Thirteenth Street Presbyterian Church noted that free congregations were usually "built for poor people and the self supporting element" and experienced high turnover because many of the newly converted members simply "would not remain." Rev. S. D. Burchard, *The Centennial Historical Discourse Preached in the Thirteenth Street Presbyterian Church, July 1876* (New York: Arthur & Bonner, 1877), p. 8. For a discussion of interdenomination strains between Protestant churches over questions of doctrine and politics, see Amy Bridges, *A City in The Republic: Antebellum New York and the Origins of Machine Politics* (Cambridge: Cambridge University Press, 1984), pp. 85–90.

82 Such transiency of church membership is a matter of community structure (devotional and local), not simply of class. People "learned to expect transiency and rapid membership turnover" and through this acceptance of social volatility, "a mobile people created a stable society." Eric H. Monkkonen, *America Become Urban: The Development of U.S. Cities & Towns, 1780–1980* (Berkeley: University of California Press, 1988), p. 92.

83 However, it would be a mistake to confuse neighborhood community entirely with church attendance. With the exception of Lower West Side wards, many residents ventured outside their home area to hear a favorite minister preach or to be among a familiar congregation. Bridge's assumed that the location of church was a strong predictor of an area's religious character by using the 1855 church census by ward, which listed average attendance, to estimate the religious affiliation of voters in the ward. See her *A City in The Republic*, pp. 64–67, 175n15.

84 "The Migration of Churches," in "New York City in Olden Time's Consisting of Newspaper Cuttings Arranged by Henry Onderdonk Jr." (Jamaica, L.I.: 1862) at the New York Public Library. Not paged.

85 Rev. Alfred H. Moment, *The New York Down-Town Presbyterian Churches* (New York: 1881), p. 10.

86 Lewis Jackson, *A Church Directory for New York City* (New York: NYC Mission Society, 1867), p. 88–89.

87 Henry Anstice, *History of St. George's Church in the City of New York, 1752–1811–1911* (New York: Harper & Bros., 1911), pp. 149–150. "The Migration of Churches," in "New York City in Olden Time's Consisting of Newspaper Cuttings Arranged by Henry Onderdonk Jr." Not paged.

88 West Presbyterian Church, *Manual* (New York: 1864), p. 9. For a full historical account of church removals and the conversion of religious structures to other uses, see Henry B. Hoffman, "Transformations of New York Churches," *New York Historical Society Quarterly* 22 (1938), pp. 3–27.

89 Bridges, *A City In the Republic*, p. 73. For a discussion of the implication of the self-separation of elites on older, socially mixed communities, see Richard Dennis,

English Industrial Cities of the Nineteenth Century: A Social Geography (Cambridge: Cambridge University Press, 1984), pp. 285–286.

90   Nash, "The Social Evolution of Preindustrial American Cities, 1700–1820," p. 41.

91   Both cited in Edward K. Spann, *The New Metropolis: New York City, 1840–1857* (New York: Columbia University Press, 1981), pp. 228–232.

92   Although the combined associations tested significantly at the .0711 level, with the strongest association occurring between the date of admission and whether the church had moved, those who joined the congregation after the move belonged to higher occupational ranks.

93   Dennis and Daniels, " 'Community' and the Social Geography of Victorian Cities," pp. 18–19. See also Dennis, *English Industrial Cities of the Nineteenth Century*, pp. 276–285.

94   Brooks, ed., *The Diary of Michael Floy Jr.*, p. 180.

95   Information on the social composition and internal organization of saloons is uncommon in the antebellum years despite the increasing frequency of temperance reformers' attacks and even period censuses of grog shops and porterhouses in particularly impoverished areas. In a study of saloons in Chicago and Boston later in the century, Perry R. Duis found that not only did these institutions meet the needs of transients, but that they also reflected the ethnic makeup surrounding neighborhoods. But while saloons could be classified according to their ethnic exclusivity, Duis's argues that saloons actually functioned as "public melting pots" that not only reflected the "heterogeneity and social class of the street life surrounding the saloon," but also made many bars "ethnic universals." Perry R. Duis, *The Saloon: Public Drinking in Chicago and Boston, 1880–1920* (Urbana: University of Illinois Press, 1983), pp. 86–113, 143–171.

96   Peter George Buckley, "To the Opera House: Culture and Society in New York City, 1820–1860" (Ph.D. diss., SUNY Stony Brook, 1984), p. 386. For a discussion of immigrant voluntary associations, see also Robert Ernst, *Immigrant Life in New York City 1825–1863* (New York: Kings Crown Press, 1849), pp. 122–134.

97   Bridges, *A City in the Republic*, p. 76. See also Eliot J. Gorn, " 'Good-Bye Boys, I Die a True American': Homicide, Nativism, and Working-Class Culture in Antebellum New York City," *Journal of American History* 74 (September 1987), p. 403.

98   Buckley, "To the Opera House: Culture and Society in New York City, 1820–1860," pp. 345–346.

99   Harlow, *Old Bowery Days*, p. 294.

100   Francis, Augustus, *History of the 71st Regiment, N.G., N.Y.* (New York: Veterans Association, 1919), pp. 10–42.

101   Buckley, "To the Opera House: Culture and Society in New York City, 1820–1860," pp. 345–346.

102   Wilentz, *Chants Democratic*, pp. 259–262; and Stott, *Workers in the Metropolis*, pp. 229–231. For a description of the early career of one of New York's most notorious fire company leaders, William M. Tweed, see Leo Hershkowitz, *Tweed's New York: Another Look* (Garden City: Anchor Books, 1978), pp. 11–14. See also Bayard Still, *Mirror for Gotham* (New York: NYU Press, 1956), pp. 136–138; and Thomas Picton, *Rose Street: Its Past, Present and Future* (New York: Russell Bros, 1873), p. 7. For a longer description of the old voluntary association, see Kenneth H. Dunshee, *As You Pass By* (New York: Hastings House, 1952); Augustine E. Costello, *Our Fire-*

men: A History of the New York Fire Department Volunteer and Paid (New York: Augustine Costello, 1887); and George W. Sheldon, *The Story of the Volunteer Fire Department of the City of New York* (New York: Harper and Bros, 1882).

103   Bridges, *A City in the Republic*, pp. 75–76. The records of fire companies provide a useful source on voluntary associations and a great potential for the study of proximity in relations. See Chief Engineer of the Fire Department, *Annual Report for 1865*, in Board of Alderman Documents (New York: 1865).

104   [Burns], *Three Years Among the Working-Classes in the United States During the War*, pp. 48–49. See also Stott, *Workers in the Metropolis*, pp. 217–222.

105   [Jackson], *A Church Directory for New York*, p. 6, and *A Guide to the Mission Stations for the Use of The Director* (New York: N.Y. Mission Society, n.d.), Doc. no. 7, p. 6. See also *The Night Side of New York: A Picture of the Great Metropolis After Nightfall By Members of the New York Press* (New York: Excelsior Press, [1866]), pp. 28–32.

106   [Burns], *Three Years Among the Working-Classes in the United States During the War*, p. 48.

107   Alvin Harlow, *Old Bowery Days* (New York: Appleton 1931), p. 188.

108   Gorn, " 'Good-Bye Boys, I Die a True American," pp. 388–410; Joel T. Headley, *The Great Riots of New York 1712–1873* (Indianapolis: Bobbs-Merrill, 1970; reprint of 1873 ed., pp. 131–134; and Stott, *Workers in the Metropolis*, pp. 230–235. See also Edward Spann, *The New Metropolis: New York City 1840–1857* (New York: Columbia University Press, 1981), pp. 393–394; and Herbert Asbury, *The Gangs of New York* (Garden City: Garden City Publications, 1928), pp. 112–117.

109   Amy Bridges, *A City in The Republic*, pp. 76–77.

110   "Terrible Riot in the Ninth Ward," *New York Times*, July 6, 1853; and H. Wilson, comp., *Trow's New York City Directory 1853–54* (New York: H. Trow, 1853).

111   Bernstein, "The New York City Draft Riots of 1863," pp. 75–75, 78n183ff.

112   Charles H. Haswell, *Reminiscences of New York By an Octogenarian* (New York: Harper & Bros., 1896), pp. 262, 355.

113   Wilentz, *Chants Democratic*, pp. 300–301, 257–271. For an extensive discussion of Bowery subculture and its implication to women, see Stansell, *City of Women*, pp. 89–101.

114   The importance of the Bowery as a milieu is discussed in Stott, *Workers in the Metropolis*, pp. 213, 245–246.

115   Stuart Blumin, "Explaining the New Metropolis: Perception, Depiction, and Analysis in Mid-Nineteenth-Century New York City," *Journal of Urban History* 11 (November 1984), p. 22. Buckley, "To the Opera House: Culture and Society in New York City, 1820–1860," p. 296, 316, 323–337, 351–335, 408–409. Buckley notes that: "The very reproducibility of the accounts of Bowery B'hoy life may not testify to 'reality' but rather to a set of literary conventions and a way of handling the experience of observation through narrative. This is not to claim, of course, that the b'hoy is simply the product of literary and graphic imagination, rather that his appearance on the street and his arrival in print were part of the same social transformation." Buckley has subsequently revised his views to downgrade the importance of the Bowery. Comments, Meeting of the Organization of American Historians, Louisville, April 13, 1991. See also Wilentz, *Chants Democratic*, p. 270.

116   Stansell, *City of Women*, pp. 90–98. Stansell labels the Bowery Boy as "a mem-

ber of youth culture, a milieu characterized by a symbiotic relationship to its own symbolic elaboration."

117 Even in the arena of political activity, the nineteenth-century urban neighborhood was the site for both local and trans-local social interaction. Despite the selection of a Common Council and Board of Alderman on the basis of ward, New York's wards did not truly function as bases for political power until the emergence of political machines late in the 1850s—a decade when professional politicians finally learned to exploit their positions on local school committees and fire companies to win elections. Up until that time, even if residential segregation allowed contemporaries to attribute "certain kinds of character to particular wards," the city retained "a kind of social wholeness that was both symbolic and real." Bridges, *A City in the Republic*, pp. 43–44, 73, 146–150. Bridges gives the example of German representatives of the Seventeenth Ward who, when they organized politically, spoke in terms of "the city wide German League or German Democracy" rather than in terms of local area.

118 Buckley, "To the Opera House: Culture and Society in New York City, 1820–1860," p. 334.

7 Conclusion

1 Thomas Jesse Jones, *The Sociology of a New York City Block* (New York: Published by the Author, 1904), pp. 98–99, 108–111, 113–114; and Thomas Bender, *Community and Social Change in America* (New Brunswick, N.J.: Rutgers University Press, 1978).

2 Elsa G. Herzfeld, *Family Monographs: The History of Twenty-Four Families Living in the Middle West Side of New York City* (New York: James Kemster Printing, 1905), pp. 48–50. The discovery of working-class mobility may be dated back even further to Charles Loring Brace, who credited "the fact that tenants must forever be 'moving' in New York" with preventing "some of the worst evils among the lower poor," namely the inheritance of pauperism and crime from "bad" parents and siblings. See his work, *The Dangerous Classes of New York, and Twenty Years' Work Among Them* (New York: Wynkoop & Hallenbeck, 1872), p. 47.

3 Blackmar concedes that "trade" and "tenant" neighborhoods were "perceptions of the period" rather than "territories of the city" that "spatially and socially enclosed the everyday lives of their residents." However, she also contends that by the mid-nineteenth century, "the elaboration of localized networks and institutions fostered . . . a spatial sense of collective identity" that linked "an extensive neighborhood geography with social identity." Elizabeth Blackmar, *Manhattan for Rent, 1785–1850* (Ithaca: Cornell University Press, 1990), pp. 11–12.

4 See chap. 1.

5 The debate over what constitutes a neighborhood has become ideologically charged given the popular connotation of the terminology. Segregation, Dennis notes, commonly signifies "constraint, management, and social engineering" compared with "community," which invariably connotes "choice, freedom, and harmony," leading to a view in which "segregation is assumed to be bad" and "community is always good." Richard Dennis, *English Industrial Cities of the Nineteenth Century: A Social Geography* (Cambridge: Cambridge University Press, 1984), pp. 285–286.

6 Little is know about the role of individuals in the city at this crucial juncture—

although historians have learned much about their behavior as members of groups and classes. Dennis, *English Industrial Cities of the Nineteenth Century*, pp. 285–296.

7 For a discussion of the relationship between social problems and ecological processes formulated by the Chicago School, see David Ward, *Poverty, Ethnicity, and the American City, 1840–1925: Changing Conceptions of the Slum and the Ghetto* (Cambridge: Cambridge University Press, 1989), pp. 158–170.

8 Matthew Hale Smith, *Sunshine and Shadow in New York* (Hartford: J. B. Burr, 1868), pp. 26–27.

Appendix A   A Note on Method and Sources

1 The manuscript census for the county is housed in the County Clerk's Office located in the Hall of Records, Chambers Street, in New York City.

2 Deciding upon a sampling fraction is one of the most difficult decisions that a researcher may make, since no sampling text gives any clear rule on this matter. My decision was guided by the realization that repeated stratification might produce tables with too few cases to be analyzed successfully by multivariate techniques. For a description of how many to select, see James A. Davis, "Statistical Inference with Proportions" (unpublished paper, 1975); and C. A. Moser and G. Kalton, *Survey methods in Social Investigation* (New York: Basic Books, 1972), 2d ed., pp. 81, 146.

3 The random numbers employed came from the Rand Corporation, *A Million Random Digits with 100,000 Normal Deviates* (Glencoe, Ill.: Free Press, 1955). For more information on this procedure, see Moser and Kalton, *Survey Methods in Social Investigation*, pp. 152–154.

4 See Michael Katz, *The People of Hamilton, Canada West: Family and Class in a Mid-Nineteenth-Century City* (Cambridge: Harvard University Press, 1975); Kathleen Neils Conzen, *Immigrant Milwaukee, 1836–1860: Accommodation and Community In a Frontier City* (Cambridge: Harvard University Press, 1976); and Clyde and Sally Griffen, *Natives and Newcomers: The Ordering of Opportunity in Mid-Nineteenth-Century Poughkeepsie* (Cambridge: Harvard University Press, 1978). For a description of hierarchical data sets in historical research, see Michael Anderson, "Family and Class in the Nineteenth Century Cities," *Journal of Family History*, 2 (1977), pp. 139–150.

5 Theodore Hershberg and Robert Dockhorn, "Occupational Classification," *Historical Methods Newsletter* 9 (1976), pp. 59–98.

6 See New York Secretary of State, *Census of the State of New York for 1865* (Albany, 1867); and Franklin B. Hough, *Statistics of Population of the City and County of New York As Shown by the State Census of 1865* (New York: New York Printing, 1867).

7 Rev. Henry Chase, Mariners Church Marriages 1830–1853, manuscript volumes (15) at the New-York Historical Society.

8 For a discussion of problems with uncommon *last* names, see Richard S. Alcorn and Peter R. Knight, "Most Uncommon Bostonians: A Critique of Stephan Thernstrom's *The Other Bostonians: Poverty and Progress in the American Metropolis 1880–1970*," *Historical Methods Newsletter* 8 (June 1975), pp. 98–114.

Appendix B   A Note on Presentation and Analysis

1   For information on both, see David Knoke and Peter J. Burke, *Log-Linear Models* (Beverly Hills: Sage Publishers, 1980), Sage University Papers series on Quantitative Applications in the Social Sciences, series no. 07-020; Graham J. G. Upton, *The Analysis of Cross-Tabulated Data* (New York: John Wiley & Sons, 1978); B. Fingleton, *Models of Category Counts* (Cambridge: Cambridge University Press, 1984); Stephen E. Fienberg, *The Analysis of Cross-Classified Categorical Data*, 2d ed. (Cambridge: MIT Press, 1980); Leo A. Goodman, "New Methods for Analyzing the Intrinsic Character of Qualitative Variables Using Cross-Classified Data," *American Journal of Sociology* 93 (November 1987), pp. 529–583; Clifford C. Clogg and Scott R. Eliason, "Some Common Problems in Log-Linear Analysis," *Sociological Methods & Research* 16 (August 1987), pp. 8–44; and Richard D. Alba, "Interpreting the Parameters of Log-Linear Models," *Sociological Methods & Research* 16 (August 1987), pp. 45–77.

2   For information on iterative proportional fitting, see James A. Davis, "Hierarchical Models for Significance Tests in Multivariate Contingency Tables: An Exegesis of Goodman's Recent Paper," in H. L. Costner, ed., *Sociological Methodology 1973–1974* (San Francisco: Jossey-Bass, 1974), pp. 189–231. Also Robert L. Kaufman and Paul G. Schervish, "Variations on a Theme: More Uses of Odds Ratios to Interpret Log-Linear Parameters," *Sociological Methods & Research* 16 (November 1987), pp. 218–255.

Bibliography

Manuscripts

Ackerman, Abraham, Manuscript Census Book of the Fifth Ward, 1819–1820, New-York Historical Society.

Allen Street Memorial Methodist Church, Records 1830–1875, New-York Historical Society.

Allen Street Presbyterian Church, Records 1830–1872, Presbyterian Historical Society, Philadelphia.

Annunciation Protestant Episcopal Church, Records 1847–1875, New York Episcopal Diocese Archives.

Bedford Street Methodist Church, Records 1828–1875, New York Annual Conference Center, Rye, New York.

Bowery Savings Bank, Savings Account Ledger Book, Volumes 1, 2, and 8, 1833–1838, 1840, 1850–1854, Archives of the Bowery Savings Bank, New York City.

Bowery Savings Bank, Transfer Volumes 1 and 2, 1846–1853, Archives of the Bowery Savings Bank, New York City.

Chapel of the Holy Comforter Protestant Episcopal Church, Records 1846–1875, Seaman's Institute, New York City.

Chase, Rev. Henry, Mariners Church Marriage Records 1830–1853, 15 vols., New-York Historical Society.

Chase, Rev. Henry, Diaries 1820–1833, New-York Historical Society.

Christ Episcopal Church, Records 1830–1868, Christ and St. Stephen's Church, New York City.

Duane Methodist Church, Records 1830–1875, Metropolitan-Duane Methodist Church, New York City.

Duane Street Presbyterian Church, Letters of Dismissal and Pew Certificates 1808–1859, New-York Historical Society.

Eighth Presbyterian Church, Register 1819–1842, Presbyterian Historical Society, Philadelphia.

First German Presbyterian Mission, Records 1852–1872, Presbyterian Historical Society, Philadelphia.

First Wesleyan Church, Records 1834–1875, Metropolitan-Duane Church, New York City.

Forsyth Street Methodist Church, Records 1837–1875, Rare Books and Manuscript Division, The New York Public Library, Astor, Lenox and Tilden Foundations.

Forsyth Street Reformed Dutch Church (German Reformed Church), Records 1830–1875, Gardner Sage Library, New Brunswick Theological Seminary, New Brunswick, New Jersey.

Fourth Free Presbyterian Church (Ward 4), Treasurer's Account Book 1834–1838, Presbyterian Historical Society, Philadelphia.

French Church of St. Espirit, Copy of Marriage Records 1830–1835, New-York Historical Society.

Greenwich Reformed Church, Records 1830–1866, Gardner Sage Library, New Brunswick Theological Seminary, New Brunswick, New Jersey.

Holy Evangelist Episcopal Church (Free Church of St. George), Records 1860–1867, Trinity Parish Archives, New York City.

Hope Presbyterian Church, Records 1846–1870, Presbyterian Historical Society, Philadelphia.

Jane Street Methodist Church, Records 1844–1875, New York Annual Conference Center, Rye, New York.

Laight Street Baptist Church, Membership Records 1843–1870, Central Baptist Church, New York City.

Laight Street Presbyterian Church, Records 1830–1843, Presbyterian Historical Society, Philadelphia.

Madison Avenue Reformed Church, Records 1830–1875, Gardner Sage Library, New Brunswick Seminary, New Brunswick, New Jersey.

Madison Street Methodist Church, Records 1843–1855, Rare Books and Manuscript Division, The New York Public Library, Astor, Lenox and Tilden Foundations.

Metropolitan Temple (Methodist), Records 1834–1875, Metropolitan-Duane Church, New York City.

New York City Clerk's Filed Papers, "Bonds of Keepers of Junkshops, 1844–1855," Box 3074, Municipal Archives, New York City.

New York City Clerk's Filed Papers, "Bonds of Second-Hand Dealers 1840–1858, 1859–1863," Boxes 3072 and 4073, Municipal Archives, New York City.

New York City, Jury Census for 1819, Historical Documents Collection, Queens College, New York City (microfilm copy at Harvard University).

New York City Police Department, "Tenth District Police Blotter May 25 to August 27, 1855, July 7, 1856 to November 29, 1856" and "List of Saloons Open on Sundays, 1855 for the Tenth District," 3 vols. in Box 4063, New York Municipal Archives.

New York State Census for 1855, County Clerk's Office, New York City.

North River Savings Bank, Signature Book and Account Ledgers for 1866, Archives of Bowery Savings Bank, New York City.

Oliver Street (Epiphany) Baptist Church, Letters of Admission, 1790–1821, New-York Historical Society.

Perry Street Methodist Church, Records for 1863–1875, New York Annual Conference, Rye, New York.

St. James Roman Catholic Church, Marriages and Baptisms, 1836–1875, St. James Roman Catholic Church, New York City.

St. John the Evangelist Lutheran Church, Records 1853–1875, St. John the Evangelist Church, New York City.

St. John's Chapel of Trinity Parish, Records 1858–1875, Trinity Parish Archives, New York City.

St. Joseph's Roman Catholic Church, Baptisms and Marriages 1833–1875, St. Joseph's Roman Catholic Church, New York City.

St. Jude's Episcopal Free Church, Records 1824–1853, St. John the Evangelist Episcopal Church, New York City.

St. Luke's Episcopal Church, Records 1820–1875, St. Luke's Episcopal Church, New York City.

St. Matthew's Episcopal Church, Records 1842–1856, New York Episcopal Diocese Archives, New York City.

St. Stephens Protestant Episcopal Church, Records 1830–1875, Christ and St. Stephen's Church, New York City.

Second Avenue Church (Church at Corner of Greene and Houston Street), Records 1852–1859, New-York Historical Society.

Seventh Avenue (Houston Street) Reformed Church, Records 1823–1859, New-York Historical Society.

Seventh Census of the United States, New York Schedules, New York County, 1860, Federal Archives and Record Center, Waltham, Massachusetts.

Shiloh Presbyterian Church, Records 1857–1869, Presbyterian Historical Society, Philadelphia.

Sixth Avenue Presbyterian Church, Records, 1835–1838, Presbyterian Historical Society, Philadelphia.

Sixth Free Episcopal Church, Record of Communicants 1852, New-York Historical Society.

Thirteenth Street Presbyterian Church, Records 1846–1875, Typescript Copy at the New York Genealogical and Biographical Society, New York City.

Union Reformed Church, Records 1859–1875, Gardner Sage Library, New Brunswick Theological Seminary, New Brunswick, New Jersey.

U.S. Department of Treasury, Internal Revenue Assessment Lists for New York 1862–1866, Reels M-603: T56-8, 67A, 216-7, 62-3, T52-8, T65-71, T213-7.

West Presbyterian Church, Records 1831–1875, West-Park Presbyterian Church, New York City.

Wheeler, Mary Ann, "Dressmaker's Account Book 1848–1854," New-York Historical Society.

Published Church and Vital Records

Kraege, Elfrida A., "Records of the Fifth Avenue Presbyterian Church, New York, 1808–1859," *The New York Genealogical and Biographical Record*, vol. 105 (1974), pp. 129–137, 224–233; vol. 106 (1975), pp. 37–42, 95–99, 146–152, 222–230; vol. 107 (1976), pp. 7–11, 96–101, 135–140, 223–228; vol. 108 (1977), pp. 37–44, 98–102, 150–156, 205–208; vol. 109 (1978), pp. 43–44, 89–97.

"Laight Street Baptist Church Marriages 1841–1850," *New York Historical Society Quarterly Bulletin* 5 (1921), pp. 19–23.

Ogilvy, C. Stanley, "Voters' List, Ward 10, New York, 1840," *The New York Genealogical and Biographical Record* 109 (1978), pp. 82–84, 168–172.

Stryker-Rodda, Kenneth, "Membership of the Thirteenth Street Presbyterian Church, New York City, 1839–1844," *The New York Genealogical and Biographical Record* 103 (1972), pp. 53–59, 117–122, 160–167.

United States Documents and Reports

[Claghorn, Kate H], "The Foreign Immigrant in New York City," Industrial Commission on Immigration, *Report*, vol. 15 (Washington, D.C., 1901).

[Cox, John Jr.], Historical Records Survey, *New York City: Church Archives, Religious Society of Friends Catalogue* (New York, 1940).

Historical Records Survey, *Guide to Vital Statistics of New York, Borough of Manhattan: Churches* (New York, 1942).

Historical Records Survey, *Inventory of Borough Archives in the City of New York* (New York, 1942).

Historical Records Survey, *Inventory of the Church Archives in New York City: Lutheran* (New York, 1940).

Historical Records Survey, *Inventory of the Church Archives in New York City: Methodist* (New York, 1940).

Historical Records Survey, *Inventory of the Church Archives in New York City: Protestant Episcopal Church, Diocese of New York, Manhattan, Bronx, Richmond* (New York, 1940).

Historical Records Survey, *Inventory of the Church Archives in New York City: Reformed Church* (New York, 1940).

Historical Records Survey, *Inventory of the Church Archives in New York City: Roman Catholic Archdiocese of New York* (New York, 1941).

New York and New Jersey State Documents and Reports

Assembly, *Documents, Report of the Select Committee Appointed to Examine Conditions of Tenant Houses in New York and Brooklyn*, 1857, vol. 3, no. 205 (Albany, 1857).

Assembly, *Documents, Report of the Special Committee on Tenement Houses in New York and Brooklyn*, 1856, vol. 3, no. 199 (Albany, 1856).

Commissioners of Emigration, *Reports*, 1847–1860 (New York: John F. Trow, 1861).

Metropolitan Board of Health, *Annual Reports*, 1866–1868 (Albany: Charles Van Benthuysen, 1867–1869).

Metropolitan Fire Department, *Annual Report of the Board of Commissioners 1865–1867* (New York, 1867–1870).

Metropolitan Police Commissioner, *Annual Reports*, 1858–1872 (Albany, 1858–1872).

New Jersey Department of State, *Compendium of Censuses, 1726–1905* (Trenton, 1906).

Secretary of State, *Census of the State of New York for 1835* (Albany, 1837).

Secretary of State, *Census of the State of New York for 1845* (Albany, 1847).

Secretary of State, *Census of the State of New York for 1855* (Albany, 1857).

Secretary of State, *Census of the State of New York for 1865* (Albany, 1867).

Secretary of State, *Census of the State of New York for 1875* (Albany, 1877).

Secretary of State, *Instructions for Taking the Census of the State of New York in the Year 1855* (Albany: Weed Parson, 1855).

Secretary of State, *Instructions for Taking the Census of the State of New York in the Year 1865* (Albany, 1865).

Senate, *Documents, Annual Report of the Secretary of State Relating to the Statistics of the Poor for 1855*, vol. 3, no. 72 (Albany, 1865).

Senate, *Documents, Report of the Select Committee Appointed to Investigate the Health Department of the City of New York, 1859*, vol. 2, no. 49 (Albany, 1859).

Senate, *Documents, Report on the Tenement-House Problem in New York, 1888*, vol. 3, no. 16 (Albany, 1888).

New York City and County Documents and Reports

Alms House Commissioners, *Annual Reports, 1846–1859* (New York, 1846–1859).

Board of Health, *A History of the Proceeding of the Board of Health of the City of New-York in the Summer and Fall of 1822; Together With an Account of the Rise and Progress of the Yellow Fever, Which Appeared During that Season* (New York: P & H Van Pelt, 1823).

Board of Health, *Report of the Sanitary Committee in Relation to the Cholera as it Prevailed in New York in 1849* (New York: McSpedon and Bates, 1849).

Board of Health, *Statement of Facts Relative to the Late Fever Which Appeared in Bancker-Street and Its Vicinity* (New York: Elam Bliss, 1821).

Building Department, *Communication from the Superintendent of Building and Annual Report of the Superintendent 1862–1872* (New York, 1863–1873).

Chief Engineer of the Fire Department, *Annual Report 1858–1865* (New York, 1859–1866).

Chief of Police, *Semi-Annual Report, 1850–1858* (New York, 1850–1858).

City Inspector's Office, *Annual Report 1845–1865* (New York, 1846–1866).

City Inspector's Office, *Annual Report of the City Inspector, of the New Buildings Erected in the City and County of New York, 1839, 1840, 1843, 1848* (New York, 1840, 1841, 1844, 1849).

City Inspector's Office, *Annual Report of Deaths in the City of New York, 1832–1844* (New York: Peter Van Pelt, 1833–1845).

City Inspector's Office, *Census of the Electors and Total Population of the City and County of New York* (New York, 1807).

Common Council, Board of Aldermen, *Report of a Special Committee on the Re-Organization of the Police 1844*, Document No. 53 (New York, 1844).

Common Council, *Minutes 1789–1831* (New York, 1911), 19 vols. and 2 of index.

Common Council, *Report of A Special Committee Appointed on Greenwich Village in Common Council, September 7, 1818* (New York: Thomas O. Low, 1818).

Fire Marshall, *Annual Report 1854–1860* (New York, 1854–1860).

Landmark Preservation Commission, *Charleton-King-Vandam Historic District, Borough of Manhattan* (New York, 1966).

Landmark Preservation Commission, *Chelsea Historic District Designation Report* (New York, 1970).

Landmark Preservation Commission, *Greenwich Village Historical District Designation Report* (New York, 1969), 2 vols.

Landmark Preservation Commission, *Soho Cast-Iron Historical District Designation Report* (New York, 1973).

Planning Commission, *A Plan for New York City* (Cambridge: MIT Press, 1969), 6 vols.

Valentine, David T. (compiler), *Manual of the Corporation of the City of New York 1841–1870* (New York, 1841–1870).

Private Agencies' Documents and Reports

Bowery Savings Bank, *Annual Reports 1835–1838, 1840–1844, 1850–1851* (New York, 1836–1839, 1841–1845, 1851–1852).

Bowery Savings Bank, *Manual* (New York, 1888).

Citizens Association of New York, *Report of the Council of Hygiene and Public Health Upon the Sanitary Condition of the City* (New York: Appleton, 1866).

Citizens Association of New York, *Wholesale Corruption! Sale of Situations in Fourth Ward Schools, Report of the Committee Appointed by the Board of Education* (New York: Citizens Association of New York, 1864).

City Mission and Tract Society, *Christian Work in New York (First Annual Report of the City Mission)* (New York: City Mission Society, n.d.).

City Mission and Tract Society, *City Evangelization* (New York: City Mission Society, 1866).

City Mission and Tract Society, *A Guide to the Churches and Missions in the City of New York* (New York: City Mission Society, 1870, 1873), Document No. 19.

City Mission and Tract Society, *A Guide to the Mission Station for the Use of the Director* (New York: City Mission Society, n.d.), Document No. 7.

Eastern Dispensary, *Annual Reports 1841–1843, 1846–1848, 1850* (New York: 1842–1844, 1847–1849, 1851).

Fourth Ward Industrial School for Girls (Association for Improvement and Protection of Destitute Children), *Annual Report 1854–1855, 1860* (New York, 1854, 1856, 1860).

Greenwich Savings Bank, *Annual Reports 1833–1841, 1843–1844* (New York, 1834–1842, 1844–1845).

Jackson, Lewis E., *Gospel Work in New York City: A Memorial of Fifty Years in City Missions* (New York: New York City Mission, 1878).

Jackson, Lewis E., *A Missionary Field* (New York: City Mission, 1866), City Mission Doc. 6.

Jackson, Lewis, *Walks About New York: Facts and Figures Gathered From Various Sources* (New York: City Mission Society, 1865).

New York Association for Improving the Condition of the Poor, *Annual Reports 1844–1861, 1864–1875* (New York, 1845–1862, 1865–1876).

New York Association for Improving the Condition of the Poor, *First Report of a Committee on the Sanitary Condition of the Laboring Classes in the City of New York with Remedial Suggestions* (New York: John F. Trow, 1853).

Ninth Ward Temperance Association, *Temperance in the City of New York* (New York, 1844).

Northern Dispensary, *Annual Report of Trustees, 1827, 1834, 1841–1858, 1860–1867* (New York, 1828, 1835, 1842–1859, 1861–1868).

Water Street Home for Women, *First Report, Rev. W. H. Boole Superintendent* (New York: Egbert, Bourne, 1870).

New York City Directories

Carroll, O. Danielson, *Carroll's New York City Directory* (New York: Carroll, 1859).

Directory to the Seraglios in New York, Philadelphia, Boston and All the Principal Cities in the Union By a Free Lover (New York, 1859).

Doggett's New York City Directory 1842–1851 (New York: John Doggett, 1842–1851).

Doggett's Street Directory for New York City, 1851 (New York: John Doggett, 1851).

[Eastman, H. D.], *Fast Man's Directory and Lover's Guide by the Ladies Man* (New York: May, 1853).

The Gentleman's Directory (The Gentleman's Companion) (New York: John F. Murray, 1870).

Goulding's New York City Directory 1875–1877 (New York: Lawrence Goulding, 1875–1876).

Jackson, Lewis, *A Church Directory for New York City* (New York: New York City Mission, 1867), Mission Document No. 9.

Longworth's American Almanac, New York Register, and City Directory, 1829–1842 (New York: Thomas Longworth, 1829–1842).

Rode's New York City Directory, 1850–1854 (New York: Charles R. Rode, 1850).

Trow's New York City Directory, 1853–1870 (New York: H. Trow, 1853–1870).

New York City Atlases

Perris, William, *Maps of the City of New York, Surveyed Under the Direction of the Insurance Companies of Said City* (New York: William Perris, 1853), 5 vols.

Newspapers

New York Evening Post, 1833, 1838, 1839.

New York Illustrated News, 1860.

The Subterranean, 1845–1847.

New York Times, 1851–1875.

Contemporary Sources

Abbott, Jacob, *Marco Paul's Travels and Adventures in the Pursuit of Knowledge . . . City of New York* (Boston: Benjamin B. Mussey, 1844).

Aiken, George, *Cythia: The Pearl of the Points—A Tale of New York* (Boston: Elliott, Thomas & Talbot, 1867).

Alvarez, *Guia de Nueva York Para Usa de los Españoles e Hispanoamericanos* (New York: John A. Gray, 1863).

Bannard, Rev. William, *Discourse on the Moral Aspects and Destitution of the City of New York—Delivered at the Opening of the Presbytery of New York* (New York: Charles Scribner, 1851).

Barltran, F. S., *Retrographics* (New Haven: Yale Publishing, 1888).

Beck, Louis J., *New York's Chinatown* (New York: Bohemia Publishing, 1898).

Belden, E. Porter, *New York: Past, Present, and Future* (New York: G. P. Putnam, 1849).

Benedict, Francis, "Boarding-House Experience in New York," *Packard's Monthly* 1 (1869), new series, pp. 100–103.

Bobo, William M., *Glimpses of New-York City by a South Carolinian* (New York: J. J. McCarter, 1852).

Boutwell, George S., *A Manual of the Direct and Excise Tax System of the United States* (Boston: Little, Brown, 1863).

Boyd, William H., *Boyd's New York City Tax Book* (New York: William Boyd, 1857).

Brace, Charles Loring, *The Dangerous Classes of New York and Twenty Years Work Among Them* (New York: Wynkoop & Hallenbeck, 1872).

Brace, Charles L., *Short Sermons to Newsboys* (New York: Charles Scribner, 1866).

Brainerd Presbyterian Church, *Manual* (New York: West & Trow, 1836).

Bremer, Frederika, *The Homes of the New World: Impressions of America*, trans. Mary Howitt (New York: Harper Bros., 1853), vol. 1 and 2.

A Brief History of the Presbyterian Church, Corner of Fifth Avenue and Nineteenth Street in the City of New York with a List of Officers and Members, April 1862 (New York: Anson D. F. Randolph, 1862).

A Brief History of the Fifth Avenue Presbyterian Church, November 1877, Published by the Session (New York: Anson D. F. Randolph, 1877).

The British Mechanic's and Labourer's Hand Book and True Guide To the United States (London: Chas. Knight, 1840).

Bromley, Clara F., *A Woman's Wanderings in the Western World* (London: Saunders, Olley, 1861).

Brooks, Richard A. E., ed., *The Diary of Michael Floy Jr., Bowery Village 1833–1837* (New Haven: Yale University Press, 1941).

Buckingham, J. S., *America, Historical, Statistic and Descriptive* (London: Fisher, Son, 1841), vol. 1.

Burchard, Rev. S. D., *Discourse Preached in the Thirteenth Street Presbyterian Church* (New York: Arthur & Bonnel, 1877).

Burford, Robert, *Description of a View of the City of New York* (London: T. Brettell, 1834).

[Burns, James D.], *Three Years Among the Working-Class in the United States During the War* (London: Smith, Elder, 1865).

Burns, William, *Life in New York in Doors and Out of Doors* (New York: Bunce and Bros., 1851).

Burton, Thomas, *Greenwich Village, and Landmarks in Its Vicinity* (New York, 1894).

Bussing, Mrs. Ann Van Nest, *Reminiscences of the Van Nest Homestead* (New York: Private Circulation, 1897).

Byrnes, Clara, *Block Sketches of New York City* (New York: Radbridge, 1918).

Campbell, Helen, *Darkness and Daylight: Or Lights and Shadows of New York Life* (Hartford: A. D. Worthington, 1893).

Child, L[ydia] Maria, *Letters from New York* (New York: C. S. Francis, 1845), second series.

Child, L[ydia] Maria, *Letters from New York* (New York: C. S. Francis, 1846).

City Election Hand-Book of Votes for Mayor 1834–1843 (New York: Burgess, Stinger, 1844).

A Clear & Concise Statement of New-York & the Surround Country Containing a Factual Account of Many of those Base Imports Which Are So Constantly & Unfortunately Practiced upon British Emigrants by Crafty Designers and Unprincipled Adventurers (New York: John Wilson, 1819).

Connors, Chuck, *Bowery Life* (New York: Richard Fox, 1904), comp. and ed. Frederick A. Wilson.

Crapsey, Edward, *The Neither Side of New York or, the Vice, Crime, and Poverty of the Great Metropolis* (Montclair, N.J.: Patterson Smith, 1969; reprint of 1872 ed.).

[Crapsey, Edward], "Public Lodgers," *Harpers Monthly* 39 (1869), pp. 753–759.

[Davenport, John I.], *Registry of Voters in the City of New York by Ward, Assembly District, and Electoral District* (New York: John I. Davenport, 1874).

[De Forest, T. R.], *Olden Time in New York By Those Who Knew It* (New York: Anderson & Smith, 1833).

De Voe, Thomas Farrington, *The Market Book* (New York: Printed by the Author, 1862).

Dix, John A., *The City of New York, Its Growth, Destinies, and Duties* (New York, 1853).

Dixon, Edward H., *Scenes in the Practice of a New York Surgeon* (New York: DeWitt & Davenport, ca. 1855).

Duer, William A., *New-York As It Was During the Latter Part of the Last Century* (New York: Stanford & Swords, 1849).

Duer, William A., *Reminiscences of an Old New Yorker* (New York: W. L. Anders, 1867).

Dunning, Mrs. Jane, *Brands from the Burning: An Account of a Work Among the Sick and Destitute in Connection with Providence Mission, New York City* (New York: J. N. Pratt, 1877).

Dyer, Oliver, *The 'Wickedest Man' in New York or the Great Awakening in Water Street* (New York: P. Dwight, 1868), reprinted from *Packard's Magazine*.

The 1866 Guide to New York City (New York: Schocken Books, 1975).

Ellington, George, *The Women of New York: Social Life in the Great City* (New York: N.Y. Book, 1870).

Everts, William Wallace, *The Life of Rev. W. W. Everts D.D.* (Philadelphia: Louis H. Everts, 1891).

The Fancy Ball Given By Mrs. Sxxxxx: A Description of the Characters, Dresses &c Assumed on the Occasion (New York: Morning Courier, 1829).

Fay, Theodore Sedgwick, *Hoboken: A Romance of New-York* (New York: Harper Bros, 1843), 2 vols.

Fay, Theodore S., *Views of the City of New York And Its Environs* (New York: Peabody, 1831).

Fearon, Henry Bradshaw, *Sketches of America—A Narrative of a Journey of Five Thousand Miles through the Eastern and Western States of America* (London: Longman, Hust, Rees, Orm & Brown, 1819).

Felton, Mrs., *American Life: A Narrative of Two Years' City and Country Residence in the United States* (London: Simpkin, Marshall, 1842).

"The Five Points," *The National Magazine* 3 (1853), pp. 169–173, 267–271, 370–374.

[Five Points Mission], *The Old Brewery and the New Mission House at the Five Points. By Ladies of the Mission* (New York: Stringer and Townsend, 1854).

Foster, George G., *Celio: Or New York Above Ground and Under Ground* (New York: DeWitt & Davenport, 1850).

Foster, George G., *Fifteen Minutes Around New York*, (New York: Robert M. DeWitt, ca. 1853).

Foster, George G., *New York by Gas-Light with Here and There a Streak of Sunshine* (New York: M. J. Ivers, 1849?).

Foster, George G., *New York Naked* (New York: Robert De Witt, 185?).

[Foster, George G.], *New York in Slices by an Experienced Carver Being the Original Slices Published in the NY Tribune* (New York: William H. Graham, 1849).

Francis, John W., *Old New York: Or Reminiscences of the Past* (New York: Charles Roe, 1858).

Frothingham, W., "Stewart, and the Dry Goods Trade in New York," *Continental Monthly* 2 (1862), p. 528.

Fry, James B., *New York and the Conscription of 1863* (New York: G. P. Putnam's Sons, 1885).

Gallier, James, *The American Builder's General Price Book and Estimator* (Boston: Marsh Caper & Lyes, 1834).

Gerard, James Watson, *The Impress of Nationalities Upon the City of New York, A Paper Read Before the New York Historical Society* (New York: Columbia Spectator Publishing, 1883).

Gerard, J. W., *London and New York: Their Crime and Police* (New York: William C. Bryant, 1853).

[Goodrich, Andrew T.], *The Picture of New-York and Strangers Guide to the Commercial Metropolis of the United States* (New York: A. T. Goodrich, 1828).

[Goodrich, Samuel Griswald], *Peter Parley's Visit to the City of New York* (New York: Mahlon Day, 183?).

Gough, John B., *Autobiography and Personal Recollections* (Springfield, Mass.: Bill, Nichols, 1870).

Gould, Edward S., *John Doe and Richard Roe: Or, Episodes of Life in New York* (New York: Carleton, 1862).

Gouverneur, Marian, *As I Remember: Recollections of American Society during the Nineteenth Century* (New York: D. Appleton, 1911).

Greatorex, Elize, and M. Despard, *Old New York from the Battery to Bloomingdale* (New York: G. P. Putnam's, 1875).

[Greene, Asa], *A Glance at New York* (New York: A. Greene, 1837).

Greene, Asa, *The Perils of Pearl Street Including a Taste of the Dangers of Wall Street by a Late Merchant* (New York: Betts & Anstice & Peter Hill, 1834).

Griesinger, Theodor, *Lebende Bilder aus Amerika* (Stuttgart: Wilh. Ritzschke, 1858).

Griesinger, Theodor, *New York vor Zwanzig Jahren: Oder Die Alte Brauerie* (New York: H. Ziches, 1873).

Griscom, John H., *Condition of the Laboring Population of New York* (New York: Harper & Bros., 1845).

Griscom, John H., *A History, Chronological and Circumstantial, of the Visitation of Yellow Fever at New York* (New York: Hall, Clayton, 1858).

Griscom, John H., *Sanitary Legislation Past and Future: The Value of Sanitary Reform, and the True Principles for its Attainment* (New York: Edmund Jones, 1861).

Gunn, Thomas Butler, *The Physiology of New York Boarding-Houses* (New York: Mason Bros., 1857).

Gurowski, Adam G. de, *America and Europe* (New York: D. Appleton, 1857).

Hale, Edward E., *Letters on Irish Emigration* (Freeport, N.Y.: Books for Libraries Press, 1972; reprint of 1852 ed.).

Halliday, Samuel B., *The Lost and Found or Life Among the Poor* (New York: Blakeman & Mason, 1859).

Hancock, William, *An Emigrant's Five Years in the Free States of America* (London: T. Cautley, 1860).

Hansel, George H., *Reminiscences of Baptist Churches and Baptist Leaders in New York City and Vicinity from 1835 to 1898* (Philadelphia: American Baptist Publication Society, 1899).

Hardie, James, *An Account of the Malignant Fever Lately [sic] Prevalent in the City of New-York* (New York: Hurtin & M'Farline, 1799).

Hardie, James, *Account of the Malignant Fever which Prevailed in the City of New York During the Autumn of 1805* (New York: Southwick & Hardcastle, 1805).

Hardie, James, *An Account of the Yellow Fever, Which Occurred in the City of New York, in the Year 1822* (New York: Samuel Marks, 1822).

Hardie, James, *A Census of New Buildings Erected in this City in the Year 1824 Arranged in Distinct Classes According to Their Material and Number of Stories* (New York: Samuel Marks, 1825).

Hardie, James, *The Description of New York* (New York: Samuel Marks, 1827).

Harris, Charles Townsend, *Memories of Manhattan in the Sixties and Seventies* (New York: Derrydale Press, 1928).

[Hastings, Thomas], *New York Magdelen Benevolent Society Missionary Labors Through a Series of Years Among Fallen Women* (New York, 1870).

Haswell, Charles H., *Reminiscences of New York by an Octogenarian* (New York: Harper & Bros., 1896).

Holley, O. L., *A Description of the City of New York* (New York: J. Disturnell, 1847).

Holloway, Emmory, and Adimori, Ralph, eds., *New York Dissected by Walt Whitman* (New York: Wilson, 1936).

Hough, Franklin B., *Statistics of Population of the City and County of New York as Shown by the State Census of 1865* (New York: New York Printing, 1866).

Howe, Julia Ward, *Reminiscences 1819–1899* (Boston: Houghton Mifflin, 1899).

Howe, William W., *The Pasha Papers: Epistles of Mohamed Pasha* (New York: Charles Scribner, 1859).

Hubbard, N. T., *Autobiography of N. T. Hubbard with Personal Reminiscences of New York City from 1798 to 1875* (New York: John F. Trow, 1875).

The Income Record: A List Giving the Taxable Income for the Year 1863 of Every Resident of New York (New York: American News, 1865).

Jay, Cornelia, *The Diary of Cornelia Jay 1861–1873, Rye, Westchester County, N.Y.* (New York: Privately Printed, n.d.).

Jones, Charles J., *From the Forecastle to the Pulpit: Fifty Years Among Sailors* (New York: Tibbals & Sons, 1884).

Judson, Edward Z. C., *The Mysteries and Miseries of New York: A Story of Real Life By Ned Buntline* (New York: Bedford, 1848).

Kapp, Frederick, *Geschichte der Deutschen im Staate New York bis zum Aufgange des Neunzehnten Jahrhunderts* (New York: A. Steiger, 1869).

Kennion, John, *The Architects and Builders Guide* (New York: Fitzpatrick & Huston, 1868).

King, Moses, *King's Handbook of New York City* (Boston: Moses King, 1893), 2d ed.

Lander, S. W., *Spectacles for Young Eyes: New York* (New York: Sheldon, 1869).

Lening, Gustav, *The Dark Side of New York Life and Its Criminal Classes from Fifth Avenue Down to the Five Points* (New York: Fred'k Oerhard, 1873).

Lester, Rev. Charles Edward, *Glances at the Metropolis* (New York: Isaac D. Gayer, 1854).

Lippard, George, *The Midnight Queen: or Leaves from New-York Life* (New York: Garrett, 1853).

Lippard, George, *New York: Its Upper Ten and Lower Million* (New York: H. M. Rulinson, 1853).

London v. New York by an English Workman (London: Bosworth & Harrison, 1859).

Lutz, Henry T., "Reminiscences of the Fifth Ward," in Henry Collins Brown, ed., *Valentine's Manual of Old New York* (New York: Valentine, 1916).

[Lyon, Isaac S.], *Recollection of an Ex Carter* (Newark, N.J.: Daily Journal, 1872).

Mackay, Charles, *Life and Liberty in America* (London: Smith, Elder, 1859), 2 vols.

Mackeever, Samuel A., *Glimpses of Gotham and City Characters* (New York: National Police Gazette, 1880).

Macy, Silvanus J., *Memories of Old New York* (Rochester, 1899), scrapbook of newspaper clippings at the New-York Historical Society.

McCabe, James D., Jr., *Sights and Shadows of New York Life or Sights and Sensations of the Great City* (New York: Farrar, Straus and Giroux, 1970; reprint of 1872 ed.).

Maguire, John F., *The Irish in America* (New York: Longmans Green, 1868).

McVickar, William A., *City Missions* (New York: Pott & Amery, 1868).

"A Physician of New York," *Madame Restell: An Account of Her Life and Horrible Practice Together with Prostitutes in New York* (New York: Proprietor—Charles Smith, 1847).

"The Mariner's Church, Roosevelt Street, New York," *The National Magazine* 4 (1854), pp. 112–113.

[Martin, William R.], *The Growth of New York* (New York: George W. Wood, 1865).

Martin, Winslow Martin, *The Secrets of the Great City . . . New York City* (Philadelphia: Jones, Brothers, 1868).

Mason, Cyrus, *A Brief History of the Duane Street, Late Cedar Street Presbyterian Church and a Manual for Its Members* (New York: James Van Norden, 1835).

Matrimonial Brokerage in the Metropolis: Being True Narratives of Strange Adventures in New York and Startling Facts in City Life by a Reporter of the New York Press (New York: Thatcher & Hutchinson, 1859).

Melville, Herman, "Bartleby the Scrivener: A Story of Wall-Street," in Warner Berthoff, ed., *The Great Short Stories of Herman Melville* (New York: Harper and Row, 1970), pp. 39–74.

Miller's New York As It Is in 1864: Or Stranger's Guide-Book to the Cities of New York, Brooklyn and Adjacent Places (New York: James Miller, 1864).

Mitchell, D. W., *Ten Years Residence in the United States* (London: Smith, Elder, 1862).

Mitchell, Samuel Latham, *The Picture of New York or the Traveller's Guide* (New York: I. Riley, 1807).

Moment, Rev. Alfred H., *The New York Down-Town Presbyterian Churches* (New York, 1881).

Nevins, Allan, ed., *The Diary of Philip Hone* (New York: Dodd, Mead, 1927) 2 vols.

Nevins, Allan, and Milton H. Thomas, eds., *The Diary of George Templeton Strong* (New York: Octagon Press, 1974; reprint of 1952 edition), 4 vols.

Newman, R. W., *Old New York, The City in '32: Its People and Public Institutions* (New York: Evening Mail, 1873), clipping scrapbook at the New-York Historical Society.

New-York: A Historical Sketch of the Rise of Progress of the Metropolitan City of America by a New Yorker (New York: Carlton & Phillips, 1853).

"New York Daguerreotyped," *Putnam's Monthly* 1 (1853), pp. 121–136, 353–368, 678–686.

"New York—Private Residences," *Putnam's Monthly* 3 (1854), pp. 233–248.

New York Scene's: Designed for the Entertainment and Instruction of City and Country Children (New York: Mahlon Day, 1833).

The Night Side of New York: A Picture of the Great Metropolis After Nightfall by Members of the New York Press (New York: Excelsior Press, [1866]).

O'Brien, F. J., "Tenement House," in *Harpers Magazine* 23 (1861), pp. 732–734.

O'Donovan, Jeremiah, *A Brief Account of the Author's Interview with His Countrymen, and the Parts of the Emerald Isle Whence They Emigrated Together with a Direct Reference to their Present Location in the Land of Their Adoption, During Travels through Various States of the Union in 1854 and 1855* (Pittsburgh: Published by the Author, 1864).

O'Donovan, Jermiah, *A History of Ireland Containing a Compendious Account of Her Woes, Afflictions and Suffering . . . in Epic Verse* (Pittsburgh: published by the author, 1854).

Oldest New York's Past and Present: Racial and Religious Conditions (New York: N.Y. Federation of Churches, 1904).

Oliver Street Baptist Church, *Names of Members of the Baptist Church Meeting in Oliver Street* (New York, 1835).

Onderdonk, Henry, Jr., *New York City in Olden Time's Consisting of Newspaper Cutting Arranged by Henry Onderdonk Jr.* (Jamaica, L.I., 1862), Newspaper Scrapbook at the New York Public Library.

Oran the Outcast or a Season in New York (New York: Peabody, 1833).

Osgood, Samuel, *New York in the Nineteenth Century: A Discourse Before the New-York Historical Society* (New-York: J. F. Trow, 1868).

Outline of the Title of Samuel Ruggles to His Land Between 15th Street on South, 28th Street on North, The Bloomingdale Road, and Old Post Road on West, and First Avenue on the East (New York, 1834).

Pachmann, Joseph, *Leben und Treiben der Stadt New-York mit Hinweis auf der Hinwanderung und das deutche Element* (Hamburg: Hermann Grunig, 1874).

Palmer, Elizabeth Story, *My Memories of Old New York* (New York: Edwin S. Gorham, 1923).

A Peep Into Catherine Street or Mysteries of Shopping by A Late Retailer (New York: John Slater, 1846).

Picton, Thomas, *Rose Street: Its Past, Present and Future* (New York: Russell Bros., 1873).

Price, Joseph H., *An Historical Sketch Delivered at the Closing Service in St. Stephen's Church, New York* (New York: Vinten, 1866).

Prime, Samuel, *Life in New York* (New York: Robert Carter, 1847).

Reese, David, *A Plain and Practical Treatise on the Epidemic Cholera, As It Prevailed in the City of New York, in the Summer of 1832* (New York: Conner & Cook, 1833).

Reid, Walter C., "Recollections of Old Sixth Avenue," in *Valentine's Manual of Old New York* (New York: Valentine, 1919), vol. 3, pp. 27–44.

Richmond, Rev. J. M., *New York and Its Institutions 1609–1873* (New York: E. B. Treat, 1872).

Ritchie, James, *The Tax-Payer's Guide* (Boston: William H. Forbes, 1864).

Robinson, Solon, *Hot Corn: Life Scenes in New York Illustrated* (New York: De Witt and Davenport, 1853).

Ross, Joel H., *What I Saw in New York: Or a Bird's Eye View of City Life* (Auburn, N.Y.: Dervy and Miller, 1851).

[Ruggles, E.], *Picture of New York in 1846* (New York: Homans & Ellis, 1846).

Sainsbury, Pauline C., *Chronicles: A Tale of Old Chelsea* (New York: Friebale Press, 1932).

Scott, Franklin D., ed., *Baron Klinkowstrom's America 1818–1820* (Evanston, Ill.: Northwestern University Press, 1952).

[Scoville, Joseph], *The Old Merchants of New York By Walter Barrett* (pseud.), (New York: Carleton Publications, 1860–1865), 4 vols.

Seaman, Valentine, "An Inquiry into the Case of the Prevalence of the Yellow Fever in New York," *Medical Repository* 1 (1798), pp. 315–332.

Shea, John Gilmary, *The Catholic Churches of New York City* (New York: Lawrence G. Goulding, 1878).

Skillman, John B., *Skillman's New-York Police Report Written in 1828–1829* (New York: Ludwig & Tolefree, 1830).

Smith, —— , *Rambling Recollections of a Trip to America* (Edinburgh: David S. Steward, 1875).

Smith, Eliza Yale, "Residents on the West Side of Greenwich Street (Early Nineteenth Century)," Typescript, 1940, N.P., New-York Historical Society.

Smith, Matthew Hale, *Sunshine and Shadow in New York* (Hartford: J. B. Burr, 1868).

[Smith, Seba], *May Day in New York: Or House Hunting and Moving* (New York: Burgess, Stringer, 1845).

Some Very Gentle Touches to Some Very Gentle-men by a Humble Country Cousin of Peter Pinday Dedicated to All the Little Girls and Boys of the City (New York, 1820).

Stephens, Ana S. W., *High Life in New York* (New York: Burgess, Stringer, 185?).

Stryker, Rev. Peter, *The Lower Depth of the Great American Metropolis: A Discourse Delivered at the Thirty-Fourth St. Reformed Dutch Church, New York City, 1866* (New York: Schermerhorn Bancroft, 1866).

A Summary Geographical and Statistical View of the City of New York (New York: J. H. Colton, 1836).

Taylor, Henry, *New York As It Was Sixty Years Ago: Reminiscences* (Brooklyn: Nolan, 1894).

Techla, Georg, *Drei Jahre in New-York, Eine Skizze für das Volk nach der Natur gezeichnet* (Zwickau: Volkschriften, 1862).

Thornburn, Grant, *Fifty Years' Reminiscences of New York or Flower from the Garden of Lawrence Todd* (New York: Daniel Fanshaw, 1845).

Townsend, Percy, *Appleton's Dictionary of New York City* (New York: D. Appleton, 1880).

Townsend, Peter S., *An Account of the Yellow Fever as It Prevailed in the City of New York Summer and Autumn 1822* (New York: O. Halstead, 1823).

Tramps in New York by Rebecca (New York: American Tract Society, 1863).

Tricks and Traps of New York City (Boston: C. H. Brainard, 1857).

Trollope, Mrs. Francis, *Domestic Manners in the Americas* (London: Whittaker, Treacher, 1832).

The Value of Real Estate in the City of New York Past, Present and Prospective by a Retired Merchant (New York: J. W. Orr, 1860).

Vetter, Christoph, *Zwie Jahre in New York* (Hof: Published by the Author, 1849).

A Vindication and Defense of the German Reformed Church in the City of New-York and its Pastor, Against the Repeated Attacks Made Upon them by Certain Members of the Classis of New York (New York: G. B. Maign, 1851).

Vose, John D., *Fresh Leaves from the Diary of a Broadway Dandy* (New York: Bunnell & Price, 1852).

Wallys, Philip, *About New York: An Account of What A Boy Saw in His Visit to the City* (New York: Dix, Edwards, 1857).

Warren, John R., *Thirty Year's Battle with Crime, or the Crying Shame of New York* (Poughkeepsie: A. J. White, 1875).

West Presbyterian Church, *Manual of the West Presbyterian Church* (New York, 1864).

White, Alfred T., *Improved Dwellings for the Laboring Classes* (New York: Putnam's Sons, 1879).

Williams, Edwin, *New York As It Is in 1834* (New York: J. Disternell, 1834).

Willis, N. Parker, *The Rag-Bag, A Collection of Ephemera* (New York: Charles Scribner, 1855).

Wiswall, Rev. Alvah, *The Poor and Criminal Classes of the 5th and 8th Wards of New York: A Sermon Preached in St. John's Chapel* (Sixth Annual Report of St. John's Guild) (New York: Chatterton and Parker, 1872).

Wright, Mabel Osgood, *My New York* (New York: Macmillan, 1926).

Secondary Works On New York City: Books

Adams, Thomas, *The Building of the City* (New York: Regional Plan for New York and its Environs, 1931), vols. 2.

Albion, Robert G., *The Rise of New York Port 1815–1860* (New York: Charles Scribner's Sons, 1939).

Anderson, Alexandra, and B. J. Archer, *Soho: The Essential Guide to Art and Life in Lower Manhattan* (New York: Simon and Schuster, 1979).

Anstice, Henry, *History of St. George's Church in the City of New York 1752–1811–1911* (New York: Harper & Bros., 1911).

Asbury, Herbert, *The Gangs of New York* (Garden City: Garden City Publishing, 1928).

Atkins, Gordon, *Health, Housing and Poverty in New York City 1865–1898* (Ann Arbor: Edward Brothers, 1947).

Bailey, Rosalie F., *Guide to Genealogical and Biographical Sources for New York City (Manhattan) 1783–1898* (New York: Published by Author, 1954).

Bayley, James R., *Brief Sketch of the Early History of the Catholic Church on the Island of New York* (New York: Catholic Publishing Society, 1870).

Bayor, Ronald H., *Neighbors in Conflict: The Irish, Germans, Jews, and Italians of New York City, 1929–1941* (Baltimore: Johns Hopkins University Press, 1978).

Berg, Barbara J., *The Remembered Gate: Origins of American Feminism: The Woman and the City 1800–1860* (New York: Oxford University Press, 1978).

Berger, Meyer, *Growth of an Ideal 1850–1950: The Story of the Manhattan Savings Bank* (New York: Published by the Bank, 1950).

Bernstein, Ivar, *The New York City Draft Riots: Their Significance for American Society and Politics in the Age of the Civil War* (New York: Oxford University Press, 1990).

Black, Mary, *Old New York in Early Photographs* (New York: Dover Publications, 1973).

Blackmar, Elizabeth, *Manhattan for Rent, 1785–1850* (Ithaca: Cornell University Press, 1989).

Block, George Ashton, *The History of Municipal Ownership of Land on Manhattan Island*, Studies in History, Economics, and Public Law (New York: Columbia College, 1891).

Bonner, Arthur, *Jerry McAiley and His Mission* (Neptune, N.J.: Loizeaux Bros., 1967).

Booth, Mary, *History of the City of New York* (New York: E. P. Dutton, 1880).

Bridges, Amy, *A City in the Republic: Antebellum New York and the Origins of Machine Politics* (Cambridge: Cambridge University Press, 1984).

Bromwell, William J., *History of Immigrants to the United States* (New York: J. S. Refield, 1856).

Brooks Brothers, *Chronicles 1818–1909: Being a Record of Sundry Happenings Which Have Had Place Since A.D. 1818 in that Part of Greater New York Which Is Distinguished as the Borough of Manhattan* (New York: Brooks Bros., 1909).

Brown, Henry Collins, *Brownstones and Saratoga Trunks* (New York: E. P. Dutton, 1935).

Callow, Alexander B., Jr., *The Tweed Ring* (New York: Oxford University Press, 1966).

Campbell, Doras Elizabeth, *The First Hundred Years: The Chronicle of a Mutual Savings Bank* (New York: East River Savings Bank, 1949).

Caro, Robert A., *The Power Broker: Robert Moses and the Fall of New York* (New York: Vintage Books, 1974).

Chapin, Ann, *Greenwich Village* (New York: Dodd, Mead, 1917).

Citizen's Savings Bank: Its Founders, History and Homes 1860–1924 (New York: Published by the Bank, 1924).

Comer, John P., *New York City Building Control 1800–1941* (New York: Columbia University Press, 1941).

Connolly, Harold X., *A Ghetto Grows in Brooklyn* (New York: New York University Press, 1977).

Costello, Augustine E., *Our Firemen: A History of the New York Fire Department, Volunteer and Paid* (New York: Augustine Costello, 1887).

Cromley, Elizabeth C., *Alone Together: A History of New York's Early Apartments* (Ithaca: Cornell University Press, 1990).

Danielson, Michael N., and Jameson W. Doig, *New York: The Politics of Urban Regional Development* (Berkeley: University of California Press, 1982).

Deforest, Robert W., and Lawrence Veiller, eds., *The Tenement House Problem* (New York: MacMillan, 1903), 2 vols.

Denison, John Hopkins, *Besides the Bowery* (New York: Dodd Mead, 1914).

Denison, Lindsay, and Max Fischell, *Village and Hamlets Within New York City* (New York: N.Y. Evening World, 1925).

Dix, John A., *A History of the Parish of Trinity Church in the City of New York* (New York: Columbia University Press, 1950), vols. 3,4,5.

Dolan, Jay, *Catholic Revivalism in the United States 1830–1900* (South Bend, Ind.: University of Notre Dame Press, 1978).

Dolan, Jay P., *The Immigrant Church: New York's Irish and German Catholics 1815–1865* (Baltimore: Johns Hopkins University Press, 1975).

Duffy, John, *A History of Public Health in New York City 1625–1966* (New York: Russell Sage Foundation, 1968–1974), 2 vols.

Dunshee, Kenneth Holcomb, *As You Pass By* (New York: Hastings House, 1952).

Emmet, Thomas A., *Memoir of Thomas and Robert Emmet* (New York: Emmet Press, 1915), vol. 1.

Ernst, Robert, *Immigrant Life in New York City 1825–1863* (New York: Kings Crown Press, 1949).

Evans, Rev. Anthony, *Celebration of the 100th Anniversary of the West Presbyterian Church and the 75th Anniversary of the Park Presbyterian Church, Now United in the West Park Presbyterian Church* (New York, 1930).

A Familiar Conversational History of the Evangelical Churches of New York (New York: Robert Carter, 1839).

Ferris, Louise M., *Tales of Other Days* (New York: Privately Printed, 1939).

Francis, Augustus, *History of the 71st Regiment, N.G., N.Y.* (New York: Veterans Association, 1919).

Gilje, Paul A., *The Road to Mobocracy: Popular Disorder in New York City, 1763–1834* (Chapel Hill: Institute of Early American History and Culture and University of North Carolina Press, 1987).

Goldberger, Paul, *The City Observed: New York City* (New York: Vintage Books, 1979).

Goodman, Cary, *Choosing Sides: Playground and Street Life on the Lower East Side* (New York: Schocken Books, 1979).

Grand-Pierre, Charles, *The Fascinating History of Fourth Street, Greenwich Village: The Street with "a Past"* (New York: Greenwich Village News, 1940).

Grand-Pierre, Charles, *The Little Book of Greenwich Village* (New York: Greenwich Village News, 1935).

Grand-Pierre, Charles, *Rambling Through Greenwich Village* (New York: Greenwich Village Weekly News, 1935).

Greenleaf, Jonathan, *A History of the Churches of All Denominations of New York* (New York: E. French, 1846).

Greenwich Savings Bank (New York: Published by the Bank, 1958).

Grinstein, Hyman, *The Rise of the Jewish Community of New York, 1654–1860* (Philadelphia: Jewish Publication Society of America, 1945).

A Guide Book to Saint Luke's Chapel, Trinity Parish (New York: Published by the Parish, 1949).

Gurock, Jeffrey, *When Harlem Was Jewish 1870–1930* (New York: Columbia University Press, 1979).

Hadley, Samuel H., *Down in Water Street* (New York: Fleming H. Revell, 1902).

Harlow, Alvin, *Old Bowery Days* (New York: D. Appleton, 1931).

Hartog, Hendrik, *Public Property and Private Power: The Corporation of the City of New York in American Law, 1730–1870* (Chapel Hill: University of North Carolina Press, 1983).

Headley, Joel Tyler, *The Great Riots of New York 1712–1873* (Indianapolis: Bobbs-Merrill, 1970).

Hemstreet, Charles, *Nooks and Corners of Old New York* (New York: Charles Scribner's Sons, 1899).

Hershkowitz, Leo, *Tweed's New York: Another Look* (Garden City: Anchor Books, 1978).

Hodges, Graham Russell, *New York Cartman, 1667–1850* (New York: New York University Press, 1986).

Jackson, Anthony, *A Place Called Home: A History of Low Cost Housing in Manhattan* (Cambridge: MIT Press, 1976).

Jessup, Henry W., *History of the Fifth Avenue Presbyterian Church of New York City, New York 1808–1908* (New York: Published by the Church, 1909).

Kaestle, Carl F., *The Evolution of the Urban Schools System, New York City, 1750–1850* (Cambridge: Harvard University Press, 1973).

Kessner, Thomas, *The Golden Door: Italian and Jewish Immigrant Mobility in New York City 1880–1915* (New York: Oxford University Press, 1977).

Klein, Milton M., ed., *New York: The Centennial Years 1676–1976* (Port Washington, N. Y.: Kennikat Press, 1976).

Kneerim, Arthur, *Old New York: Our Neighborhood* (New York: New York Savings Bank, 1932).

Knowles, Charles E., *History of the Bank for Savings in the City of New York 1819–1929* (New York: Bank for Savings, 1929).

Kouwenhoven, John A., *The Columbia Historical Portrait of New York* (New York: Harper and Row, 1972).

Kraege, Elfrieda A., *A New History of the Fifth Avenue Presbyterian Church* (New York, 1975).

Lamb, Mary J., *History of the City of New York* (New York: A. S. Barnes, 1894), 3 vols.

Levenson, Joseph, "History of the Lower East Side of Manhattan and Grand Street, Its Leading Thoroughfare," in *Souvenir Journal of the Grand Street Boys Association of New York* (New York, 1921).

Lockwood, Charles, *Bricks and Brownstones: The New York Row House 1783–1929— An Architectural and Social History* (New York: McGraw-Hill Book, 1972).

Lockwood, Charles, *Manhattan Moves Uptown: An Illustrated History* (Boston: Houghton Mifflin, 1976).

Lossing, Benson J., *History of the City of New York* (New York: George E. Perine, 1884), 2 vols.

Mandlebaum, Seymour J., *Boss Tweed's New York* (New York: John Wiley & Sons, 1965).

Manning, James Hilton, *Century of American Savings Banks* (New York: B. F. Buck, 1917), 2 vols.

Maynard, John A. F., *The Huguenot Church of New York: A History of the French Church of Saint Espirit* (New York: Published by Church, 1938).

Miller, Wilbur R., *Cops and Bobbies: Police Authority in New York and London 1830–1870* (Chicago: University of Chicago Press, 1977).

Minnigerode, Meade, *The Fabulous Forties 1840–1850: A Presentation of Private Life* (New York: G. P. Putnam's Sons, 1924).

Mohl, Raymond A., *Poverty in New York 1783–1825* (New York: Oxford University Press, 1971).

Moore, Deborah Dash, *At Home in America: Second Generation New York Jews* (New York: Columbia University Press, 1981).

Morris, Lloyd, *Incredible New York* (New York: Random House, 1951).

Moss, Frank, *The American Metropolis: New York City Life* (New York: P. F. Collier, 1897), 3 vols.

Nadel, Stanley, *Little Germany: Ethnicity, Religion, and Class in New York City, 1845–80* (Urbana: University of Illinois Press, 1990).

Nash, Gary, *The Urban Crucible: Social Change, Consciousness, and the Origins of the American Revolution* (Cambridge: Harvard University Press, 1979).

Nevins, Allan, *The Evening Post: A Century of Journalism* (New York: Boni and Liveright, 1922).

Nineteenth Century Dwelling Houses of Greenwich Village (New York: Association of Village Homeowners Landmark Committee, 1968).

The Old Merchants House (New York: Historic Landmark Society, 1963).

Olmstead, Alan L., *New York City Mutual Savings Banks, 1819–1861* (Chapel Hill: University of North Carolina Press, 1976).

Orcutt, William D., *The Miracle of Mutual Savings: As Illustrated by One Hundred Years of the Bowery Savings Bank* (New York: Bowery Savings Bank, 1934).

Ottley, Roi, and William J. Weatherby, *The Negro in New York: An Informal History, 1626–1940* (New York: Prager Publishers, 1969).

Patterson, Jerry E., *The City of New York: A History Illustrated from the Collections of the Museum of the City of New York* (New York: Harry N. Abrams, 1978).

Perkins, J. Newton, *History of St. Stephen's Parish in the City of New York 1805–1905* (New York: Edwin S. Gorham, 1906).

Pessen, Edward, *Riches, Class, and Power Before the Civil War* (Lexington, Mass.: D.C. Heath, 1973).

Pine, John B., *The Story of Gramercy Park 1831–1921* (New York: Valentine's Manual Reprinted by Gramercy Park Association, 1921).

Pluntz, Richard, *A History of Housing in New York City* (New York: Columbia University Press, 1990).

Pomerantz, Sidney, *New York an American City 1783–1803* (New York: Columbia University Press, 1938).

Pound, Arthur, *The Golden Earth: The Story of Manhattan's Landed Wealth* (New York: McMillan, 1935).

A History of Real Estate, Building and Architecture in New York City During the Last Quarter Century (New York: Arno Press, 1967; reprint of 1898 edition).

Richardson, James F., *The New York Police: Colonial Times to 1901* (New York: Oxford University Press, 1970).

Rieder, Jonathan, *Canarsie: The Jews and Italians of Brooklyn Against Liberalism* (Cambridge: Harvard University Press, 1985).

Rischin, Moses, *The Promised City: New York's Jews, 1870–1914* (Cambridge: Harvard University Press, 1977).

Rock, Howard B., *Artisans of the New Republic: The Tradesmen of New York City in the Age of Jefferson* (New York: New York University Press, 1979).

Rosenberg, Carroll S., *Religion and the Rise of the American City: The New York City Mission Movement, 1812–1870* (Ithaca, New York: Cornell University Press, 1971).

Rosenberg, Charles, *The Cholera Years: The United States in 1832, 1849, and 1866* (Chicago: University of Chicago Press, 1971).

Rosenwaike, Ira, *Population History of New York City* (Syracuse: Syracuse University Press, 1972).

Rothschild, Nan A., *New York City Neighborhoods: The 18th Century* (San Diego: Academic Press, 1990).

Sanger, William W., *The History of Prostitution: Its Extent, Causes, and Effects Throughout World* (New York: Medical Publishing, 1897; reprint of 1859 ed.).

Savage, Theodore Fiske, *The Presbyterian Church in New York City* (New York: Presbytery of New York, 1949).

Schecter, Elaine, *Perry Street Then and Now* (New York: Published by Author, 1972).

Schisgall, Oscar, *Out of One Small Chest: A Social and Financial History of the Bowery Savings Bank* (New York: AMACOM, 1975).

Seaman, Samuel, *Annals of New York Methodism: A History of the Methodist Episco-*

pal Church in the City of New York From A.D. *1766 to* A.D. *1890* (New York: Hunt & Eaton, 1892).

Sheldon, George W., *The Story of the Volunteer Fire Department of the City of New York* (New York: Harper & Bros., 1882).

Shumway, Floyd M., *Seaport City: New York in 1775* (New York: South Street Seaport Museum, 1975).

Smith, Stephan, *The City That Was* (Metuchen, N.J.: Scarecrow Reprint, 1973; reprint of 1911 ed.).

Spann, Edward K., *The New Metropolis: New York City, 1840–1857* (New York: Columbia University Press, 1981).

Stansell, Christine, *City of Women: Sex and Class in New York, 1789–1860* (New York: Alfred A. Knopf, 1986).

Still, Bayard, *Greenwich Village: A Brief Architectural and Historical Guide* (New York: New York University, 1976).

Still, Bayard, *Mirror for Gotham* (New York: New York University Press, 1956).

Stokes, I. N. Phelps, *The Iconography of Manhattan Island 1498–1909* (New York: Robert H. Dodd, 1915–1928), 6 vols.

Stott, Richard B., *Workers in the Metropolis: Class, Ethnicity, and Youth in Antebellum New York City* (Ithaca: Cornell University Press, 1990).

[Stout, Charles B.], *A History of the Stanton Street Baptist Church in the City of New York* (New York: Shelon, 1860).

Tuttle, Mrs. A. Croswell, *History of Saint Luke's Church in the City of New York, 1820–1920* (New York: Appeal Printing, 1927).

Van Pelt, Daniel, *Leslie's History of the Greater New York, New York to the Consolidation* (New York: Arkell Publishing, 1898).

Veiller, Lawrence, *Tenement House Reform in New York, 1834–1900, Prepared for the Tenement House Commission of 1900* (New York: Evening Post Job Printing House, 1900).

Weinbaum, Paul O., *Mobs and Demagogues: The New York Response to Collective Violence in the Early Nineteenth Century* (New York: UMI Research Press, 1979).

Wenner, George U., *Lutherans of New York: Their Story and Their Problems 1848–1918* (New York: Peterfield Press, 1918).

Werner, M. R., *It Happened In New York* (New York: Coward-McCann, 1957).

White, Norval, and Willensky, Eliot, *AIA Guide to New York City* third edition (New York: Harcourt Brace Jovanovich, 1988).

White, Shane, *Somewhat More Independent: The End of Slavery in New York City, 1770–1810* (Athens: University of Georgia Press, 1991).

Whittemore, Henry, *History of the Seventy-First Regiment, N.G.S.N.Y.* (New York: Willis McDonald, 1886).

Wilentz, Sean, *Chants Democratic: New York City & the Rise of the American Working Class, 1788–1850* (New York: Oxford University Press, 1984).

Wilson, James Grant, *The Memorial History of the City of New York* (New York: N.Y. History, 1893), 3 vols.

Secondary Sources: Articles on New York City History

Abbott, Carl, "The Neighborhoods of New York, 1760–1775," *New York History* 55 (1974), pp. 35–54.

Adams, Grace, and Edward Hutter, "Sex in Old New York," *American Mercury* 52 (1941), pp. 500–507.

Bender, Thomas, "James Fenimore Cooper and the City," *New-York History* 51 (1970), pp. 287–305.

"Bond Street Three-Score Years Ago," *The New York Evening Post*, July 13, 1889 (clippings at the New-York Historical Society).

"The Bowery," in Henry Collins Brown, ed., *Valentine's Manual of Old New York, 1916–1917*, vol. 1 (New York: Valentine, 1916), pp. 107–112.

Berrol, Selma, "Who Went to School in Mid-Nineteenth Century New York? An Essay in the New Urban History," in Irwin Yellowitz, ed., *Essays in the History of New York City: A Memorial to Sidney Pomerantz* (Port Washington, New York: Kennikat Press, 1978), pp. 43–60.

Blackmar, Betsy, "Re-Walking the 'Walking City': Housing and Property Relations in New York City, 1780–1840," *Radical History Review* 21 (1979), pp. 131–148.

Blumin, Stuart M. "Exploring the New Metropolis: Perceptions, Depiction, and Analysis in Mid-Nineteenth-Century New York City," *Journal of Urban History* 11 (1984), pp. 9–38.

Bremmer, Robert H., "The Big Flat: A History of a New York Tenement," *American Historical Review* 64 (1958), pp. 54–62.

Dickstein, Morris, "Neighborhoods," *Dissent* 34, no. 1 (Fall 1987), pp. 602–607.

Duffy, John, "An Account of the Epidemic Fever that Prevailed in the City of New York From 1791–1822," *New-York Historical Society Quarterly* 50 (1966), pp. 333–364.

Dunbar, Seymour, "Historical Greenwich Village," *Le Dernier Cri* 2 (1917), pp. 38–44.

Eisenstein, J. D., "The History of the First Russian-American Jewish Congregation: The Beth Hamdrash Hagadol," *Publications of the American Jewish Historical Society* 9 (1901), pp. 63–74.

Ernst, Robert, "The Economic Status of New York City Negroes, 1850–1863," in August Meier and Elliot Rudwicks, eds., *The Making of Black America: Essays in Negro Life and History* (New York: Atheneum, 1969), vol. 1.

Gabaccia, Donna R., "Sicilians in Space: Environmental Change and Family Geography," *Journal of Social History* 16 (1982), pp. 53–66.

Gorn, Eliot J., " 'Good-Bye Boys, I Die a True American': Homicide, Nativism, and Working-Class Culture in Antebellum New York City," *Journal of American History* 74 (September 1987), pp. 388–410.

Ginsberg, Stephen F., "The Police and Fire Protection in New York City 1800–1850," *New York History* 52 (1971), pp. 133–150.

Hersey, Harold, "The Greenwich Village of Today," *Le Dernier Cri* 2 (1917), pp. 45–53.

Hodges, Graham, "May Day in Manhattan," *Seaport* 21, no. 4 (Spring 1988), pp. 29–33.

Hoffman, Henry B., "Changed House Numbers and Lost Street Names in New York of the Early Nineteenth Century and Later," *New-York Historical Society Quarterly* 21 (1937), pp. 67–92.

Hoffman, Henry B., "Transformation of New York Churches," *New-York Historical Society Quarterly* 22 (1938), pp. 3–27.

Jones, Alexander, "Two Journals of Alexander Jones Esq of Providence Rhode Island," *Historical Magazine of the Protestant Episcopal Church* 10 (1941), pp. 6–30.

Katsaros, John, "New York City Wards, History Arranged Chronologically," Typescript at the New York Public Library, 1950.

Leach, Richard, "The Impact of Immigration Upon New York 1840–1860," *New York History* 31 (1950), pp. 15–30.

Lekachman, Robert, "The West Side of My Youth," *Dissent* 34 (Fall 1987), p. 611.

Liebermann, Richard K., "A Measure of the Quality of Life: Housing," *Historical Methods* 11 (1978), pp. 129–134.

Lockwood, Charles, "The Bond Street Area," *New-York Historical Society Quarterly* 56 (1972), pp. 309–320.

McMaster, J. B., "A Boyhood in New York," *New York History* 20 (1939), pp. 316–324.

Miller, Douglas T., "Immigration and Social Stratification in Pre-Civil War New York," *New York History* 49 (1968), pp. 157–168.

"New York City in 1842 Described by Samuel Dexter Ward (1821–1905)," *New-York Historical Society Quarterly* 21 (1937), pp. 111–117.

"New York City in July, 1845," *New-York Historical Society Quarterly Bulletin* 16 (1933), pp. 99–111.

New York Public Library, "Checklist of Works Relating to New York City," *Bulletin of the New York Public Library* 5 (1901), pp. 2–30, 60–73, 74–76, 90–127, 141–146, 151–159, 190–210, 261–293.

Pessen, Edward, "The Marital Theory and Practice of the Ante-Bellum Urban Elite," *New York History* 53 (1972), pp. 389–410.

Purcells, Richard J., "The Irish Emigrant Society of New York," *Studies Dublin* 27 (1938), pp. 583–599.

Schwab, John C., "History of the New York Property Tax," *American Economic Association Publications* 5 (1890), p. 67.

Stansell, Christine, "The Origins of Sweatshops: Women and Early Industrialization in New York City," in Michael H. Frisch and Daniel J. Walkowitz, eds., *Working-Class America: Essays on Labor, Community and American Society* (Urbana: University of Illinois Press, 1983), pp. 78–103.

Stevens, John Austin, "New York in the Nineteenth Century," Bound Series of Articles from *American Historical Magazine* 2 (1906–1907), pp. 97–109, 201–215, 292–314, 407–426, 500–517.

Stevenson, Lloyd G., "Putting Disease on the Map: The Early Use of Spot Maps in the Study of Yellow Fever," *Journal of the History of Medicine and Allied Sciences* 20 (1965), pp. 226–261.

Still, Bayard, "New York City in 1824: A Newly Discovered Description," *New-York Historical Society Quarterly* 46 (1962), pp. 137–169.

Thomas, Milton Halsey, "Mid-Nineteenth Century Life in New York: More Revelations from the Diary of George Templeton Strong," *New-York Historical Society Quarterly* 37 (1953), pp. 5–39.

Weitenkamph, Frank, "The Bowery Had Two Sides," *New-York Historical Society Quarterly* 43 (1959), pp. 328–333.

White, Shane, " 'We Dwell in Safety and Pursue Our Honest Calling': Free Blacks in New York City, 1783–1810," *Journal of American History* 75 (September 1988), pp. 445–479.

Wilentz, Sean, "Artisan Republican Festivals and the Rise of Class Conflict in New York City, 1788–1837," in Michael H. Frisch and Daniel J. Walkowitz, eds., *Working-Class America: Essays on Labor, Community and American Society* (Urbana: University of Illinois Press, 1983), pp. 37–77.

Wilentz, Sean, "Document: Crime, Poverty and the Streets of New York City: The Diary of William H. Bell 1850–51," *History Workshop* 7 (1979), pp. 126–155.

Zunz, Olivier, "Technology and Society in an Urban Environment: The Case of the Third Avenue Elevated Railway," *Journal of Interdisciplinary History* 3 (1972), pp. 89–102.

Dissertations and Theses on New York

Becker, Dorothy, "The Visitor to the New York City Poor 1843–1920," Ph.D. diss., Columbia University, 1960.

Buckley, Peter George, "To the Opera House: Culture and Society in New York City, 1820–1860," Ph.D. diss., SUNY Stony Brook, 1984.

Danforth, Brian J., "The Influence of Socio-Economic Factors upon Political Behavior: A Quantitative Look at New York City Merchants, 1828–1844," Ph.D. diss., New York University, 1974.

Dierick, Mary, "Manhattan's Wooden Buildings," Master's thesis, Historical Preservation, Columbia University School of Architecture, 1976.

Freeman, Rhoda G., "The Free Negro in New York City in the Era Before the Civil War," Ph.D. diss., Columbia University, 1966.

Gutman, Herbert, "Early Effects of the Depression of 1873 upon the Working Classes in New York City," Master's thesis, Columbia University, 1950.

Lapham, James S., "The German-Americans of New York City 1860–1890," Ph.D. diss., St. John's University, 1977.

Lomax, Lucille G., "A Social History of the Negro Population Living in the Section of New York Known as Greenwich Village," Master's thesis, Columbia University, 1931.

Lubitz, Edward, "The Tenement House Problem in New York City and the Movement for its Reform, 1856–1867," Ph.D. diss., New York University, 1970.

Muse, Martha Twitchell, "New York City: 1830–1837—Its Religion and Social Reform," Master's thesis, Columbia University, 1955.

Pernicone, Carol Groneman, "The 'Bloody Ould Sixth': A Social Analysis of A New York City Working-Class Community in the Mid-Nineteenth Century," Ph.D. diss., University of Rochester, 1973.

Schoenebaum, Eleanor, "Emerging Neighborhoods: The Development of Brooklyn's Fringe Area 1850–1930," Ph.D. diss., Columbia University, 1977.

Swanson, Charles Glenn, "The Social Background of the Lower West Side of New York City," Ph.D. diss., New York University, 1934.

Tabachnik, Leonard, "Irish and German Immigrant Settlement in New York City, 1815–1828," Master's thesis, Columbia University, 1960.

Sociological Works on New York City

Drachscher, Julius, "Intermarriage in New York City," *Studies in History, Economics and Political Science of Columbia University* 94 (1921).

Glazer, Nathan, and Daniel P. Moynahan, *Beyond the Melting Pot: The Negroes, Puerto Ricans, Jews, Italians, and Irish of New York City* (Cambridge: MIT Press, 1970), 2d ed.

Herzfeld, Elsa G., *Family Monographs: The History of Twenty-Four Families Living in the Middle West Side of New York City* (New York: James Kempster Printing, 1905).

Hoover, Edgar, and Raymond Vernon, *Anatomy of a Metropolis* (Garden City, N.Y.: Doubleday Anchor, 1962).

Jones, Thomas Jesse, *The Sociology of a New York City Block* (New York: Published by the Author, 1904).

Kantrowitz, N., "Ethnic and Racial Segregation in the New York Metropolis," in Ceri Peach, ed., *Urban Social Segregation* (New York: Longman Publications, 1975).

Lyford, Joseph, *The Airtight Cage: A Study of New York's West Side* (New York: Harper & Row, 1968).

Reynolds, M. T., *Housing of the Poor in American Cities* (Ithaca: American Economical Association, 1893).

Tolman, William H., and William I. Hull, *Handbook of Sociological Information with Especial Reference to New York City Prepared for the City Vigilance League, New York City* (New York: Knickerbocker Press, 1894).

Ware, Caroline F., *Greenwich Village 1920–1930* (New York: Harper Colophon, 1965).

Other Secondary Historical, Sociological and Methodological Works

Abrams, Ray H., "Residential Propinquity as a Factor in Marriage Selection: Fifty Year Trends in Philadelphia," *American Sociological Review* 8 (1953), pp. 288–294.

Adams, Bert N., "Interaction Theory and the Social Network," in Martin Sussman, ed., *Marriage and Family* (Boston: Houghton Mifflin, 1974), pp. 342–350.

Ahlbrandt, Roger S., *Neighborhoods, People, and Community* (New York: Plenum Press, 1984).

Alwin, Duane F., and Robert M. Hauser, "The Decomposition of Effects in Path Analysis," *American Sociological Review* 40 (1975), pp. 37–47.

Anderson, Michael, "Family and Class in Nineteenth-Century Cities," *Journal of Family History* 2 (1977), pp. 139–150.

Anderson, Michael, *Family Structure in Nineteenth-Century Lancashire* (Cambridge: Cambridge University Press, 1971).

Anderson, Theodore, and Janice Egeland, "Spatial Aspects of Social Area Analysis," *American Sociological Review* 26 (1961), pp. 392–397.

Babchuk, Nicholas, "Primary Friends and Kin: A Study of the Associations of Middle Class Couples," *Social Forces* 43 (1965), pp. 483–493.

Babchuk, Nicholas, and Alan Booth, "Voluntary Associations: A Longitudinal Analysis," *American Sociological Review* 34 (1969), pp. 31–45.

Baldassare, Mark, ed., *Cities and Urban Living* (New York: Columbia University Press, 1983).

Baldassare, Mark, "Residential Density, Local Ties and Neighborhood Attitudes: The Findings of Micro-Studies Generalizable to Urban Areas," *Sociological Symposium* 14 (1975), pp. 93–104.

Banerjee, Tridib and William C. Baer, *Beyond the Neighborhood Unit: Residential Environments and Public Policy* (New York: Plenum Press, 1984).

Barth, Gunther, *City People: The Rise of Modern City Culture in Nineteenth-Century America* (New York: Oxford University Press, 1980).

Barton, Joseph J., *Peasants and Strangers: Italians, Rumanians, and Slovaks in an American City, 1890–1950* (Cambridge: Harvard University Press, 1975).

Berarida, Francois, and Anthony Sutcliffe, "The Street in the Structure and Life of the City: Reflections on Nineteenth-Century London and Paris," *Journal of Urban History* 6 (1980), pp. 379–396.

Bell, Marion, *Crusade in the City: Revivalism in Nineteenth-Century Philadelphia* (Lewisburg, Pa.: Bucknall University Press, 1977).

Bell, Wendell, and Marion Boat, "Urban Neighborhoods and Informal Social Relations," *American Journal of Sociology* 62 (1956), pp. 391–398.

Bell, Wendell, and Maryann Force, "Urban Neighborhood Types and Participation in Formal Associations," *American Sociological Review* 21 (1956), pp. 25–34.

Bell, Wendell, "Social Structure and Participation in Different Types of Formal Associations," *Social Forces* 34 (1956), pp. 345–350.

Bender, Thomas, *Community and Social Change in America* (New Brunswick, N.J.: Rutgers University Press, 1978).

Bernard, Richard M., and John B. Sharpless, "Analyzing Structural Influence on Social History Data," *Historical Methods* 11 (1978), pp. 113–122.

Berry, Brian J., *The Human Consequences of Urbanization* (New York: St. Martin Press, 1973).

Berthoff, Rowland T., *British Immigrants in Industrial America 1790–1950* (Cambridge: Harvard University Press, 1953).

Bestor, Theodore C., *Neighborhood Tokyo* (Stanford: Stanford University Press, 1989).

Bieder, Robert, "Kinship as a Factor in Migration," *Journal of Marriage and the Family* 35 (1973), pp. 429–439.

Bissell, Lydia A., "Family, Friends and Neighbors: Social Interaction in Seventeenth-Century Windsor, Connecticut" (Ph.D. diss., Brandeis University, 1973).

Blalock, Hubert M., Jr., *Social Statistics* (New York: McGraw Hill, 1972) 2d ed.

Blum, Allan F., "Social Structure, Social Class, and Participation in Primary Relationships," in William Goode, ed., *The Dynamics of Modern Society* (New York: Atherton Press, 1966), pp. 77–98.

Blumin, Stuart, *The Emergence of the Middle Class: Social Experience in the American City, 1760–1900* (Cambridge: Cambridge University Press, 1989).

Blumin, Stuart, "Mobility and Change in Ante-Bellum Philadelphia," in Stephan Thernstrom and Richard Sennett, eds., *Nineteenth-Century Cities: Essays in the New Urban History* (New Haven: Yale University Press, 1970), pp. 165–208.

Blumin, Stuart M., *The Urban Threshold: Growth and Change in a Nineteenth-Century American Community* (Chicago: University of Chicago Press, 1976).

Bodnar, John, Roger Simon, and Michael P. Weber, *Lives of Their Own: Blacks, Italians, and Poles in Pittsburgh, 1900–1960* (Urbana: University of Illinois Press, 1982).

Bodnar, John, *The Transplanted: A History of Immigrants in Urban America* (Bloomington: University of Indiana Press, 1985), chap. 6.

Boissevain, Jeremy, *Friends of Friends: Networks, Manipulators and Coalitions* (New York: St. Martins Press, 1974).

Boissevain, Jeremy, and J. Clyde Mitchell, eds., *Network Analysis: Studies in Human Interaction* (The Hague: Mouton, 1973).

Borchert, James, *Alley Life in Washington: Family, Community, Religion, and Folklife in the City, 1850–1970* (Urbana: University of Illinois Press, 1980).

Bossard, James H., "Residential Propinquity As a Factor in Marriage Selection," *American Journal of Sociology* 38 (1932), pp. 219–224.

Bott, Elizabeth, *Family and Social Network: Roles, Norms and External Relationships in Ordinary Families* (New York: Free Press, 1972), 2d ed.

Boulton, Jeremy, *Neighbourhood and Society: A London Suburb in the Seventeenth Century* (Cambridge: Cambridge University Press, 1987).

Bowden, Martyn J., "The Growth of the Central Districts in Large Cities," in Leo F. Schnore and Eric E. Lampard, eds., *The New Urban History: Quantitative Explorations by American Historians* (Princeton: Princeton University Press, 1975), pp. 110–142.

Boyer, Paul, *Urban Masses and Moral Order in America* (Cambridge: Harvard University Press, 1978).

Breton, Raymond, "Institutional Completeness of Ethnic Communities and the Personal Relations of Immigrants," *American Journal of Sociology* 70 (1964), pp. 193–205.

Bulmer, Martin, ed., *Neighbours: The Work of Philip Abrams* (Cambridge: Cambridge University Press, 1986).

Burstein, Alan N., "Residential Distribution and Mobility of Irish and German Immigrants in Philadelphia 1850–1880" (Ph.D. diss., University of Pennsylvania, 1975).

Calhoun, C. J., "History, Anthropology and the Study of Communities: Some Problems in Macfarlane's Proposal," *Social History* 3 (1978), pp. 363–373.

Carson, Gerald, *The Golden Egg: The Personal Income Tax, Where it Came from, How it Grew* (Boston: Houghton Mifflin, 1977).

Carwardine, Richard, "The Second Great Awakening in the Urban Centers: An Examination of Methodism and the 'New Measures'," *Journal of American History* 59 (1972), pp. 327–340.

Choldin, Harvey, "Kinship Networks in the Migration Process," *International Migration Review* 7 (1973), pp. 163–175.

Chudacoff, Howard, "A New Look at Ethnic Neighborhoods: Residential Dispersion and the Concept of Visibility in a Medium Sized-City," *Journal of American History* 60 (1973), pp. 72–93.

Chudacoff, Howard P., *Mobile Americans: Residential and Social Mobility in Omaha 1880–1920* (New York: Oxford University Press, 1972).

Chudacoff, Howard P., "Newlyweds and Family Extension: The First Stage of the Family Cycle in Providence, Rhode Island, 1864–1865 and 1879–1880," in Tamara K. Hareven and Maris A. Vinovskis, eds., *Family and Population in Nineteenth-Century America* (Princeton: Princeton University Press, 1978), pp. 179–205.

Cinel, Dino, *From Italy to San Francisco: The Immigrant Experience* (Stanford: Stanford University Press, 1982).

Clark, Christopher, *The Roots of Rural Capitalism: Western Massachusetts, 1780–1860* (Ithaca: Cornell University Press, 1990).

Cohen, Lizabeth, *Making a New Deal: Industrial Workers in Chicago, 1919–1939* (New York: Cambridge University Press, 1990).

Connell, John, "Social Networks in Urban Society," in B. D. Clark and M. B. Gleave, eds., *Social Patterns in Cities, Institute of British Geographers Special Publication*, London, March 1973 (no. 5), pp. 41–52.

Conner, Margaret Egan, "Their Own Kind: Family and Community in Albany, New York 1850–1915" (Ph.D. diss., Harvard University, 1975).

Conway, Alan, "Welsh Emigration to the United States," *Perspectives in American History* 7 (1973), pp. 177–271.

Conzen, Kathleen Neils, *Immigrant Milwaukee, 1836–1860: Accommodation and Community in a Frontier City* (Cambridge: Harvard University Press, 1976).

Conzen, Kathleen Neils, "Immigrants, Immigrant Neighborhoods, and Ethnic Identity: Historical Issues," *Journal of American History* 66 (1979), pp. 603–615.

Conzen, Kathleen N., "Patterns of Residence in Early Milwaukee," in Leo F. Schnore and Eric E. Lampard, eds., *The New Urban History: Quantitative Explorations by American Historians* (Princeton: Princeton University Press, 1975), pp. 145–183.

Cottrell, Leonard S., Jr., Albert Hunter, and James F. Short, Jr., eds., *Ernest W. Burgess on Community, Family, and Deliquency: Selected Writings* (Chicago: University of Chicago Press, 1973).

Cox, Peter, *Demography* (Cambridge: Cambridge University Press, 1970), 4th ed.

Craven, Paul, and Barry Wellman, "The Network City," *Sociological Inquiry* 43 (1973), pp. 57–88.

Crenson, Matthew A., "Social Networks and Political Processes in Urban Neighborhoods," *American Journal of Political Science* 22 (1978), pp. 578–594.

Davenport, David Paul, "Duration of Residence in the 1855 Census of New York State," *Historical Methods* 18 (1985), pp. 5–12.

Davenport, David Paul, "Tracing Rural New York's Out-Migrants, 1855–1860," *Historical Methods* 17 (1984), pp. 59–67.

Davie, Maurice, and Ruby Jo Reeves, "Propinquity of Residence Before Marriage," *American Journal of Sociology* 44 (1939), pp. 510–517.

Davis, James A., "Analyzing Contingency Tables With Linear Flow Graphs: D. Systems," in D. R. Heise, ed., *Sociological Methodology 1975–1976* (San Francisco: Jossey-Bass, 1976), pp. 111–145.

Davis, James A., "Extending Rosenberg's Technique for Standardizing Percentage Tables," *Social Forces* 62 (1984), pp. 679–708.

Davis, James A., "Hierarchical Models for Significance Tests in Multivariate Contingency Tables: An Exegesis of Goodman's Recent Paper," in H. L. Costner, ed., *Sociological Methodology 1973–1974* (San Francisco: Jossey-Bass, 1974), pp. 189–231.

Davis, James A., "Statistical Inference with Proportions" (unpublished paper, 1975).

Davis, Susan G., *Parades and Power: Street Theatre in Nineteenth-Century Philadelphia* (Philadelphia: Temple University Press, 1986).

Demos, John, and Sarane Spence Boocock, eds., *Turning Points: Historical and Sociological Essays on the Family* (Chicago: University of Chicago Press, 1978).

Dennis, Richard, and Stephen Daniels, "'Community' and the Social Geography of Victorian Cities," *Urban History Yearbook* (1981), pp. 7–23.

Devine, Edward T., "The Shiftless and Floating City Population," *Annals of American Academy of Political and Social Sciences* 10 (1897), pp. 149–164.

Diner, Hasia R., *Erin's Daughters in America: Irish Immigrant Women in the Nineteenth Century* (Baltimore: Johns Hopkins University Press, 1983).

Dogan, Mattes, and Stein Rokkan, eds., *Quantitative Ecological Analysis* (Cambridge: MIT Press, 1969).

Doherty, Robert, "Sociology, Religion, and Historians," *Historical Methods Newsletter* 6 (1973), pp. 161–169.

Doherty, Robert, *Society and Power: Five New England Towns 1800–1860* (Amherst: University of Massachusetts Press, 1977).

Doherty, Robert W., *The Hicksite Separation: A Sociological Analysis of Religious*

Schism in Early Nineteenth Century America (New Brunswick, N.J.: Rutgers University Press, 1967).

Doherty, Robert W., "Social Bases for the Presbyterian Schism of 1837–1838: The Philadelphia Case," Journal of Social History 2 (1968), pp. 69–79.

Doyle, Don H., "The Social Functions of Voluntary Associations in a Nineteenth-Century American Town," Social Science History 3 (1977), pp. 333–355.

Doyle, Don H., The Social Order of a Frontier Community: Jacksonville, Illinois 1825–1870 (Urbana: University of Illinois Press, 1978).

Dublin, Thomas, "Rural-Urban Migrants in Industrial New England: The Case of Lynn, Massachusetts, in the Mid-Nineteenth Century," Journal of American History 73 (1986), pp. 623–644.

Dublin, Thomas, Women at Work: The Transformation of Work and Community in Lowell, Massachusetts, 1826–1860 (New York: Columbia University Press, 1979).

Duis, Perry, "The Saloon and the Public City: Chicago and Boston" (Ph.D. diss., University of Chicago, 1975), 2 vols.

Duncan, Beverly, and Otis Duncan, "Residential Distribution and Occupational Stratification," in Robert Gutman and David Poponoe, eds., Neighborhood, City and Metropolis (New York: Random House, 1970), pp. 70–83.

Edel, Matthew, Elliott D. Sclar, and Daniel Luria, Sharky Places: Homeownership and Social Mobility in Boston's Suburbanization (New York: Columbia University Press, 1984).

Ellsworth, John S., "The Relationship of Population Density to Residential Propinquity as a Factor in Marriage Selection," American Sociological Review 13 (1948), pp. 444–448.

Erickson, Charlotte, Invisible Immigrants: The Adaptation of English Immigrants in Nineteenth Century America (London: Weidenfield and Nicholson, 1972).

Faler, Paul G., Mechanics and Manufacturers in the Early Industrial Revolution: Lynn, Massachusetts, 1780–1860 (Albany: State University of New York Press, 1981).

Fellin, Phillip, and Eugene Litwak, "Neighborhood Cohesion Under Conditions of Mobility," American Sociological Review 28 (1963), pp. 364–376.

Festinger, Leon, Stanley S. Schacter, and Kurt Back, "The Spatial Ecology of Group Formation," in Herbert Hyman and Eleanor Singer, eds., Readings in Reference Group Theory (New York: Free Press, 1968), pp. 268–277.

Fienberg, Stephen E., The Analysis of Cross-Classified Categorical Data, 2d ed. (Cambridge: MIT Press, 1980).

Fingleton, B., Models of Category Counts (Cambridge: Cambridge University Press, 1984).

Firey, Walter, "Sentiments and Symbolism as Ecological Variables," in Scott and Ann L. Greer, eds., Neighborhood and Ghetto: Their Local Area in Large-Scale Society (New York: Basic Books, 1974), pp. 284–296.

Fischer, Claude S., Networks and Places: Social Relations in Urban Settings (New York: Free Press, 1977).

Fischer, Claude S., "On Urban Alienation and Anomie: Powerlessness and Social Isolation," American Sociological Review 38 (1973), pp. 311–326.

Fischer, Claude S., To Dwell Among Friends: Personal Networks in Town and City (Chicago: University of Chicago Press, 1982).

Fischer, Claude S., "The Study of Urban Community and Personality," Annual Review of Sociology 1 (1975), pp. 67–89.

Fischer, Claude S., *The Urban Experience* (New York: Hartcourt Brace Jovanovich, 1976).

Formissano, Ronald P., *The Birth of Mass Political Parties: Michigan, 1827–1861* (Princeton: Princeton University Press, 1971).

Fried, Marc, *The World of the Urban Working Class* (Cambridge: Harvard University Press, 1973).

Friedkin, Noah, "A Test of Structural Features of Granovetter's Strength of Weak Ties Theory," *Social Networks* 2 (1980), pp. 411–423.

Frisch, Michael, *Town Into City: Springfield, Massachusetts, and the Meaning of Community, 1840–1880* (Cambridge: Harvard University Press, 1972).

Gans, Herbert J., *The Urban Villagers: Group and Class in the Life of Italian-Americans* (New York: Free Press, 1962).

Gans, Herbert J., "Urbanism and Suburbanism as Ways of Life: A Re-Evaluation of Definitions," in Robert Gutman and David Poponoe, eds., *Neighborhood, City and Metropolis* (New York: Random House, 1970), pp. 70–83.

Gans, Herbert J., and Mark Granovetter, "Commentary and Debate: Gans on Granovetter's 'Strength of Weak Ties'; Granovetter Replies to Gans; Gans Responds to Granovetter," *American Journal of Sociology* 80 (1974), pp. 524–523.

Garrioch, David, *Neighborhood & Community in Paris, 1740–1790* (Cambridge: Cambridge University Press, 1986).

Gilchrist, David T., ed., *The Growth of the Seaport Cities 1790–1825* (Charlotteville: University of Virginia Press, 1967).

Glasco, Laurence A., "Ethnicity and Social Structure: Irish, Germans and Native-born in Buffalo, 1850–1860" (Ph.D. diss., State University of Buffalo, 1973).

Glasco, Laurence A., "The Life Cycles and Household Structure of American Ethnic Groups: Irish, Germans, and Native-born Whites in Buffalo, New York, 1855", in Tamara K. Hareven, ed., *Families and Kin in Urban Communities, 1700–1930* (New York: New Viewpoints, 1977), pp. 122–143.

Glasco, Laurence A., "Migration and Adjustment in the Nineteenth-Century City: Occupation, Property, and Household Structure of Native-born Whites, Buffalo, New York, 1855," in Tamara K. Hareven and Maris A. Vinovskis, eds., *Family and Population in Nineteenth-Century America* (Princeton: Princeton University Press, 1978).

Glazer, Walter S., "Cincinnati in 1840: A Community Profile" (Ph.D. diss., University of Michigan, 1968).

Glazer, Walter S., "Participation and Power: Voluntary Association and the Functional Organization of Cincinnati in 1840," *Historical Methods Newsletter* 5 (1972), pp. 151–168.

Godfrey, Brian J., *Neighborhoods in Transition: The Making of San Francisco's Ethnic and Nonconformist Communities* (Berkeley: University of California Press, 1988).

Goheen, Peter G., *Victorian Toronto, 1850 to 1900: Patterns and Process of Growth* (Chicago: University of Chicago Press, 1970).

Golab, Carolina, *Immigrant Destinations* (Philadelphia: Temple University Press, 1977).

Goldstein, Sidney, "City Directories as Sources of Migration Data," *American Journal of Sociology* 60 (1954), pp. 169–176.

Goldstein, Sidney, *Patterns of Mobility 1910–1950: The Norristown Study* (Philadelphia: University of Pennsylvania Press, 1958).

Granovetter, Mark S., "The Strength of Weak Ties," *American Journal of Sociology* 78 (1973), pp. 1360–1380.

Granovetter, Mark, "The Strength of Weak Ties: A Network Theory Revisited," in Peter V. Marsden and Nan Lin, eds., *Social Structure and Network Analysis* (Beverly Hills: Sage Publications, 1982) pp. 105–130.

Gray, Malcolm, "Scottish Emigration: The Social Impact of Agrarian Change in the Rural Lowlands, 1775–1875," *Perspectives in American History* 3 (1973), pp. 95–174.

Greenbaum, Susan D., "Bridging Ties at the Neighborhood Level," *Social Networks* 4 (1982), pp. 367–384.

Greenbaum, Susan D., and Paul E. Greenbaum, "The Ecology of Social Networks in Four Urban Neighborhoods," *Social Networks* 7 (1985), pp. 47–76.

Greer, Scott, "Urbanism Reconsidered: A Comparative Study of Local Areas in a Metropolis," in Scott and Ann L. Greer, eds., *Neighborhood and Ghetto: The Local Area in Large-Scale Society* (New York: Basic Books, 1974).

Griffen, Clyde, and Sally Griffen, *Natives and Newcomers: The Ordering of Opportunity in Mid-Nineteenth-Century Poughkeepsie* (Cambridge: Harvard University Press, 1978).

Grigg, Susan, "Towards a Theory of Remarriage: A Study of Newburyport at the Beginning of the Nineteenth Century," *Journal of Interdisciplinary History* 8 (1977), pp. 183–220.

Guest, Avery M., "Patterns of Family Location," *Demography* 9 (1972), pp. 159–171.

Gulliver, P. H., *Neighbours and Networks: The Idiom of Kinship in Social Action among the Ndendeuli of Tanzania* (Berkeley: University of California Press, 1971).

Haines, Michael R., "Fertility, Marriage, and Occupation in the Pennsylvania Anthracite Region, 1850–1880," *Journal of Family History* 2 (1977), pp. 28–55.

Hallman, Howard W., *Neighborhoods: Their Place in Urban Life* (Beverly Hills: Sage Publications, 1984).

Handlin, Oscar, *Boston's Immigrants: A Study in Acculturation* (New York: Atheneum, 1972).

Handlin, Oscar, "The Modern City As a Field of Historical Study," in Oscar Handlin and John Burchard, eds., *The Historian and the City* (Cambridge: MIT Press, 1963), pp. 1–26.

Hannerz, Ulf, *Exploring the City: Inquiries Towards an Urban Anthropology* (New York: Columbia University Press, 1980).

Hareven, Tamara K., "Cycles, Courses and Cohorts: Reflections on Theoretical and Methodological Approaches to the Historical Study of Family Development," *Journal of Social History* 11 (1978), pp. 97–109.

Hareven, Tamara K., "The Family as Process: The Historical Study of the Family Cycle," *Journal of Social History* 7 (1974), pp. 322–329.

Hareven, Tamara K., *Family Time & Industrial Time: The Relationship Between the Family and Work in a New England Industrial Community* (Cambridge: Cambridge University Press, 1982).

Hareven, Tamara K., "Introduction," in Tamara K. Hareven, ed., *Family and Kin in Urban Communities, 1700–1930* (New York: New Viewpoints, 1977), pp. 1–15.

Hareven, Tamara, and Maris A. Vinovskis, "Marital Fertility, Ethnicity, and Occupation in Urban Families: An Analysis of South Boston and the South End in 1880," *Journal of Social History* 9 (1974), pp. 69–93.

Hareven, Tamara K. and Maris A. Vinovskis, "Patterns of Childbearing in Late Nineteenth-Century America: The Determinants of Marital Fertility in Five Massachusetts Towns in 1880," in Tamara K. Hareven and Maris A. Vinovskis, eds., *Family and Population in Nineteenth-Century America* (Princeton: Princeton University Press, 1978), pp. 85–125.

Harry, Joseph, "Family Localism and Social Participation," *American Journal of Sociology* 75 (1970), pp. 821–827.

Herbert, David, *Urban Geography: A Social Perspective* (New York: Praeger, 1972).

Herlihy, Patricia, *Odessa: A History, 1794–1914* (Cambridge: Harvard University Press, 1986).

Hershberg, Theodore, Alan M. Burstein, and Susan M. Drobis, "The Historical Study of Urban Space," *Historical Methods Newsletter* 9 (1976), pp. 99–136.

Hershberg, Theodore, Michael Katz, Stuart Blumin, Laurence Glasco, and Clyde Griffen, "Occupation and Ethnicity in Five Nineteenth-Century Cities: A Collaborative Inquiry," *Historical Methods Newsletter* 7 (1974), pp. 174–216.

Hershberg, Theodore, and Robert Dockhorn, "Occupational Classification," *Historical Methods Newsletter* 9 (1976), pp. 59–98.

Hershberg, Theodore, ed., *Philadelphia: Work, Space, Family, and Group Experience in the 19th Century* (New York: Oxford University Press, 1981).

Hollingsworth, T. H., "Historical Studies of Migration," *Annals de Demographie Historique* (Paris, 1970), pp. 87–96.

Holt, Glen E., "The Changing Perception of Urban Pathology: An Essay on the Development of Mass Transit in the United States," in Kenneth T. Jackson and Stanley K. Schultz, eds., *Cities in American History* (New York: Alfred A. Knopf, 1972), pp. 324–343.

Hunter, Albert, "The Loss of Community: An Empirical Test Through Replication," *American Sociological Review* 40 (1975), pp. 537–552.

Hunter, Albert, *Symbolic Communities: The Persistence and Change of Chicago's Local Community* (Chicago: University of Chicago Press, 1974).

Hunter, Albert, "The Urban Neighborhood: Its Analytical and Social Contexts," *Urban Affairs Quarterly* 14 (1979), pp. 267–288.

Irving, Henry W., "Social Networks in the Modern City," *Social Forces* 55 (1977), pp. 867–880.

Jackson, Kenneth T., *Crabgrass Frontier: The Suburbanization of the United States* (New York: Oxford University Press, 1985).

Jackson, Kenneth T., "Urban Decentralization in the Nineteenth Century: A Statistical Inquiry," in Leo F. Schnore and Eric E. Lampard, eds., *The New Urban History: Quantitative Explorations by American Historians* (Princeton: Princeton University Press, 1975), pp. 110–142.

Jacobs, Jane, *The Death and Life of Great American Cities* (New York: Vintage Books, 1961).

Janis, Ralph, "The Brave New World That Failed: Patterns of Parish Social Structure in Detroit, 1880–1940" (Ph.D. diss., University of Michigan, 1972).

Janowitz, Morris, *The Community Press in an Urban Setting* (Glencoe, Ill.: Free Press, 1952).

Janson, Carl-Gunnar, "Factorial Social Ecology: An Attempt at Summary and Evaluation," *Annual Review of Sociology* 6 (1980), pp. 433–456.

Jarausch, Konrad H., and Kenneth A. Hardy, *Quantitative Methods for Historians: A Guide to Research, Data, and Statistics* (Chapel Hill: University of North Carolina Press, 1991).

Jensen, Richard, "Found: Fifty Million Missing Americans" (Paper Presented at the Social Science History Association Meeting, Rochester, New York, November, 1980).

Johnson, Paul E., *A Shopkeeper's Millennium: Society and Revivals in Rochester, New York 1815–1837* (New York: Hill and Wang, 1978).

Johnson, R. Christian, "A Procedure for Sampling the Manuscript Census Schedules," *Journal of Interdisciplinary History* 8 (1978), pp. 515–530.

Johnston, R. J., *Urban Residential Patterns* (New York: Praeger, 1971).

Jones, Maldwyn A., "The Background of Emigration from Great Britain in the Nineteenth Century," *Perspectives in American History* 7 (1973), pp. 3–92.

Jones, Wendy L., "Couples Network Patterns of Newcomers in an Australian City," *Social Networks* 2 (1980), pp. 357–370.

Kantrowitz, Nathan, "The Index of Dissimilarity: A Measurement of Residential Segregation for Historical Analysis," *Historical Methods Newsletter* 7 (1974), pp. 285–289.

Kapp, Frederick, "Immigration," *Journal of Social Science* 2 (1870), pp. 1–30.

Kasarda, John D., and Morris Janowitz, "Community Attachment in Mass Society," *American Sociological Review* 39 (1974), pp. 328–339.

Kasson, John F., *Rudeness & Civility: Manners in Nineteenth-Century Urban America* (New York: Hill and Wang, 1990).

Katz, Michael B., Michael J. Doucet, and Mark J. Stern, "Migration and Social Order in Erie County, New York: 1855," *Journal of Interdisciplinary History* 8 (1978), pp. 669–701.

Katz, Michael B., *The People of Hamilton, Canada West: Family and Class in a Mid-Nineteenth Century City* (Cambridge: Harvard University Press, 1975).

Katz, Michael B., Michael J. Doucet, and Mark J. Stern, *The Social Organization of Early Industrial Capitalism* (Cambridge: Harvard University Press, 1982).

Kayssar, Alexander, *Out of Work: The First Century of Unemployment in Massachusetts* (New York: Cambridge University Press, 1986).

Keller, Suzanne, *The Urban Neighborhood: A Sociological Perspective* (New York: Random House, 1968).

Kennedy, Robert E., Jr., *The Irish: Emigration, Marriage, and Fertility* (Berkeley: University of California Press, 1973).

Kennedy, Ruby Jo Reeves, "Premarital Residential Propinquity and Ethnic Endogamy," *American Journal of Sociology* 48 (1943), pp. 580–584.

Kennedy, Ruby Jo Reeves, "Single or Triple Melting Pot: Inter-Marriage in New Haven," *American Journal of Sociology* 58 (1952), pp. 56–59.

Keyfitz, Nathan, *Applied Mathematical Demography* (New York: John Wiley, 1977).

Kim, Jae-om, and Mueller, Charles W., *Factor Analysis: Statistical Methods and Practical Issues* (Beverly Hills: Sage Publications, 1978).

Kim, Jae-om, and Mueller, Charles W., *Introduction to Factor Analysis: What It Is and How to Do It* (Beverly Hills: Sage Publications, 1978).

Knights, Peter R., *The Plain People of Boston, 1830–1860* (New York: Oxford University Press, 1971).

Knights, Peter R., "Population Turnover, Persistence, and Residential Mobility in Boston, 1830–1860," in Stephan Thernstrom and Richard Sennett, eds., *Nineteenth-Century Cities: Essays in the New Urban History* (New Haven: Yale University Press, 1969), pp. 258–274.

Knights, Peter R., and Leo F. Schnore, "Residential and Social Structure in the Ante-Bellum Period," in Stephan Thernstrom and Richard Sennett, eds., *Nineteenth-Century Cities: Essays in the New Urban History* (New Haven: Yale University Press, 1969), pp. 247–257.

Knoke, David, and Peter J., Burke, *Log-Linear Models* (Beverly Hills: Sage Publications 1980).

Kollman, Wolfgang, and Peter Marschalck, "German Emigration to the United States," *Perspectives in American History* 7 (1973), pp. 499–554.

Komarovsky, Mirra, "The Voluntary Associations of Urban Dwellers," *American Sociological Review* 11 (1946), pp. 686–698.

Kousser, J. Morgan, Gary W. Cox, and David W. Galenson, "Log-linear Analysis of Contingency Tables: An Introduction for Historians with an Application to Thernstrom on the 'Floating Proletariat'," *Historical Methods* 15 (1982), pp. 152–169.

Kraut, Alan, *The Huddled Masses: The Immigrant in American Society, 1880–1921* (Arlington Heights, Ill: Harlan Davidson, 1982).

Lane, Roger, *Policing the City: Boston, 1822–1885* (Cambridge: Harvard University Press, 1967).

Langbein, Laura I., and Allan Lichtman, *Ecological Inference* (Beverly Hills: Sage Publications, 1978).

Lansing, John B., and Eva Mueller, *The Geographic Mobility of Labor* (Ann Arbor: Survey Research Center, Institute for Social Research, 1973).

Laslett, Barbara, "Household Structure on an American Frontier: Los Angeles, California in 1850," *American Journal of Sociology* 81 (1975), pp. 109–128.

Laumann, Edward O., *Bonds of Pluralism: The Form and Substance of Urban Social Networks* (New York: John Wiley & Sons, 1973).

Laumann, Edward O., "The Sociological Structure of Religion," *American Sociological Review* 34 (1969), pp. 182–197.

Lazersfeld, Paul F., and Robert K. Merton, "Friendship as Social Process: A Substantive and Methodological Analysis," in Monroe Berger, Theodore Abel, and Charles Page, eds., *Freedom and Control in Modern Society* (New York: Van Nostrand, 1954), pp. 18–66.

Lees, Lynn Hollen, *Exiles of Erin: Irish Migrants in Victorian London* (Ithaca, N.Y.: Cornell University Press, 1979).

Lee, T. R., "Cities in the Mind," in D. T. Herbert and R. J. Johnston, *Spatial Perspectives on Problems and Policies* (London: John Wiley & Sons, 1976), vol. 2, pp. 159–187.

Leinhardt, Samuel, ed., *Social Networks: A Developing Paradigm* (New York: Academic Press, 1977).

Lenski, Gerhart, *The Religious Factor: A Sociological Study of Religion's Impact on Politics, Economics and Family Life* (New York: Doubleday, 1961).

Lieberman, Stanley, *Ethnic Patterns in American Cities* (Glencoe, Ill.: Free Press, 1963).

Lindstrom, Diane, *Economic Development in the Philadelphia Region 1810–1850* (New York: Columbia University Press, 1978).

Litwak, Eugene, "Geographic Mobility and Extended Family Cohesion," *American Sociological Review* 25 (1960), pp. 385–394.

Litwak, Eugene, "Occupational Mobility and Extended Family Cohesion," *American Sociological Review* 25 (1960), pp. 9–21.

Litwak, Eugene, and Ivan Szelenyi, "Primary Group Structures and Their Functions:

Kin, Neighbors, and Friends," *American Sociological Review* 35 (1969), pp. 465–481.

Lynch, Kevin, *The Image of the City* (Cambridge: MIT Press, 1960).

McClelland, Robyn, *Bibliography: Social Network, Social Planning and Community Needs* (Monticello, Ill.: Council of Planning Librarians, 1976).

MacDonald, John S., and Leatrice D. MacDonald, "Chain Migration, Ethnic Neighborhoods Formation, and Social Networks," in Charles Tilly, ed., *An Urban World* (Boston: Little, Brown, 1974), pp. 226–236.

MacDonagh, Oliver, "The Irish Famine Emigration to the United States," *Perspectives in American History* 10 (1976), pp. 357–446.

Macfarlane, Alan, "History, Anthropology, and the Study of Community," *Social History* 4 (1977), pp. 631–652.

McGahan, Peter, "The Neighbor Role and Neighboring in a Highly Urban Area," *The Sociological Quarterly* 13 (1972), pp. 397–408.

McGee, Thomas D'Arch, *A History of the Irish Settlers in North America* (Boston: Patrick Donahoe, 1852).

Macionis, John J., "The Search for Community in Modern Society: An Interpretation," *Qualitative Sociology* 1 (1978), pp. 130–143.

Manning, James H., *Century of American Savings Banks: Retrospective-Prospective* (New York: B. F. Buck, 1917).

Martin, Edgar W., *The Standard of Living in 1860* (Chicago: University of Chicago Press, 1942).

Merriman, John M., *The Margins of City Life: Explorations on the French Urban Frontier, 1815–1851* (New York: Oxford University Press, 1991).

Miller, Randall M., and Thomas D. Marzik, *Immigrants and Religion in Urban America* (Philadelphia: Temple University Press, 1977).

Miller, Ruth, "Social Cohesion and Political Activism in Two Low Income City Neighborhoods" (Ph.D. diss., Columbia University, 1972).

Mills, Dennis R., "The Residential Propinquity of Kin in a Cambridgeshire Village, 1841," *Journal of Historical Geography* 4 (1978), pp. 265–276.

Mitchell, J. Clyde, *Social Networks in Urban Situations: Analysis of Personality Relations in Central African Towns* (Manchester, England: Manchester University Press, 1969).

Modell, John, "An Ecology of Family Decisions: Suburbanization, Schooling, and Fertility in Philadelphia, 1880–1920," *Journal of Urban History* 6 (1980), pp. 397–417.

Modell, John, "Patterns of Consumption, Acculturation, and Family Income Strategies in Late Nineteenth-Century America," in Tamara K. Hareven and Maris A. Vinovskis, eds., *Family and Population in Nineteenth-Century America* (Princeton: Princeton University Press, 1978), pp. 206–240.

Modell, John, "The People of a Working-Class Ward: Reading, Pennsylvania, 1850," *Journal of Social History* 5 (1971), pp. 71–95.

Modell, John, and Tamara Hareven, "Urbanization and the Malleable Household: An Examination of Boarding and Lodging in American Families," *Journal of Marriage and the Family* 35 (1973), pp. 467–479.

Monkkonen, Eric H., *America Become Urban: The Development of U.S. Cities & Towns, 1780–1980* (Berkeley: University of California Press, 1988).

Morrison, Peter A., "Duration of Residence and Prospective Migration: The Evaluation of a Stochastic Model," *Demography* 4 (1967), pp. 553–562.

Moser, C. A., and G. Kalton, *Survey Methods in Social Investigation* (New York: Basic Books, 1972), 2d ed.

Murdie, R. A., *The Factorial Ecology of Metropolitan Toronto 1951–1961* (Chicago: University of Chicago Press, 1969).

Murphy, Raymond E., *The Central Business District: A Study in Urban Geography* (London: Longman, 1972).

Nash, Gary B., *Forging Freedom: The Formation of Philadelphia's Black Community, 1720–1840* (Cambridge: Harvard University Press, 1988).

Nash, Gary, "The Social Evolution of Preindustrial American Cities, 1700–1820," in Raymond A. Mohl, ed., *The Making of Urban America* (Wilmington, Del.: Scholarly Resources, 1988), pp. 24–44.

Nisbet, Robert, *The Sociological Tradition* (New York: Basic Books, 1966).

Norusis, Marija J., *SPSS-X Advanced Statistical Guide* (New York: McGraw-Hill, 1985).

Pack, Janet Rothenberg, "The Transformation of Urban Neighborhoods, 1850–1880 Philadelphia: Heterogeneity to Homogeneity?" (Paper Presented at American Historical Association Annual Meeting, Washington, D.C. 1982).

Page, William F., "Interpretation of Goodman's Log-Linear Model Effects," *Social Methods and Research* 5 (1977), pp. 419–435.

Park, Robert E., Ernest W. Burgess, and Roderick D. McKenzie, *The City* (Chicago: University of Chicago Press, 1925).

Park, Robert E., *Human Communities: The City and Human Ecology* (Glencoe, Ill.: Free Press, 1952).

Parkerson, Donald H., "America's 'Strange Unrest'" (Paper Presented at the American Historical Association Pacific Coast Branch Meeting, Seattle, 1984).

Pessen, Edward, "Did Fortunes Rise or Fall Mercurially in Antebellum America? A Tale of Two Cities, Boston and New York," *Journal of Social History* 4 (1971), pp. 339–357.

Pessen, Edward, "The Occupations of the Ante-Bellum Rich: A Misleading Clue to the Sources and Extent of Their Wealth," *Historical Methods Newsletter* 5 (1972), pp. 49–52.

Pessen, Edward, "The Social Configuration of the Antebellum City: An Historical and Theoretical Inquiry," *Journal of Urban History* 2 (1978), pp. 267–306.

Pleck, Elizabeth H., "The Two-Parent Household: Black Family Structure in Late Nineteenth Century Boston," *Journal of Social History* 6 (1972), pp. 3–31.

Pomer, Marshall I., "Demystifying Loglinear Analysis: Four Ways to Assess Interaction in a 2x2x2 Table," *Sociological Perspectives* 27 (1984), pp. 111–135.

Poponoe, David, "Urban Residential Differentiation: An Overview of Patterns, Trends, Problems," *Sociological Inquiry* 43 (1973), pp. 33–55.

Pred, Allan, *Making Histories and Constructing Human Geographies: The Local Transformation of Practice, Power Relations, and Consciousness* (Boulder, Colo.: Westview Press, 1990).

Pred, Allan R., *The Spatial Dynamics of U.S. Urban-Industrial Growth, 1800–1914* (Cambridge: MIT Press, 1966).

Pred, Allan R., *Urban Growth and the Circulation of Information: The United States System of Cities, 1790–1840* (Cambridge: Harvard University Press, 1973).

The Rand Corporation, *A Million Random Digits with 100,000 Normal Deviates* (Glencoe, Ill.: Free Press, 1955).

Reed, John Shelton, *The Enduring South: Subcultural Persistence in Mass Society* (Lexington: D. C. Heath, 1972).

Reese, Philip H., *Residential Patterns in American Cities: 1960*, Department of Geography Research Paper No. 189 (Chicago: University of Chicago, 1979).

Reynolds, H. T., *Analysis of Nominal Data* (Beverly Hills: Sage Publications, 1977).

Reynolds, H. T., "Some Comments on the Causal Analysis of Surveys with Log-Linear Models," *American Journal of Sociology* 83 (1978), pp. 127–143.

Ritchey, P. Neal, "Explanations of Migration," *Annual Review of Sociology* 2 (1976), pp. 363–404.

Robson, B., *Urban Analysis: A Study of City Structure* (Cambridge: Cambridge University Press, 1969).

Rosenthal, Naomi, Meryl Fingrutd, Michele Ethier, Roberta Karant, and David McDonald, "Social Movements and Network Analysis: A Case Study of Nineteenth-Century Women's Reform in New York State," *American Journal of Sociology* 90 (1985), pp. 1022–1054.

Ross, H. Laurence, "The Local Community: A Survey Approach," in Scott and Ann L. Greer, eds., *Neighborhood and Ghetto: The Local Area in Large-Scale Society* (New York: Basic Books, 1974), pp. 46–60.

Ross, Steven J., *Workers on the Edge: Work, Leisure, and Politics in Industrializing Cincinnati, 1788–1890* (New York: Columbia University Press, 1985).

Rutman, Darrett B., "Community Study," *Historical Methods* 13 (1980), pp. 29–42.

Ryan, Mary P., *Cradle of the Middle Class: The Family in Oneida County, New York, 1780–1865* (Cambridge: Cambridge University Press, 1981).

Samuel, Raphael, "Comers and Goers," in H. J. Dyos and Michael Wolf, eds., *The Victorian City: Images and Realities* (London: Routledge & Kegan Paul, 1973) vol. 1, pp. 123–160.

Schnepp, Gerald, and Louis A. Roberts, "Residential Propinquity and Mate Selection of a Parish Basis," *American Journal of Sociology* 58 (1952), pp. 45–50.

Schnore, Leo F., *The Urban Scene: Human Ecology and Demography* (New York: Free Press, 1965).

Schwarz, L. D., "Social Class and Social Geography: The Middle Classes in London at the End of the Eighteenth Century," *Social History* 7, no. 1 (May 1982), pp. 167–185.

Sennett, Richard, *Families Against the City: Middle Class Homes of Industrial Chicago, 1872–1890* (New York: Vintage Books, 1972).

Sewell, William H., Jr., "Social Change and the Rise of Working-Class Politics in Nineteenth-Century Marseille," *Past and Present* 65 (1974), pp. 75–109.

Sharpe, William, and Leonard Wallock, eds., *Visions of the Modern City: Essays in History, Art, and Literature* (Baltimore: Johns Hopkins University Press, 1987).

Shulman, Norman, "Life-Cycle Variations in Patterns of Close Relationships," *Journal of Marriage and the Family* 37 (1975), pp. 813–821.

Shulman, Norman, "Network Analysis: A New Addition to an Old Bag of Tricks," *Acta Sociologica* 19 (1976), pp. 307–323.

Shuval, Judith, "Class and Ethnic Correlates of Casual Neighboring," *American Sociological Review* 21 (1956), pp. 453–458.

Singh, Andrea Menefee, *Neighbourhood and Social Networks in Urban India* (New Delhi: Marwah, 1976).

Slovak, Jeffrey S., "Attachments in the Nested Community: Evidence from a Case Study," *Urban Affairs Quarterly* 21 (1986), pp. 575–597.

Smith, Judith, *Family Connections: A History of Italian & Jewish Immigrant Lives in Providence, Rhode Island, 1900–1940* (Albany: SUNY Press, 1985).

Smith, R. M., "Kin and Neighbors in a Thirteenth-Century Suffolk Community," *Journal of Family History* 4 (1979), pp. 219–256.

Smith, Timothy L., "Religion and Ethnicity in America," *American Historical Review* 83 (1978), pp. 1155–1185.

Smith, Timothy L., *Revivalism and Social Reform in Mid-Nineteenth-Century America* (New York: Abingdon Press, 1957).

Smith-Rosenberg, Carol, "The Female World of Love and Ritual," *Signs* 1 (1975), pp. 1–29.

Soltow, Lee, *Men and Wealth in the United States 1850–1870* (New Haven: Yale University Press, 1975).

Spear, Alden, Jr., "Residential Satisfaction As an Intervening Variable in Residential Mobility," *Demography* 11 (1974), pp. 173–188.

Stack, Carol B., *All Our Kin: Strategies for Survival in a Black Community* (New York: Harper & Row, 1974).

Stephenson, Charles, "Tracing Those Who Left: Mobility Studies and the Soundex Indexes to the U.S. Census," *Journal of Urban History* 1 (1974), pp. 73–85.

Stern, Mark J., "Homeownership: A Multivariate Analysis," in Michael Katz, ed., *York Social History Project Second Research Report* (Toronto: York University Institute of Behavioral Research, 1976), pp. 177–213.

Stinchcomb, Arthur L., *Constructing Social Histories* (New York: Harcourt Brace & World, 1968).

Stinchcomb, Arthur L., *Theoretical Methods in Social History* (New York: Academic Press, 1978).

Strickland, Donald, "The Scial Structure of Urban Neighborhoods," *Urban Affairs Quarterly* 14 (1979), pp. 391–400.

Sudman, Seymour, *Applied Sampling* (New York: Academic Press, 1976).

Sussman, Marvin, "Family, Kinship, and Bureaucracy," in Marvin Sussman, ed., *Marriage and the Family* (Boston: Houghton Mifflin, 1974), pp. 233–251.

Suttles, Gerald D., *The Social Construction of Communities* (Chicago: University of Chicago Press, 1972).

Suttles, Gerald D., *The Social Order of the Slum: Ethnicity and Territory in the Inner City* (Chicago: University of Chicago Press, 1968).

Swafford, Michael, "Three Parametric Techniques for Contingency Table Analysis: A Nontechnical Commentary," *American Sociological Review* 45 (1980), pp. 664–690.

Taeuber, Karl, and Alma F. Taeuber, *Negroes in Cities: Residential Segregation and Neighborhood Change* (New York: Atheneum, 1972).

Tapp, Robert B., *Religion Among the Unitarian Universalists: Converts in the Stepfathers' House* (New York: Seminar Press, 1973).

Taub, Richard P., George P. Surgeon, Sara Lindhol, Phylis B. Otti, and Ann Bridge, "Urban Voluntary Associations, Locality Based and Externally Induced," *American Journal of Sociology* 83 (1977), pp. 425–442.

Teaford, John, *City and Suburb: The Political Fragmentation of Metropolitan America, 1850–1970* (Baltimore: Johns Hopkins University Press, 1979).

Teaford, John C., *The Municipal Revolution in America: Origins of Modern Urban Government 1650–1825* (Chicago: University of Chicago Press, 1975).

Thernstrom, Stephan, *The Other Bostonians: Poverty and Progress in the American Metropolis, 1880–1970* (Cambridge: Harvard University Press, 1973).

Thernstrom, Stephan, *Poverty and Progress: Social Mobility in a Nineteenth-Century City* (New York: Atheneum, 1969).

Thernstrom, Stephan, "Reflections on the New Urban History," in Alexander B. Callow, ed., *American Urban History* (New York: Oxford University Press, 1973), 2d ed., pp. 672–684.

Thernstrom, Stephan, and Peter R. Knights, "Men in Motion: Some Data and Speculations About Urban Population Mobility in Nineteenth-Century America," *Journal of Interdisciplinary History* 1 (1970), pp. 7–36.

Thernstrom, Stephan, Ann Orlov, and Oscar Handlin, eds., *Harvard Encyclopedia of American Ethnic Groups* (Cambridge: Harvard University Press, 1980).

Thompson, E. P., *The Making of the English Working Class* (New York: Vintage Books, 1963).

Tiller, John, "Record Linkage for Everyman: A Semi-Automated Process," *Historical Methods Newsletter* 6 (1972), pp. 114–150.

Tilly, Charles, *The Vendee* (Cambridge: Harvard University Press, 1964).

Tilly, Charles, "What is Good Urban History?" *New School for Social Research Center for Studies of Social Change*, Working Paper no. 99 (July 1990).

Tilly, Charles, and C. Harold Brown, "On Uprooting, Kinship, and the Auspices of Migration," in Charles Tilly, ed., *An Urban World* (Boston: Little, Brown, 1974), pp. 108–133.

Timms, Duncan, *The Urban Mosaic: Towards a Theory of Residential Differentiation* (Cambridge: Cambridge University Press, 1971).

Turner, Ralph H., ed., *Robert E. Park On Social Control and Collective Behavior* (Chicago: University of Chicago Press, 1967).

Uhlenberg, Peter R., "A Study of Cohort Life Cycles: Cohorts of Native-Born Massachusetts Women, 1830–1920," *Population Studies* 23 (1969), pp. 407–420.

Upton, Graham J. G., *The Analysis of Cross-Tabulated Data* (New York: John Wiley & Sons, 1978).

van Leeuwen, Marco H. D., and Ineke Maas, "Log-linear Analysis of Changes in Mobility Patterns: Some Models with an Application to the Amsterdam Upper Classes in the Second Half of the Nineteenth Century," *Historical Methods* 24 (1991), pp. 66–79.

Vinovskis, Maris A., "Marriage Patterns in Mid-Nineteenth-Century New York State: A Multivariate Analysis," *Journal of Family History* 4 (1978), pp. 51–61.

Vinovskis, Maris A., "Socioeconomic Determinants of Interstate Fertility Differentials in the United States in 1850 and 1860," in Maris A. Vinovskis, ed., *Studies in American Historical Demography* (New York: Academic Press, 1979), pp. 459–480.

Vinyard, JoEllen M., "The Irish on the Urban Frontier: Detroit 1850–1880" (Ph.D. diss., University of Michigan, 1972).

Walkowitz, Daniel J., *Worker City, Company Town: Iron and Cotton-Worker Protest in Troy and Cohoes, New York, 1855–84* (Urbana: University of Illinois Press, 1981).

Ward, David, *Cities and Immigrants: A Geography in Nineteenth-Century America* (New York: Oxford University Press, 1971).

Ward, David, "Environs and Neighbours in the 'Two Nations' Residential Differentiation in Mid-Nineteenth-Century Leeds," *Journal of Historical Geography* 6 (1980), pp. 133–162.

Ward, David, "The Internal Spatial Differentiation of Immigrant Residential Districts," in Northwestern University, Department of Geography, *Special Publications*, no. 3 (1970), pp. 24–42.

Ward, David, *Poverty, Ethnicity, and the American City, 1840–1925: Changing Conceptions of the Slum and the Ghetto* (Cambridge: Cambridge University Press, 1989).

Ward, David, "Victorian Cities: How Modern?" *Journal of Historical Geography* 1 (1975), pp. 135–151.

Warner, Sam Bass, Jr., *The Private City: Philadelphia in Three Periods of Its Growth* (Philadelphia: University of Pennsylvania Press, 1968).

Warner, Sam Bass, Jr., and Colin Burke, "Cultural Change and the Ghetto," *Journal of Contemporary History* 4 (1969), pp. 173–187.

Webber, Melvin M., "Order in Diversity: Community Without Propinquity," in Robert Gutman and David Poponoe, eds., *Neighborhood, City and Metropolis* (New York: Random House, 1970), pp. 791–811.

Wellman, Barry, "The Community Question: The Intimate Networks of East Yorkers," *American Journal of Sociology* 84 (1979), pp. 1201–1231.

Wellman, Barry, and S. D. Berkowitz, eds., *Social Structures: A Network Approach* (Cambridge: Cambridge University Press, 1988).

Wellman, Barry, and Barry Leighton, "Networks, Neighborhoods, and Communities: Approaches to the Study of the Community Question," *Urban Affairs Quarterly* 14 (1979), pp. 363–390.

Wetherell, Charles, "Network Analysis Comes of Age," *Journal of Interdisciplinary History* 19 (Spring 1989), pp. 645–651.

White, Michael J., *American Neighborhoods and Residential Differentiation* (New York: Russell Sage Foundation, 1987).

Wilkinson, Leland, *SYSTAT: The System for Statistics*, Statistics Volume (Evanston, Ill., Systat, 1990).

Winship, Christopher, and Robert D. Mare, "Structural Equations and Path Analysis for Discrete Data," *American Journal of Sociology* 89 (1983), pp. 54–110.

Wireman, Peggy, *Urban Neighborhoods, Networks, and Families: New Forms for Old Values* (Lexington, Mass.: Lexington Books, 1984).

Wirth, Louis, "Urbanism As a Way of Life," *American Journal of Sociology* 44 (1938), pp. 1–24.

Wolf, Stephanie G., *Urban Village: Population, Community, and Family Structure in Germantown, Pennsylvania 1683–1800* (Princeton: Princeton University Press, 1976).

Woods, Robert A., and Albert J. Kennedy, *The Zone of Emergence: Observations of the Lower Middle and Upper Working Class Communities of Boston, 1905–1914* (Cambridge: MIT Press, 1969).

Wrigley, E. A., ed., *Identifying People in the Past* (London: Edward Arnold, 1973).

Yans-McLaughlin, Virginia, *Family and Community: Italian Immigrants in Buffalo, 1880–1930* (New York: Cornell University Press, 1977).

Young, Michael, and Peter Wilmott, *Family and Kinship in East London* (London: Routledge & Kegan Paul, 1957).

Zunz, Olivier, *The Changing Face of Inequality: Urbanization, Industrial Development, and Immigrants in Detroit, 1880–1920* (Chicago: University of Chicago Press, 1982).

Zunz, Olivier, "Detroit en 1880: Espace Et Segregation," *Annales E.S.C.* 32 (1977), pp. 106–136.

Zunz, Olivier, "The Organization of the American City in the Late Nineteenth Century: Ethnic Structure and Spatial Arrangements in Detroit," *Journal of Urban History* 3 (1977), pp. 443–466.

Zunz, Olivier, "Sampling for a Study of the Population and Land Use of Detroit in 1880–1885," *Social Science History* 1 (1977), pp. 307–332.

Zunz, Olivier, "The Synthesis of Social Change: Reflections on American Social History," in Olivier Zunz, ed., *Reliving the Past: The Worlds of Social History* (Chapel Hill: University of North Carolina Press, 1985), pp. 86–92.

Index

Kenneth A. Scherzer is Assistant Professor of
History at Middle Tennessee State University.

Library of Congress Cataloging-in-Publication Data
Scherzer, Kenneth A., 1953–
The unbounded community : neighborhood life and
social structure in New York City, 1830–1875 /
Kenneth A. Scherzer.
Includes bibliographical references and index.
ISBN 0-8223-1228-X (acid-free paper)
1. New York (N.Y.)—Social conditions.
2. Neighborhood—New York (N.Y.)—History—
19th century. 3. Community life—New York (N.Y.)
—History—19th century. 4. Social structure—New
York (N.Y.)—History—19th century. I. Title.
HN80.N5S27 1992
307.3′362′097471—dc20   91-40452CIP